Marketing and Mobile Financial Services

Mobile financial services (MFS) are of major importance for both academics and practitioners. The role played by nonbanking actors – telecoms and FinTech firms as well as other participants, such as PayPal and Amazon, in developing and deploying innovative financial and payment services is undeniable. Peer2peer (P2P) payments from a nonbank service are becoming commonplace and will shortly be codified by EC regulations requiring banks to provide access to consumer data for third-party app developers and service providers.

Three major mobile financial systems – mobile banking, mobile payments, and branchless banking – currently dominate the electronic retail banking sector. Although interconnected and interrelated, their business models, regulatory frameworks, and target markets are distinct. This book provides a unified perspective on MFS and discusses its evolution, growth, and future, as well as identifying the frameworks, stakeholders, and technologies used in financial information systems in general and MFS in particular.

Academics and researchers in digital and financial marketing will find this book an invaluable resource, as will bank executives, regulators, policy makers, FinTech companies, and anyone interested in how mobile technology, social media, and financial services will increasingly intersect.

Aijaz A. Shaikh is a University Lecturer (Marketing) at the University of Jyväskylä, Finland. He has more than 15 years of professional, teaching, and research experience. His research interests include customer behavior, mobile financial services, shared-economy, and social media technologies and their usage.

Heikki Karjaluoto is a Professor of Marketing at the University of Jyväskylä, Finland, and the leader of the Digital Marketing Research group. His research interests include customer relationship management, marketing communications, mobile communications, and retail banking.

Routledge Studies in Marketing

This series welcomes proposals for original research projects that are either single or multi-authored or an edited collection from both established and emerging scholars working on any aspect of marketing theory and practice and provides an outlet for studies dealing with elements of marketing theory, thought, pedagogy and practice.

It aims to reflect the evolving role of marketing and bring together the most innovative work across all aspects of the marketing 'mix' – from product development, consumer behaviour, marketing analysis, branding, and customer relationships, to sustainability, ethics and the new opportunities and challenges presented by digital and online marketing.

Addiction as Consumer Choice
Exploring the Cognitive Dimension
Gordon R. Foxall

The Psychology of Consumer Profiling in a Digital Age
Barrie Gunter

Contemporary Consumer Culture Theory
Edited by John F. Sherry, Jr. and Eileen Fischer

Marketing and Mobile Financial Services
A Global Perspective on Digital Banking Consumer Behavior
Edited by Aijaz A. Shaikh and Heikki Karjaluoto

Ethic Marketing
Theory, Practice and Entrepreneurship
Guilherme D. Pires and John Stanton

Relationship Marketing in the Digital Age
Robert W. Palmatier and Lena Steinhoff

Marketing and Mobile Financial Services

A Global Perspective on Digital Banking Consumer Behavior

**Edited by Aijaz A. Shaikh
and Heikki Karjaluoto**

LONDON AND NEW YORK

First published 2019
by Routledge
2 Park Square, Milton Park, Abingdon, Oxon OX14 4RN

and by Routledge
52 Vanderbilt Avenue, New York, NY 10017

First issued in paperback 2020

Routledge is an imprint of the Taylor & Francis Group, an informa business

British Library Cataloguing-in-Publication Data
A catalogue record for this book is available from the British Library

Library of Congress Cataloging-in-Publication Data
Names: Shaikh, Aijaz A., editor. | Karjaluoto, Heikki, editor.
Title: Marketing and mobile financial services: a global perspective
    on digital banking consumer behaviour/edited by Aijaz A. Shaikh
    and Heikki Karjaluoto.
Description: Abingdon, Oxon; New York, NY: Routledge, 2019. |
    Includes bibliographical references and index. |
Identifiers: LCCN 2018043068 (print) | LCCN 2018044294 (ebook) |
    ISBN 9781351174466 | ISBN 9780815386940 (hbk: alk. paper)
Subjects: LCSH: Banks and banking, Mobile. | Banks and banking,
    Mobile – Marketing.
Classification: LCC HG1616.M54 (ebook) | LCC HG1616.M54
    M37 2019 (print) | DDC 332.1068/8 – dc23
LC record available at https://lccn.loc.gov/2018043068

ISBN 13: 978-0-367-66282-0 (pbk)
ISBN 13: 978-0-8153-8694-0 (hbk)

Typeset in Sabon
by Apex CoVantage, LLC

Contents

Figures

Tables

Contributors

Editor biographies

Dr. Aijaz A. Shaikh is University Lecturer (in Marketing) at the University of Jyväskylä in Finland. He earned his PhD (with a major in marketing) from the Jyväskylä University School of Business and Economics in Finland. Prior to that, he earned his MSc from the AACSB-accredited Hanken School of Economics in Finland. Dr. Shaikh has more than 15 years of professional (mostly banking), teaching, and research experience. His primary research interests include both qualitative and quantitative studies in the broader areas of consumer behavior, mobile banking, branchless banking, shared economy, payment systems, and social media. He has published in *International Journal of Information Management*, *Journal of Retailing and Consumer Services*, *Computers in Human Behavior*, *Telematics and Informatics*, and other refereed journals, such as the *Journal of Financial Services Marketing*, the *International Journal of E-Business Research*, and the *International Journal of Bank Marketing*.

Heikki Karjaluoto is Professor of Marketing at the University of Jyväskylä, Finland, and the leader of the Digital Marketing and Communication research group. His research interests include customer relationship management, marketing communications, mobile communications, and retail banking. His previous publications have appeared in *Business Strategy and the Environment*, *Computers in Human Behavior*, the *European Journal of Marketing*, *Industrial Marketing Management*, and others.

Contributor biographies

Salimat Modupe Abass is a doctoral student at the University of Zaria, Nigeria. She is a senior internal auditor in the Federal Radio Corporation of Nigeria. She has her BSc and MSc from the University of Illorin, Nigeria. She has a certification as an Associate Accounting Technician (AAT). She is experienced in administrative as well as customer service.

Tommi Auvinen is a lecturer in management and leadership at the Jyväskylä University School of Business and Economics, Finland, and a docent in narrative leadership research at the University of Lapland. His teaching focuses on leadership and human resource management, and research on such leadership themes as storytelling and discursive power. Auvinen has published in national and international journals – including *Journal of Management Learning, Accounting and Business Research* and *Journal of Business Ethics* – and book chapters published by such esteemed institutions as Routledge and Springer.

Shounak Basak is a doctoral student at Indian Institute of Management Calcutta in the Operations Research area. His research is in the area of omni-channel and game theory. His research has been published in the journal *Decision Support Systems*.

Robert Ciuchita, PhD, is Assistant Professor in the Department of Marketing at Hanken School of Economics. His research revolves around customer experience and customer engagement with a focus on (digital) service innovation.

Olayinka David-West, PhD, is Senior Fellow in Information Systems at Lagos Business School, Pan-Atlantic University. She also serves as the Academic Director and leads the Sustainable and Inclusive Digital Financial Services Initiative. She obtained a Doctor of Business Administration Degree from Manchester Business School and is the author of several case studies and learned academic journals

Richard Glavee-Geo graduated with MSc and PhD degrees in business logistics from Molde University College, Norway. He also has a postgraduate diploma in marketing (CIM-UK) and advanced marketing diploma from Harstad University College (now the Arctic University of Norway). He is Associate Professor (marketing, logistics, & supply chain management) at the Department of International Business, Faculty of Economics and Management, Norwegian University of Science and Technology (NTNU), Norway. His research interests include global logistics and SCM, technology/innovation adoption and usage, social media, financial services and bank marketing, interorganizational relationships, and consumer and organizational buying behavior. His publications include book chapters published by Palgrave Macmillan, Springer, IGI-Global, and articles published in *International Journal of Export Marketing, British Food Journal, International Journal of E-Business Research, Research in International Business and Finance*, and *International Journal of Bank Marketing*, among others.

Hannele Haapio is a PhD Student of Marketing at the University of Jyväskylä School of Business and Economics, Finland. Her research interests include digital marketing, customer relationship management, emotions and digitalization, omnichannel communication, and retail banking. She has over

30 years of experience in different levels of customer and managerial positions in international banking. Before joining the university in 2017, she was an executive level manager, heading the international customer service.

Robert Ebo Hinson holds a doctorate in Marketing from the University of Ghana and another in International Business from Aalborg University in Denmark. He is a Professor and Head of the Department of Marketing and Entrepreneurship at the University of Ghana Business School.

Nkemdilim Iheanachor is currently Doctoral Student at Pan-Atlantic University as well as Research Fellow in Lagos Business School's sustainable and inclusive digital financial services initiative. He has authored several book chapters, articles, and case studies.

Marko Järvenpää is currently Professor of accounting at the University of Vaasa School of Accounting and Finance, Finland, formerly of Jyväskylä School of Business and Economics, Finland. He studies management accounting, like management accountants' role transformation, performance measurement, strategy and management accounting change, and sustainability and accounting, typically by conducting qualitative case and field studies and employs interpretative theories like institutional, stakeholder, and cultural theories.

Hanna Komulainen is Associate Professor at Oulu Business School, University of Oulu, Finland. She obtained her PhD in marketing from University of Oulu in 2010. Her research interests include digitalization, service experience, and value co-creation in emergent service contexts, e.g., new health care and financial services. She has published, among others, in *Journal of Service Management, Journal of Business Market Management, Management Decision*, and *Journal of Business and Industrial Marketing*.

Ilkka Lähteenmäki works at the moment as a Post-Doctoral Researcher at Aalto University and is associated with CERS, Hanken. He has over 20 years experience in banking on the executive level. His main research interests include banking and financial services development, manager's mental models, and FinTech. He has published in such journals as *Journal of Service Theory and Practice, Management & Organizational History, International Journal of Bank Marketing*, and *Business Horizons*.

Dominik Mahr is Associate Professor at Maastricht University and the Scientific Director of the Service Science Factory (SSF). His research centers on digital marketing, service design, co-creation, and innovation management.

Bhupesh Manoharan is Doctoral Student at Indian Institute of Management Calcutta in the Marketing area. His research is the areas of digital marketing and consumer behavior.

Felix Adamu Nandonde, PhD, is Lecturer in Marketing at Sokoine University of Agriculture, Morogoro, Tanzania. He teaches graduate and undergraduate courses at the university level. His research works appeared in *Journal of African Business*, *African Management Review*, *Journal of Business Research*, *British Food Journal*, *Journal of Language*, *Technology & Entrepreneurship in Africa*, and *International Journal of Retail & Distribution Management*. Before joining academia he worked with National Bank of Commerce (NBC) 1997, Tanzania Limited as Sales Consultant Business Banking.

Satu Nätti is Professor of Marketing at the Oulu Business School, University of Oulu, Finland. Her main research interests include innovation network orchestration, professional services, and bank industry. She has published in such journals as *Industrial Marketing Management*, *Journal of Business and Industrial Marketing*, *Journal of Service Management*, *Journal of Services Marketing*, *Service Industries Journal*, and *International Journal of Bank Marketing*.

Gaby Odekerken-Schröder holds a chair in customer-centric service science at Maastricht University and she is co-founder of Maastricht University's Service Science Factory. Her main research interests are innovations in (health care) services and customer loyalty.

Sunday A. Olaleye has a Master of Science in Information Systems from the Åbo Akademi University, Turku, Finland. Currently doing his doctoral studies at the Department of Marketing, Management, and International Business, Oulu Business School, Finland. He has presented papers at conferences and published in academic journals. His research interests are Emerging Mobile Technologies, Electronic and Mobile Commerce, Social Commerce, and Mobile Apps.

Mia Olsen is PhD Fellow at the Department of Management, Society, and Communication at Copenhagen Business School, Denmark. She wrote her Master's thesis on mobile wallets in 2010–2011 and has since then been studying and writing about the cashless society, payments, mobile payments, and user perspectives on these topics.

Mikko Riikkinen is a last-year Doctoral Student at the University of Tampere, Finland. He has more than 10 years of work experience in banking and start-ups and is currently researching value creation in banking, insurance and FinTech start-ups. Mikko has published in *International Journal of Bank Marketing*.

Pasi Sajasalo, PhD, is Lecturer in Management and Leadership at the Jyväskylä University School of Business and Economics, Finland. His teaching and research interests focus on various aspects of strategy in differing contexts, such as forest industry, engineering industry, media industry, and financial sector. More recently, he has focused on strategy-as-practice inspired work, including cognitive aspects of strategy, such as strategy-related sensemaking and sensegiving, in addition to networked strategy-making. His work appears in national and international journals as well as in book chapters of volumes published by national and international publishers.

Saila Saraniemi is Senior Lecturer of Marketing at Oulu Business School, University of Oulu, Finland. She obtained her PhD from University of Eastern Finland in 2009. Her main research interests relate to value creation and digitalization of services as well as corporate, service, and place branding. She has published, among others, in *Industrial Marketing Management*, *Journal of Brand Management*, and *Journal of Business and Industrial Marketing*.

Sudhanshu Shekhar is a Doctoral Student at Indian Institute of Management Calcutta in the Organizational Behavior area. His research is in the area of institutional theory and business history.

Teppo Sintonen is Lecturer of Management and Leadership at the Jyväskylä University School of Business and Economics, Finland. His research focuses on organizational change, identity, strategy, and creativity, and he has specialized on narrative research methods. He has published in national and international volumes, including *Journal of Business Ethics*, *Management Learning*, *Qualitative Research*, and *Journal for Critical Organization Inquiry*.

Tuomo Takala is Professor of Management and Leadership at the University of Jyväskylä School of Business and Economics, Finland. He has executed several administrative duties, e.g., Vice Dean and Dean of the faculty. He is the editor in chief of EJBO (*Electronic Journal of Business Ethics and Organizational Studies*). He has conducted research on several areas, including business ethics, qualitative research, responsible management, leadership studies, and charisma studies. He has published numerous articles, e.g., in the *Journal of Business Ethics*.

Dandison C. Ukpabi is a PhD Student in the Digital Marketing Research Group of the University of Jyväskylä, Finland. He did his Master's degree programme in the University of Plymouth, United Kingdom, in Marketing Management and Strategy. His most recent publications appeared in Telematics and Informatics and Tourism Management Perspectives. He has also presented papers in reputable conferences such as ENTER e-Tourism conferences, Bled eConferences, and the European Marketing Academy Conference (EMAC). His research interest focuses on e-tourism, digital marketing and social media, relationship marketing, and marketing strategy.

Pauliina Ulkuniemi is Professor of Marketing at Oulu Business School, University of Oulu, Finland. She obtained her PhD in marketing from University of Oulu in 2003. Her research interests lie in the value creation in business relationships in different industry contexts, especially in services and digitalization. She has recently published in, e.g., *Industrial Marketing Management*, *The Journal of Service Management*, *Scandinavian Journal of Management*, and *Management Decision*.

Immanuel Ovemeso Umukoro is Doctoral Student in information systems at the Africa Regional Centre for Information Science (ARCIS) and also a Research Fellow at the Lagos Business School's sustainable and inclusive digital financial services initiative. His research cuts across digital financial services, financial inclusion, technology adoption and use, digital platforms, innovation and technology transfer studies, business intelligence and analytics, business information systems, process management, consumer studies, development information systems, ergonomics and man-machine interaction, and management information.

Martin Wetzels is Professor in Marketing and Supply Chain Research at the School of Business and Economics of Maastricht University. His main research interests are services marketing, marketing research, B2B marketing, marketing channels, and digital marketing.

Acknowledgments

For many, it is either mobile or nothing

First and foremost, we would like to thank various contributing authors for generously contributing and sharing their time and insights on mobile financial services in different markets. We especially thank the reviewers for their careful reading of the book chapters and their valuable comments, suggestions, and feedback.

We would like to express our deep gratitude to Jacqueline Curthoys, Commissioning Editor, Business and Management, Routledge, for providing essential guidelines, encouragement, and timely feedback on the book proposal.

We are also thankful to Laura Hussey and Jess Harrison, Editorial Assistants, Business and Management, Routledge, for assisting in organizational matters including documentation.

This edited collection would not have been possible without the unwavering support, motivation, and resources provided by the Jyväskylä University School of Business and Economics, University of Jyväskylä, Finland.

Thank you all.☺

Jyväskylä, Finland
Aijaz A. Shaikh
Heikki Karjaluoto

Part I
Mobile financial services

1 Mobile financial services

Introduction, definition, and conceptualization

Aijaz A. Shaikh* and Heikki Karjaluoto

Introduction

Over the last two decades, researchers and practioners have paid great attention to understanding and examining innovative mobile financial technologies and mobile financial services (MFS). The underline reason for this devotion from the research and the industry is attributed to the momentous shift seen in the technological culture and the rise of smartphones. Because of the availability and affordability of smartphones and tiny but smart wearables, customers are now more empowered and have endless virtual and physical options for accessing information, researching, choosing, buying, as well as using new financial and payment products and value-added services at the convenience of anytime anywhere.

This rapidly converging financial landscape was earlier dominated by branch-oriented banking, which provided services to customers who maintained a formal relationship (bank account) with the banks. Paper-based instruments, such as checks, payment drafts, dominated the transactions mode and a transactions cycle was completed in days. The rise of the digital natives during late 1980s, birth of the Internet and Internet-based business models during early 1990s, mobile technology, and the retail agent network (in case of branchless banking) have transformed delivery of financial services. Internet banking, point-of-sale banking, and telephone banking were introduced and added to the repertoire of banking channels. These innovative banking channels, commonly known as 'alternative delivery channels' or 'digital banking channels,' became the lingua franca of banking business globally.

Historically, these developments in the domain of digital banking were originally started in the 1960s and received a tremendous momentum during the late 1980s. The climax was in the 1990s, and slowly eroded the need for branch-oriented banking. In the 2000s, portable and wearable devices brought a major revolution in the consumer mindset and lifestyle in general because of their massive social and economic impact (Liébana-Cabanillas, Sánchez-Fernández, & Muñoz-Leiva, 2014). Similarly, digital banking channels including mobile were developed and deployed in most of the developed world. Later on, their deployment and usage has been noticed in emerging and developing countries as well. Perhaps, this diffusion of financial digital services including MFS in the developing markets is essentially due to the increasing usage of smartphones as well as the presence of the digital native segment.

According to Helsper and Eynon (2010), the digital natives (also known as net generation, the Google generation, or the millennials) are those consumers or users who were born during the late 1980s and have always been surrounded by, and interacted with, new technologies such as mobile. On the other hand, the people who were born before this new digital era, which began around 1980, are called 'digital immigrants' (Helsper & Eynon, 2010). According to Prensky (2001), digital immigrants may learn to use new and innovative technologies but will still be in some way located within the past, unable to fully understand the digital natives.

In tandem with these global advancements seen in the mobile technology, the financial institutions located in emerging and developing countries started developing mobile-based innovative solutions and offering retail mobile financial banking services to a more heterogeneous, demographically disbursed, and relatively less-privileged population. A significant impediment to reaching the remote customer segment was the non-availability of infrastructure, high security risks, and low deposit rate. The adoption of mobile telephony to provide financial services in Africa and other developing regions of the world has become instrumental in integrating the hitherto less-inclusive or unbanked and underbanked segments of the population to the mainstream financial systems (Ouma, Odongo, & Were, 2017).

Earlier, the strategy to reach the underbanked and unbanked was the part of financial inclusion programs, which were introduced and motivated by the government agencies and regulators. These financial programs were undertaken by banks, other financial institutions, mobile network operators (MNO), and retail agent networks with an underlying purpose to increase the financial and social inclusion, increase the financial well-being of the underbanked (and even unbanked consumers), and entice the customers to access and use the mainstream banking and payment services. These developments have gradually designated 'mobile' as absolutely necessary for many banks, MNOs, and other nonbanking institutions.

Despite these developments and the availability of extensive literature on MFS, there has been no effort to date to comprehensively define and conceptualize the term 'MFS.' This chapter extends the depth of previous studies and demonstrates the need for defining and conceptualizing the term 'MFS' and investigating what constitutes the field of MFS. In doing so, this chapter provides an analysis and synthesis of the past literature in the field of MFS. Because the prior research has not defined the term 'MFS' – at least until recently, researchers often overlook the potential of MFS, especially the branchless banking. This chapter seeks to answer the following research questions:

- What is the mobile financial services landscape?
- What are MFS and how are they conceptualized in the marketing and IT literature?

- How has prior literature segregated MFS into different types?
- How do the different types of MFS differ from each other?

Attention is given to the contemporary and relevant published sources including journal articles and conference proceedings published during the last decade, i.e., 2008 till 2017 (inclusive) defining and conceptualizing the term 'MFS.' Within the broader scope of this conceptualization, we have used the term 'mobile financial services' or 'mobile banking services' or 'retail mobile financial services,' or 'mobile banking and payment services' interchangeably.

The chapter is organized as follows: the next section offers the definition and conceptualizes the term 'MFS' and its different facets. This is followed by a discussion on how to differentiate the terms 'mobile banking,' 'mobile payments,' and 'branchless banking services.' The chapter ends with a conclusion.

Mobile financial services landscape

This section addresses the first research question: What is the mobile financial services landscape?

The retail banking sector is considered the backbone of the financial services industry, economy, and it permeates different realms of social, private, and economic life. Retail banking fulfills everyday banking and payment needs of the consumers and encompasses high-volume and low-value transactions. Retail banking sector facilitates both electronic and paper-based transactions, and it includes a horde of delivery channels with variant capabilities to promote, for example, financial inclusion as well as the financial well-being of the customers. Historically, the development and the deployment of these multiple digital banking delivery channels by the financial companies, including banks, is based on a very simple notion, i.e., the bank-customer relationship is built on interaction between the partners and should not (metaphorically and literally) end at the bank branch door (Feinberg, Hokama, Kadam, & Kim, 2002).

Mobile devices have added the element of pure mobility to digital services consumption and have provided motivation and several business opportunities to the retail financial sector to expand their business portfolio. Resultantly, the widespread penetration and use of portable devices as an information-rich tool created a new payment environment, a new revenue stream for banks, and became a central payment business strategy. Using the functions of the cell phones – payment – mobile financial systems became the next big thing and an ultimate choice for the consumers.

Figure 1.1 depicts the landscape of the retail MFS and how these services are segregated in different types by the research and the industry. Figure 1.1 segregates the consumers (such as banked, de-banked, and unbanked) who access and use the MFS. These segregations are largely based on the evidences collected from the prior research (e.g., Demirgüç-Kunt & Klapper, 2013) that have identified two functional domains in the financial system:

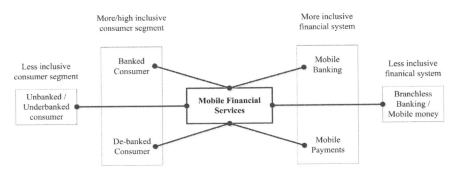

Figure 1.1 Retail mobile financial services landscape

(1) more inclusive mobile financial systems and (2) less inclusive mobile financial systems.

More inclusive mobile financial systems include mobile banking and mobile payments, including its advanced version called mobile wallets. Banked and de-banked consumers with an easy and always access to the infrastrusture, Internet, and mobile devices are generally considered as the inclusive consumer base. On the other hand, a less-inclusive mobile financial system consists of branchless banking or mobile money. Here unbanked and underbanked consumers using their cell phones perform basic banking and payment transactions. Since banks could not manage the mobile network by themselves, mobile money services allow greater collaboration between and among various banking and nonbanking players, such as mobile network operators (MNOs), software houses, and newly emerging Fintech start-ups.

There have been some assertions that the MFS, including more-inclusive and less-inclusive, provide several benefits to the consumers, such as MFS provide more personalize experiences, better customer service, reduced costs, the increased reactivity of the bank and other financial institutions, increased market share, reinforced brand image, and provide the unbanked with new opportunities to access financial services (Morawczynski, 2009). Furthermore, Kumar, Lall, and Mane (2017) discuss wider benefits from using MFS, such as increasing customer satisfaction, increasing profitability, sustaining competitive advantage, providing a higher level of convenience, and also as a tool to cater to unbanked customers.

Mobile financial services – definition and conceptualization

This section addresses the second research question: What are MFS and how are they conceptualized in the marketing and IT literature?

Mobility is the cornerstone of the MFS. It refers to the higher degree of independence from space and time achieved in banking and payment processes by the employment of mobile devices (Fenu & Pau, 2015). MFS was developed in the backdrop of 'mobility,' introduced a new breed of consumers popularly known as 'always-on' or 'always-connected,' as well as introduced new trends in the financial sector, revolutionized the payment mechanisms, and allowed the development of mobile-based banking and payment solutions. On the same lines, the portable or mobile devices have become an inseparable component of consumer life. Against this transformation, the banks are designing new marketing strategies to entice customers including the banked and unbanked using MFS.

According to Duncombe (2012), MFS is an umbrella term that incorporates mobile cash transfers and payments and other financial transactions undertaken using portable devices such as mobile phones and tablets. In the understanding of Dass and Pal (2011), MFS encompasses a broad range of financial and payment transactions that consumers engage in or access using their mobile phones or tablets. McKinsey and Co. (2017) argue that these mobile financial transactions include the full spectrum of financial services, ranging from payments and current accounts to savings, loans, investments, and insurance. Here, MFS are classified in three major but overlapping types: m-banking, m-payment, and the latterly included branchless banking or mobile money, which until now was considered the subset of m-payments.

Most scholars who have identified and endorsed the classification within the MFS (e.g., Petrauskas & Zumaras, 2008; Selvadurai, 2014) concur that this classification is due to different consumer preferences and access methods to information, size or the volume of the transactions or payments (retail payment or wholesale payment), nature of the transactions (financial and non-financial), the time of payment (prepaid, postpaid), the place of purchase (real-time, online), the medium of payment (paper, electronic, mobile), and the method of payments (point-of-sale, proximity payments, remote payments).

Major types of mobile financial services

In this section, we address the second research question by discussing how prior literature has segregated MFS into different types, such as mobile banking (m-banking), mobile payment (m-payment), and branchless banking.

M-banking technology and services

The most extensively researched area within the MFS is m-banking. By collecting and analyzing the contemporary scientific literature including journal articles and conferene proceedings, we have identified and summarized 27 definitions proposed by the research on m-banking (see Table 1.1).

The definitions of m-banking (Table 1.1) suggest that prior research has considered m-banking a multivariate service in terms of application that falls under many domains. For instance, Riivari (2005) considered

Table 1.1 Mobile banking literature summary

S. No.	Citation	Definition	Contemplated as
1	Chung and Kwon (2009)	MB is the convergence of mobile technology and financial services, which have emerged after the advent of the wireless Internet and smart-chip-embedded handsets, and it is for people on the move who want to access their bank accounts and transfer funds anytime, anywhere through their phones without visiting banks in person.	. . . a convergence of mobile technology and financial services.
2	Mehrad and Moham-madi (2016)	MB is an application of mobile commerce that enables customers to bank virtually at any convenient time and place.	. . . an application of mobile commerce.
3	Tiwari and Buse (2007)	MB is the provision of banking and related financial services such as savings, funds transfer, and stock market transactions among others on mobile devices.	–
4	Chaouali, Souiden, and Ladhari (2017)	MB is an emerging application of mobile commerce that could become an additional revenue source to both banks and telecom service providers. It is a form of service convergence enabled by innovative technologies.	. . . an emerging application of mobile commerce.
5	Al-Ajam and MdNor (2015)	MB is a cost-effective banking and financial service which allows users to break free of the constraints of time, place, and queues.	. . . a cost-effective banking and financial service.
6	Moham-madi (2015)	MB enables consumers to gain convenient access to value-added and banking services, even in countries with low incomes.	–
7	Boor, Oliveira, and Veloso (2014)	MB is a natural evolution of electronic banking which empowers consumers to complete financial transactions via mobile or handheld devices.	. . . a natural evolution of electronic banking.
8	Muñoz-Leiva, Climent-Climent, and Liébana-Cabanillas (2017)	MB is considered a remote service (via mobile phone, PDAs, tablets, etc.) offered by financial entities to meet the needs of their customers located in different demographic locations.	. . . considered as a remote service.

Table 1.1 (Continued)

S. No.	Citation	Definition	Contemplated as
9	Zhou, Lu, and Wang (2010)	MB is defined as the use of mobile devices such as cell phones and personal digital assistants (PDAs) to access banking networks via the wireless application protocol (WAP).	–
10	Veríssimo (2016)	MB is a banking product or service to conduct financial and non-financial transactions using a mobile device such as a mobile phone or tablet.	. . . a banking product or service.
11	Malaquias and Hwang (2016)	MB promotes better efficiency and improved service quality, and it also benefits customers through time optimization, immediate information, instant connectivity, great convenience, and interactivity.	–
12	Shaikh and Karjaluoto (2015)	MB, also referred to as cell phone banking, is the use of mobile devices such as personal digital assistants (PDA), mobile telephones, smartphones, and tablet computers to access banking networks via the wireless application protocol (WAP) for financial services.	. . . a cell phone banking.
13	Tam and Oliveira (2016)	MB is defined as the subset of applications of mobile e-commerce offered by the financial industry. MB enables users to access account balances, pay bills, transfer funds, and perform other financial services, at any time and anywhere.	. . . a subset of mobile e-commerce application.
14	Lee, Harindranath, Oh, and Kim (2015)	MB is an extension of banking and financial services onto mobile networks and devices. Characteristics such as time and location independence as well as secured transactions through the use of a personal mobile phone to identify the account owner and to confirm the transaction led to rapid growth in mobile banking.	. . . an extension of banking and financial services.
15	Gu, Lee, and Suh (2009)	With the improvement of mobile technologies and devices, MB has been considered as a salient system because of such attributes of mobile technologies as ubiquity, convenience, and interactivity.	. . . a salient system.

(*Continued*)

Table 1.1 (Continued)

S. No.	Citation	Definition	Contemplated as
16	Oliveira, Faria, Thomas, and Popovič (2014)	MB is an instance of a mobile commerce application by which financial institutions enable their customers to carry out banking activities via mobile devices. It relies on technologies (e.g., short messaging services) and communication protocols (e.g., wireless applications protocols, WAP) for providing banking services (e.g., transfer of funds), and related inquiries (e.g., searching for the closest ATM location).	. . . an instance of a mobile commerce application.
17	Baptista and Oliveira (2015)	MB can be defined as a type of execution of financial services in the course of which, within an electronic procedure, the customer uses mobile communication techniques in conjunction with mobile devices or as a service whereby customers use a mobile phone or mobile device to access banking services and perform financial transactions.	–
18	Masrek, Mohamed, Daud, and Omar (2014)	MB, which is also referred to as cell phone banking is the use of mobile terminals such as cell phones and personal digital assistants (PDAs) to access banking networks via the wireless application protocol (WAP). MB is also considered similar to Internet banking in that it provides a fast and convenient way of performing common banking transactions. MB allows customers to perform three fundamental transactions: (i) storing money in an account that is accessible by the mobile device, (ii) completing cash-in and cash-out transactions with the stored account, and (iii) transferring money among different accounts.	. . . a cell phone banking.
19	Oliveira et al. (2014)	MB includes mobile accounting (e.g., checkbook requests, blocking lost cards, money transfers or insurance policies subscription), mobile brokerage (selling and purchasing financial instruments), and mobile financial information services (balance inquiries, statement requests, credit card information, branches, and ATM locations, foreign exchange rates or commodity prices).	–

Table 1.1 (Continued)

S. No.	Citation	Definition	Contemplated as
20	Baptista and Oliveira (2017)	MB can be defined as a type of execution of financial services in the course of which, within an electronic procedure, the customer uses mobile communication techniques in conjunction with mobile devices, or as the ability to bank virtually anytime and anywhere.	–
21	Chawla and Joshi (2017)	MB is a digital delivery channel where the bank customer interacts with his/her bank via a mobile device such as a smartphone or a personal digital assistant to access financial information and conduct transactions.	. . . a digital delivery channel.
22	Bhas (2014)	MB is the provision of banking services (operation of bank current and deposit or savings accounts, encapsulating services such as deposits, withdrawals, account transfers and balance inquiry) to customers on their mobile devices.	–
23	Gupta, Yun, Xu, and Kim (2017); Riivari (2005)	MB, considered as a new marketing and CRM tool, refers to the conduct of banking activities using a mobile device whereby customers can access their accounts to verify balances, transfer funds, pay bills, and perform various other transactions.	. . . a new marketing and CRM tool.
24	Sharma (2017)	MB refers to a service provided by banks or other financial institutions that allows its customers to conduct a range of financial and non-financial transactions. These transactions can be realized remotely using a mobile device such as a mobile phone or tablet on dedicated mobile applications (apps), provided by the financial institutions.	–
25	Yuan, Liu, Yao, and Liu (2016); Dahlberg, Mallat, Ondrus, and Zmijewska (2008)	MB means that users adopt mobile terminals such as cell phones to access payment services including account inquiry, transference and bill payment. Compared to traditional/online banking, the main advantages of m-banking are ubiquity and immediacy. That is, m-banking can free users from temporal and spatial limitations, and enable them to conduct payment at any time from anywhere.	–

Table 1.1 (Continued)

S. No.	Citation	Definition	Contemplated as
26	Glavee-Geo, Shaikh, and Karjaluoto (2017)	M-banking is defined as a service offered by a banking company, telecom company, or mobile network operator to conduct transactions via a mobile terminal.	–
27	Barnes and Corbitt (2003)	MB can be defined as a channel whereby the customer interacts with a bank via a mobile device, such as a mobile phone or personal digital assistant (PDA).	. . . a delivery channel.

m-banking as a new marketing and CRM tool, whereas Shaikh (2016) considered it as a successful business-to-consumer application. Research has additionally considered m-banking as a subset of mobile commerce (Mehrad & Mohammadi, 2016; Tam & Oliveira, 2016), an important information system (e.g., Luo, Li, Zhang, & Shim, 2010), an extension of e-payment system (Schierz, Schilke, & Wirtz, 2010), an innovative banking channel (Chawla & Joshi, 2017), and a subset of electronic finance (e.g., Ratten, 2012). Chung and Kwon (2009) discuss m-banking from the perspective of convergence of mobile technology and financial services. Baptista and Oliveira (2015) state m-banking to be a vital electronic banking channel.

In addition to SMS banking, prior literature has referred to the term 'm-banking' as cell phone banking (Masrek et al., 2014), smartphone banking (Park, Shin, & Lee, 2014), pocket banking (Amin, Hamid, Tanakinjal, & Lada, 2006), WAP Banking (Ratten, 2008), m-finance (Donner & Tellez, 2008), and digital banking (Olanrewaju, 2014).

The earlier variant of m-banking, known as SMS (short-message-service), first appeared during the late 1990s (Birch, 1999) when banks located in Scandinavian countries started offering financial services to mobile handsets. These mobile-based financial services were at the beginning related to notifications such as sending customers balance alerts. The first m-banking service was developed and introduced in Finland during early 1992 (Barnes & Corbitt, 2003). This first-ever m-banking application allowed the bank customers of MeritaNordbanken (later known as Nordea Bank) to make utility bill payments and check account balances using a cell phone. Further review of the past literature (e.g., Chawla & Joshi, 2017) reveals that the first self-service technologies in the world emerged in the 1970s when banks deployed ATMs. This was followed by telephone banking services introduced in the 1980s and the emergence of television, Internet, and an early browser-based version on m-banking called 'WAP-banking' in the 1990s (Suoranta & Mattila, 2004). After the development of smartphones in 2007 (notably the launch of the first iPhone), m-banking services transformed radically and allowed a host of innovative and value-added services via mobile applications (apps) that can easily be downloaded onto smartphones. These developments have largely inverted other banking channels, such as telephone and SMS banking.

M-banking is defined as the execution of banking services to conduct financial and non-financial transactions on a mobile phone or tablet (Veríssimo, 2016; Shaikh, Hanafizadeh, & Karjaluoto, 2017). M-banking offers an element of ubiquitousy as well as increased convenince and low-cost transactions for the consumers (Luo, Li, Zhang, & Shim, 2010). Lin (2013) considers m-banking a subset of m-commerce, facilitating consumers to conduct both conventional banking transactions (such as balance checks and fund transfers) and more advanced banking transactions (such as insurance and portfolio management services). Gu et al. (2009) treat m-banking as a 'salient system' considering its unique attributes: ubiquity, convenience, and interactivity. M-banking is often used to refer only to customers with bank accounts, and m-banking services perform various transactions on a bank customer's mobile phone or tablet. Despite the definitional divergence, a relative consensus is found in the literature that sees the m-banking as the provision of banking services on portable devices anytime anywhere.

M-banking benefits the consumer through anytime, anywhere banking convenience (time and location independence), with increasing ubiquity, immediacy, value-added banking service, low-cost banking, time optimization, immediate information, instant connectivity, and interactivity (Akturan & Tezcan, 2012). For banking and financial institutions, the benefits of introducing m-banking include an additional source of revenue, better efficiency and improved service quality, better customer relationship management, and better security.

The access methods in m-banking, however, differ from one demographic location to another and it largely relies on technologies and communication protocols for providing banking services (e.g., transfer of funds), and related inquiries (e.g., searching for the closest ATM location) to a demographically disbursed population (Oliveira et al., 2014). In most of the developed markets, m-banking applications provide various innovative, secure, and high-value banking services and support to consumers. The banking companies and other financial institutions located in the global south in developing and low-income countries are leveraging their experience and offering m-banking applications in addition to SMS notifications and various alerts. Therefore, the m-banking applications are also gaining popularity in emerging and developing countries.

In sum, m-banking is considered as one of the core components of the retail MFS sector, and it has rapidly emerged as the most preferred and separate bank channel by banks and customers, a powerful CRM tool used to build loyalty and mutually rewarding relationships with customers.

M-payments technology and services

One promising area of m-commerce that is receiving attention globally from consumers to merchants as an alternative to using cash, check instrument, or payment cards is *mobile payment* (Oliveira, Thomas, Baptista, & Campos, 2016). According to Allied Market Research (2017), the global mobile payments market is estimated to reach $3.388 trillion by 2022, growing at a rate of 33.4% from 2016 to 2022. Considering its prolific benefits, Nokia Corporation invested USD 70 million in Obopay to enter the m-payment market in April 2009; China mobile bought 20% of PuDong bank stake in May 2010 to develop m-payment services; Google ventures invested USD 100 million in May 2010 into m-payment business (Yang, Lu, Gupta, Cao, & Zhang, 2012). The first mobile-based non-cash payment transaction was conducted using a mobile device in 1997 (Dahlberg, Guo, & Ondrus, 2015) when Coca-Cola Beverages Company experimented with vending machines that accepted SMS-based payments in Finland (Dahlberg et al., 2015).

One of the significant observations made while synthesizing the literature of mobile payment is that a radical shift has been noticed where the mobile device was earlier used as a browser, accessing existing Internet-based banking and retail systems (known as Internet banking) to the use of downloadable mobile application as a payment form, thereby reducing the need for paper-based instruments such as checks, pay orders, as well as cash and plastic cards.

According to Thakur and Srivastava (2014) m-payment refers to making payments for goods and services using mobile devices including smart cell phones, radio frequency enabled and near-field communication-based devices. Dahlberg et al. (2015) define m-payments as mobile-based payments for goods, services, information, and bills with a mobile device by taking advantage of wireless and other communication technologies. Table 1.2 summarizes a host of definitions proposed by the research on m-payment.

M-payments, also known as mobile wallet, have been divided into two major domains: proximity and remote. Proximity, contactless, or on-site m-payment mechanism is largely performed by using various innovative technologies such as Bluetooth, near-field communications (NFC), and radio frequency identification (RFID) (Morosan & DeFranco, 2016; Pham & Ho, 2015). Here the presence of both buyers' and sellers' at one physical location is essential. Remote or off-site payments are performed through text messages, downloadable m-banking applications, wireless payment network requiring wireless application protocol, and mobile data exchange.

Branchless banking technology and services

According to Dermish, Kneiding, Leishman, and Mas (2011), branchless banking involves building a payment infrastructure that allows customers and businesses to deposit and withdraw funds and make electronic

Table 1.2 Mobile payment literature summary

S. No.	Citation	Definition	Contemplated as
1	Chen (2008)	MP refers to making payments using mobile devices including wireless handsets (e.g., cell phones and Blackberry devices), Personal Digital Assistants (PDA), Radio Frequency (RF) devices and Near-Field Communication (NFC) based devices.	–
2	Au and Kauffman (2008)	MP is any payment where a mobile device is used to initiate, authorize and confirm an exchange of financial value in return for goods and services.	–
3	Weber and Darbellay (2010)	MP is a range of mobile commerce services that entail initiated or confirmed payment transactions by means of a mobile phone.	. . . a range of mobile commerce services.
4	Gerpott and Kornmeier (2009)	MP is a solution utilizing mobile devices to make transactions, for example, banking transactions or pay bills.	–
5	Liébana-Cabanillas, Sánchez-Fernández, & Muñoz-Leiva, 2014 (2014)	MP is a business activity involving an electronic device with a connection to a mobile network enabling the successful completion of an economic transaction.	. . . a business activity.
6	Zhou (2011)	MP means that users adopt mobile terminals to conduct payment at anytime from anywhere.	–
7	Amoroso and Magnier-Watanabe (2012)	MP is defined as any payment in which a mobile device, such as a mobile phone or any other device capable of connecting to mobile communication networks, is utilized to initiate, authorize, and confirm a commercial transaction. A mobile wallet is a type of electronic wallet which carries out transactions using a mobile device, and the former is an evolution of the latter.	–
8	Dahlberg et al. (2008); Tan, Ooi, Chong, and Hew (2014)	MP is the payment for goods, services, and bills with a mobile device such as mobile phone, smartphone, or personal digital assistant by taking advantage of wireless and other communication technologies.	–

(Continued)

Table 1.2 (Continued)

S. No.	Citation	Definition	Contemplated as
9	Kim, Mirus-monov, and Lee (2010)	MP is defined as any payment in which a mobile device is utilized to initiate, authorize, and confirm a commercial transaction.	–
10	Dennehy and Sammon (2015)	MP is the transfer of funds in return for a good or service, where the mobile phone is involved in both the initiation and confirmation of the payment.	–
11	Liébana-Cabanillas and Lara-Rubio (2017); Ghezzi, Renga, and Balocco (2010)	MP is considered by many experts as one of the applications with the greatest potential in this sector, even referring to it as the future "star" or "killer" application in mobile communications. Mobile payment can be defined as any type of individual or business activity involving an electronic device connected to a mobile network thus enabling the successful completion of an economic transaction.	. . . a "star" or "killer" application.
12	Ting, Yacob, Liew, and Lau (2016)	MP, which is a particular form of e-payment, utilizes communication technology by enabling mobile users to make payment using Internet-connected mobile devices.	. . . a particular form of e-payment.
13	Ondrus and Pigneur (2005)	MP is the wireless transactions of a monetary value from one party to another using a mobile device whose physical form can vary from a mobile phone to any wireless enabled device (e.g., PDA, laptop, key ring, watch) which are capable of securely processing a financial transaction over a wireless network.	. . . a wireless transactions of a monetary value.

payments using a portable device, such as cell phone, from everyday retail stores or agents, thus eliminating the need for bank branches. Branchless banking, also referred to as mobile money, is a supply side innovation that potentially supports the needs of the poor or unbanked through financial inclusion initiatives that are useful for managing their lives and livelihoods (Duncombe, 2012). Therefore, the notion that branchless banking increases the financial inclusion among the underbanked and unbanked consumer segment in developing countries is substantively important. Despite its growing importance and need, the analysis of the areas covered by the articles included in this review indicated a dearth of published work in the area of branchless banking and similar other areas, such as mobile money.

Several titles have been attributed to bank-led and MNO-led branchless banking technology and services. For instance, in Africa, branchless banking is known as 'mobile money,' 'M-PESA,' 'mKesk,' or 'Wizzit.' In Asia, it is known as 'Easypaisa' or 'agent banking.' In emerging markets such as Brazil, branchless banking is known as 'correspondent banking.' In some countries, branchless banking is considered as a variant of m-banking that is conducted through SMS notification on both basic cell phones and smartphones with a GSM connection. Figure 1.2 depicts various branchless-banking-based models deployed in various countries. These models have been segregated into two major domains: bank-led and MNO-led. Since banks and other financial institutions are adequately regulated, the bank-led branchless banking models are considered more secure than MNO-led branchless banking models.

The growing use of branchless banking in emerging and developing countries is considered inevitable and the most relevant alternative banking channel, since most remotely located population segments have no other way to access banking services. Although it is less certain whether large numbers of the unbanked poor will adopt and use this alternative channel for financial services (Pickens, Porteous, & Rotman, 2009), it is generally agreed that branchless banking has facilitated an unprecedented growth in bank outreach especially in Africa and has become a reference worldwide (Jayo, Diniz, Zambaldi, & Christopoulos, 2012). In fact, there is a tremendous opportunity for banking technology to streamline banking processes,

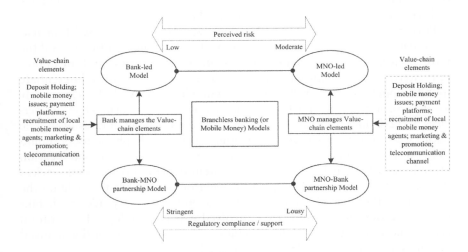

Figure 1.2 Branchless banking landscape

connect lower-income citizens at reduced costs, and bring millions of consumers to the formal financial marketplace through digital channels such as branchless banking (Diniz, Birochi, & Pozzebon, 2012).

Mobile money allows financial and non-financial institutions such as MNO to offer banking and payment services outside traditional bank premises. Despite steep challenges for the government, banks, and other financial institutions, it is considered important to reach the underbanked and unbanked consumer segment when the consumption of formal banking products and services is considered an important prerequisite to improving economic activities, helping the less privileged to increase their household income, building their asset base, and improving their resilience to shocks (Abramovay, 2004; Morawczynski, 2009).

The increasing importance and success of the mobile money model are largely attached to the non-access to the formal banking and payment services (such as conventional or branch-oriented banking, ATM banking, Internet banking, and m-banking) to a larger segment of the population also known as 'financial excluded' living in remote areas. This motivates the banking industry to expand its outreach by developing and deploying banking and payment services that can be conveniently accessed using cell phones by a largely unserved and unexplored consumer segment, which is often referred to as the underbanked or unbanked.

In branchless banking the African continent is considered the global leader in mobile money, followed by the South Asian countries such as Pakistan and India. According to McKinsey and Co. (2017), over half of the 282 mobile money services operating worldwide are located in the African continent. Moreover, there are over 100 million active mobile money accounts in Africa and 40 million active mobile money accounts in South Asia. Majority of these mobile money users in Africa and South Africa are those who have little or no access to a bank branch or ATMs.

Prior research (e.g., Tobbin, 2012; Suárez, 2016) has discussed four reasons that allow the development of branchless banking, a different and the most preferred banking channel in low-income countries, and an important alternative for financial inclusion. These four reasons also differentiate mobile money from other domains that fall within the MFS. First, remotely located consumer segments have no other way to access formal banking services and conduct transactions. Second, there must be high rates of mobile phone diffusion. In other words, the number of mobile phone users should long exceed the number of people with bank accounts at a certain location (Tobbin, 2012). Third, there must be a latent demand for financial services (Suárez, 2016). Fourth, the regulatory environment needs to facilitate the banks and other financial and non-financial entities (supply side) while taking into account the possible risks involved when technological innovation is introduced to masses with low literacy and awareness about the financial products and technology (Heyer & Mas, 2011).

Differences between the m-banking, m-payments, and branchless banking

In this section, we address the third research question by discussing how these three types of MFS differ from each other. First, we will bring into discussion the major difference between the first two mobile financial technologies, i.e., m-banking and m-payments.

M-banking is always considered a formal digital bank channel which means all the value chain elements, i.e., product development and deployment, digital customer service, m-banking application, and deposit holding, are owned and managed by a diligently regulated banking company. M-payment on the other hand follows a less stringent regulatory framework that allows greater collaboration and partnership with nonbanking entities. To retain and expend the market share and consumer base, banking companies develop different m-banking and m-payment applications and provide various value-added services to banked and de-banked consumers. To access and conduct m-payment transactions, the user does not necessarily need a bank account. De-banked consumers – those who do not wish to maintain a formal bank account with any bank – prefer to opt and use the m-payment services. Prominent m-payment models include mobile wallet.

Adopting a different perspective, Hepola, Karjaluoto, and Shaikh (2016) consider m-wallet a much-advanced versatile m-payment application. For example, unlike m-banking applications, m-wallet applications can include several innovative elements, such as conducting m-payments that contain information related to membership cards, loyalty cards, travel cards, and usually also store-sensitive and personal information in the form of passports, credit card information, PIN codes, and encrypted online shopping accounts.

Second, when looking at the difference between m-banking and branchless banking, the latter is considered a viable alternative payment service supporting the financial inclusion programs initiated in developing countries as well as providing scalable financial services, markets, and information to the poor. These financial inclusion programs are enabling the demographically disbursed and remotely located population where the presence of bank branches and ATMs are very uncommon. Here mobile money technology and services allow the widespread use of money transfers, credit, and savings (Karippacheril, Nikayin, De Reuver, & Bouwman, 2013) on a basic cell phone set.

Despite many benefits of using mobile money services, the mobile money transactions have presented regulatory challenges that could potentially hinder their potential benefits (Nyaga, 2014). For example, unlike m-banking that is offered by the banks, mobile money blurs the traditionally distinct and independent sectors of regulation such as telecommunications and financial sectors (Nyaga, 2014). Furthermore, prior research (e.g., Porteous, 2006) has segregated mobile money from other subsets of MFS, such as m-banking and m-payments, by proposing two models, i.e., additive and transformational. Mobile money is largely considered as transformational. The term 'transformational' is defined as one of the banking and payment models in which the financial product is linked to the use of the phone and is targeted at the unbanked and underbanked with the largely low-income user. All other MFS are considered additive.

Conclusion

The underline purpose of this chapter was to present a conceptualization of the term 'MFS' and investigate what constitutes the field of MFS. Globally, the mobile financial services – which are largely seen as convenient extension of services over the phone – are offered by a large portion of banks and financial institutions either as stand-alone or in collaboration with different service providers. Moreover, the term 'mobility' in the MFS is less referred to any specific device and more about providing new opportunities and wider options to augment customer interactions with the delivery channels available now, with more to come in the near future (Srinivas, Friedman, & Eckenrode, 2014).

Two types of MFS, i.e., m-banking and m-payments, dominate the digital retail banking sector. These are largely interconnected and interrelated to each other since they use the cell phone as the primary communication channel. However, the business models, regulatory frameworks, consumer and service concentration, and target market make them distinct from each other. The success of the m-banking in developed countries is largely attributed to an extensive usage of smart portable devices and the availability of infrastructure and communication services offered by the mobile network operators. This infrastructure facilitates an uninterrupted access to the consumers to use the banking services on their cell phones at the convenience of their office and home.

Branchless banking or mobile money services, unlike m-banking and m-payment, provided a different perspective. Our discussion suggests that mobile money was primarily targeted at the underbanked and unbanked population segments with very low-income sources. However, this assertion is now gradually changing. For example, the use of branchless banking is not limited to low-income segments of the population, but other customer segments and income earners are making use of branchless banking financial services due to its simplicity, convenience, innovativeness, and low-cost transactions.

Branchless banking allows customers also without a formal bank account to conduct low-value, high-volume financial transactions, such as deposits and transfers, at designated retail stores known as branchless banking agents or third-party outlets. These outlets can be a small retailer, a post office, and so forth. In some cases, the mobile network operators also act as an agent as well as co-marketing and branding with banks and other financial institutions. Therefore, unlike other digital banking channels, such as ATMs which require large investments and maintenance costs, mobile money services largely rely on the agent network by providing an alternative banking delivery mechanism using cell phones with a GSM connection. According to GSMA (2017), the branchless banking industry, including technology and services, is now processing over a billion USD of transactions a day and generating direct revenues of over USD 2.4 billion, which makes branchless banking a leading payment platform for the digital economy in many emerging markets.

The banking industry and customers have realized the growing importance and necessity of the MFS. Here the development and the deployment of innovative digital banking channels has provided an innovative option for facilitating customers to remotely access and use various banking and payment products at their convenience. This convenience and freedom of choice of accessing and using digital banking channels allows greater levels of customer empowerment (Loonam & O'Loughlin, 2008), provide an unprecedented breadth and depth of consumer choice opportunities in a wide range of domains (Broniarczyk & Griffin, 2014).

Note

* *Corresponding/primary contact author*

References

Abramovay, R. (2004). As finanças na luta contra a pobreza. *Desafios do Desenvolvimento, 1*(3), 66–67.

Akturan, U., & Tezcan, N. (2012). Mobile banking adoption of the youth market: Perceptions and intentions. *Marketing Intelligence & Planning, 30*(4), 444–459.

Al-Ajam, A. S., & MdNor, K. (2015). Challenges of adoption of Internet banking service in Yemen. *International Journal of Bank Marketing, 33*(2), 178–194.

Allied Market Research. (2017). Retrieved from www.alliedmarketresearch.com/mobile-payments-market

Amin, H., Hamid, M. R. A., Tanakinjal, G. H., & Lada, S. (2006). Undergraduate attitudes and expectations for mobile banking. *The Journal of Internet Banking and Commerce, 11*(3), 1–10.

Amoroso, D. L., & Magnier-Watanabe, R. (2012). Building a research model for mobile wallet consumer adoption: The case of mobile Suica in Japan. *Journal of Theoretical and Applied Electronic Commerce Research, 7*(1), 94–110.

Au, Y. A., & Kauffman, R. J. (2008). The economics of mobile payments: Understanding stakeholder issues for an emerging financial technology application. *Electronic Commerce Research and Applications, 7*(2), 141–164.

Baptista, G., & Oliveira, T. (2017). Why so serious? Gamification impact in the acceptance of mobile banking services. *Internet Research, 27*(1), 118–139.

Baptista, G., & Oliveira, T. (2015). Understanding mobile banking: The unified theory of acceptance and use of technology combined with cultural moderators. *Computers in Human Behavior, 50*, 418–430.

Barnes, S. J., & Corbitt, B. (2003). Mobile banking: Concept and potential. *International Journal of Mobile Communications, 1*(3), 273–288.

Bhas, N. (2014). Digital banking: Mobile and beyond, white paper. *Juniper Research, Basingstoke, Hampshire.* [Google Scholar]. Retrieved February 10, 2016, from www.juniperresearch.com/whitepaper/digital-banking-mobile-and-beyond

Birch, D. G. W. (1999, October). Mobile financial services: The Internet isn't the only digital channel to consumers. *Journal of Internet Banking and Commerce, 4*(1).

Boor, p. V. D., Oliveira, P., & Veloso, F. (2014). Users as innovators in developing countries: The global sources of innovation and diffusion in mobile banking services. *Research Policy, 43*, 1594–1607.

Broniarczyk, S. M., & Griffin, J. G. (2014). Decision difficulty in the age of consumer empowerment. *Journal of Consumer Psychology, 24*(4), 608–625.

Chaouali, W., Souiden, N., & Ladhari, R. (2017). Explaining adoption of mobile banking with the theory of trying, general self-confidence, and cynicism. *Journal of Retailing and Consumer Services, 35*, 57–67.

Chawla, D., & Joshi, H. (2017). Consumer perspectives about mobile banking adoption in India: A cluster analysis. *International Journal of Bank Marketing, 35*(4), 616–636.

Chen, L. D. (2008). A model of consumer acceptance of mobile payment. *International Journal of Mobile Communications, 6*(1), 32–52.

Chung, N., & Kwon, S. J. (2009). The effects of customers' mobile experience and technical support on the intention to use mobile banking. *Cyberpsychology & Behavior, 12*(5), 539–543.

Dahlberg, T., Guo, J., & Ondrus, J. (2015). A critical review of mobile payment research. *Electronic Commerce Research and Applications, 14*(5), 265–284.

Dahlberg, T., Mallat, N., Ondrus, J., & Zmijewska, A. (2008). Past, present and future of mobile payments research: A literature review. *Electronic Commerce Research and Applications, 7*(2), 165–181.

Dass, R., & Pal, S. (2011). *Exploring the factors affecting the adoption of mobile financial services among the rural under-banked.* ECIS 2011. Proceedings of the European Conference on Information Systems. Paper 246. Retrieved from http://www.aisel.aisnet.org/ecis2011/246

Demirgüç-Kunt, A., & Klapper, L. (2013). Measuring financial inclusion: Explaining variation in use of financial services across and within countries. *Brookings Papers on Economic Activity, 2013*(1), 279–340.

Dennehy, D., & Sammon, D. (2015). Trends in mobile payments research: A literature review. *Journal of Innovation Management, 3*(1), 49–61.

Dermish, A., Kneiding, C., Leishman, P., & Mas, I. (2011). Branchless and mobile banking solutions for the poor: A survey of the literature. *Innovations: Technology, Governance, Globalization, 6*(4), 81–98.

Diniz, E., Birochi, R., & Pozzebon, M. (2012). Triggers and barriers to financial inclusion: The use of ICT-based branchless banking in an Amazon county. *Electronic Commerce Research and Applications, 11*(5), 484–494.

Donner, J., & Tellez, C. A. (2008). Mobile banking and economic development: Linking, adoption, impact, and use. *Asian Journal of Communication, 18*(4), 318–332.

Duncombe, R. (2012). An evidence-based framework for assessing the potential of mobile finance in sub-Saharan Africa. *The Journal of Modern African Studies, 50*(3), 369–395.

Feinberg, R. A., Hokama, L., Kadam, R., & Kim, I. (2002). Operational determinants of caller satisfaction in the banking/financial services call center. *International Journal of Bank Marketing, 20*(4), 174–180.

Fenu, G., & Pau, p. L. (2015). An analysis of features and tendencies in mobile banking apps. *Procedia Computer Science, 56*, 26–33.

Gerpott, T., & Kornmeier, K. (2009). Determinants of customer acceptance of mobile payment systems. *International Journal of Electronic Finance, 3*(1), 1–30.

Ghezzi, A., Renga, F., & Balocco, R. p. (2010). Pescetto mobile payment applications: Offer state of the art in the Italian market. *Info, 12*(5), 3–22.

Glavee-Geo, R., Shaikh, A. A., & Karjaluoto, H. (2017). Mobile banking services adoption in Pakistan: Are there gender differences? *International Journal of Bank Marketing, 35*(7), 1090–1114.

GSMA. (2017). *2017 state of the industry report on mobile money*. Retrieved from www. gsma.com/mobilefordevelopment/sotir/?gclid=EAIaIQobChMI9Nnrh6-02gIVyM qyCh13UwALEAAYAiAAEgIjMPD_BwE

Gu, J. C., Lee, S. C., & Suh, Y. H. (2009). Determinants of behavioral intention to mobile banking. *Expert Systems with Applications, 36*(7), 11605–11616.

Gupta, S., Yun, H., Xu, H., & Kim, H. W. (2017). An exploratory study on mobile banking adoption in Indian metropolitan and urban areas: A scenario-based experiment. *Information Technology for Development, 23*(1), 127–152.

Helsper, E. J., & Eynon, R. (2010). Digital natives: Where is the evidence? *British Educational Research Journal, 36*(3), 503–520.

Hepola, J., Karjaluoto, H., & Shaikh, A. A. (2016). *Consumer engagement and behavioral intention toward continuous use of innovative mobile banking applications: A case study of Finland.* Thirty Seventh International Conference on Information Systems, AISel, Dublin.

Heyer, A., & Mas, I. (2011). Fertile grounds for mobile money: Towards a framework for analysing enabling environments. *Enterprise Development and Microfinance, 22*(1), 30–44.

Jayo, M., Diniz, E. H., Zambaldi, F., & Christopoulos, T. p. (2012). Groups of services delivered by Brazilian branchless banking and respective network integration models. *Electronic Commerce Research and Applications, 11*(5), 504–517.

Karippacheril, T. G., Nikayin, F., De Reuver, M., & Bouwman, H. (2013). Serving the poor: Multisided mobile service platforms, openness, competition, collaboration and the struggle for leadership. *Telecommunications Policy, 37*(1), 24–34.

Kim, C., Mirusmonov, M., & Lee, I. (2010). An empirical examination of factors influencing the intention to use mobile payment. *Computers in Human Behavior, 26*(3), 310–322.

Kumar, V. R., Lall, A., & Mane, T. (2017). Extending the TAM Model: Intention of management students to use mobile banking: Evidence from India. *Global Business Review, 18*(1), 238–249.

Lee, H., Harindranath, G., Oh, S., & Kim, D. J. (2015). Provision of mobile banking services from an actor: Network perspective: Implications for convergence and standardization. *Technological Forecasting and Social Change, 90*, 551–561.

Liébana-Cabanillas, F., & Lara-Rubio, J. (2017). Predictive and explanatory modeling regarding adoption of mobile payment systems. *Technological Forecasting and Social Change, 120*, 32–40.

Liébana-Cabanillas, F., Sánchez-Fernández, J., & Muñoz-Leiva, F. (2014). Antecedents of the adoption of the new mobile payment systems: The moderating effect of age. *Computers in Human Behavior, 35*, 464–478.

Lin, H. F. (2013). Determining the relative importance of mobile banking quality factors. *Computer Standards & Interfaces, 35*(2), 195–204.

Loonam, M., & O'Loughlin, D. (2008). An observation analysis of e-service quality in online banking. *Journal of Financial Services Marketing, 13*(2), 164–178.

Luo, X., Li, H., Zhang, J., & Shim, J. p. (2010). Examining multi-dimensional trust and multi-faceted risk in initial acceptance of emerging technologies: An empirical study of mobile banking services. *Decision Support Systems, 49*(2), 222–234.

Malaquias, R. F., & Hwang, Y. (2016). An empirical study on trust in mobile banking: A developing country perspective. *Computers in Human Behavior, 54*, 453–461.

Masrek, M. N., Mohamed, I. S., Daud, N. M., & Omar, N. (2014). Technology trust and mobile banking satisfaction: A case of Malaysian consumers. *Procedia-Social and Behavioral Sciences, 129*, 53–58.

McKinsey and Co. (2017). *Mobile financial services in Africa: Winning the battle for the customer.* Retrieved from www.mckinsey.com/industries/financial-services/our-insights/mobile-financial-services-in-africa-winning-the-battle-for-the-customer

Mehrad, D., & Mohammadi, S. (2016). Word of Mouth impact on the adoption of mobile banking in Iran. *Telematics and Informatics, 34*(7), 1351–1363.

Mohammadi, H. (2015). A study of mobile banking usage in Iran. *International Journal of Bank Marketing, 33*(6), 733–759.

Morawczynski, O. (2009). Exploring the usage and impact of "transformational" mobile financial services: The case of M-PESA in Kenya. *Journal of Eastern African Studies, 3*(3), 509–525.

Morosan, C., & DeFranco, A. (2016). It's about time: Revisiting UTAUT2 to examine consumers' intentions to use NFC mobile payments in hotels. *International Journal of Hospitality Management, 53*, 17–29.

Muñoz-Leiva, F., Climent-Climent, S., & Liébana-Cabanillas, F. (2017). Determinants of intention to use the mobile banking apps: An extension of the classic TAM model. *Spanish Journal of Marketing-ESIC, 21*(1), 25–38.

Nyaga, J. K. (2014). Mobile banking services in the East African Community (EAC): Challenges to the existing legislative and regulatory frameworks. *Journal of Information Policy, 4*, 270–295.

Olanrewaju, T. (2014). *The rise of the digital bank.* Retrieved from www.mckinsey.com/insights/business_technology/the_rise_of_the_digital_bank

Oliveira, T., Faria, M., Thomas, M. A., & Popovič, A. (2014). Extending the understanding of mobile banking adoption: When UTAUT meets TTF and ITM. *International Journal of Information Management, 34*(5), 689–703.

Oliveira, T., Thomas, M., Baptista, G., & Campos, F. (2016). Mobile payment: Understanding the determinants of customer adoption and intention to recommend the technology. *Computers in Human Behavior, 61*, 404–414.

Ondrus, J., & Pigneur, Y. (2005, January). *A disruption analysis in the mobile payment market.* System Sciences. HICSS'05. Proceedings of the 38th Annual Hawaii International Conference on (pp. 84c–84c). IEEE.

Ouma, S. A., Odongo, T. M., & Were, M. (2017). Mobile financial services and financial inclusion: Is it a boon for savings mobilization? *Review of Development Finance, 7*(1), 29–35.

Park, K. C., Shin, J. W., & Lee, B. G. (2014). Analysis of authentication methods for smartphone banking service using ANP. *KSII Transactions on Internet and Information Systems (TIIS), 8*, 2087–2103.

Petrauskas, R., & Zumaras, L. (2008). Comparative analysis of mobile payments in the European Union. *Intelektine Ekonomika*, 2(4).

Pham, T. T. T., & Ho, J. C. (2015). The effects of product-related, personal-related factors and attractiveness of alternatives on consumer adoption of NFC-based mobile payments. *Technology in Society*, 43, 159–172.

Pickens, M., Porteous, D., & Rotman, S. (2009). *Scenarios for branchless banking in 2020*. Washington, DC: CGAP.

Porteous, D. (2006). The enabling environment for mobile banking in Africa. Paper Commissioned by United Kingdom Department for International Development (DFIP). Retrieved from www.bankablefrontier.com/assets/ee.mobil.banking.report.v3.1.pdf

Prensky, M. (2001). Digital natives, digital immigrants part 1. *On the Horizon*, 9(5), 1–6.

Ratten, V. (2008). Technological innovations in the m-commerce industry: A conceptual model of WAP banking intentions. *The Journal of High Technology Management Research*, 18, 111–117.

Ratten, V. (2012). Entrepreneurship, e-finance and mobile banking. *International Journal of Electronic Finance*, 6, 1–12.

Riivari, J. (2005). Mobile banking: A powerful new marketing and CRM tool for financial services companies all over Europe. *Journal of Financial Services Marketing*, 10(1), 11–20.

Schierz, p. G., Schilke, O., & Wirtz, B. W. (2010). Understanding consumer acceptance of mobile payment services: An empirical analysis. *Electronic Commerce Research and Applications*, 9(3), 209–216.

Selvadurai, J. (2014). Security risks and protection mechanisms in mobile payments. *International Journal of Technology and Research*, 2(3), 93.

Shaikh, A. A. (2016). Examining consumers' intention, behavior, and beliefs in mobile banking adoption and continuous usage. *Jyväskylä Studies in Business and Economics*, 172.

Shaikh, A. A., Hanafizadeh, P., & Karjaluoto, H. (2017). Mobile banking and payment system: A conceptual standpoint. *International Journal of E-Business Research*, 13.

Shaikh, A. A., & Karjaluoto, H. (2015). Mobile banking adoption: A literature review. *Telematics and Informatics*, 32(1), 129–142.

Sharma, S. K. (2017). Integrating cognitive antecedents into TAM to explain mobile banking behavioral intention: A SEM-neural network modeling. *Information Systems Frontiers*, 1–13.

Srinivas, V., Friedman, S., & Eckenrode, J. (2014). *Mobile financial services: Raising the bar on customer engagement*. Westlake, TX: Deloitte University Press. [Google Scholar].

Suárez, S. L. (2016). Poor people's money: The politics of mobile money in Mexico and Kenya. *Telecommunications Policy*, 40(10), 945–955.

Suoranta, M., & Mattila, M. (2004). Mobile banking and consumer behaviour: New insights into the diffusion pattern. *Journal of Financial Services Marketing*, 8(4), 354–366.

Tam, C., & Oliveira, T. (2016). Understanding the impact of m-banking on individual performance: DeLone & McLean and TTF perspective. *Computers in Human Behavior*, 61, 233–244.

Tan, G. W. H., Ooi, K. B., Chong, S. C., & Hew, T. S. (2014). NFC mobile credit card: The next frontier of mobile payment? *Telematics and Informatics, 31*(2), 292–307.

Thakur, R., & Srivastava, M. (2014). Adoption readiness, personal innovativeness, perceived risk and usage intention across customer groups for mobile payment services in India. *Internet Research, 24*, 369–392.

Ting, H., Yacob, Y., Liew, L., & Lau, W. M. (2016). Intention to use mobile payment system: A case of developing market by ethnicity. *Procedia-Social and Behavioral Sciences, 224*, 368–375.

Tiwari, R., & Buse, S. (2007). *The mobile commerce prospects: A strategic analysis of opportunities in the banking sector.* Hamburg, Germany: Hamburg University Press.

Tobbin, p. (2012). Towards a model of adoption in mobile banking by the unbanked: A qualitative study. *Info, 14*(5), 74–88.

Veríssimo, J. M. C. (2016). Enablers and restrictors of mobile banking app use: A fuzzy set qualitative comparative analysis (fsQCA). *Journal of Business Research, 69*(11), 5456–5460.

Weber, R. H., & Darbellay, A. (2010). Legal issues in mobile banking. *Journal of Banking Regulation, 11*, 129–145.

Yang, S., Lu, Y., Gupta, S., Cao, Y., & Zhang, R. (2012). Mobile payment services adoption across time: An empirical study of the effects of behavioral beliefs, social influences, and personal traits. *Computers in Human Behavior, 28*(1), 129–142.

Yuan, S., Liu, Y., Yao, R., & Liu, J. (2016). An investigation of users' continuance intention towards mobile banking in China. *Information Development, 32*(1), 20–34.

Zhou, T. (2011). The effect of initial trust on user adoption of mobile payment. *Information Development, 27*(4), 290–300.

Zhou, T., Lu, Y., & Wang, B. (2010). Integrating TTF and UTAUT to explain mobile banking user adoption. *Computers in Human Behavior, 26*(4), 760–767.

2 Engaging non-active consumers to use mobile financial services

A developed country perspective

Hanna Komulainen, * *Saila Saraniemi and Pauliina Ulkuniemi*

Introduction

The marketing landscape has changed significantly with the rise of digital technologies, and along with this development, mobile financial services (MFS) have become a key issue in the financial sectors. MFS can be defined as a service provided by a financial institution that enables customers to conduct various financial transactions remotely using a mobile device (i.e., a smartphone or tablet) and mobile software (Yen & Wu, 2016). As in other previous studies (e.g., Chemingui & Iallouna, 2013; Yen & Wu, 2016), we use the concept of MFS as a synonym for mobile banking services, and thus MFS refers to financial, bank-related services that are used via a mobile channel (excluding laptops or other devices used in online banking services).

Mobile banking has gained a growing amount of interest among information systems (IS) and marketing scholars (Laukkanen & Kiviniemi, 2010). The majority of empirical studies explore consumer acceptance of mobile banking services (see extensive reviews in Baptista & Oliveira, 2015; Shaikh & Karjaluoto, 2015) through quantitative methodologies. Customer acceptance refers to customers' behavioral intention to adopt mobile banking (Jeong & Yoon, 2013), and most studies thus focus on consumers' intentions to use the service (Laukkanen, 2016). However, recent literature criticizes this and suggests that research should focus more on actual usage behavior, since behavioral intention might not accurately predict actual usage (Wu & Du, 2012; Laukkanen, 2016). We agree and suggest that examining intentions does not provide profound understanding of the customers using (or not using) mobile banking services. Therefore, a qualitative approach and a focus on actual usage of MFS is needed to gain more in-depth knowledge.

In addition, existing research on mobile banking is mostly centered on early adopters (see Rogers, 2003), i.e., active consumers interested in new technologies. However, in addition to early adopters, there exists also non-active consumers who are currently reluctant to use mobile financial services, and their role in the markets needs to be considered as well. There are a few surveys that have addressed the non-usage of Internet banking services (e.g., Laukkanen, 2016) or more generally resistant behavior of individuals (e.g., Kleijnen, Lee, N., & Wetzels, 2009), but in order to make MFS a thriving business, a more thorough understanding of the non-active consumers and their reasons for not using MFS needs to be achieved.

Empirically, the present study focuses on studying the non-active users of MFS in Finland. One of the key features of the Finnish financial markets has been the emergence of large financial conglomerates offering banking, finance, and insurance services, and also actively developing their digital service offerings. For example, a Finnish bank OP launched its Internet banking services in 1996, being the second bank in the world to do so and the first in Europe (Deloitte Review, 2017). Although Finland is one of the leading European countries in MFS adoption, according to the Digital Payments Report (2016), 53% of consumers are still not using any mobile payment services. The non-active users of MFS form a vast group of people who represent massive unutilized potential for mobile financial service providers. Although non-active MFS users can be identified in all age groups, these people are often identified as the elderly (see, e.g., Laukkanen, 2016) who may also have substantial wealth. This raises the critical question of how to get the non-active consumers to start using mobile financial services and to continue using them. Answering this question is the purpose of the present study.

We use the literature related to innovations and MFS in particular and complement it with recent marketing studies related to customer's service experience, value creation, and engagement in order to get a more comprehensive understanding of the researched phenomenon. Although past research has identified numerous different drivers (e.g., Jeong & Yoon, 2013), barriers (e.g., Laukkanen & Kiviniemi, 2010), demographic features (e.g., Yen & Wu, 2016), and other antecedents (Lin, 2011) influencing mobile banking service acceptance, this study proposes a wider viewpoint by extending the perspective beyond the intention to use. In our qualitative research, we take a look at a diverse set of consumers, their attitudes, service experiences, and future expectations at three different phases: before service usage, during it, and afterwards. In other words, we do not concentrate only on the factors that are important for intentions in pre-usage phase but also on factors that are emphasized in the customers' actual use experiences and specifically factors critical from the perspective of continued use and long-term engagement to the mobile banking service. This is highly important in light of our aim to unveil how to get non-active consumers to start using and continue to use MFS.

In the empirical part, we have conducted qualitative research in order to get an in-depth understanding of the non-active consumers and the reasons behind their reluctance to use MFS. Empirical data was collected through 24 semi-structured theme interviews and three focus groups. Both active users (those who currently use or had used any mobile banking service) and non-active users (those who have not used any mobile banking service) were included to complement the big picture. Theory-based content analysis was used to analyze the data, adopting also an abductive approach.

The present study contributes to existing bank marketing research by empirically and through a qualitative approach exploring the non-active consumers and the use of MFS. By extending the view from pre-usage towards examining the actual usage and continuation of usage through active users, the study provides a more holistic view of the phenomenon, which currently is lacking in the existing research. The study also provides implications for banks and other actors developing new MFS by indicating what elements to focus on in the service development in order to get also non-active consumers to use and continue using their services.

The remainder of the study is organized as follows. First, the previous literature is reviewed, and based on that, a tentative theoretical framework is developed. Thereafter, the methodology used is described. The chapter then presents the empirical findings of the study and suggests an empirically grounded framework of how to engage non-active customers to use mobile financial services. Finally, we outline the theoretical and managerial implications of our findings and present some avenues for future research.

Theoretical foundations

Mobile banking is one of the major technological innovations for financial institutions (Lin, 2011). Moving customers to the mobile channel is an important issue for banks because it allows them to reduce operational costs (Calisir & Gumussoy, 2008), but more importantly, it provides a convenient means for customers to meet their banking needs flexibly and with better quality, availability, and usability (Chemingui & Iallouna, 2013). In order to increase understanding on how to get the non-active consumers to start using and continue to use mobile financial services, we use the innovation diffusion literature as a broad starting point for our study, as it is an often-used theory in MFS studies exploring different aspects that affect an individual's adoption of new technology (e.g., Al-Jabri & Sohail, 2012). Innovation as a concept can be broadly understood, but basically it refers to a product or service that a consumer perceives as new (e.g., Laukkanen, 2016) and can thus be also applied to new MFS.

The diffusion of innovation theory (DIT) focuses on the five-stage decision-making process that an individual consumer passes through in the innovation adoption process (Rogers, 2003). This adoption occurs through (1) the knowledge stage, where the individual is first exposed to an innovation but lacks information about it; (2) the persuasion stage, where the individual is interested in innovation and actively seeks related information; (3) the decision stage, where the individual decides to adopt or reject the innovation based on weighing the advantages against the disadvantages; (4) the implementation stage, where the individual employs the innovation and determines its usefulness; and (5) the confirmation stage, where the individual finalizes his or her decision to continue using the innovation (Rogers, 2003).

To examine the non-active consumers and the factors related to their initial and continuing use of mobile financial services, we focus on the three critical phases: (1) *pre-usage phase* of the service (including knowledge, persuasion, and decision stages of the DIT model), (2) *actual usage* of the service (referred the as the implementation stage in the DIT), and (3) *continued usage of the service* (referred to as the confirmation stage in the DIT).

First, concerning the *pre-usage phase* of the MFS, it is important to find out what are the critical aspects at this phase that (1) positively influence the intention to start using MFS and (2) prevent consumers from starting to use MFS. Based on the existing literature, we identified a number of studies addressing pre-usage phase–related issues in the MFS context. Several distinct theoretical models, theories, and constructs have been used in various, mainly quantitative studies (Baptista & Oliveira, 2015). For example, the technology acceptance model (TAM) developed by Davis (1989) is widely used to explore the determinants influencing the use of technology, i.e., how users come to accept and use a technology. Also the unified theory of acceptance and use of technology (UTAUT) formulated by Venkatesh, Morris, Davis, and Davis (2003) aims to explain user intentions to use an information system and subsequent usage behavior. In addition to these well-established models, several other technological and social psychological adoption theories and frameworks can also be identified in the field of mobile banking (see Shaikh & Karjaluoto, 2015, for a literature review). However, as Baptista and Oliveira (2015) found out in their recent weight and meta-analysis on mobile banking acceptance research, these studies are scattered in nature, and more than 520 different relationships could be identified. Based on their analysis, the best predictors of the intention to use mobile banking services are attitude, initial trust, perceived risk, and performance expectancy. In terms of use of mobile banking, they found intention and performance expectancy as the best predictors.

Another critical aspect of the studies related to the pre-usage phase of the MFS is the customer's choice to either adopt or reject the service. Since we are interested in customers who are not using mobile banking services (hereinafter referred to as 'non-active users'), the choice to decline using the service needs further attention. Innovation resistance is about customers' reactions against innovation due to potential changes in a comfortable habit or to a conflict with their own beliefs (Ram & Sheth, 1989; Chemingui & Iallouna, 2013). Existing studies suggest that instead of only viewing innovation resistance as a basic 'not-trying,' it can be divided into three types of consumer behavior: rejection, postponement, and opposition (Szmigin & Foxall, 1998; Kleijnen et al., 2009). Thus, postponers may find the innovation acceptable, but they postpone the adoption, whereas rejecters do not even intend to adopt the innovation. Those consumers who oppose the innovation may be convinced that the innovation is unsuitable and even attack it, e.g., in the form of negative word-of-mouth. As adoption postponement suggests potential future intention, rejection and opposition terminate the adoption process.

Moreover, several drivers of resistance or barriers to adoption have also been identified in the MFS context (Chemingui & Iallouna, 2013; Laukkanen, 2016; see also Kleijnen et al., 2009). First, *usage barrier* refers to difficulty in using the service due to a small screen or the user interface, for example. Secondly, *value barrier* is related to benefits obtained from the service compared to sacrifices such as monetary costs or learning effort. Thirdly, *risk barrier* may include (1) physical risk, referring to concern that innovation might be harmful mentally (e.g., in terms of privacy) or physically, (2) economic risk of losing money, (3) functional risk related to performance uncertainty, and (4) social risk that innovation will not be approved by relevant others. Fourthly, *tradition barrier* is related to customers' desire to maintain the status quo and traditional customs. Finally, *image barrier* refers to beliefs that MFS are difficult to use or otherwise hold an unfavorable image in the minds of the customers. In addition, Laukkanen (2016) also identified demographic factors (i.e., gender and age) as factors influencing innovation adoption and rejection, as young men seem to be more likely to adopt MFS than older people and women.

We suggest that it is not enough to concentrate only on the factors in the pre-usage phase, but in order to understand how to get consumers to actually use and furthermore to engage in the continuous use of MFS, we need to take a look at the following phases as well. Therefore, concerning the *actual usage phase* of the MFS, a more in-depth understanding of the existing customer's use experiences (both positive and negative) is needed. It provides valuable information for the providers of MFS on how to develop their services to provide better experiences and thus more value for their current and potential customers.

In reviewing the existing literature, we could not find many studies addressing the customer experience in MFS (Komulainen, Saraniemi, Still, & Uusipaikka, 2016 being an exception) as most of the studies in this field focus on use intention instead of actual experiences. For this reason, we looked at the previous marketing literature on customer's service experience to find the essence of the phenomenon. Customer experience can be understood as an individual's internal and subjective awareness or perception of a service (Holbrook & Hirschman, 1982; Lemke, Clark, & Wilson, 2011). Experience is thus created in the mind of an individual who is connected to a service on an emotional, physical, intellectual, and/or spiritual level, and participates in the service (ibid.). Keiningham et al. (2017) identify cognitive, emotional, physical, sensorial, and social elements as the key factors that comprise customer experience. Experience is also closely tied to the concept of value because value is constructed on experience that is gained from the service (see Frow & Payne, 2007). Primarily, value can be considered to be experiential in nature (Vargo & Lusch, 2008), and customer perceived value influences the cumulative customer service experience, and vice versa (Helkkula & Kelleher, 2010). Therefore, in order to understand customer value, it is essential to also understand the customer's experiences.

According to Keiningham et al. (2017), the principal goal of companies' efforts to improve and enhance customer experience is to engender a greater loyalty and commitment. They suggest that commitment can be understood as a customer's attitude that managers are seeking to influence in the hope of engendering increased purchase behaviors. It has been suggested in previous studies that there is a progression from cumulative customer experience to customer commitment (Lemon & Verhoef, 2016). Wang (2015) proposes that optimizing the service experience fosters the continued use of different mobile services. However, Keiningham et al. (2017) point out that there is an interplay between customer experience and commitment and that customer commitment may be affected by customer experience, and the other way round. From the perspective of the present study, it is important to understand customers' experiences related to MFS as we consider that positive experiences lead to long-term usage of these services, whereas negative experiences may, in the worst case, result in ending MFS usage.

Thirdly, in relation to *continued usage of MFS*, it is important to understand the drivers that enhance customers' long-term use of MFS as well as the factors that hinder it. When considering the customers' service experiences and their relationship with continued use, a diverse set of concepts is being used; for example, commitment, loyalty, satisfaction, involvement, participation, and engagement are often used as synonyms for continued use. We chose to focus on the phenomenon itself, i.e., the critical factors from the perspective of continued usage and long-term engagement to MFS. In other words, we concentrate here on the phase where the acceptance and adoption decision is already made and engagement (or continued use) consists of the users' ongoing activities, attitudes, and intrinsic interests (Kim, Kim, & Wachter, 2013).

Engagement is closely related to user experience (Kim et al., 2013), and it can be seen as a series of emotional and behavioral activities that include cognitive process, reasoning, decision-making, problem-solving, and evaluation (Kearsley & Shneiderman, 1998). Kunz et al. (2017) point out that prior engagement research has been strongly firm-centric, i.e., focused on firm-beneficial engagement from customers. They suggest that adopting a value co-creation perspective emphasizing both the customer's and the firm's perspectives would help to more fully capture value generated by engagement.

In order to understand how service value is formed for customers and how it can enhance the continued use of the service, it is necessary to understand how service is "embedded in the customer's context, activities, practices and experiences" (Heinonen et al., 2010, p. 533). In this study, we adopt the customer-dominant approach (Heinonen et al., 2010) and acknowledge that the history and future of a particular service, as well as customer activities and experiences beyond the specific service use, are highly important in continued service use.

Even though there are some studies that have investigated service experiences in the mobile service continuance context (Wang, 2015) and mobile users' engagement (Kim et al., 2013), research related to continued service use or engagement in the field of mobile financial services is still scarce. One exception is the study by Thakur (2014), which suggests that the loyalty of mobile banking customers is directly affected by satisfaction with the mobile banking services. He further puts forward that banks should invest in building customer trust and initial usage, which will further lead to loyalty based on satisfying usage experiences. This is in line with the study of Kim et al. (2013), who found out that perceived value is strongly related to users' satisfaction and continued engagement intention in the context of mobile technologies. Thus, it can be concluded that customers need to perceive value in the mobile service to continue its usage also in the future.

It has been noted that even though a large number of customers may have registered for mobile banking, the continuance of usage post-registration remains a challenge (Thakur, 2014). This makes it a critical issue for banks and other financial institutions to understand how the continued use of MFS could be advanced. We will continue by examining this as well as factors related to pre-usage and actual usage of MFS in our empirical study. The theoretical framework (Figure 2.1) provides a broad starting point for the empirical exploration. Before that, the methodology of the study is described.

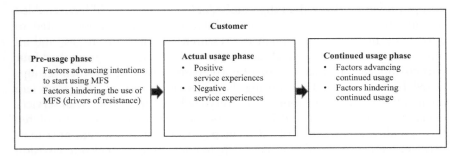

Figure 2.1 Factors influencing the use of MFS

Methodology

The qualitative empirical approach was adopted to collect versatile and in-depth information about the phenomenon. Data set 1 included 24 interviews of Finnish bank customers. In terms of the empirical context, the banking services in Finland can be described as highly digital and accessible for the citizens. In 2015, 86% of 16- to 74-year-old Finns used online banking services. Volunteer consumers interested in sharing their views and experiences of banking and financial services were invited to participate through researchers' Facebook pages. Participants were 21 to 70 years old, and both genders as well as various occupational groups were represented equally. Interviews were carried out as semi-structured theme interviews, and they varied in length between 20 and 55 minutes. All interviews were recorded and transcribed word-for-word. The transcribed material totaled 528 pages. All the participants had an existing relationship with one or more banks, which was checked to be able to treat them as existing bank customers, (and not as new customers).

In the preliminary analysis, the interviewees were first divided into two groups. Those who had used at least one mobile banking application were classified as 'active users/customers,' and those who had never used any mobile banking application were classified as 'non-active users/customers.' Both groups had 12 participants. Studying both active and non-active users was essential, as this study focuses not only on customers' intentions to use MFS (in the pre-usage phase) but also actual use experiences and long-term engagement. Examining only non-active customers would have given merely partial understanding about the reasons why they have not started using MFS, whereas active customers can complete our understanding of how to get non-active customers to adopt the use and continue using MFS.

Data set 2 consisted of three focus groups that were arranged to get an in-depth understanding of the participants' mobile banking and financial service use. Focus group method was used to reveal open-ended thoughts of consumer participants, while researchers engaged them to in-depth discussion as moderators. Particularly, the method allowed interaction within groups providing richer data than individual responses would have enabled (Liamputtong, 2011, p. 6). Again, volunteer consumers were invited to participate in the study through the researchers' Facebook pages, and all interested consumers were included in the study. Each focus group had four participants, leading to a total of 12 participants involved. The focus groups lasted 1.5 to 2 hours. First, during the focus group session, the group had an interactive discussion about their everyday banking and financial services experiences. Discussion and imagination of participants were stimulated through showing pictures of different payment situations, e.g., at a marketplace, at a desert, and at a spaceship, to encourage them also to envision their future financial and payment habits. In the second phase, a digital storytelling method (e.g., Gregori-Signes & Pennock-Speck, 2012) was used where each participant was able to describe and reflect their thoughts about their personal financial and banking habits by utilizing digital tools available in the research lab and sharing this story with the group. All the focus group discussions were video-recorded. Data set 2 was mainly used to complement the understanding gained from the interviews.

All interviews and focus group sessions were recorded and transcribed verbatim. We followed an abductive approach, including constantly going back and forth between empirical observations and theoretical concepts (Dubois & Gadde, 2002, p. 556). In the first phase of data analysis, initial interpretations of the interview data were created based on multiple readings of each transcript. When a holistic understanding of the data was acquired, the data was organized in categories created based on theoretical pre-understanding (pre-usage, actual usage, and continuing usage phases). Also new themes were allowed to freely emerge from the data related to factors impacting the use within the three stages. As a result, Figure 2.2 was formed. Thus, as in a typical qualitative study, empirical analysis and theoretical understanding have developed in parallel.

Empirical findings

In the following, we will present the results of our empirical analysis of the factors influencing the use of mobile services structured around the pre-usage phase of the service, actual use of the service, and continued use of the service.

Pre-usage phase of the service

First, we will examine the factors related to the stage preceding the use of the mobile service and the emergence of the need for the service – why the need emerges and becomes identified, or why this does not take place.

The origin of the need to use a mobile banking service is typically based on the added value that the service offers relative to the existing methods for conducting the banking services, such as Internet banking. The need can thus arise from the customer's own value creation processes and challenges that they encounter in their everyday lives. In case of such a challenge, the customer is more likely to observe related services and recall a service that they have encountered while not having a need for such a service, as the following quotation illustrates.

> *I started to use [MFS] because I expected to gain some kind of benefit. I very rarely start using any new mobile services just because of some wow-effect of "look how cool user interface!" [. . .] Once I was considering budgeting issues and noticed that [the mobile banking service application of a certain Finnish bank] apparently provides these tools and so I started to tap in the application to my phone.*
>
> *(Man, 40 years)*

The importance of references was emphasized in our data, both based on friends and family as well as evaluations provided by different media. References appear to have a strong impact on all types of customers and more importantly the references can be in many forms, including evaluations, comments, suggestions, etc., and can be provided by different actors. Interestingly, the multiple sources for reference were considered as important. On the other hand, the role of a single reference in the actual service trial experience may become very important. The extent of referencing applies to both positive and negative perceptions, as the following quotations illustrate.

> *If 90% of my friends would say that a certain application is really poor and that one should not try that at all, most likely I would not even try to use that.*
>
> (Man, 29 years)

> *In the long run, if I hear from multiple directions about a certain application, I start to think whether I also should try that. Oftentimes when I first try an application, I notice how useful it is. Especially if there is someone sitting next to me recommending the first trial, the service experience can become very pleasant.*
>
> (Man, 36 years)

In addition to personal references, public sources were also considered important. Based on our data, for example, social media such as blogs may be useful because they function as communities of users with similar interests and perhaps similar concerns and goals in their value creation processes, as the following quotation illustrates:

> *I started to use this MobilePay application based on reading in a blog something about this. They were recommending this for situations such as a flea market, where it is handy to pay straight away through a text message, even though you don't have any cash on you.*
>
> (Woman, 24 years, focus group)

Our data indicates that there is considerable variability in the characteristics of customers who adopt mobile banking services, ranging from active and eager novelty-seeking individuals to more passive ones who expect an impulsive or explicit reason before adopting new applications. These approaches were also related in the way referencing functioned in terms of starting to use a new mobile banking service. Customers that considered themselves as forerunners within their circle of friends easily adopt new applications based on a positive reference. It may also be the case that they adopt a tutoring role as well and help others to start using the new mobile banking services, too.

> *I am typically the one that has to show everyone [introduce a new application], whereas I myself usually very easily start to try new applications. I have in my phone all kinds of eBays and AliExpresses and there I go on ordering hats for my children.*
>
> *(Woman, 26 years)*

The usefulness and value provided by the mobile service are crucial in adopting the use of a new application. In case the customer is hesitant in terms of the usage, the security aspect of the mobile banking service becomes an issue. Based on our data, the user typically relies on the service because it is provided by a bank or a well-known and reliable service provider.

> *Regarding banking services, one is somehow inclined to think that the bank must have worked out the security issues. It is of course a gut feeling, but I do have a kind of assumption that since it is a Finnish bank, their information security is bound to be in order and thus I dare to use their mobile services.*
>
> *(Man, 36 years)*

Based on our data of non-active users, several reasons for not perceiving a need to adopt mobile banking services can be identified. First of all, a generally conservative outlook and protective attitude towards money and privacy were connected to the non-active users, as the informants described their perceptions of the mobile banking services. Such an approach may be visible in other aspects of their daily life as well, preventing the adoption of new services. However, especially as far as money and privacy is concerned, the critical attitude seems to be especially high. Another identified reason relates to the users' reservation towards security issues. In the case of users, these reservations were typically overcome through reliance on banks as service providers, but this did not apply to non-active users. On the other hand, mistrust towards other people and criminals was also raised in our data. However, there seemed to be hesitation in this as well, and the users also reported being willing to overcome their reservations, as the following quotation illustrates:

> *Actually I don't even know myself where this fear [towards security issues in mobile banking services] comes from, but it is very important to me. I guess I would need more emotional support from service providers, like "You can do it!"*
>
> *(Woman, 39 years)*

A third type of reason for remaining a non-active user of mobile banking services relates to habits and principles that users have in relation to their behavior. For example, avoiding using excess time with mobile devices was raised as an important objective by the non-active users. Also, merely the feeling of falling behind technological developments prevented the respondents from becoming active users of mobile banking services. This was also connected to the personality of the customers and their courage to try new things.

Finally, based on our data, an important reason for not starting to use a mobile banking service was the obliviousness to the potential benefits of the service. Of course this is the other side of the same coin if we think of the reasons why the active users have adopted the use – because they perceive value in it. However, obliviousness to the benefits is not merely an information issue – that they are just not aware of the benefits – but rather it is deeply embedded in the person's own personality, habits, and outlook on life.

> *I am just not the kind of person who is out there all the time with a mobile device in my hand. I have so many other more important things to do than just stare at the phone. I don't need it. What would the mobile bank give to me? Would it give something? How would it expand my use of banking services? What would I do with that? I just don't understand what I could do with it. [. . .] There really should be a real benefit explicitly available for me to start using it.*
>
> *(Man, 70 years)*

All in all, in relation to non-users in our data, different kinds of traditions, prejudices, attitudes, as well as insecurities are related to the need to handle banking services in a different way than they have become used to. Customers do not see the benefits offered by mobile banking service as significant enough compared to the practices that they have become acquainted with, for example Internet banking services. In addition, insecurities related to security or losing their phones, viruses, and all sorts of other risks were emphasized.

Actual use of the service

In the following, we will discuss the users' experiences and perceptions regarding the actual usage of the mobile banking services, both positive and negative. From the data related to active users, we identified the positive experiences related to the actual usage of the services. Among the most evident reasons for positive experiences was the speed and time-savings that the customers perceived. The time-savings were perceived as relative to the other means of conducting banking services, most often the Internet banking services, but also in relation to other means requiring the customer to go to a certain place – such as a bank branch or their desktop computer.

> *You don't need to start your computer, but you can quickly check the issue through a phone or tablet.*
>
> *(Woman, 37 years)*

> *It's always available when needed; one doesn't need to go anywhere.*
>
> *(Man, 40 years)*

The ease of conducting banking affairs through mobile banking compared to Internet banking was also among the most typical reasons for using mobile banking. This was related to activities like checking the account balance or paying bills, and also more broadly, for example, transactions with other individuals or even connecting to other services such as insurance services. Customers reported highly positive experiences in terms of the speed and ease of mobile banking services. Mobile banking also provided the informants with a clear and explicit outlook on their money affairs. Especially those customers that wanted to continuously follow the money flows in their account reported being very satisfied with mobile banking, as it allowed them to easily see the transactions.

The mobile bank user interfaces were perceived as very clear and easy by the users in our data. They reported different kinds of functions that they felt were very useful for them.

> *I think the mobile bank is so easy, for example there's a spinning orange circle that indicates that a bill has arrived, and all I need to do is accept it, no need to look for it anywhere.*
>
> *(Woman, 26 years, focus group)*

Overall, the positive user experiences were connected to the usefulness of the mobile banking service. It helps in taking care of one's personal financial affairs, especially compared to the Internet.

Negative service experiences identified in our data can be described as annoyances. If negative experiences were encountered, the customers associated feelings of irritation or annoyance. Typical sources of such feelings were related to failure or malfunctioning of the service in certain situations or physical surroundings. In a similar vein, missing functionalities compared to the existing customary method (e.g., Internet banking) also raised annoyance, as the following quotation illustrates:

> *I do not think that it [mobile banking services] facilitates the handling of one's banking affairs; after all, the Internet banking services offer a lot more extensive opportunities to do things.*
>
> *(Man, 36 years)*

The perception of the value provided by the mobile device as a channel for service delivery was of course connected to the extent and nature of the user's willingness to engage in banking services. Some customers were disappointed with the lack of functions compared to Internet banking, whereas some were looking for a more limited version for their daily needs. A limited version would enable a smoother transfer of data in the mobile networks. Overall, negative experiences while using the service were connected to the perceived value of the service or the lack of it. In fact, high expectations in relation to the utility were connected to low value perception, as indicated in the following quote:

> *Actually I have downloaded that [certain] mobile banking service application. I saw it as rather unclear to use [. . .] I was not able to get into its idea, as apparently there was mostly only discount coupons to a hamburger restaurant. I felt as if there was nothing else.*
>
> *(Woman, 26 years, focus group)*

Continued use of the service

Thirdly, we examined the factors related to the service experience in terms of the continuation of the use of the service, both advancing and hindering factors. Regarding the factors advancing the continuous use and engagement with the mobile banking service, much of the same issues were raised related to starting the use and the actual usage stage as well; the utility of the service, ease of use and functionalities were perceived as valuable (e.g., the budgeting function, graphics, and technical functioning).

Continuously introducing new functionalities also adds to the customer's commitment to the service, especially in the case of active and novelty-seeking customers. In addition to these, tailoring opportunities also emerged as particularly valuable in terms of continuation of the usage and commitment by the customers:

> *When you are logging into the service, it would be nice if the system would ask what I'm interested in, I mean whether I'd like to receive specific information or discounts or something else. I think it is quite substantial that I will get tailored and targeted service when I'm using it [mobile banking service].*
>
> *(Man, 36 years)*

Trust plays an important role, as many interviewees pointed out how essential it is to be able to use the service without constantly thinking whether it is safe or not. Also the trust in banks and other 'big players' in the field was seen as increasing the reliability of the mobile banking services:

I'm actually very confident about using this service because the services downloaded from the AppStore are so controlled. They are developed by big national banks and I believe I can also trust them in the future.

(Man, 29 years)

In terms of factors hindering the continuous use and engagement, security issues were unsurprisingly raised. It is fair to say that perceived security of the service serves as a basic requirement for the usage in all of the three phases: intention, actual usage, and continued usage. So if there were problems in security, that would likely influence the use of the mobile banking services in the future. Moreover, the infrastructure required were reported as potentially affecting the use of the services, as indicated in the following quote:

For me, making payments in a mobile bank has been impossible, as I haven't so far used such an mobile device that it would have been reasonable. If the services aren't very simple to use and one tries to use them with an old phone, it may not be worthwhile. I guess it's a different thing when you have a new and well-functioning phone.

(Woman, 22 years, focus group)

Dysfunctionalities of the service are also one major threat for the continuance of mobile banking service use. Any uncertainty or technical problems in using the service causes a lot of confusion for the user, as the following quotation illustrates:

If it is not coded well and if there are constantly these different kinds of faults and malfunctions . . . then I quite easily would just stop using it.

(Man, 31 years)

Development of future MFS

Finally, our analysis revealed different types of future development ideas related to the three phases of service use. First, in relation to the *pre-usage phase*, service providers should provide hands-on guidance for the customers who feel uncomfortable or insecure about using mobile banking services, guidance on both the use and the technology.

I would like to see for example a short video about how the service functions on a concrete level. All this kind of guidance and support would be good for me. Showing all the possibilities of the service with the help of examples. It would definitely make it easier for me (to start using it).

(Woman, 36 years)

Some non-active interviewees also felt that the mobile banking service providers should be more proactive in informing them about new services in general and about security-related issues in particular.

I think the bank should convince me. If they would advertise it and inform me properly that their mobile systems are really reliable and secure and that you can easily use them with a mobile phone. Or in a same way as with credit cards, if they could give the same kind of back-up that if somebody misuses it, they would take responsibility for it. That could make me start using it [mobile banking service].

(Woman 36 years)

Concerning the *actual usage phase*, to make sure the customer actually uses the service, the service providers of course need to develop ways to provide customers with valuable services that are easy to use. Furthermore, they need to understand the heterogeneity of customers, not only in terms of their technical abilities and resources but also in terms of their value perceptions. Our data indicated that all customers valued the smooth handling of daily banking affairs that the mobile service provided. However, in relation to the extent of the services offered, the customers' perceptions varied. For example, some respondents appreciated new and interesting functionalities, whereas some saw all kinds of advertisements or 'extra' stuff as very negative. Therefore, the user interface needs to be tailorable for different types of customers.

All the unnecessary information, advertisements and animations or anything like that are very confusing to older people. It needs to be as simple as possible; include only the most relevant functions such as basic payments so that you can use it without any fear of pressing a wrong button.

(Woman, 36 years)

On the concrete level, the use of the mobile banking service is highly dependent on the user interface. According to respondents, whether they will start using it on a regular basis often depends on their first experiences with the service. In other words, the user interface needs to be as simple and easy as possible to encourage further usage.

Banks should invest in the user interface an awful lot. It is The Thing that defines whether you like to use the service and whether you will use it again.

(Man, 36 years)

The factors important for the *continuous use* are closely related to the actual use, but here the focus is more on the ideas related to future usage of the MFS. Based on our data, the tailoring and provisioning of customer-specific services was emphasized. To engage customers with continuous use of the MFS, it is important that the service provider develops such modular services that each customer can be offered a tailored customer experience. Similarly to actual usage, some value a simple service, whereas others would like to have several different features related to banking and financial affairs.

> *At the moment, mobile banking service is not that important to me, but in the future I hope I could increase my understanding about where my money goes and how I spend it. It could have different features, e.g., about average consumers, how others use their money. Or how many times I have eaten in the restaurant last month. These kinds of interesting facts and funny stuff would make me use it more regularly.*
>
> *(Man, 40 years)*

Also, the importance of utilizing different social aspects of mobile banking services was found to be related to continued usage. Other customers' experiences, recommendations, and comments play a big role in both the active consumers' and the inactive consumers' behavior and attitudes towards new MFS.

New innovative technological features that would make customers' everyday life easier were highlighted by respondents as increasing the continued use of the service. Since banking affairs are such an integral part of a consumers' life, banks need to keep up with what is going on in their customers' lives and how they could efficiently utilize new technological possibilities to make those activities even more simple and effortless.

> *I would really appreciate if in the future I could pay bills by using only one 'click.' Or even better, by using a fingerprint or maybe even with the help of a microchip that would be installed under my skin!*
>
> *(Man, 33 years)*

To sum up, the empirically grounded framework in Figure 2.2 illustrates the main findings of the study. It identifies the critical factors in engaging inactive customers to continuously use MFS, first from the customer's perspective, and second by suggesting the key points of future development for financial service providers. Both of these are related to three phases – pre-usage, actual usage, and continued usage – to provide an understanding on what is important at each stage of MFS use from the perspective of customers and service providers.

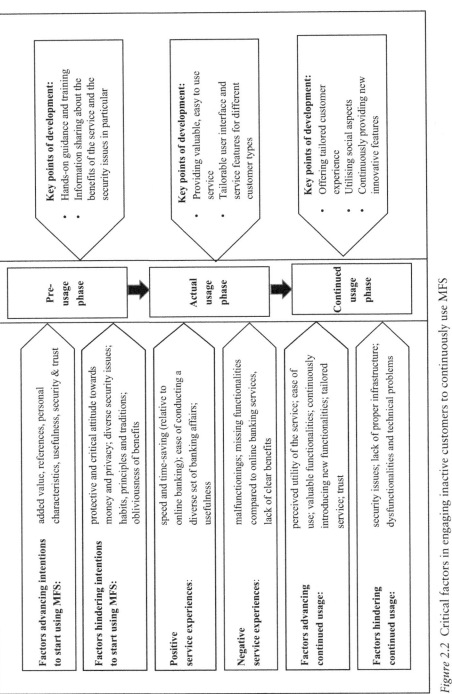

Key points of development:
- Hands-on guidance and training
- Information sharing about the benefits of the service and the security issues in particular

Key points of development:
- Providing valuable, easy to use service
- Tailorable user interface and service features for different customer types

Key points of development:
- Offering tailored customer experience
- Utilising social aspects
- Continuously providing new innovative features

Pre-usage phase

Actual usage phase

Continued usage phase

Factors advancing intentions to start using MFS: added value, references, personal characteristics, usefulness, security & trust

Factors hindering intentions to start using MFS: protective and critical attitude towards money and privacy; diverse security issues; habits, principles and traditions; obliviousness of benefits

Positive service experiences: speed and time-saving (relative to online banking); ease of conducting a diverse set of banking affairs; usefulness

Negative service experiences: malfunctionings; missing functionalities compared to online banking services, lack of clear benefits

Factors advancing continued usage: perceived utility of the service; ease of use; valuable functionalities; continuously introducing new functionalities; tailored service; trust

Factors hindering continued usage: security issues; lack of proper infrastructure; dysfunctionalities and technical problems

Figure 2.2 Critical factors in engaging inactive customers to continuously use MFS

Conclusions

The purpose of this study was to find out how to get non-active consumers to start using and engaging in continued usage of MFS. In answering this question, we developed an empirically grounded framework (Figure 2.2) that provides novel insights into the critical factors that either advance or hinder customers in starting the use of new MFS and to engage in continuously using them. Our findings show that there is a diverse set of factors that influence customers' attitudes and behaviors in relation to MFS. The most important factors are related first to the need for mobile banking services to be truly useful and to provide added value for customers compared to other banking services. In addition, it needs to be easy to use, function flawlessly, and be tailorable for diverse customer segments and their varying needs. Security issues are also highly emphasized because the service is closely related to customers' money and privacy. Finally, the social aspects are important because recommendations, suggestions, evaluations, and encouragement from others may have a strong impact on the decision to start (or not to start) using and continuing the use of the service.

The present study contributes to the existing research in several ways. First, most of the prior research in the field of MFS has focused on consumers' intentions to adopt or use these services (e.g., Chemingui & Iallouna, 2013; Jeong & Yoon, 2013; Shaikh, Karjaluoto, & Chinje, 2015; Glavee-Geo, Shaikh, & Karjaluoto, 2017), i.e., merely to the phase preceding the use of MFS. We suggest that focusing only on intentions is not enough if the aim is to really understand non-active customers and how they could be activated to start using and becoming engaged in the continued use of MFS. Therefore, we also included actual usage and continued usage phases into the study instead of focusing only on the pre-usage phase. This way, the present study creates a wider and more comprehensive understanding of the topic instead of focusing merely on use intentions.

Second, the common interest in both the innovation literature and mobile banking research in particular seems to lie in active customers or early adopters (see, e.g., Rogers, 2003) who are principally interested in adopting new technological solutions. We focused our attention on the other extreme, i.e., consumers who are reluctant to use new MFS and thus represent a vast unutilized potential for banks and other financial service providers. There are only a few recent studies that have addressed these types of consumers and their decision to either adopt or reject mobile banking service (e.g., Laukkanen, 2016), and our study is one of the first attempts to reveal underlying attitudes, experiences, and future expectations of the non-active customers.

Third, previous studies on MFS are mainly quantitative in nature (see a recent review in Baptista & Oliveira, 2015), and therefore our study answers the call for more in-depth qualitative empirical research. By using interviews and focus groups as data collection methods, we explored both the users and non-users of mobile banking services to gain a more in-depth understanding of their reasons for using and not using these services. In addition, we explored their positive and negative experiences of the service as well as ideas concerning the future usage of MFS. This enabled us to gain various versatile viewpoints about the attitudes, intentions, actual use experiences, and future expectations (and fears) in the field of MFS compared to survey data based on strictly predetermined concepts and models.

Our findings provide important implications for providers of MFS on how they could get non-active customers to start using and to further engage in the continuous use of MFS. First, one of the reasons why non-active customers are not using MFS is that they seem to be satisfied with their present situation and way of handling bank-related affairs. Therefore, it is important that service providers connect the value proposition to those services (in most cases online banking) they are currently using. In practice this means that the benefits of MFS need to be clearly communicated and emphasized compared to online banking services. For example, speed and time-savings, ease of conducting a diverse set of banking affairs, and useful features should be clearly described and demonstrated to the non-active customers whenever and wherever the service provider is in contact with them. In addition, all kinds of encouragement is needed both from the bank and the social network of the customer because non-active customers are often unsure about their technological skills and abilities to use MFS. Hands-on guidance and mental support could help them in crossing the first threshold of starting to use the service. Hence, service providers should pay attention to social aspects specifically in the pre-usage phase, where the recommendations, suggestions, and back-up from others may have a strong impact on the decisions to start (or not to start) using the service.

Another important factor to pay attention to is the tailoring of MFS for different types of customer needs. According to our findings, non-active customers value a simple and easy-to-use service that does not have anything 'extra' (e.g., advertisements, animations, and an overload of information) in it that could distract them from handling the basic banking activities. This is important both in the starting phase as well as for the continued usage. On the contrary, most of the active customers want to constantly have new technological features added to the service in order to find it interesting in the long run and to continuously use it. Therefore, we suggest that the providers of MFS could create different versions of the mobile banking service designed for different kinds of customers. For example, it could include a beginner's version for new MFS users and a more advanced, professional version for active users.

Finally, we found that security is a highly important matter in all phases of the service use. Our data reveals that the fear of security breaches, viruses, thefts, and all kinds of external threats was present in both the active and the non-active customer groups. Interestingly, these fears often seem to be quite irrational and inconsistent in both groups and even in individuals themselves.

For example, some non-active customers use other mobile services without any problems, but with mobile banking services they become overly skeptical. Active users also expressed fears concerning security; but on the other hand they, overcome these fears as they perceived their bank as a trusted and reliable service provider. We think this is in connection with the barriers to adoption and the perceived risks related to MFS. This also seems to be the most crucial factor in getting non-active customers to start using and continue using MFS. We therefore suggest that this is an issue that definitely deserves further attention in future research, i.e., how could service providers better understand and influence their customers' mental states related to security issues and perceived risk in order to help them to overcome their fears.

Note

* *Corresponding /primary contact author*

References

Al-Jabri, I. M., & Sohail, M. S. (2012). Mobile banking adoption: Application of diffusion of innovation theory. *Journal of Electronic Commerce Research*, *13*(4), 379–391.

Baptista, G., & Oliveira, T. (2015). Understanding mobile banking: The unified theory of acceptance and use of technology combined with cultural moderators. *Computers in Human Behavior*, *50*, 418–430.

Calisir, F., & Gumussoy, C. A. (2008). Internet banking versus other banking channels: Young consumers' view. *International Journal of Information Management*, *28*(3), 215–221.

Chemingui, H., & Iallouna, H. (2013). Resistance, motivations, trust and intention to use mobile financial services. *International Journal of Bank Marketing*, *31*(7), 574–592.

Davis, F. D. (1989). Perceived usefulness, perceived ease of use and user acceptance of information technology. *MIS Quarterly*, *13*(3), 319–340.

Deloitte Review. (2017). *FinTech in the Nordics*. Retrieved from www2.deloitte.com/content/dam/Deloitte/se/Documents/financial-services/FinTech_Publikation_A4_WEB_FINAL.PDF

Digital Payments Report. (2016). Retrieved September 14, 2017, from http://gotech.fi/2016/10/12/mobiilimaksamisen-suosio-kolminkertaistui-vuodessa

Dubois, A., & Gadde, L. E. (2002). Systematic combining: An abductive approach to case research. *Journal of Business Research*, *55*(7), 553–560.

Frow, P., & Payne, A. (2007). Towards the "perfect" customer experience. *Journal of Brand Management*, *15*(2), 89–101.

Glavee-Geo, R., Shaikh, A. A., & Karjaluoto, H. (2017). Mobile banking services adoption in Pakistan: Are there gender differences? *International Journal of Bank Marketing*, *35*(7), 1090–1114.

Gregori-Signes, C., & Pennock-Speck, B. (2012, December). Digital storytelling as a genre of mediatized self-representations: An introduction. *Digital Education Review*, *22*.

Heinonen, K., Strandvik, T., Mickelsson, K. J., Edvardsson, B., Sundström, E., & Andersson, p. (2010). A customer-dominant logic of service. *Journal of Service Management, 21*(4), 531–548.

Helkkula, A., & Kelleher, C. (2010). Circularity of customer service experience and customer perceived value. *Journal of Customer Behavior, 9*(1), 37–53.

Holbrook, M. B., & Hirschman, E. C. (1982). The experiential aspects of consumption: Consumer fantasies, feelings, and fun. *Journal of Consumer Research, 9*(2), 132–140.

Jeong, B. K., & Yoon, T. E. (2013). An empirical investigation on consumer acceptance of mobile banking services. *Business and Management Research, 2*(1), 31.

Kearsley, G., & Shneiderman, B. (1998). Engagement theory: A framework for technology-based teaching and learning. *Educational Technology, 38*(5), 20–23.

Keiningham, T., Keiningham, T., Ball, J., Ball, J., Benoit, S., Benoit, S., & Dzenkovska, J. (2017). The interplay of customer experience and commitment. *Journal of Services Marketing, 31*(2), 148–160.

Kim, Y. H., Kim, D. J., & Wachter, K. (2013). A study of mobile user engagement (MoEN): Engagement motivations, perceived value, satisfaction, and continued engagement intention. *Decision Support Systems, 56*, 361–370.

Kleijnen, M., Lee, N., & Wetzels, M. (2009). An exploration of consumer resistance to innovation and its antecedents. *Journal of Economic Psychology, 30*(3), 344–357.

Komulainen, H., Saraniemi, S., Still, J., & Uusipaikka, M. (2016). *Value dimensions related to customer experience in mobile banking service.* Proceedings of the ANZMAC 2016 Conference, Christchurch, New Zealand.

Kunz, W., Aksoy, L., Bart, Y., Heinonen, K., Kabadayi, S., Ordenes, F., Sigala, M., Diaz, D., & Theodoulidis, B. (2017). Customer engagement in a Big Data world. *Journal of Services Marketing, 31*(2), 161–171.

Laukkanen, T. (2016). Consumer adoption versus rejection decisions in seemingly similar service innovations: The case of the Internet and mobile banking. *Journal of Business Research, 69*(7), 2432–2439.

Laukkanen, T., & Kiviniemi, V. (2010). The role of information in mobile banking resistance. *International Journal of Bank Marketing, 28*(5), 372–388.Lemke, F., Clark, M., & Wilson, H. (2011). Customer experience quality: An exploration in business and consumer contexts using repertory grid technique. *Journal of the Academy of Marketing Science, 39*(6), 846–869.

Lemon, K. N., & Verhoef, p. C. (2016). Understanding customer experience throughout the customer journey. *Journal of Marketing: AMA/MSI Special Issue, 80*, 69–96.

Liamputtong, p. (2011). *Focus group methodology: Principle and practice.* London: Sage Publications.

Lin, H. F. (2011). An empirical investigation of mobile banking adoption: The effect of innovation attributes and knowledge-based trust. *International Journal of Information Management, 31*(3), 252–260.

Ram, S., & Sheth, J. N. (1989). Consumer resistance to innovations: The marketing problem and its solutions. *Journal of Consumer Marketing, 6*(2), 5–14.

Rogers, E. M. (2003). Diffusion of innovations. *Free Press.* New York, 551.

Shaikh, A. A., & Karjaluoto, H. (2015). Mobile banking adoption: A literature review. *Telematics and Informatics, 32*(1), 129–142.

Shaikh, A. A., Karjaluoto, H., & Chinje, N. B. (2015). Continuous mobile banking usage and relationship commitment: A multi-country assessment. *Journal of Financial Services Marketing, 20*(3), 208–219.

Szmigin, I., & Foxall, G. (1998). Three forms of innovation resistance: The case of retail payment methods. *Technovation, 18*(6), 459–468.

Thakur, R. (2014). What keeps mobile banking customers loyal? *International Journal of Bank Marketing, 32*(7), 628–646.

Vargo, S. L., & Lusch, R. F. (2008). Service-dominant logic: Continuing the evolution. *Journal of the Academy of Marketing Science, 36*(1), 1–10.

Venkatesh, V., Morris, M. G., Davis, G. B., & Davis, F. D. (2003). User acceptance of information technology: Toward a unified view. *MIS Quarterly*, 425–478.

Wang, K. (2015). Determinants of mobile value-added service continuance: The mediating role of service experience. *Information & Management, 52*(3), 261–274.

Wu, J., & Du, H. (2012). Toward a better understanding of behavioral intention and system usage constructs. *European Journal of Information Systems, 21*(6), 680–698.

Yen, Y. S., & Wu, F. S. (2016). Predicting the adoption of mobile financial services: The impacts of perceived mobility and personal habit. *Computers in Human Behavior, 65*, 31–42.

3 How emotions are considered crucial on an omnichannel banking environment in gaining customer loyalty

Hannele Haapio *

Introduction

The environment of traditional banks is changing rapidly. New entrants, including nonbanking entitities, are stepping into the financial market. Banks in the European Union (EU) member countries have been compelled to open their Application Programming Interfaces (API) because of the updated Payment Services Directive (PSD2). New online channels, especially mobile channels and social media, as well as digitalization, have changed customer behavior. The need to be cost-effective has forced banks to close a tremendous number of branches. There is an urgent need for banks to find new revenue channels as well as to retain and acquire profitable customers in this new landscape. The solution cannot merely be to expand digitally by closing more branches and improving online and mobile banking solutions. Banks need to move further into the lives of their customers, not only at the moment of financial transaction (Busch & Moreno, 2014). Transformation in the digital age requires both high tech and high touch.

Customer satisfaction is a key marketing construct that has been studied from different perspectives since the early 1980s and has evolved since that time. It is commonly agreed that customer satisfaction leads to customer loyalty (Shaikh, Karjaluoto, & Häkkinen, 2018). Loyal customers buy more, they are willing to recommend the company (word-of-mouth, WOM), and they reduce cost of service, all of which directly and indirectly affects banks' financial outcomes. Emotions, which have been studied in a marketing context for years, are a key element of satisfaction. Research has been done on emotions evoked by marketing stimuli, products, and brands as well as on emotional reactions to advertising and service failures. There seems to be no research showing that emotions do not play an important role in the customers' journey. However, emotions' role in the omnichannel environment among retail banking customers and how they contribute to customer loyalty are not well understood.

The emotional relationship between customers and their banks seems to be weak (Marinkovic & Obradovic, 2015), which creates risk for banks in the changing environment. Nevertheless, in the banking sector, emotions have a direct impact on customer satisfaction and thus on customer loyalty (Marinkovic & Obradovic, 2015). Emotionally involved customers are more loyal to their banks, and more satisfied customers maintain longer-lasting relationships with their banks and spread positive comments by word of mouth (Levy & Hino, 2016; Marinkovic & Obradovic, 2015).

Emotions have been studied for years in the context of marketing. Research has been done on the emotions that marketing stimuli, products, and brands evoke (Holbrook & Hirschman, 1982); on customers' emotional reactions to advertising (e.g., Derbaix, 1995); and on emotions' effects on consumer satisfaction (e.g., Phillips & Baumgartner, 2002), complaining (e.g., Stephens & Gwinner, 1998), and response to service failures (e.g., Zeelenberg & Pieters, 1999; Gohary, Hamzelu, Pourazizi, & Hanzaee, 2016). However, there does not seem to be research on emotions' impact on the omnichannel environment and thus on customer loyalty and companies' financial performance. Limited research has been done on the banking sector and among omnichannel customers in general.

In an omnichannel environment, customers expect a consistent, uniform, and integrated customer experience, including both online and off-line experience when needed. However, research has found that heavy online usage without human touch weakens the bank-customer relationship (Levy, 2014). Banks have started the digital transformation mainly for cost saving reasons and are now facing a new situation in which the power that companies used to have is moving to the customers. Technology has changed customer behavior, and the financial sector has been at the forefront of this movement. The use of mobile phones and tablets in particular has had a major impact on customer behavior in the financial sector (Liu, Abhishek, & Li, 2015). According to Juniper Research (2016), mobile banking users are expected to reach 2 billion by 2020, representing more than one in three adults worldwide. At the same time, the natural borders between different channels are disappearing and the channels are becoming blurred (Verhoef, Kannan, & Inman, 2015). Customers are becoming more demanding in online environments (McLean & Wilson, 2016), and they want to use channels seamlessly. For companies that is a challenge, because they have almost no ability to control that usage (Verhoef et al., 2015).

The omnichannel approach includes all mobile, online, and traditional channels and the key question is how providers can strengthen the emotional relationship in the omnichannel environment in a profitable manner. Even though emotions and customer loyalty, in both off-line and online contexts, have been examined for many years (e.g., Amin, 2016; Bapat, & Bapat, 2017; Bloemer, De Ruyter, & Peeters, 1998), a lack of information regarding how emotions affect customer experience in an omnichannel environment still exists.

This chapter shows that understanding the impact of emotions in an omnichannel environment is crucial to gain loyalty in retail banking. This study aims to fill the potential gaps in the existing literature, such as how emotions affect an omnichannel environment, by looking at emotions and the omnichannel environment in retail banking and their contribution to customer loyalty.

This chapter examines the relevant literature keywords: emotions, omnichannel, customer satisfaction, customer loyalty, and customer dominant logic. Using these keywords and the context of banking and services led to focus mainly on the *International Journal of Bank Marketing*, *Journal of Marketing*, *Journal of Retailing*, and *Journal of Retailing and Consumer Services*. These journals naturally expanded the list of references covered. This chapter is organized as follows: after the introduction the second paragraph is a review of the element of omnichannel environment. The third paragraph is a review of different approaches of emotions and the fourth paragraph concentrates on customer satisfaction and loyalty. Next, there is the conclusion and discussion with theoretical and managerial implications. The last paragraph is the future research agenda based on the findings and identified questions.

Elements of an omnichannel environment

The literature includes different definitions of omnichannel. 'Omni' is a Latin word meaning 'all' or 'universal' (Lazaris & Vrechopoulos, 2014). In an omnichannel environment, customers move among the various channels. The environment emphasizes the connection between the customers and the brand (Piotrowicz & Cuthbertson, 2014). In an omnichannel environment, customers expect a consistent, uniform, and integrated experience. They want to move seamlessly among different channels and find it confusing to see a lack of consistency in elements such as pricing, marketing, and brand building. All distinct channels (human and technology based, including sales personnel) should complement each other to have a joint influence on customer experience perception (Pantano & Viassone, 2015).

I have examined the omnichannel environment through five elements. First is the components of the omnichannel experience: humans plus technology. The second element involves touchpoints, and the third focuses on channel choice. The fourth element emphasizes customers' value creation, and the fifth element explores the leadership required to ensure a good omnichannel experience. These elements are described in more detail in the following paragraphs. Table 3.1 summarize the findings.

Omnichannel environment

An omnichannel environment does not focus on the channels themselves like a multichannel environment does. However, the literature does not always make a clear distinction between multichannel and omnichannel, and the interchanging use of those words is sometimes confusing. The crucial factor for distinguishing multichannel and omnichannel strategies is where the

Table 3.1 Five elements of an omnichannel environment

Element	Description	Citations
Omnichannel environment	Common descriptions of omnichannel attributes: uniform, consistent, integrated. Heavy online banking usage without human touch weakens the relationship between customer and company.	Pantano and Viassone (2015), Herington and Weaven (2009), Verhoef et al. (2015), Juaneda-Ayensa, Mosquera, and Murillo (2016), Melero et al. (2016), Lazaris and Vrechopoulos (2014), Levy (2014), Buttle and Maklan (2015)
	Personal relationships improve security with complex financial products.	
	Sales personnel and technology should have a joint influence on customer experience.	Pantano and Viassone (2015)
Touchpoints	Customer touchpoint categories: brand-owned, partner-owned, customer-owned, and social/external/independent	Lemon and Verhoef (2016)
	Touchpoint elements: atmosphere, technology, communication, process, employee-customer interaction, customer-customer interaction, product interaction	Stein and Ramaseshan (2016)
	Customers have experiences whenever they "touch" any aspect of the service, product, or brand across multiple channels and at various points in time.	Pantano and Viassone (2015), Zomerdijk and Voss (2010)
Channel choice	Channel attributes and marketing characteristics, marketing activities, customer channel experience, social effects, customer heterogeneity in buying behavior	Melero et al. (2016), Juaneda-Ayensa et al. (2016), Estrella-Ramon, Sánchéz-Perez, and Swinnen (2016)
	Personal innovativeness, effort expectancy, performance expectancy	
	Easy cancellation of products	
Value creation	Value creation stages: value in pre-use, value in use, value in post-use	Jain, Aagja, and Bagdare (2017)
	Co-creation, where customer is co-creating the process	Martovoy and Santos (2012), Sandström, Edvardsson, Kristensson, and Magnusson (2008)
	Recovery situations and how those are handled effect value creation	Gohary et al. (2016) Forbes, Kelley, and Hoffman (2005)
	Value is created during consumption	Vargo and Lusch (2004)
	Value formation, value continuously emerge when offering is used	Heinonen and Strandvik (2018)

(Continued)

Table 3.1 (Continued)

Element	Description	Citations
Leadership	Silo mentality, where different players defend their "silos" instead of collaboration.	Piotrowicz and Cuthbertson (2014)
	Systematic mistakes that include overestimation of customer satisfaction and loyalty as well as misunderstanding of key drivers effecting customer experience.	Hult, Morgeson, Morgan, Mithas, and Fornell (2017)
	Managerial mindset, how managers view their customers	Heinonen and Strandvik (2018), Rydén, Ringberg, and Wilke (2015)
	Challenges with channel synergies	Verhoef et al. (2015), Carlson and O'Cass (2011), Pantano and Viassone (2015), Zhang et al. (2010)
	Customers weak emotional connection with their bank	Marinkovic and Obradovic (2015)
	Customer dominant logic (CDL)	Heinonen and Strandvik (2018)
	Online customers have higher expectations of service than off-line customers	McLean and Wilson (2016)

customer focus is. In multichannel strategy, managerial objectives are set for each channel, whereas in omnichannel strategy, the objective is to offer a holistic customer experience in which all the channels work together seamlessly (Juaneda-Ayensa et al., 2016). Lazaris and Vrechopoulos (2014) have studied several descriptions of omnichannel and found that they all agree that the prevailing theme is an integrated and seamless experience across all channels. In other words, multichannel involves a number of channels used one at a time, whereas omnichannel allows for seamless usage among the channels, with a focus on customers' lives.

In an omnichannel environment, it is crucial that the channels work together seamlessly, e.g. according to Herington & Weaven (2009), good e-service performance does not override unsatisfactory performance in other areas. Favorable behavior (e.g., purchase, WOM) is based on the consumers' interactions with each channel. A customer needs to be able to choose the best possible channel for him or her in each situation, and those channels then need to communicate with each other (Pantano & Viassone, 2015). Combining this with the thinking of Verhoef et al. (2015) that different channels are becoming blurred due to the disappearance of natural borders between channels and adding Cao and Li (2015) findings that positive synergies among channels tend to generate stronger sales growth, it is obvious the omnichannel approach becomes the new normal. To create best possible result, all channels customers are using must work synergistically.

The omnichannel approach includes both human and technology aspects. Modern bank customers desire to conduct their business anywhere they choose, while also requiring a deeper personal relationship with their bank advisors, creating complexity for banks (Accenture, 2015). Customers feel more secure when they have a good relationship and rapport with an advisor, especially if he or she specializes in complex financial products (Buttle & Maklan, 2015). However, customers operating online also have high expectations of timely service (McLean & Wilson, 2016). Thus, some researchers see human relationships with customers as becoming less relevant in the future (Ostrom, Parasuraman, Bowen, Patricio, & Voss, 2015). They assume that machines and robots will replace employees (Ostrom et al., 2015) in both traditional service and sales functions (Brynjolfsson & McAfee, 2014). Yet, recent research about employee presence and its impact on customer satisfaction shows that the practice of replacing employees with robots calls for caution (Söderlund, 2017).

Touchpoints

Both customers and firms use different channels and touchpoints constantly, interchangeably, and simultaneously to facilitate the customer experience. The increasingly complex customer journey and myriad touchpoints across multiple channels are forcing companies to put increasing focus on the customer experience (Lemon & Verhoef, 2016). Customers have experiences every time they encounter any part of a service, product, or brand, regardless of the channel (Pantano & Viassone, 2015; Zomerdijk & Voss, 2010). These moments of interaction between the customer and any part of the company are known as touchpoints and can be divided into four categories: (1) brand-owned (customer interactions during the experience, designed, controlled, and managed by the company), (2) partner-owned (customer interactions during the experience, jointly designed, controlled or managed by the company and one or more partners), (3) customer-owned (customer actions, which the company or its partners does not influence or control), and (4) social/external/independent (customers are surrounded by external touchpoints, like other customers, that may influence the process) (Lemon & Verhoef, 2016).

A more detailed approach to touchpoints can be found in the work of Stein and Ramaseshan (2016), who identified seven touchpoint elements: atmosphere, technology, communication, process, employee-customer interaction, customer-customer interaction, and product interaction. The nature of the omnichannel environment, with its human and technology aspects, suggests that emotions will influence each touchpoint element. However, the most relevant elements from the touchpoint elements of Stein and Ramaseshan for how emotions influence the retail banking context, are technological, process, customer-customer interaction, and employee-customer interaction. According to Stein and Ramaseshan (2016) the technological element describes customers' direct interactions with any form of technology during an encounter and involves ease of use, convenience, and self-service. Further, the process element describes the steps customers need to take to achieve the desired outcome. It plays an important role in shaping customers' perceptions and evaluations of service. Offline, it involves aspects such as the checkout wait time and the service process. In a digital environment, process elements include the way customers navigate the site or technology platform. Another element is the customer-customer interaction, which describes the direct and indirect exchanges customers have with other customers. It involves elements such as customer reviews and WOM. Further, the employee-customer interaction describes the direct and indirect communications customers have with employees and is not limited to face-to-face interaction. Such interactions could also be by phone or online chat, for example. This element involves the helpfulness or argumentativeness of employees and personalized services.

Channel choice

The customer experience in an omnichannel environment brings up a question of key drivers of customers to adopt/choose different channels. Although the key drivers for different channels have been researched, it is still unclear how to adapt these findings to an omnichannel environment. Another study by Melero, Sese, and Verhoef (2016) found the drivers of customer channel choice to be channel attributes and characteristics, marketing activities, customer channel experience, social effects, and customer heterogeneity (in buying behavior as well as in psychographics and demographics). Juaneda-Ayensa et al. (2016) studied purchases in a retail omnichannel context (not banking) and found the key drivers to be personal innovativeness, effort expectancy, and performance expectancy. Venkatesh, Thong, and Xu (2012) describe that the personal innovativeness is the degree to which a person prefers to try new and varied products or channels, effort expectancy is the ease of use, and performance expectancy refers to the benefits consumers will get by using different channels. Furthermore, Estrella-Ramon et al. (2016) found that one reason banking customers choose online channel is for easy cancellation of products or services. Overall, research thus far has mostly focused on individual channels, indicating that there is still a lack of understanding drivers in an omnichannel environment, especially in banking.

Value creation

Customer value is holistic in nature; it is created by the total experience of all elements (Grönroos, 2006). Three value creation stages exist: value in pre-use, value in use, and value in post-use (Jain et al., 2017). Jain et al. (2017) define the stages as follows: Value in pre-use refers to the pre-purchase stage in the consumer decision-making process in which customers seek out and become familiar with the service/product. Value in use is the stage in which the actual consumption happens, and the third stage, value in post-use, includes after-sales activities, customer complaint and feedback handling, loyalty programs, and regular communication. Collective value creation across all three stages has important implications for customer loyalty, overall customer satisfaction, and WOM (Jain et al., 2017). Excellent customer experiences require excellence in all stages at all touchpoints.

Value creation also happens in service recovery, which seems to be one of the top issues in the literature. Emotions play a significant role in these situations, and inviting customers to actively participate in the recovery process may increase the level of positive emotions. Gohary et al. (2016) studied positive and negative emotions' effects on the process of co-recovery in mobile banking settings and found that positive reactions promote the reuse of mobile banking and co-creation in the future, whereas negative emotions typically eliminate this tendency. Human interaction seems to be particularly appreciated in cases of service failure or dissatisfaction (Forbes et al., 2005). Customers do not want to feel left alone without any reliable company representatives to monitor their emotional climates in service failure situations (Levy, 2014).

Furthermore, the customer dominant logic (CDL) views value creation from the customer point of view (Heinonen & Strandvik, 2018). CDL finds that value-in-use continuously emerges during the usage of the service/product offer. CDL also emphasizes that value is formed in the customer's ecosystem, not the provider's service ecosystem. Customer ecosystem refers to a network of activities, practices, and actors where the focus is not on the individual but on the whole ecosystem. In CDL, the customer's perspective is primary, which highlights customer activities and how providers can engage in these activities and tasks. There are three levels of customer activities according to CDL: core activities, related activities, and other activities (Heinonen & Strandvik, 2015). In contrast, Vargo and Lusch (2004) find that value is always created in cooperation with customers. Companies can only offer value proposition for customers. According to this assumption, the value is created during the consumption, so they emphasize customer interaction and co-creation activities.

A study of the banking sector confirms the importance of co-creation, while customers who are engaged in co-creation processes tend to be committed to their banks (Martovoy & Santos, 2012). Banks can use new digital channels combined with digital literacy to enable customers to act as co-designers and co-producers of the services (Straker & Wrigley, 2016). Sandström et al. (2008) identified a model of total technology-based service experience, where the customer is in the center as an active co-creator. Their model shows that value-in-use is the result of a cognitive assessment of the total service experience, which includes both the functional and emotional dimensions.

Kumar and Reinartz (2016) wrote about customer treatment and undesired consequences (costs). They found that digitalization in particular provides new facets for customer value creation. They raised the very interesting subject of the customers' understanding of the value they offer by providing their personal information. Some customers may value their privacy so much that they are willing to pay extra for it, which creates a market for privacy. This issue taps into the basic emotion of fear. If customers worry about their privacy and do not find a solution, that could impact loyalty.

Leadership

Enhancing experiences in an omnichannel environment requires new forms of leadership. In the omnichannel environment, the ultimate goal is to deliver a holistic customer experience, so targets need to be set according to the holistic customer experience, not according to the goals of each channel. Leaders should avoid a silo mentality in which online and off-line channels are treated separately, as it can easily destroy the holistic customer experience (Piotrowicz & Cuthbertson, 2014). Managerial mindset, or how managers view customers, plays a crucial role in how companies act towards customers (Heinonen & Strandvik, 2018). Rydén et al. (2015) identified four managerial mindsets: business-to-customers, business-from-customers, business-with-customers, and business-for-customers. Their study reveals the completely different mindsets of managers as they consider the role of customers.

Leaders tend to make two systematic mistakes when trying to understand their customers. According to Hult et al. (2017), leaders systematically overestimate levels of customer satisfaction and loyalty as well as misunderstand key drivers of their customers. By doing so, managers risk missing trouble signs (e.g., customers partly transfer their business) as they appear as well as seeing some issues as less dangerous than they really are (e.g., service delivery). In an omnichannel environment, e.g., the seamless use of channels makes it almost impossible for managers to have control of customer behavior (Verhoef et al., 2015), which could lead to misunderstanding of customers' key drivers of channel choice. Managers are facing challenges with opportunities for synergies across channels, including decisions that must be made as well as rapid changes in customer behavior in the new environment (Carlson, O'Cass, & Ahrholdt, 2015; Pantano & Viassone, 2015; Zhang et al., 2010).

It is also important to understand who the omnichannel customers are. Marinkovic and Obradovic (2015) found that many customers have weak emotional connections with their banks, but they are willing to continue working with them. This lack of emotional connection could be a risk for banks, especially when new competitors like FinTech companies are entering the market. A recent study by Estrella-Ramon et al. (2016) found that customers with higher average monthly assets as well as customers who own high-risk products tend to engage in online banking more slowly than other customers. In other words, customers with savings and investments find the traditional channel important. According to Estrella-Ramon et al. (2016), that behavior correlates with the risk. In contrast, home loans and transaction accounts as well as debit and credit cards have a significant positive impact on the adoption of online banking, which is an interesting and important topic for banks to consider.

Emotions

This section concentrates on explaining: what is an emotion? what are the different aspects of emotions and how could the knowledge gain on 'emotions' be utilized to understand retail banking customers' behavior in an omnichannel environment?

Emotions have numerous definitions, and there does not seem to be any distinct agreement on what emotions really are (Figure 3.1). That seems to

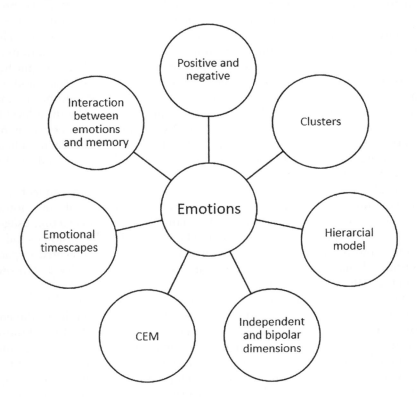

Figure 3.1 Different approaches to emotions

be dependent on the discipline and researcher. The most widely used conceptualization of emotions is the classification into positive and negative. In the literature, positive and negative emotions are considered independent and are treated as different constructs. An advantage is that the model is simple, and the combination also indicates one's attitude (Laros & Steenkamp, 2005). A disadvantage is that one may lose important information (e.g., negative emotions could be anger, fear, and sadness), because different emotions have different behavioral consequences (e.g., Bagozzi, Gopinath, & Nyer, 1999). There is an interaction between emotion and memory (Lewis, Haviland-Jones, & Barrett, 2008), and people tend to remember emotional experiences better than non-emotional ones, and they tend to re-experience emotional situations.

Furthermore, emotions can also be grouped into three major clusters (Shaver, Schwartz, Kirson, & O'Connor, 1987; Storm & Storm, 1987). First is the most general, superordinate level, which consists of positive and negative affect. Second is the basic emotion level like anger, fear, love, and sadness. The third level consists of groups of individual emotions, e.g., fear consists of scared, afraid, panicky, nervous, worried, and tense. This construct is consistent with that of Laros and Steenkamp (2005), who proposed a hierarchical model. They found that nuances can be lost if emotions are only conceptualized on a very general level as positive or negative. The model of Laros and Steenkamp of consumer experience describes emotions at three levels of generality. First is the superordinate level, which distinguishes between positive and negative affect. The next level divides basic emotions into four positive categories (contentment, happiness, love, and pride) and four negative categories (sadness, fear, anger, and shame). The third level is the subordinate level, which distinguishes 42 specific emotions. For studying emotions of retail banking customers, the first two levels, slightly modified, are sufficient (love does not seem to be relevant for this type of study and it should be changed to trust).

It is also possible to classify emotions based on three independent and bipolar dimensions: pleasure/displeasure, arousal/non-arousal, and dominance/submissiveness (Russell & Mehrabian, 1977). For marketing usage, the pleasure/displeasure dimension could be useful. That dimension includes positive and negative emotions, which past research has indicated impact consumer behavior (e.g., their adoption of e-services) (Beaudry & Pinsonneault, 2010; Gelbrich, 2010).

One aspect could also be managerial as such. Grønholdt, Martensen, Jørgensen, and Jensen (2015) identified eight customer experience dimensions in their conceptual Customer Experience Model (CEM). Two of those dimensions are directly emotional: emotional customer experience and emotional skills of employees. In general, the analyzed companies in their study were good at rational components but poor at emotional components. There is a clear connection between performance and the ability to engage in both emotional and rational dimensions; top-performing companies excel in both. Retail bank managers should ensure that both components are used in their businesses.

Another aspect is the emotional timescapes. Maguire and Geiger (2015) studied emotional timescapes in service industries. They found that consumers can experience various and diverse emotions both simultaneously and successively during service encounters. Their study identified consumption emotions (emotions that are created within consumers during service encounter) occurring throughout the experiences. They found that during service encounters, consumption emotions change rapidly, causing overlay with incomplete effects. Their study also showed that the uncertainty that exists in consumers before a service encounter commences can lead to the consumers' experiencing conflicting or mixed emotions. People tend to react negatively to mixed emotions (Lau-Gesk, Kramer, & Mukherjee, 2011), so these feelings may lead customers to avoid the service situation in the future.

Satisfaction and loyalty

This paragraph discusses satisfaction and loyalty. Clearly, satisfaction leads to loyalty. A recent study by Bapat and Bapat (2017) shows the strong link between satisfaction and loyalty also in the banking context. Loyal customers buy more, are willing to recommend the company (WOM), and reduce the cost of service, all of which has direct and indirect effects on banks' financial outcomes. There is also a clear understanding that emotions (positive and negative) are significantly related to customer satisfaction (e.g., Hassan, Ramayah, Mohamed, & Maghsoudi, 2015; Yim, Tse, & Chan, 2008; Bügel, Verhoef, & Buunk, 2011; Akgün, Keskin, & Koçak, 2017) and that the emotional constituents of firm customer relationships are important drivers of customer loyalty. Furthermore, some research, particularly in the service sector, shows that customer loyalty originates from positive emotional experiences (Kandampully, Zhang, & Bilgihan, 2015) and that emotions drive consumer behaviors (Razzaq, Yousaf, & Hong, 2017). Recent research also emphasizes that customers' positive affective experiences in banks seem to enhance customers' perceptions, especially via word-of-mouth, which initiates customer loyalty (Reydet & Carsana, 2017).

In the banking sector, emotions have a direct impact on customer satisfaction and through that on customer loyalty. Bloemer et al. (1998 p. 277) define bank loyalty as "the biased (i.e. nonrandom) behavioral response (i.e. revisit), expressed over time, by some decision-making unit with respect to one bank out of a set of banks, which is a function of psychological (decision-making and evaluative) processes resulting in brand commitment." Emotionally involved customers are more loyal to their banks, and customers who are more satisfied maintain long-lasting relationships with their banks and spread positive comments by word-of-mouth (Levy & Hino, 2016; Marinkovic & Obradovic, 2015). In banking, emotions drive customer behavior and are crucial to predicting customer loyalty intentions (Razzaq et al., 2017). Marinkovic and Obradovic (2015) also found that customer satisfaction is a strong driver of behavioral intentions (including WOM and repurchase intentions) in banking. Their study showed that intangible elements (trust, social bonds, image, and service quality) are highly valuable in establishing long-term relationships. These elements have a significant impact on customer satisfaction. They also found satisfaction and affective commitment to be variables reflecting the customers' emotional responses. Similar findings regarding the important variables in customer satisfaction also appear in the work of Zalfa, Siew, and Sedigheh (2017), who studied perceived overall service quality in retail banking. Several studies also found trust to be of particular importance in satisfaction, especially in banking (Marinkovic & Obradovic, 2015; Zalfa et al., 2017).

Young, tech-savvy consumers are less loyal and more demanding than ever. According to Moreno (2014), one-fifth of customers change some or all of their retail banking products each year. These customers expect their service providers to know and understand them, which is consistent with CDL. By studying e-lifestyle customers' loyalty, Hassan et al. (2015) found that e-values have the most significant impact on e-loyalty. Interestingly, finding is also that economic value has a greater influence on customer loyalty in the real world than in the virtual world, where social value is more important (Piyathasanan, Mathies, Wetzels, Patterson, & de Ruyter, 2015). Further, the same research shows that loyalty can be generated in the virtual world independently from the real world, but brand loyalty is needed in both worlds to truly maintain loyalty (Piyathasanan et al., 2015).

Customer loyalty to a bank is relatively low in customers who engage in high levels of online banking service activities but lack direct face-to-face interactions. Heavy online usage without human touch weakens the bank-customer relationship (Levy, 2014), which affects loyalty. This is consistent with previous research that shows online customers still value human interaction (e.g., Gerrard, Barton Cunningham, & Devlin, 2006; Holloway & Beatty, 2003; Forbes et al., 2005). Perceived ease of use and branch service quality (Carlson & O'Cass, 2011; Herington & Weaven, 2009; Kaura, Durga Prasad, & Sharma, 2015; Amin, 2016) as well as customer service in banking sector (Ganguli & Roy, 2011; Ngoc & Nguyen, 2010) are antecedents for customer satisfaction and loyalty. Technological factors mediate these factors and influence customer satisfaction. Customers want new online and mobile services, but at the same time, that could deteriorate loyalty via weakening relationship, and customers may be easily tempted by rival banks. For banks, that is a big risk and paradox.

On the other hand, research does show that Internet banking service quality has a positive relationship with e-customer satisfaction (Carlson & O'Cass, 2011; Herington & Weaven, 2009; Kaura et al., 2015; Amin, 2016). Four key dimensions of Internet banking quality influence e-customer satisfaction and loyalty: personal need, site organization, user friendliness, and website efficiency (Amin, 2016). The relationships among Internet banking service quality, e-customer satisfaction, and e-customer loyalty are significant. Accordingly, research also shows that satisfaction with mobile banking affects customer loyalty (Thakur, 2014).

Discussion and conclusion

Emotions are key in relationships between customers and companies in the banking sector and especially in the omnichannel environment. It could be useful for banks to use the division of emotions into two general categories – positive and negative – in order to better understand customer relationships. To ensure important nuances are not lost, the division of basic emotions into four positive and four negative categories is also helpful. Of these, trust has been found to be a crucial issue in banking. Useful categories of basic emotions in banking context could be contentment, happiness, trust, pride, sadness, fear, anger, and shame. Emotions affect customer loyalty and therefore banks would benefit of better understanding the issue.

There is a wide agreement that satisfaction leads to loyalty, especially in service industries such as banking. Numerous studies show that emotions have a direct effect on satisfaction and thus direct or indirect effects on loyalty. Emotionally involved customers are more loyal, and emotions drive banking customer behavior. There is also a connection between emotions and memory, which indicates that emotional experiences (positive and negative) are easier to remember, and people tend to repeat positive memorable experiences. There are clear connections among emotions, omnichannel experiences, and loyalty, as evidenced by the studies discussed herein. Emotions may be positive or negative, but they always affect the experience in an omnichannel environment as well as loyalty. Loyalty or disloyalty is the outcome of both emotions and the experience in an omnichannel environment.

The literature shows that banks should provide customers with both high technology and high human touch to make a successful digital transformation. Customers require a consistent, uniform, and integrated experience in omnichannel environment. Research has been conducted to determine key drivers of customers' use of different channels. However, the research has mostly focused on single channels, and the key drivers in an omnichannel banking environment remain unclear. Customers seem to want an omnichannel experience, but providing it might be a double-edged sword for banks. Customers may see the offering of omnichannel possibilities as a commitment to effective, convenient, and high-quality service. If the bank does not meet these expectations, the customer will not be satisfied, leading to a decrease in customer loyalty.

Particularly in service recovery situations, customers appreciate the opportunity to actively participate in the process and to experience human interaction. The literature also shows that heavy online usage weakens the emotional relationship between customer and bank, which in turn affects customer loyalty. One possibility to avoid the loyalty deterioration is by giving the customer opportunities to engage in the service process and co-create it. Customer co-creation and value formation seem to help to build emotional relationships.

Customer behavior is undergoing fundamental changes, and the power has moved to the customers. In an omnichannel environment, banks have little ability to control customer usage and behavior. A new form of leadership is required, one in which the focus is on customers and no silo mentality regarding channels exists. Banks should understand the managerial mindset, the systematically overestimated levels, and the key drivers of customer satisfaction in order to take needed actions that ensure customer loyalty. Accordingly, managers also need to understand the different customer touchpoints and the importance of the emotional relationship between the customer and the bank. From the customer's point of view, all channels and marketing activities merge to form one impression. CDL looks at customers holistically and emphasizes understanding how customers compose their lives and use logic in purchasing situations. According to CDL, it is the customers who decide which providers they invite into their ecosystems. Customer empowerment gives customers the ability to use their emotions to show providers how they prefer them to become involved in their lives.

This chapter started with the hypotheses that understanding the impact of emotions in an omnichannel environment is crucial to gain loyalty in retail banking. This chapter shows that is true. Figure 3.2 describes that the basic emotions that are relevant in a banking context need to be considered in each element of an omnichannel environment to gain loyalty.

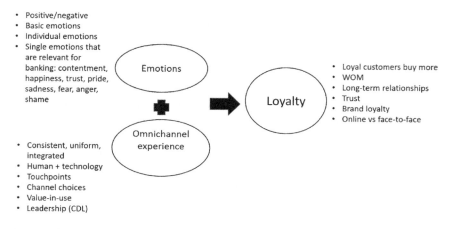

Figure 3.2 Emotions in omnichannel banking to gain loyalty

Theoretical and managerial implications

Theoretically, this study describes what elements define the omnichannel environment and that emotions have a strong effect. This study gives managers advice on how to describe and approach the omnichannel environment and to consider the effect of emotions on each element on the omnichannel environment. It also implicates the importance of emotions in banking, where most transactions could be handled through technology, but with more complex issues, customers still want to have possibility to human interactions. Omnichannel behavior, where all the channels are truly integrated and emotions are not neglected is the key to customer loyalty.

Directions for future research

To further research in this area, several possible directions are outlined. First, it will be interesting to study the weight of the effect of each basic emotion (contentment, happiness, trust, pride, sadness, fear, anger, and shame) on each element of an omnichannel environment. Second, the effect of emotions in each touchpoint would be interesting to study. That is to find out the main strengths and weaknesses according to different touchpoints. Third, it would be interesting to find out what changes are needed in the organization to ensure that emotions in an omnichannel environment are in focus. In other words, e.g., how to avoid silos and ensure that customer emotions are not neglected.

CDL offers many possibilities for future research. In the changing environment, it might be beneficial for banks to focus on customers as drivers and find out how banks could better enter customers' ecosystem. The CDL mindset could help banks to ensure that emotions are involved in customer interactions.

Note

* *Corresponding/primary contact author*

References

Accenture. (2015). *Banking shaped by the customer.* [Online] Retrieved August 2017, from www.accenture.com/us-en/insight-consumer-banking-survey

Akgün, A. E., Keskin, H., & Koçak A. A. (2017). Emotional prototypes, emotional memory usages, and customer satisfaction. *The Service Industries Journal, 37*(7–8), 494–520.

Amin, M. (2016). Internet banking service quality and its implication on e-customer satisfaction and e-customer loyalty. *International Journal of Bank Marketing, 34*(3), 280–306.

Bagozzi, R. P., Gopinath, M., & Nyer, p. U. (1999). The role of emotions in marketing. *Journal of the Academy of Marketing Science, 27*(2), 184–206.

Bapat, D., & Bapat, D. (2017). Exploring the antecedents of loyalty in the context of multi-channel banking. *International Journal of Bank Marketing, 35*(2), 174–186.

Beaudry, A., & Pinsonneault, A. (2010). The other side of acceptance: Studying the direct and indirect effects of emotions on information technology use. *MIS Quarterly,* 689–710.

Bloemer, J., De Ruyter, K., & Peeters, p. (1998). Investigating drivers of bank loyalty: The complex relationship between image, service quality and satisfaction. *International Journal of Bank Marketing, 16*(7), 276–286.

Brynjolfsson, E., & McAfee, A. (2014). *The second machine age: Work, progress, and prosperity in a time of brilliant technologies.* New York: WW Norton & Company.

Bügel, M. S., Verhoef, p. C., & Buunk, A. p. (2011). Customer intimacy and commitment to relationships with firms in five different sectors: Preliminary evidence. *Journal of Retailing and Consumer Services, 18*(4), 247–258.

Busch, W., & Moreno, J. p. (2014). Banks' new competitors: Starbucks, Google, and Alibaba. *Harvard Business Review, 2,* 1–3.

Buttle, F., & Maklan, S. (2015). *Customer relationship management: Concepts and technologies* (3rd ed.). Abingdon, UK: Routledge.

Cao, L., & Li, L. (2015). The impact of cross-channel integration on retailers' sales growth. *Journal of Retailing, 91*(2), 198–216.

Carlson, J., & O'Cass, A. (2011). Developing a framework for understanding e-service quality, its antecedents, consequences, and mediators. *Managing Service Quality: An International Journal, 21*(3), 264–286.

Carlson, J., O'Cass, A., & Ahrholdt, D. (2015). Assessing customers' perceived value of the online channel of multichannel retailers: A two country examination. *Journal of Retailing and Consumer Services, 27,* 90–102.

Derbaix, C. M. (1995). The impact of affective reactions on attitudes toward the advertisement and the brand: A step toward ecological validity. *Journal of Marketing Research,* 470–479.

Estrella-Ramon, A., Sánchez-Pérez, M., & Swinnen, G. (2016). How customers' offline experience affects the adoption of online banking. *Internet Research, 26*(5), 1072–1092.

Forbes, L. P., Kelley, S. W., & Hoffman, K. D. (2005). Typologies of e-commerce retail failures and recovery strategies. *Journal of Services Marketing, 19*(5), 280–292.

Ganguli, S., & Roy, S. K. (2011). Generic technology-based service quality dimensions in banking: Impact on customer satisfaction and loyalty. *International Journal of Bank Marketing, 29*(2), 168–189.

Gelbrich, K. (2010). Anger, frustration, and helplessness after service failure: Coping strategies and effective informational support. *Journal of the Academy of Marketing Science, 38*(5), 567–585.

Gerrard, P., Barton Cunningham, J., & Devlin, J. F. (2006). Why consumers are not using Internet banking: A qualitative study. *Journal of Services Marketing, 20*(3), 160–168.

Gohary, A., Hamzelu, B., Pourazizi, L., & Hanzaee, K. H. (2016). Understanding effects of co-creation on cognitive, affective and behavioral evaluations in service recovery: An ethnocultural analysis. *Journal of Retailing and Consumer Services, 31,* 182–198.

Grønholdt, L., Martensen, A., Jørgensen, S., & Jensen, p. (2015). Customer experience management and business performance. *International Journal of Quality and Service Sciences, 7*(1), 90–106.

Grönroos, C. (2006). Adopting a service logic for marketing. *Marketing Theory*, 6(3), 317–333.

Hassan, S. H., Ramayah, T., Mohamed, O., & Maghsoudi, A. (2015). E-lifestyle, customer satisfaction, and loyalty among the generation Y mobile users. *Asian Social Science*, 11(4), 157–168.

Heinonen, K., & Strandvik, T. (2015). Customer-dominant logic: Foundations and implications. *Journal of Services Marketing*, 29(6/7), 472–484.

Heinonen, K., & Strandvik, T. (2018). Reflections on customers' primary role in markets. *European Management Journal*, 36(1), 1–11.

Herington, C., & Weaven, S. (2009). E-retailing by banks: E-service quality and its importance to customer satisfaction. *European Journal of Marketing*, 43(9/10), 1220–1231.

Holbrook, M. B., & Hirschman, E. C. (1982). The experiential aspects of consumption: Consumer fantasies, feelings, and fun. *Journal of Consumer Research*, 9(2), 132–140.

Holloway, B. B., & Beatty, S. E. (2003). Service failure in online retailing: A recovery opportunity. *Journal of Service Research*, 6(1), 92–105.

Hult, G. T. M., Morgeson, F. V., Morgan, N. A., Mithas, S., & Fornell, C. (2017). Do managers know what their customers think and why. *Journal of the Academy of Marketing Science*, 45(1), 37–54.

Jain, R., Aagja, J., & Bagdare, S. (2017). Customer experience: A review and research agenda. *Journal of Service Theory and Practice*, 27(3), 642–662.

Juaneda-Ayensa, E., Mosquera, A., & Murillo, Y. S. (2016). Omnichannel customer behavior: Key drivers of technology acceptance and use and their effects on purchase intention. *Frontiers in Psychology*, 7.

Juniper Research. (2016). *Mobile banking users to reach 2 billion by 2020: Representing more than 1 in 3 of global adult population.* Retrieved May 2017, from www.juniper-research.com/press/press-releases/mobile-banking-users-to-reach-2-billion-by-2020

Kandampully, J., Zhang, T., & Bilgihan, A. (2015). Customer loyalty: A review and future directions with a special focus on the hospitality industry. *International Journal of Contemporary Hospitality Management*, 27(3), 379–414.

Kaura, V., Durga Prasad, C. S., & Sharma, S. (2015). Service quality, service convenience, price and fairness, customer loyalty, and the mediating role of customer satisfaction. *International Journal of Bank Marketing*, 33(4), 404–422.

Kumar, V., & Reinartz, W. (2016). Creating enduring customer value. *Journal of Marketing*, 80(6), 36–68.

Laros, F. J., & Steenkamp, J. B. E. (2005). Emotions in consumer behavior: A hierarchical approach. *Journal of Business Research*, 58(10), 1437–1445.

Lau-Gesk, L., Kramer, T., & Mukherjee, S. (2011). *Coping with mixed emotions: Exploring the temporal arousal of positive emotion relative to negative emotion.* ACR North American Advances, USA.

Lazaris, C., & Vrechopoulos, A. (2014, June). *From multi-channel to "omnichannel" retailing: Review of the literature and calls for research.* The 2nd International Conference on Contemporary Marketing Issues (ICCMI), Athens, Greece.

Lemon, K. N., & Verhoef, p. C. (2016, November). Understanding customer experience throughout the customer journey. *American Marketing Association*, 69–96.

Levy, S. (2014). Does usage level of online services matter to customers' bank loyalty? *Journal of Services Marketing*, 28(4), 292–299.

Levy, S., & Hino, H. (2016). Emotional brand attachment: A factor in customer-bank relationships. *International Journal of Bank Marketing, 34*(2), 136–150.

Lewis, M., Haviland-Jones, J. M., & Barrett, L. F. (Eds.). (2008). *Handbook of emotions*. New York: Guilford Press.

Liu, J., Abhishek, V., & Li, B. (2015). *The influence of mobile channel on customer behavior in omni-channel banking services*. 2015 International Conference on Mobile Business (p. 7). Retrieved from August 2017, http://aisel.aisnet.org/icmb2015/7

Maguire, L., & Geiger, S. (2015). Emotional timescapes: The temporal perspective and consumption emotions in services. *Journal of Services Marketing, 29*(3), 211–223.

Marinkovic, V., & Obradovic, V. (2015). Customers' emotional reactions in the banking industry. *International Journal of Bank Marketing, 33*(3), 243–260.

Martovoy, A., & Dos Santos, J. (2012). Co-creation and co-profiting in financial services. *International Journal of Entrepreneurship and Innovation Management 1, 16*(1–2), 114–135.

McLean, G., & Wilson, A. (2016). Evolving the online customer experience . . . is there a role for online customer support? *Computers in Human Behavior, 60*, 602–610.

Melero, I., Sese, F. J., & Verhoef, p. C. (2016). Recasting the customer experience in today's omni-channel environment 1/Redefiniendo la experiencia del cliente en el entorno omnicanal. *Universia Business Review, 50*, 18–37.

Moreno, J. p. (2014). Banking at the digital crossroads. *Financial Times*, 11–21.

Ngoc T. P., & Nguyen H. L. (2010). Service personal values and customer loyalty: A study of banking services in a transitional economy. *International Journal of Bank Marketing, 28*(6), 465–478.

Ostrom, A. L., Parasuraman, A., Bowen, D. E., Patricio, L., & Voss, C. A. (2015). Service research priorities in a rapidly changing context. *Journal of Service Research, 18*(2), 127–159.

Pantano, E., & Viassone, M. (2015). Engaging consumers on new integrated multichannel retail settings: Challenges for retailers. *Journal of Retailing and Consumer Services, 25*, 106–114.

Phillips, D. M., & Baumgartner, H. (2002). The role of consumption emotions in the satisfaction response. *Journal of Consumer Psychology, 12*(3), 243–252.

Piotrowicz, W., & Cuthbertson, R. (2014). Introduction to the special issue information technology in retail: Toward omnichannel retailing. *International Journal of Electronic Commerce, 18*(4), 5–16.

Piyathasanan, B., Mathies, C., Wetzels, M., Patterson, p. G., & de Ruyter, K. (2015). A hierarchical model of virtual experience and its influences on the perceived value and loyalty of customers. *International Journal of Electronic Commerce, 19*(2), 126–158.

Razzaq, Z., Yousaf, S., & Hong, Z. (2017). The moderating impact of emotions on customer equity drivers and loyalty intentions: Evidence of within sector differences. *Asia Pacific Journal of Marketing and Logistics, 29*(2), 239–264.

Reydet, S., & Carsana, L. (2017). The effect of digital design in retail banking on customers' commitment and loyalty: The mediating role of positive affect. *Journal of Retailing and Consumer Services, 37*, 132–138.

Russell, J. A., & Mehrabian, A. (1977). Evidence for a three-factor theory of emotions. *Journal of Research in Personality, 11*(3), 273–294.

Rydén, P., Ringberg, T., & Wilke, R. (2015). How managers' shared mental models of business: Customer interactions create different sensemaking of social media. *Journal of Interactive Marketing, 31,* 1–16.

Sandström, S., Edvardsson, B., Kristensson, P., & Magnusson, p. (2008). Value in use through service experience. *Managing Service Quality: An International Journal, 18*(2), 112–126.

Shaikh, A. A., Karjaluoto, H., & Häkkinen, J. (2018). Understanding moderating effects in increasing share-of-wallet and word-of-mouth: A case study of Lidl grocery retailer. *Journal of Retailing and Consumer Services, 44,* 45–53.

Shaver, P., Schwartz, J., Kirson, D., & O'Connor, C. (1987). Emotion knowledge: Further exploration of a prototype approach. *Journal of Personality and Social Psychology, 52*(6), 1061–1086.

Söderlund, M. (2017). Employee display of burnout in the service encounter and its impact on customer satisfaction. *Journal of Retailing and Consumer Services, 37,* 168–176.

Stein, A., & Ramaseshan, B. (2016). Towards the identification of customer experience touch point elements. *Journal of Retailing and Consumer Services, 30,* 8–19.

Stephens, N., & Gwinner, K. p. (1998). Why don't some people complain? A cognitive-emotive process model of consumer complaint behavior. *Journal of the Academy of Marketing Science, 26*(3), 172–189.

Storm, C., & Storm, T. (1987). A taxonomic study of the vocabulary of emotions. *Journal of Personality and Social Psychology, 53*(4), 805–816.

Straker, K., & Wrigley, C. (2016). Designing an emotional strategy: Strengthening digital channel engagements. *Business Horizons, 59*(3), 339–346.

Thakur, R. (2014). What keeps mobile banking customers loyal? *International Journal of Bank Marketing, 32*(7), 628–646.

Vargo, S. L., & Lusch, R. F. (2004). Evolving to a new dominant logic for marketing. *Journal of Marketing, 68*(1), 1–17.

Venkatesh, V., Thong, J. Y., & Xu, X. (2012). Consumer acceptance and use of information technology: Extending the unified theory of acceptance and use of technology. *MIS Quarterly, 36*(1), 157–178.

Verhoef, p. C., Kannan, p. K., & Inman, J. J. (2015). From multi-channel retailing to omni-channel retailing: Introduction to the special issue on multi-channel retailing. *Journal of Retailing, 91*(2), 174–181.

Yim, C. K., Tse, D. K., & Chan, K. W. (2008). Strengthening customer loyalty through intimacy and passion: Roles of customer: Firm affection and customer: Staff relationships in services. *Journal of Marketing Research, 45*(6), 741–756.

Zalfa, L. H., Siew, p. L., & Sedigheh, M. (2017). Elucidating perceived overall service quality in retail banking. *International Journal of Bank Marketing, 35*(5), 781–804.

Zeelenberg, M., & Pieters, R. (1999). Comparing service delivery to what might have been: Behavioral responses to regret and disappointment. *Journal of Service Research, 2*(1), 86–97.

Zhang, J., Farris, p. W., Irvin, J. W., Kushwaha, T., Steenburgh, T. J., & Weitz, B. A. (2010). Crafting integrated multichannel retailing strategies. *Journal of Interactive Marketing, 24*(2), 168–180.

Zomerdijk, L. G., & Voss, C. A. (2010). Service design for experience-centric services. *Journal of Service Research, 13*(1), 67–82.

Part II

Mobile banking and payment services

4 The development of mobile banking services in a large Finnish financial organization

Pasi Sajasalo, * *Tommi Auvinen, Marko Järvenpää, Tuomo Takala and Teppo Sintonen*

Introduction

It has been said that the digital revolution has challenged traditional business models in most industries (e.g., The Economist, 2012), and banking is no exception. With the pressures caused by digitalization (e.g., Sajasalo, Auvinen, Takala, Järvenpää, & Sintonen, 2016), financial institutions have recently invested considerable resources into developing their mobile financial service offerings (Shaikh, Hanafizadeh, & Karjaluoto, 2017). The entire financial sector seems to be undergoing a transformation in which the overall digitalization of business and resulting digital service provisions have paved the way for new ways of interacting with clientele.

Migrating customers from face-to-face transactions to computer-mediated transactions – more recently, to mobile device-based transactions – has been ongoing in banking for some time (cf. Koenig-Lewis, Palmer, & Moll, 2010; Robinson, 2009). The first wave of digital transformation took place at the turn of the millennium when the use of online banking services exceeded face-to-face interactions in physical bank branches. Online banking services grew steadily and peaked around 2010, at which point mobile banking (m-banking) services[1] were rolled out (OP Financial Group, 2015). The swift technological development and end-user adoption of m-banking services aptly highlights the revolutionary nature of m-banking. To maintain their relevance in the economy, banking incumbents must remain at the developmental forefront of m-banking services to fend off threats posed by newer, more agile players in their traditional domain.

In general, digitalization is portrayed as one of the major megatrends of our time that affects businesses and societies alike (Hajkowicz, 2015, p. 107). OP Financial Group (henceforth OP Group), the largest Finnish-owned financial organization and the principal company studied herein, estimates that as much as 30 to 40% of current financial services' business volume will be wiped out in the next five to ten years as digitalization continues (OP Financial Group, 2016). In response to this projected development, OP Group crafted an updated long-term strategy in summer 2016, stressing the importance of customer experience enhancement by digitizing services and processes (OP Financial Group, 2017a). According to OP Group, the rationale for the chosen strategy lies in "the changing customer behavior and the dramatic and fast digital disruption underway in the financial sector which will attract new market entrants on an ongoing basis." At the same time, digitalization is seen to provide "an opportunity to improve customer experience, create new business and streamline the current processes" (OP Financial Group, 2017a).

OP Group's chosen strategy coincides with the industry's current developments. For instance, Deutsche Bank announced not only a reduction in its bank branches in Germany from 700 to 500 to adapt to digitalization, but also an investment program of one billion euro into developing digital services (Banking Technology, 2016). Furthermore, Banco Santander in Spain announced a closure of 450 bank branches (Financial Times, 2016) and contracted an advisory team to lead their transformation towards digitalization (OP Financial Group, 2016).

The explosion in customers' use of m-banking services (Yen & Wu, 2016) highlights the importance of understanding how m-banking service development takes place in financial institutions, as well as show they integrate customer perspectives into the development of these services. This massive increase is also reflected in the usage statistics of our case organization's m-banking services: its m-banking application called OP-mobile, which was launched in 2012, surpassed its Internet-based e-banking service (OP.fi) in March 2016 by hitting 14.5 million monthly instances of use compared to OP.fi's 10 million (OP Financial Group, 2017b). Furthermore, the fast-paced changes in consumers' use of banking services is all the more evident by examining how OP.fi initially developed in 1995, as it took five years for patrons to use OP.fi more than traditional physical banks for accessing their banking services (Tivi, 2016; OP Financial Group, 2016; OP Financial Group, 2017b). This makes the transition from physical to electronic, and later to mobile banking, rather striking.

As the number of smartphone users worldwide is forecast to pass five billion by 2019 (Statista, 2017), actors in the financial sector will have to monitor this development closely. M-banking appears to be the fastest-growing digital banking channel worldwide (Wonglimpiyarat, 2014; Shaikh et al., 2017), and this is why we focus on the development of OP Group's mobile financial services in this chapter. The specific goal is to shed light on how developers regard and incorporate consumer perspectives into m-banking services so that service adoption can take place effortlessly, thereby encouraging the use of m-banking services. Previous studies (e.g., Koenig-Lewis et al., 2010) have pointed out that perceived risks and trust-related issues, such as fears of personal information or funds being given to third parties without consent, have formed barriers in the adoption of mobile financial services (e.g., Chen, 2013; Laukkanen, 2016; Kim, Shin, & Lee, 2009; Hoehle, Scornavacca, & Huff, 2012).

Despite such barriers, this chapter dissects the rationale for the continued promotion and development of m-banking services as expressed by developers within our case organization, as well as those operating at the frontline. Among other things, earlier research has pointed to saved time and costs (on the sides of both service providers and end users), a lack of limitations from time and space (cf. Moser, 2015), ease of access, and increasing customer demand, especially among younger generations (Calisir & Gumussoy, 2008), as driving forces behind increased m-banking service usage.

Theoretical framing

Mobile banking and payment systems (MBPS)

Mobile banking and payment systems refer primarily to new channels of distribution for regular bank customers or account holders (Shaikh et al., 2017). In this chapter, we primarily focus on OP Group's two existing MBPS services and their development. These services are OP-mobile, a secure service channel to manage banking and insurance transactions, and Pivo, a mobile service app that allows OP Group customers to keep track of all account transactions. Unlike OP-mobile, Pivo is open to customers from all banks, regardless of their patronage to OP Group. In addition, Pivo gives users access to various offers from OP Group's partners, as well as the opportunity to perform instant payments using the recipient's mobile phone number.

Digital service design and development

The competitive setting in banking services is rapidly transforming from one containing few established local service providers into one with seemingly innumerable providers, all unlimited by time or space (see Sajasalo et al., 2016). As such, digitalization poses major challenges for incumbents of the financial sector. The digital revolution has challenged several established business tenets that financial institutions have relied on for decades. For instance, changes in regulation, such as the directive on payment services in the internal market (PSD2), are projected to revolutionize the relationships between banks and their customers by allowing third-party agents, the so-called Payment Initiation Service Providers (PISPs) and Account Information Service Providers (AISPs), access to consenting customers' banking information without incumbents having a say in it (see EUR-Lex, 2015).

Furthermore, the digital revolution in banking services is predicted to elevate customers' influence on banks by setting them at the center stage of future banking services. Instead of simply being *provided* banking services, customers are in a new position of being able to *demand* services that fulfill their current and future needs. Banks must find ways of catering to such needs to build and secure outstanding customer experiences and relationships (OP Financial Group, 2016). The financial landscape favoring customer influence has placed heightened pressure on financial service providers; they must offer innovative new services to not only retain their current clientele but also to attract new customers.

Several service innovation models have been proposed in existing literature with varying emphasis on the drivers of such models, whether external or internal to the organization (e.g., Darmanpour, Walker, & Avellaneda, 2009). For instance, Barras (1986, p. 165) proposes that service innovation follows what he calls a "reverse product cycle," and he ended up applying the model to innovation in financial services (Barras, 1990). Instead of following the Schumpeterian model of technological revolution progressing from radical product innovation to more incremental process innovation – which is typical in manufacturing industries – Barras (1986, 1990) argues the following process cycle in service industries: first are incremental process innovations meant specifically for boosting productivity and driving down costs, then comes innovation meant to improve efficacy and quality, and the final step is emphasis on radical service innovation aimed at generating new and competitive services; this creates differentiation from other firms trying to enter and capture new markets.

Research setting

Our research task is to empirically dissect the development of OP Group's mobile financial services. The goal is to shed light on how customer perspectives are regarded and incorporated in the development of m-banking services by their developers so that adopting services – and eventually using them – would be effortless for consumers, thereby encouraging them to use m-banking services. We seek to complete our research task by obtaining answers to the following research questions:

1   What are OP Group's rationales in developing mobile banking services?
2   How are customer perspectives considered in developing mobile banking services?
3   What are the implications of digitalization and m-banking for the bank and the client?

Our research strategy follows qualitative thematic analysis (e.g., Eriksson & Kovalainen, 2016) to analyze the data. Empirical data were collected from interviews to access in-depth information about the processes involved in the development of m-banking services. To investigate the phenomena of interest empirically, we have constructed a qualitative data set.[2] Using purposeful sampling (Flick, 2007a, 2007b), we invited members of the organization involved with digital and m-banking to participate in our study. Table 4.1 categorizes our interviewees by organizational rank and professional field.

Table 4.1 Interview data

Description	Middle/top management	Specialist/teller	Total
Financial professionals	15	3	18
IT professionals	2	3	5
Total			23

The interviews lasted 30 to 60 minutes each and resulted in some 220 sheets of transcriptions. Moreover, in addition to the interview data, our analysis is supported by internal documents (management strategy presentations, e-banking, and m-banking usage statistics) provided by OP Group. We have covered several organizational echelons' perspectives on m-banking services and their development to better understand various actors' roles in developing their services, as well as how the developers make sense of their customers' perspectives.

Findings

We structure our analysis and present our findings following our research questions. For clarity and concision of presentation, we will present our answer(s) to each question at the end of each theme.

Rationales for developing mobile banking services

In late 2016, two financial professionals in private banking characterized the role of digital and m-banking in their line of business as follows:

> We encourage the use of m-banking to boost customer satisfaction and efficiency, as we see it as a better tool for customers than those our competitors have to offer.
>
> Our clientele are accustomed social media users. We need to keep up with our competitors and provide solutions at a fast pace. From an efficiency perspective, routines, such as automated credit checks, can be robotized to smooth out work processes. Automation makes life a bit easier for customers, and us too. That's efficiency.

Internally, digitalization and mobile services are means of improving the efficiency of back-office routines and reducing the chances of human error. Combined, they can fend off competitive pressure from various sources. For instance, the PSD2 directive that took effect in early 2018 is projected to intensify competition since new competitors riding the wave of digitalization are entering the industry (e.g., Sajasalo et al., 2016). As financial markets grow, incumbents are preparing for the post-PSD2 world by intensifying m-banking development. OP Group has also expended considerable effort in developing m-banking applications for all major mobile operating systems (Android, iOS, and Windows) to make both the OP-mobile and Pivo apps widely accessible, thereby increasing their use. A senior manager in m-banking service development describes the evolving competitive landscape and the transformation of business logic in banking:

> In 2018–2019, new regulations [PSD2, GDPR, MiFID II] will dramatically change competition. Banking will experience the same transformation as many other already digitalized industries; there will be service platforms, marketplaces and applications utilizing customer data. This is a totally foreign model for the financial sector . . . the new reality is that you have 8,000 financial service providers right at your fingertips to pick and choose from.

While there are sound reasons for an organization and its customers to transition to digital and mobile services, equally sound counterarguments appear in organizational discourse. Even some financial professionals in top management take a critical stance toward the digitalization trend that has taken over organizations, highlighting some potential risks and drawbacks:

> There's a fast-paced plan in place to make OP.fi the main sales channel by 2019. I got rather discouraged in a TMT meeting when even younger colleagues fluent with the digital world had their reservations with the plan. Our internal reporting services [Fall 2016] show merely 1.5% of sales originating from OP.fi. Is it due to lack of credibility, or just failed communication?
>
> Many have parroted the idea that "more will change in the next 3–5 years in this business than in the last 50 years," but are our systems able to keep up with the pace? What if OP.fi fails to turn into our main sales channel? Yes, housing loan applications have started coming in through OP.fi, but still, every single loan is finalized manually.

Furthermore, it appears that some members of the organization believe that the less routine solutions the customers require, the harder it is to handle their needs via digital and mobile means. This highlights the continued need for human interaction in various transactions and the importance of human expertise, as explained by two private banking professionals:

> Digitalization won't replace everything 'old.' You're able to perform various transactions digitally, but it is more important for people to have a real person to discuss and weigh alternatives to determine which is advisable. It's situations like those when you need expertise and caring people.

If you're already knowledgeable of the ropes of investments and loans, it's basically just a modification of your previous transactions. In such cases, digital transactions might work well. But if it's your first time, nothing beats personal face-to-face contact. If we have the resources to combine the two, doing so would undoubtedly be our competitive asset.

Clearly, the risks associated with transforming business models and related processes causes apprehension: even those already immersed in the digital world have doubts regarding the transformation and its speed. Moreover, while digitalization and mobile services appear to be competitive weapons, so, too, did personal face-to-face service provision. It therefore appears that both are needed, and finding a balance between the two is likely critical in the emerging competitive landscape, as a senior manager in service development notes:

> We are currently juggling two balls: we have the new digital world with its own operating logic, and we have the old world whose operating logic must be optimized. To survive, you really must win both battles.

The answer to our first research question – "What are OP Group's rationales in developing mobile banking services?" – has multiple facets. From the organization's point of view, the rationales stem from competition-related aspects; keeping up with established competitors, preparing for challenges posed by new entrants (cf. Sajasalo et al., 2016), efficiency, automating functions that are invisible to the customer as much as possible, transferring routine daily banking transactions to be performed by the customers themselves, as well as customer benefit-related issues; flexible 24/7 access to services, and ease of use. The most prominent counter-discourse about digitalization's positive aspects cite the need and longing for human interaction, which may be jeopardized by the transformation to digital and mobile service provision.

Thus, digitalization and m-banking are seen to allow ubiquitous availability and efficiency of service provision, and therefore offer a sound rationale for developing technology-assisted means of interaction with clientele. However, digital and m-banking services dilute the human interaction that has a heightened importance in establishing and maintaining trust, thus challenging the rationale of improving the customer experience. This particular tension remains unresolved and neglected in the OP Group's official strategy.

Taking the customer perspective into account

Enhancing customer experience is an integral, strategy-derived rationale for promoting m-banking in the OP Group, and more generally, an integral part of developing such services is to involve the customer in service development. The idea of integrating various customer inputs into developing software products/services is not new – quite the contrary (e.g., Alam & Perry, 2002). Software development as a field of science and practice have developed numerous models for the process of software development, and in virtually all of them, probing the existing or potential customers' needs and preferences features prominently, even to the extent of referring to co-creation, a concept popularized by service dominant logic thinking (e.g., Ordanini & Pasini, 2008; Vargo & Lusch, 2004).

To take the customer perspective into account in developing m-banking services, OP Group utilized the following established modes of engagement with the customers: (1) customer committees having a more official nature in that the members of the committees are nominated from among the customer-owners of the individual cooperative banks making up the OP Group; (2) feedback channels embedded in both the e-bank and m-banking applications allowing a more unofficial and direct channel of communication between the customer and the developers; (3) face-to-face interaction as part of both scheduled and unscheduled customer appointments with tellers in which the current services used by the customer and future needs are regularly charted as part of the meeting agenda; and (4) invited focus group panels summoned by the service design and development teams consisting of either existing customers, or a random sample for probing customer needs or conducting usability testing of m-banking applications, for instance.

The effort to involve customers in the design and development of m-banking services features recurrently in our informants' thoughts, as exemplified by two IT professionals:

> It's the customer we want to hear from how a given service should function. But then, we want to launch the first version through agile development ASAP. We refer to MVP [minimum viable product], a version that is sufficiently good for its intended use to attract the interest of the clientele.
>
> Design thinking has made a breakthrough recently. I'm not sure if our recently implemented workshop-based approach of working on ideas was copied from Google or someone else, but we now bring in actual customers to test our ideas with quick prototyping to see how they fly. It's the service designer's job to integrate customer perspective in all development. If both the designers and customers agree on the benefits, only then will a new service proceed to technical analysis and production.

Service developers, describing their work and the process through which new services are introduced to the clientele, not only emphasize the importance of involving the customer over the entire development cycle, but also refer to the need for the process to proceed quickly from idea generation to the launch of a new service. A change in the development logic is evident, as a service development manager comments:

The unwritten rule in banking was to never launch an unfinished product/service. Ever. But even as we speak, we are running end user pilots of the new OP.fi service [fully functional alongside current service]. Previously, we would have finalized the new service and tested it in the lab to a T, and only then transitioned from the existing to the new at once. Now we get feedback from the pilot to determine issues, and fix them on the go.

Regardless of the customer appearing frequently in the preceding developer excerpts, these thoughts at the same time implicitly highlight the limited role of customers in service development when it comes to innovation. There are no instances in our data of genuinely new services initiated by customers, but instead their role is to become involved in the development of already brainstormed services. As the preceding excerpts demonstrate, the role of the customer in service development could be best characterized as either a beta-tester or initiator of requests for additional features to be added to already existing services and applications. Thus, this kind of customer involvement may be seen as more about supporting the usability development of the services and applications offered by the bank, rather than initiating idea generation, which is generally the case in service development processes (e.g., Vargo & Lusch, 2004).

As the OP Group itself states, integrating customer perspectives serves as the guiding principle in developing m-banking services. However, even the Pivo application was originally coined by a developer of the mobile development unit of OP Group; obviously, the "end product" is a result of a long-term mutual development process. Typical of mobile applications, Pivo is also undergoing constant updates and feature additions as new versions are rolled out. While customers are placed at center stage in the parlance of the service developers, the idea of developing new services differs somewhat between customer-initiated and developer-initiated service development. A service developer characterizes the idea of the influence of customer feedback on development:

The inclusion of the client in the product development, ensuring that the services meet the clients' needs, and that their perspective serves as the starting point of development, is my job [as a service designer]. We constantly monitor customer feedback and wishes as we go. For instance, an e-mail billing feature was just added in OP-mobile for business users based on the wishes of our customers.

The answer to our second research question – how are customer perspectives taken into account while developing mobile banking services? – is multi-part, similar to our first research question. On the level of organizational discourse, the customer appears as the central figure in service development. Putting the customer at center stage in organizational discourse may be seen as rooted in the customer orientation discourse dominating both academic marketing discourse (see Skålén, Fougère, & Fellesson, 2008; Skålén, 2009) and more generally, business practitioner discourse stemming from the service marketing paradigm (see, e.g., Grönroos, 1978, 1982). Customer discourse offers a source of legitimation for both the organization itself and for those responsible for developing e-banking and m-banking services within the organization.

Moreover, the cooperative roots of the OP Group make the centrality of the customer in organizational discourse, especially that of the customer-owner, understandable. After all, the goal of cooperatives is to create benefits for their members (Jussila, Tuominen, & Saksa, 2008) or, more generally, to promote the economic well-being of their members (see Puusa, Mönk-könen, & Varis, 2013). However, while the customer appeared prominently in organizational discourse in relation to service development, the actual role of customers was less pronounced than the discourse would suggest. Instead of being true co-creators of services, the role assigned to the customer was to provide feedback for the improvement of existing services, as discussed previously.

In terms of the development process, while various established channels for customer participation do exist, they may be characterized as developer-initiated rather than customer-initiated, apart from some instances regarding service features reportedly added based on customer demand. Therefore, from the customer's perspective, there is an interesting tension: on the one hand, ease of use and assisting customers with their daily banking needs by allowing access on a 24/7 basis appear as driving forces for development, but on the other hand, the customer's belief is not necessarily the initiator nor the true beneficiary of the development. The customers may be seen as having been 'forced' participants in the process of digitalizing their banking services, first in the form of e-banking and, more recently, in the form of m-banking. A private banking financial professional reminisces on the process of transformation to e-banking and draws a parallel to the ongoing transformation:

> Back in the day, we taught the customers – by force, in truth – to use the online services. This [m-banking] may be the next similar thing.

The mode adopted by the OP Group in e-banking and m-banking service development reflects the tendency of much of the software industry in general: rather than involving the customer in the idea generation phase, customers are involved in the later phases of development with the aim of testing and improving the usability of the service developed by IT professionals. Service developers are, in other words, testing and improving their own service ideas to make them fit the needs and use habits of customers after-the-fact, instead of actually eliciting user needs or problems at the beginning to build appropriate services from the ground up.

Implications of digitalization and m-banking for the bank and the client

Digitalization appeared as an inevitable phenomenon, akin to a force of nature, for the members of the organization. To survive among the competition, financial institutions are portrayed as desperately needing to develop digital services for their customers – m-banking services in particular – to provide essentially ubiquitous banking and payment services to benefit the customer. While m-banking is often seen to support equality and availability, it is not universally so. In particular, some financial professionals were concerned about the exclusion of certain customer groups, most pronouncedly, the elderly, who may not possess high-speed Internet access and smartphones, nor the technological savvy required to make use of digital services. Moreover, in terms of customer feedback, there appears to be one other segment in the dark: the socially excluded. While in need of banking services in order to be able to function as members of society, they have no voice. Senior ranking financial professionals raise the following concerns:

> [Involving the older generation] is a major challenge . . . those with wealth tend to be in their 70s or over, retired entrepreneurs, and such. They are not heavy users of smartphones. Instead they tend to treat our private bankers as their personal secretaries who will get the job done.
>
> I don't think the customers relying on the physical branch for banking services will change their ways anytime soon. They may have limitations: age-related, unwillingness to learn new ways, or other. The reasons may relate to social exclusion too. These people are unable to take on new services. We encounter them at the till.

As discussed earlier, from the perspective of the OP Group, the development of m-banking services and digitalization of services more generally centers on two main rationales: competition and efficiency. Pressured by competition, no bank can divert from the trend of introducing more m-banking services. As more m-banking services are introduced to keep them in the race, it increasingly leads to services becoming commoditized, and as a result, they do not offer a source of sustained competitive advantage to any of the competitors in the long run (cf. Barney, 1991). Moreover, developing additional services means that vast amounts of resources need to be invested in improving customer experience and security.

The implications of digitalization and increased provision of m-banking services for the customer experience, elevated to top priority in the strategy of the OP Group, are twofold. It is likely that for the representatives of the younger generation, invariably referred to as Generation Y, the Internet Generation, Millennials, or Digital Natives, digital services enhance the customer experience due to this population being at ease with the digital world comprised of tools and processes – such as m-banking services – rather than technologies (Booth, 2009, pp. 3, 15). Being at ease with digital services and utilizing them almost as an extension of the individual him/herself obviously paves the way for the adoption and use of m-banking services. However, digital natives have grown very demanding of their applications through their extensive use, which places extra pressure on the development of m-banking applications in terms of their ease of use, appearance, and speed of performance (see, e.g., Ickin et al., 2012). For the older generations, the digital immigrants (Prensky, 2001), the push for m-banking services may at first diminish the customer experience, but with increased use and habituation with the use logic of the applications, it is also likely that the digital immigrants' customer experience will be enhanced. A middle management financial professional points toward the importance of truly knowing the needs of customers and what affects their experience:

> We want deeper understanding, we are on top of NPS [net promoter score] ratings as it is. That's great, but we want to know how we are able to improve even further. A single rating [NPS] doesn't help much if we want to know why someone would not recommend us; what should be done better so that s/he would? We want to tap into authentic customer feedback so that we know which aspects we need to improve.

To elaborate on the importance of knowing the customer, as well as receiving customers' firsthand feedback and fresh top-of-mind responses related to their physical or digital service encounters with the organization, the middle manager outlines ways in which a more thorough understanding of the customer experience is obtainable through relying on low-tech measures like personal contact with the customer:

> What does being customer-centered and managing customer experience mean in practice? It means, for instance, that tomorrow morning, I will pick up the phone and call several customers who have had appointments over the past couple of days. I will ask them, "How did we fare, what could we improve on, and what are your future expectations on our business hours or service channels?" and those sort of things. We, us managers and senior management alike, need to generate a true understanding of the customers' wishes by getting in touch with them personally and talking things over.

Furthermore, the development of m-banking services appears to resonate with our case organization's values. Most financial professionals from our data agree that one of the OP Group's core values, humaneness, can be fulfilled more effectively with m-banking services because mobile devices provide customers with a real-time connection to the bank. As one manager states, "[T]he bank is closer to people than ever before; it goes along in your pocket wherever you go." Therefore, the new ways of building an even stronger sense of community than was previously available to financial institutions appear as particularly interesting findings based on our data. Through m-banking, financial institutions have the capacity to employ new, virtual means for community building and engaging clientele in a meaningful dialogue to further develop such services. While m-banking promises new means of community building, it has also raised some criticism. Two senior managers comment on the discordance between digitalization and traditional humane cooperative values and challenge the perception of fit:

> There are not enough value discussions conducted at the moment . . . will there be a robot holding the hand of a senior citizen . . . how will we care for our customers when everything is changing?
>
> Those who are unable or unwilling to use digital bank services are mentioned just once in our strategy. That's all. Someone made a slightly sarcastic comment in a meeting: "Does that mean that we'll send them a Christmas card?"

Thus, the unresolved challenge is how to interact with, maintain, and further develop various services for customers who are unwilling or unable to use digital banking services. Should they be left to their own devices, or, as suggested by the cooperative value base of the organization, be cared for through either existing or new tailored services? This may be another issue to be considered explicitly in the strategy, as the issue clearly puzzles even senior managers within the organization.

The answer to our third research question – what are the implications of digitalization and m-banking for the bank and the client? – distills into three main points. First, digitalization paves the way to a self-service culture in banking services. This process leads to an increasing number of customers becoming self-service operators who provide themselves the banking services they need by working with technological platforms and tools provided by financial institutions. In a world characterized by increasing self-servitude, customers have effectively become part of their service provider's workforce. They not only constitute an unpaid workforce, but they are also paying service providers to be a workforce as service charges apply for the use of the technology platform.

Second, according to our findings, the availability and flexibility of m-banking services and the automation of routines – such as credit checks and managing properties and wealth – improves the life of the customer and streamlines the internal processes of the bank, thus providing efficiency gains. However, several informants express concern that there is also an inherent risk of losing real-life interaction and humane caring – integral parts of the value base of a cooperative organization. The real competitive advantage may therefore lie in taking both aspects into account in the development of new digital m-banking services.

Third, the change facing banking due to digitalization is likely to be dramatic as a potentially almost infinite number of competitors can enter the industry, which makes truly knowing the customer more crucial than ever. Therefore, there is a heightened need for deeply understanding the needs of the customers, be they digital natives or digital immigrants. No customer group can be neglected. Truly understanding the customer requires both quantitative and qualitative feedback, active listening, and engaging in dialogue – without forgetting the customer's role of active participation in developing and launching new services.

Discussion

It appears that the financial sector is on the verge of a major disruption brought about by digitalization. In preparation for the new competitive landscape just around the corner, in early 2018 with the PSD2 directive opening up payment services, all major banks, not just the OP Group, our case organization, have resorted to m-banking as the latest step in the digitalization of banking services in order to cushion the blows of the turmoil that is projected in the near future. The opening of financial markets through the PSD2 directive allows entry to banking for not only the incumbents of the industry worldwide but also for countless other organizations outside the traditional industry boundaries, allowing customers a new kind of leverage in their relationships with financial institutions.

Furthermore, as customers have grown used to the various applications available to them in the hundreds of thousands, they have at the same time grown increasingly demanding, which further increases the leverage of customers toward financial institutions. Sub-par performance of or user experience with any application will not be tolerated for long. This obviously places enormous pressure on banks and the m-banking applications they develop, as gold standards against which they are measured are the topmost rated applications of the Android, iOS, or Windows platforms, not necessarily other m-banking applications. The m-banking applications offered by the banking industry incumbents cannot fall too far behind in this new competitive landscape because customers will have a myriad of choices among m-banking applications; in the future, as the market opens, they will not be content with the application offered by the bank they patronize.

Furthermore, the changing relationship between the bank and the customer may be perceived to be, partly at least, a generational issue. The CEO of the OP Group recently pointed to a salient prevailing tension related to the issue: according to this CEO, the Finns love their bank branches more than they actually use them. Thus, even if customer feedback demands bank branches be retained, people still use m-banking as their primary, e-banking as secondary, and bank branches only as the last resort channel to handle their bank affairs. Whereas digital immigrants, the older generations, have become used to physical bank branches, ATMs, and later on learned to use e-banking, and most recently are learning to cope with the technological wonders of m-banking, digital natives may never have set foot in a bank branch.

However, as they live their lives online and inhabit the application space, m-banking applications offer a natural way of connecting with a bank – more specifically, the services they offer (see Booth, 2009). Unlike older generations, digital natives not being attached to a bank as an institution, may well be at ease with a possible future state in which digitalization, intensified competition, and a search for lower cost and prices lead us toward a scenario in which banking becomes permanently and irrevocably self-servitized through technology-assisted ubiquitous services operating on mobile platforms. Whether this actually leads to the dissipation of personal service by financial experts, and to a situation where all human contact is removed as we connect with banks solely via applications, service robots and artificial intelligence (AI) systems, remains to be seen.

This gloomy future – depending on the observer's viewpoint – is most likely a concern to advanced Western economies in which time and cost savings or, more generally, efficiency, is highly favored. Similarly, ease of use, 24/7 availability, individuality, and similar features dominate the development of m-banking services in advanced economies. The rationales driving the development of m-banking services in advanced economies is therefore, apart from competition, convenience, whereas the rationale in developing economies driving their development and promotion may be said to be a necessity. To be able to provide banking services at all, these services must be available on mobile platforms through partnering with mobile operators and banks (e.g., Aker & Mbiti, 2010).

While the use of m-banking services has increased almost exponentially, one must be careful when interpreting usage trends and their implications. While the use of e-banking (especially m-banking) appears to have skyrocketed recently and has seemingly displaced all other forms of interaction between banks and their customers, face-to-face human interaction – either within a physical bank branch or assisted by technology in various ways – is unlikely to disappear in the future. This is due to the different channels and forms of interaction different consumers need; the simple, routine tasks that customers have already grown used to performing themselves using self-service technology require no intervention from financial professionals. However, for the time being, e-banking and m-banking services fall short in providing customer solutions to more demanding, non-routine tasks that require true expertise and "a second opinion" to be helpful in making financial decisions. Although artificial intelligence (AI) is projected to provide such solutions, it cannot provide the degree of insight currently offered by seasoned professionals in the field.

Whether the future of banking will be application and AI-driven or something else, banking and the financial industry on a whole will inevitably change. Bill Gates reportedly made the following observation in the mid-1990s (see e.g., Filkorn, 2016): "We need banking, but we don't need banks anymore. Do you think someday we can open a bank account or ask for a loan without physically having to come to the bank?"

While we have yet to see the demise of banks, the ways in which banking is conducted have transformed considerably since the mid-1990s, and some aspects of Bill Gates' speculation are already a reality; with some limitations, one can open a bank account and apply for a loan without physically being at a bank branch. While, the claim made nearly a quarter of a century ago has not been fully realized, in that financial institutions are still necessary, ongoing technology-enabled digitalization highlights the development of m-banking services as a critical factor in the future of all financial institutions. The issue to be solved now is how to balance future digital influences on banking with the established traditional operating logics and societal norms. This requires balancing the needs of both digital immigrants and digital natives and actively immersing both groups in developing future banking services, whether they consist of e-banking, m-banking, or another form of banking entirely. As put by our informant: "To survive, you really must win both battles."

Acknowledgments

The authors wish to thank OP Group Research Foundation for their support to the SALP research group at the University of Jyväskylä School of Business and Economics.

Notes

* *Corresponding/primary contact author*
1 In this chapter, we understand mobile banking services as financial services whose access relies on cell phones, smartphones, and tablets (cf. Shaikh & Karjaluoto, 2016).
2 This chapter is part of an ongoing research project. The project, which the Strategy, Accounting, and Leadership as Practice (SALP) research group of the Jyväskylä University School of Business and Economics (https://www.jyu.fi/jsbe/en/research/research-groups/redas/salp) started in 2012, examines strategy-related issues in banking. To date, about 180 interviews within OP Group have been conducted. In this chapter, we utilize data collected between 2016 and 2017.

References

Aker, J. C., & Mbiti, I. M. (2010). Mobile phones and economic development in Africa. *The Journal of Economic Perspectives*, 24(3), 207–232.

Alam, I., & Perry, C. (2002). A customer-oriented new service development process. *Journal of Services Marketing*, 16(6), 515–534.

Banking Technology. (2016). *Deutsche Bank reduces branch network in Germany*. Retrieved July 30, 2017, from www.bankingtech.com/460382/deutsche-bank-reduces-branch

Barney, J. B. (1991). Firm resources and sustained competitive advantage. *Journal of Management, 17*(1), 99–120.

Barras, R. (1986). Towards a theory of innovation in services. *Research Policy, 15*(4), 161–173.

Barras, R. (1990). Interactive innovation in financial and business services: The vanguard of the service revolution. *Research Policy, 19*(3), 215–237.

Booth, C. (2009). *Informing innovation: Tracking student interest in emerging library technologies at Ohio University.* Chicago: The American Library Association.

Calisir, F., & Gumussoy, C. A. (2008). Internet banking versus other banking channels: Young consumers' view. *International Journal of Information Management, 28*(3), 215–221.

Chen, C. (2013). Perceived risk, usage frequency of mobile banking services. *Managing Service Quality, 23*(5), 410–436.

Darmanpour, F., Walker, R. M., & Avellaneda, C. N. (2009). Combinative effects of innovation types and organizational performance: A longitudinal study of service organizations. *Journal of Management Studies, 46*(4), 650–675.

The Economist. (2012). The third industrial revolution. Retrieved March 12, 2017, from www.economist.com/node/21553017

Eriksson, P., & Kovalainen, A. (2016). *Qualitative methods in business research: A practical guide to social research.* London: Sage Publications.

EUR-Lex. (2015). Directive (EU) 2015/2366 of the European parliament and of the council. *Official Journal of the European Union, 50,* 337/35. Retrieved August 16, 2017, from http://eur-lex.europa.eu/legal-content/EN/TXT/PDF/?uri=CELEX :32015L2366&from=en

Filkorn, M. (2016). *Banking is necessary, banks are not; how banks can survive in the digital age.* Retrieved September 22, 2017, from www.capgemini.com/consulting/2016/07/ banking-is-necessary-banks-are-not-how-banks-can-survive-in-the/

Financial Times. (2016). Santander to close 450 branches in Spain. Retrieved July 30, 2017, from www.ft.com/content/68ec8904-f7fc-11e5-96db-fc683b5e52db? mhq5j=e2

Flick, U. (2007a). *Designing qualitative research: The Sage qualitative research kit.* London: Sage Publications.

Flick, U. (2007b). *Managing quality in qualitative research: The Sage qualitative research kit.* London: Sage Publications.

Grönroos, C. (1978). A service orientated approach to marketing of services. *European Journal of Marketing, 12*(8), 588–601.

Grönroos, C. (1982). An applied service marketing theory. *European Journal of Marketing, 16*(7), 30–41.

Hajkowicz, S. (2015). *Global megatrends: Seven patterns of change shaping our future.* Melbourne: CSIRO Publishing.

Hoehle, H., Scornavacca, E., & Huff, S. (2012). Three decades of research on consumer adoption and utilization of electronic banking channels: A literature analysis. *Decision Support Systems, 54*(1), 122–132.

Ickin, S., Wac, K., Fiedler, M., Janowski, L., Hong, J.-H., & Dey, A. K. (2012). Factors influencing quality of experience of commonly used mobile applications. *IEEE Communications Magazine, 50*(4), 48–56.

Jussila, I., Tuominen, P., & Saksa, J. M. (2008). Following a different mission: Where and how do consumer cooperatives compete? *Journal of Co-Operative Studies, 41*(3), 28–39.

Kim, G., Shin, B., & Lee, H. G. (2009). Understanding dynamics between initial trust and usage intentions of mobile banking. *Information Systems Journal, 19*(3), 283–311.

Koenig-Lewis, N., Palmer, A., & Moll, A. (2010). Predicting young consumers' take up of mobile banking services. *International Journal of Bank Marketing, 28*(5), 410–432.

Laukkanen, T. (2016). Consumer adoption versus rejection decisions in seemingly similar service innovations: The case of the Internet and mobile banking. *Journal of Business Research, 69*(7), 2432–2439.

Moser, F. (2015). Mobile banking: A fashionable concept or an institutionalized channel in future retail banking? Analyzing patterns in the practical and academic mobile banking literature. *International Journal of Bank Marketing, 33*(2), 162–177.

OP Financial Group. (2015). Internal presentation materials. *Confidential, Available as a PDF-Document from the OP Financial Group Intranet.* Retrieved June 1, 2017.

OP Financial Group. (2016). Internal presentation in an annual strategy planning day. *Confidential, Available as a PDF-Document from the OP Financial Group Intranet.* Retrieved May 14, 2017.

OP Financial Group. (2017a). *Strategy.* Retrieved August 16, 2017, from www. op.fi/op/op-financial-group/op-financial-group/strategy?id=80101&srcpl=8&kie likoodi=en

OP Financial Group. (2017b). *Op Ryhmän osavuosikatsaus 1.1.2017–31.3.2017 [Interim Report Q1/2017].* Retrieved August 15, 2017, from www.op.fi/media/ liitteet?cid=-86841&srcpl=3&srcpl=3

Ordanini, A., & Pasini, p. (2008). Service co-production and value co-creation: The case for a service-oriented architecture (SOA). *European Management Journal, 26*(5), 289–297.

Prensky, M. (2001). Digital natives, digital immigrants, part 1. *On the Horizon, 9*(5), 1–6.

Puusa, A., Mönkkönen, K., & Varis, A. (2013). Mission lost? Dilemmatic dual nature of co-operatives. *Journal of Co-Operative Organization and Management, 1*, 6–14.

Robinson, T. (2009). Internet banking: Still not a perfect marriage. *Information-week.com.* Retrieved August 20, 2017, from www.informationweek.com

Sajasalo, P., Auvinen, T., Takala, T., Järvenpää, M., & Sintonen, T. (2016). Strategy implementation as fantasising: Becoming the leading bank. *Accounting and Business Research, 46*(3), 303–325.

Shaikh, A. A., Hanafizadeh, P., & Karjaluoto, H. (2017). Mobile banking and payment system: A conceptual standpoint. *International Journal of E-Business Research, 13*(2), 14–27.

Shaikh, A. A., & Karjaluoto, H. (2016). On some misconceptions concerning digital banking and alternative delivery channels. *International Journal of E-Business Research, 12*(3), 1–16.

Skålén, p. (2009). Service marketing and subjectivity: The shaping of customer-oriented employees. *Journal of Marketing Management, 25*(7–8), 795–809.

Skålén, P., Fougère, M., & Fellesson, M. (2008). *Marketing discourse: A critical perspective.* London: Routledge.

Statista. (2017). *Mobile phone users worldwide 2013–2019.* Retrieved November 30, 2017, from www.statista.com/statistics/274774/forecast-of-mobile-phone-users-worldwide/

Tivi. (2016). *Digimyrsky iskee: "pankeista voi tulla pelkkä putkisto".* Retrieved December 14, 2017, from www.tivi.fi/Kaikki_uutiset/digimyrsky-iskee-pankeista-voi-tulla-pelkka-putkisto-6593153

Vargo, S. L., & Lusch, R. F. (2004). Evolving to a new dominant logic for marketing. *Journal of Marketing, 68*(1), 1–17.

Wonglimpiyarat, J. (2014). Competition and challenges of mobile banking: A systematic review of major bank models in the Thai banking industry. *The Journal of High Technology Management Research, 25*(2), 123–131.

Yen, Y. S., & Wu, F. S. (2016). Predicting the adoption of mobile financial services: The impacts of perceived mobility and personal habit. *Computers in Human Behavior, 65,* 31–42.

5 Factors influencing mobile banking continuous use in Sub-Sahara Africa

A study of mobile banking users in Nigeria

Dandison C. Ukpabi,* Heikki Karjaluoto,
Sunday A. Olaleye and Salimat Modupe Abass

Introduction

Digital technologies are altering consumers' purchase journey in various ways (Powers, Advincula, Austin, Graiko, & Snyder, 2012). Some decades ago, a purchase decision that could take a consumer weeks and months because of information gathering on available competing products and services, prices, and locations are currently made within minutes because of the quantum of information available to the consumer through digital technology. While other digital technologies offer different benefits to the user, mobile technologies have attracted unprecedented attention in recent times (Kauffman & Techatassanasoontorn, 2005). The rapid diffusion of mobile technology is predicated on the fact that while mobile devices provide consumers with unlimited access to information, mobile apps also provide consumers with tailor-made information such as gaming, news, banking, sports, commerce, and tourism (Shaikh & Karjaluoto, 2015). While there is uniformity in the high adoption rate of mobile devices in both the developed and emerging markets, different studies however found a wide gap on consumer adoption of mobile technologies in business transactions. For instance, while nine-in-ten Nigerians and South Africans own mobile phones (Pew Research Center, 2017), around half, that is, 48%, use them for social media such as Facebook while others are use them for making and receiving calls.

In Nigeria, for instance, the rapid diffusion of mobile devices such as smartphones and tablets accentuates the impact they have made in other sectors, such as the news media and banks, which has led to a corresponding adoption by consumers in order to access these services. Specifically, all the 23 licensed money deposit banks own robust m-banking platforms that have provided a more convenient way through which customers conduct their banking transactions. Accordingly, as reported by the United Nations Conference on Trade and Development (UNCTAD, 2007), Nigeria is the leading country in Africa in terms of m-banking adoption. Additionally, a study after some few years (Bankole, Bankole, & Brown, 2011), corroborated the UNCTAD report and argued that Nigerians' use of m-banking applications varied in different forms such as balance inquiry, statement request, and money transfer, indicating that there was a frenzied rate of adoption as soon as it was introduced in the Nigerian market. However, that rate of adoption could not be sustained, as many consumers dumped the platform due to technical and regulatory challenges. For instance, a financial crisis in December 2016 saw purchases for Christmas celebrations got to a fever pitch as the rush for cash withdrawals could not be handled by the banks. Automatic teller machines (ATMs) also ran out of money, thereby casting a pale shadow on a festive season that is the most celebrated in the entire country. As a result, the multiplier effect of this economic quagmire was felt across the country. Besides the pain and hunger suffered by families, businesses such as fast food restaurants, retailers, transportation companies, and others were largely short of the expected number of customers because of the unavailability of cash. The preceding scenario paints a glaring picture of m-banking continuous usage behavior.

Accordingly, Shaikh and Karjaluoto (2015, p. 131), define m-banking as "a product or service offered by a bank or a microfinance institute (bank-led model) or MNO (non-bank-led model) for conducting financial and non-financial transactions using a mobile device, namely a mobile phone, smartphone, or tablet." The emergence of m-banking is attributed to the availability of information and communication technology tools that enabled consumers' interaction with digital devices. Thus, just like tourism, e-tailing, education, transportation, and so on, it became essential to develop mobile applications that harmonizes the different banking transactions to give the customer convenience in his/her relationship with the bank. Different studies have examined the antecedents of m-banking adoption in different contexts. Thus, Lin (2011) argues that two critical factors were responsible for m-banking adoption.

Extant studies have validated positive relationships between facilitating conditions and continuous usage of document management system (Bhattacherjee, Perols, & Sanford, 2008); social influence and continuous usage of SmartIDs and government website (Venkatesh, Thong, Chan, Hu, & Brown, 2011); hedonic features and continuous usage of Habbo, a virtual networking site (MäntymäKi & Salo, 2011). Interestingly, m-banking continuous use has been studied in different contexts particularly in the developed and technologically advanced economies (Lee & Chung, 2009; Shaikh & Karjaluoto, 2016). The reason for the preponderance of studies in such economies is that technological adoption by both individuals and corporate entities naturally follows a seamless paradigm by virtue of the technological ecosystem prevalent in such climes. However, there is empirical evidence to support that early adopters of technological innovation are not restricted to geographical boundaries but largely predicated on personal innovativeness of individuals irrespective of the prevalent socio-economic and technological profundities, and such innovation-prone consumers are more likely to adopt new technological innovations than laggards in the developed and technologically advanced economies (Akinci, Aksoy, & Atilgan, 2004; De Mooij & Hofstede, 2011; Smith & Urpelainen, 2014), therefore making our study very suitable in the Nigerian context. Accordingly, our study aims to explore the factors influencing continuous usage of m-banking in Nigeria. Specifically, our study's threefold objectives include:

- to examine the antecedents of m-banking continuous usage in a developing economy;
- to examine to what extent the hedonic features embedded on m-banking platforms influence continuous usage;
- to evaluate the differences in customer demographics in m-banking continuous usage.

Our study makes two key contributions to literature: (1) it extends the m-banking continuous use literature by integrating the UTAUT and uses and gratification models, and (2) it tests this model in an emerging market context in Africa, thus, providing new insights to underlying factors to technology use.

Figure 5.1 introduces the framework of this study and fuses the technology acceptance model, gratification model, and trust to explain the m-banking continuous use. Facilitating condition, social influence, privacy,

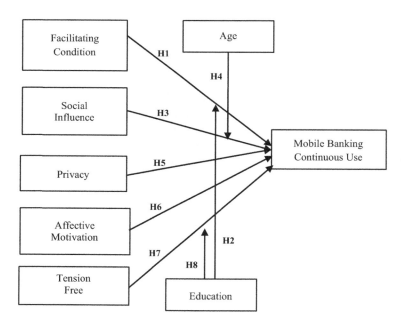

Figure 5.1 Research conceptual framework

affective motivation, and tension directly predict m-banking app continuous use. The model also examines the moderating role of user's age and user's level of education on social influence, facilitating conditions, and tension-free constructs, respectively.

Theoretical background and literature review

The unified theory of acceptance and use of technology (UTAUT) was proposed and validated in order to provide a unified theoretical basis from which to facilitate research on information system (IS) and information technology (IT) adoption and diffusion (Venkatesh, Morris, Davis, & Davis, 2003). A more complete and practical set of factors is obtained from these authors as a unified view of user adoption. By combining eight competing theoretical models, the authors derived an overarching set of four constructs that have an immediate influence on acceptance and usage behavior of technology. The theory postulates that four core constructs – performance expectancy, effort expectancy, social influence, and facilitating conditions – are direct determinants of IS/IT behavioral intention and ultimately behavior (Venkatesh et al., 2003). The theory also assumes that the effect of core constructs is moderated by gender, age, experience, and voluntariness of use (Venkatesh et al., 2003).

The theory was developed through the review and integration of eight dominant theories and models, which are the Theory of Reasoned Action (TRA), the Technology Acceptance Model (TAM), the Motivational Model (MM), the Theory of Planned Behavior (TPB), a combined Theory of Planned Behavior/Technology Acceptance Model (C-TPB-TAM), the Model of PC Utilization (MPCU), the Innovation Diffusion Theory (IDT), and the Social Cognitive Theory (SCT). These theories and models have been successfully utilized as fundamental antecedents to different branches of information science and innovation adoption, such as mobile apps, electronic shopping, mobile commerce, m-banking, and electronic financial services adoption. The motivation to define and validate the UTAUT was based on the argument that many of the constructs of existing theories are similar in nature, making it logical to map and incorporate them to create a unified theoretical basis (Venkatesh et al., 2003). UTAUT is still a relatively new model and has not been as widely used as TAM and IDT; it has gradually drawn researchers' attention and has been recently applied to exploring the users' acceptance of m-banking especially in Africa (Cudjoe, Anim, & Nyanyofio, 2015). Interestingly, while the original UTAUT conceptualization was tested in an organizational context, an extension of it, UTAUT2, was used in the consumer context (Venkatesh, Thong, & Xu, 2012). In the UTAUT2, voluntariness was dropped while hedonic motivation, experience and habit, and price value were included.

The key risks to the mobile device include malware, malicious applications, privacy violations relative to application collection and distribution of data, wireless carrier infrastructure, payments infrastructure/ecosystem, SMS vulnerabilities, hardware and operating system vulnerabilities, complex supply chain and new entrants into the mobile ecosystem, and lack of maturity of fraud tools and controls (Pegueros, 2012). The perception of risk among individuals has been proved in technology adoption literature as an important element in acquiring new technology or services (Martins, Oliveira, & Popovič, 2014). A recent study conducted by Farzianpour, Pishdar, Shakib, Hashemi, and Toloun (2014) found that users' perception of risk is a crucial driver to determine innovative/information technology acceptance. But consumers' performance risk perception, security risk perception, time loss risk perception, privacy risk perception and innovation adoption affect adoption of m-banking services. However, Martins et al. (2014) and Abadi, Kabiry, and Forghani (2013) found that risk to strongly predict behavioral intention to adopt Internet/m-banking.

Moreover, the uses and gratification theory seeks to answer the question of why and how do individuals differ in their motivations (Joo & Sang, 2013). According to Joo and Sang, the theory argues that individuals are motivated to gratify felt desires. Originally stemming from the media discipline, the importance of the theory has drawn scholarly attention to the underlying gratifications individuals derive from technological adoption. Accordingly, the theory has been used in use of social media, e-shopping, and intentions to adopt m-banking (Whiting & Williams, 2013; Amin, Supinah, Aris, & Baba, 2012; Kang, Lee, & Lee, 2012). M-banking, enabled through the use of mobile devices such as smartphones, tablets, and personal digital assistants (PDAs), is used for basic banking operations like funds transfer, account balances, bills payment, and account history (Lin, 2011; Tam & Oliveira, 2017).

Accordingly, customers who have more positive perceived relative advantage and those who find it easy to use were more favorable to its adoption. Additionally, among young people, compatibility, trust, credibility, and ease of use were major influencers of its adoption among Germans (Koenig-Lewis, Palmer, & Moll, 2010). As a matter of fact, Crabbe, Standing, Standing, and Karjaluoto (2009) found that age, educational level, and occupation influenced its adoption in a socially cohesive culture like Ghana. In order to understand the resistant factors, Laukkanen and Kiviniemi (2010) posit that bank customers' slow adoption of m-banking is as a result of lack of sufficient information. To reduce information deficit, they suggested that banks and regulatory authorities should utilize all media channels both new and traditional media to espouse the benefits of m-banking. The successful adoption of m-banking by customer, according to Shaikh, Karjaluoto, and Chinje (2015), is a vital strategy for customer retention. With the increased level of m-banking adoption in many economies including some developing countries, scholars have deemed it pertinent to examine factors that can lead to sustained use of the platform (Laukkanen, 2017). Specifically, Chen (2012) argued that post-adoption relationship quality is fundamental to sustain continuous usage. As a matter of fact, it is critical for service providers to continuously provide support services and other enabling conditions so as to sustain the usage.

Facilitating conditions

Facilitating conditions are defined as the degree to which an individual believes that an organizational and technical infrastructure exists to support use of the system (Venkatesh et al., 2003). The definition captures concepts embodied by three constructs: perceived behavioral control (TPB/DTPB, C-TAM-TPB), facilitating condition (MPCU), and compatibility (IDT). These constructs play a role in aspects of the technological and organizational environment that are designed to remove barriers to use. Taylor and Todd (1995) acknowledged the theoretical overlap by modeling facilitating conditions as a core component of perceived behavioral control in TPB/DTPB. Facilitating conditions do have a direct influence on usage beyond that explained by behavioral intentions alone, thus, when moderated by experience and age, facilitating conditions will have a significant influence on usage behavior (Deng, Liu, & Qi, 2011). As argued by Bhattacherjee et al. (2008), initial adopters of a piece of technology will likely discontinue its use if the external factors are detrimental to its continuous use. Additionally, Venkatesh et al. (2011) posit that users will seek external assistance when confronted with difficulties and are prone to discontinue its use if the assistance does not come. Similarly, in a study of mobile banking users in Ghana, Crabbe et al. (2009) found that educational level and gender significantly influence individuals' perception of facilitating conditions and intention to adopt m-banking, which also corroborates an earlier study by Haghirian and Madlberger (2005) in which education enhances consumers' interactivity and positive attitude towards mobile advertising. We thus argue that

H1:   *The facilitating conditions for m-banking app will positively influence the m-banking continuous use.*

H2:   *The higher the education status, the stronger will be the link between FC and m-banking app continuous use.*

Social influence

Venkatesh et al. (2003) stated that social influence is the degree to which an individual feels that it is important for others to believe he or she should use the new system. Three constructs are related to social influence: subjective norms (rational action theory, planned behavior theory, decomposed planned behavior theory, and technology acceptance model 2), social factors (PC utilization model) and image (innovation diffusion theory). While they have different labels each of these constructs contains the explicit or implicit notion that the individual's behavior is influenced by the way in which they believe others will view them as a result of having used the technology. The constructs are also said to behave similarly though not in voluntary context. However, each becomes significant when use is mandated (Venkatesh et al., 2003). Venkatesh and Davis (2000) suggested that such effects could be attributed to compliance in mandatory contexts that causes social influences to have a direct effect on intention, in contrast, social influence in voluntary contexts operates by influencing perceptions about the technology.

In mandatory settings, social influence appears to be important only in the early stages of individual experience with the technology, with its role becoming less significant as the user gains experience with the technology (Venkatesh & Davis, 2000). Social influence has an impact on individual behavior through compliance, internalization, and identification mechanisms (Venkatesh & Davis, 2000). The view of compliance is consistent with results in information technology, information science technology acceptance literature indicating that reliance on others' opinion is significant only in mandatory settings particularly in the early stages of experience, when an individual opinion are relatively ill-informed (Venkatesh & Davis, 2000). This pressure weakens over time as increasing experience provides a more influential basis for individual intention to use the system. Several studies found that social influence plays a significant role in behavioral intention to adopt information technology (Chang, 2013; Cheng, Yu, Huang, Yu, & Yu, 2011; Martins et al., 2014). In examining factors influencing the continuous use of mobile commerce (m-commerce), Lu (2014) posits that social influence is very critical at the initial stage of adoption, however, its effects wane as the user gains more experience with the platform, thus, corroborating Venkatesh et al. (2011), who did not find a positive relationship between social influence and continuous usage. Additionally, in a study of m-banking usage in Taipei, Yu (2012) found that age significantly moderated the relationship between effort expectancy and intention, with adults being mostly affected while younger respondents were more influenced by facilitating conditions. We thus argue that social influence is likely going to be a critical factor with age playing a dominant role in m-banking continuous usage especially in a socially cohesive culture like Nigeria. Thus,

H3: *Social influence of m-banking users will positively influence m-banking app continuous use.*

H4: *The higher the age, the stronger will be the link between social influence and m-banking app continuous use.*

Privacy

Privacy is the security that the consumer's personal information is saved and not transferred to third parties (Li & Yeh, 2010). Privacy policy should constantly be updated to increase trust and confidence amongst the customer to accept and use the mobile services (Kaitawarn, 2015). According to Li and Yeh (2010), trust and privacy play a vital role in providing satisfaction and expected outcomes for mobile commerce users. User trust and privacy as well as security are important to ensure that users have their confidence in m-banking services (Gu, Lee, & Suh, 2009; Li & Yeh, 2010). In addition to the original determinants, trust, convenience, privacy, and cost are also shown to affect behavioral intention (Min, Ji, & Qu, 2008). Customers' intention to use an innovation or mobile device can be influenced by security and privacy (Luarn & Lin, 2005). Accordingly, Cranor, Reagle, and Ackerman (2014) found that 81% of users are concerned about privacy when they are online. Mobile technology provides a great commercial potential for location-based applications and services. The capability may provide information services such as advertising and navigation based on the user's location, it also poses potential privacy problems since the service providers will know the exact location of the user and might even know the user's travel pattern. As a result, consumers are concerned about their privacy protection. Bhattacherjee (2001) suggested that service providers should permit a user to choose how his or her personal information is used. In an examination of the factors influencing continuance intention of mobile shoppers in China, Gao, Waechter, and Bai (2015) found that privacy and security significantly influence trust, flow, and satisfaction to continue mobile shopping. A conflicting finding however in an m-banking context in India was reported where risk associated with privacy concerns was not found to be a significant determinant of satisfaction but continuance intention (Kumar, Rejikumar, & Ravindran, 2012). Thus, we hypothesize that

H5: *Privacy concern of m-banking app use will negatively influence m-banking continuous use.*

Affective motivation

Affective motivation, similarly referred to as hedonic motivation, is defined as the fun or pleasure derived from using a technology, and it has been shown to play an important role in determining technology acceptance and usage (Brown & Venkatesh, 2005). It has been conceptualized as perceived enjoyment found to influence technology acceptance and use measuring m-banking as fun, enjoyable, and very entertaining (Venkatesh et al., 2012). These motivational aspects can be described as adventure, socializing, taking pleasure, having an idea, exchange of values, and roles (Arnold & Reynolds, 2003). Hedonic consumption is based on hedonism, which is a philosophy acknowledging pleasure in the content and meaning of life. Although hedonism is related to excess, unplanned, and pleasure, it is necessary for businesses to know about factors motivating consumers towards hedonic behavior. Knowledge about these factors will be of competitive advantage for businesses in the long run, as it makes it possible to understand many aspects of consumer behavior. Empirically, affective motivation has been found to be an important determinant of technology acceptance and use in consumer context (Brown & Venkatesh, 2005; Childers, Carr, Peck, & Carson, 2001). Yang (2010) found that hedonic performance expectancy, social influence, and facilitating conditions are critical determinants of US consumers' intentions to use mobile shopping services. In the m-banking context, Baptista and Oliveira (2015) found a positive relationship between affective motivation and behavioral intention on m-banking. Hedonism as a motivation for online games and mobile shopping continuance intension are well established in literature (Yang, 2010; Brown & Venkatesh, 2005; Childers et al., 2001; Gao & Bai, 2014), its application in m-banking continuous use is relatively scarce. Thus, we are arguing that embedding hedonic features in m-banking apps will increase affective interest and continuous use. Accordingly,

> H6: *Embedding affective features in m-banking apps will positively influence continuous use.*

Tension-free

Different people use the media for different reasons. The core postulation of the tension-free component of the uses and gratification theory is that besides the utilitarian reasons, the use of media is to escape tension such as listening to favorite music or watching favorite video clips in order to keep a relaxed mood (Reychav & Wu, 2014). Embedding features in mobile applications that foster users' interactivity and enjoyment will increase their cognitive and affective commitment to use the application (Kang, Mun and Johnson, 2015). Reychav and Wu (2014) posit that interactivity in digital multimedia offers sociability, benefits and involvement, and enjoyment. Interestingly, tension-free has been applied in the use of mobile tablet for road safety training (Reychav & Wu, 2014), retail apps (Kang et al., 2015), and mobile games (Sjöblom, Törhönen, Hamari, & Macey, 2017). Empirically, Reychav and Wu (2014) found that embedding enjoyment content on a road safety training application enhanced learning as perceived interactivity was a critical antecedent to users' affective involvement to use mobile retail apps. Additionally, Lu and Yu-Jen Su (2009) found that those who exhibit less anxiety on a mobile shopping site show more favorable disposition to using it. Finally, evidence abounds that educational level significantly influences patients' anxiety level with respect to the use of mobile devices (Rosen, Whaling, Rab, Carrier, & Cheever, 2013). Accordingly, we argue that embedding voice features, pleasant tones, and background music will enhance users' interactivity and enjoyment of m-banking applications just as educational level affects users' anxiety. Thus,

> H7: *Tension-free feature of m-banking app will positively influence m-banking continuous use.*

H8:   *The higher the education status, the stronger will be the link between tension-free and m-banking app continuous use.*

Continuous use

M-banking has been confirmed to be beneficial and plays a vital role in customer satisfaction, therefore retention and sustainable usage of the banking services by customers is necessary (Shaikh et al., 2015). There are several important factors that are required to be identified and designed in analyzing continuance usage intention. The adoption of m-banking can be analyzed in two stages: initial m-banking adoption and post-m-banking adoption (Kang et al., 2012). In the initial adoption process, an individual forms the attitude toward m-banking and further decides whether to adopt it or not. The post-adoption process explains an individual who has already adopted m-banking and forms the attitudes toward continuing using it or not. The available evidence within marketing literature suggests that similar to other service industries, lack of understating on determinants of customer retention can be costly to banks, which have made considerable amount of investments to provide m-banking services (Mittal & Lassar, 1998; Nazir & Shah, 2014). Retaining existing customers and making them loyal to the service providers is one the most important ways of attaining long-term profitability. Also, attracting new customers costs up to five times more than the cost of retaining an existing customer (Bansal, Irving, & Taylor, 2004; Mittal & Lassar, 1998). Regularly, it is important to banks and agencies providing m-banking services to implement effective and efficient strategies to retain existing users of their m-banking services to be able to enjoy the long-term benefits of having loyal customers. Evolving from pre-adoption to post-adoption stage, Bhattacherjee (2001) modeled an IS continuance model specifically to understand the reasons an individual continues IS usage and contends that critical factors that underpin continuous use are satisfaction, perceived usefulness, and confirmation. The framework explains that individuals continue intention is primarily determined by users' satisfaction with their prior IS use. Users' satisfaction is driven by users' perceived usefulness and confirmation of expectations following actual use.

Research design and methodology

Questionnaire development

To have an in-depth understanding of the factors responsible for an m-banking app in an emerging market, the study adopted questions from previous studies and used seven-point Likert scales (strongly disagree to strongly agree) in order to have a valid and reliable instrument for the study. The questions related to facilitating conditions and social influence were adapted from Venkatesh et al. (2003). Items for affective and tension-free were adapted from Ha, Kim, Libaque-Saenz, Chang, and Park (2015). Items from privacy and security were adapted from Flavián and Guinalíu (2006), while continuous use items were adapted from Venkatesh and Goyal (2010). To add demographic and interaction effect insights, the study added questions on gender, occupation, income, education, and age (see Table 5.1 for details).

Table 5.1 Demographic information of m-banking app users

Demography variable	Demography classification	Frequency	Percentage (%)
Gender	Male	159	65
	Female	86	35
Occupation	Armed Forces	12	5
	Teaching Professionals	40	16
	Technicians and Associate Professionals	22	9
	Clerical Support Works	19	8
	Service and Sales Workers	58	24
	Skilled Agricultural Workers	7	3
	Craft and Related Trades Workers	6	2
	Plant and Machine Operators	4	2
	Students/Researchers	66	27
	Others	11	4
Income*	Less than ₦100,000	127	52
	₦100,001–₦200,000	70	29
	₦200,001–₦300000	21	9
	₦300,001–₦400,000	12	5
	₦400,001–₦500,000	6	2
	₦500,001–₦600,000	5	2
	₦600,001 or more	4	2
Education	High School/Diploma	115	47
	Bachelor Degree	79	32
	Master's Degree	39	16
	PhD	7	3
	No Formal Education	5	2
Age	15–24	120	49
	25–34	68	28
	35–44	36	15
	45–54	19	8
	55–64	2	1

* One dollar is an equivalent of 360 Nigerian naira

Sample and data collection

Using a convenience sampling method, 300 questionnaires were administered to banking customers in the Western part of Nigeria that have used m-banking apps either to check their account balance, pay bills, or perform intra- and inter-banking money transfers. The study retrieved 250 from the respondents, which accounted for an 83% response rate, as 50 questionnaires were not returned. On further evaluation, five responses were poorly filled, had missing values, or had unengaged responses, thus, leaving 245 that were finally used for the data analysis. The study utilized nonprobability convenience sampling technique because of the inconsistency of population records of the western region of Nigeria. The participants (n = 245) consisted of 159 males (65%) and 86 females (35%). The occupation of the respondents varied; 12 respondents belonged to the armed forces (5%), 40 were teaching professionals (16%), 22 were technicians and associate professionals (9%), 19 clerical support workers (8%), 58 service and sales workers (24%), 7 skilled agricultural workers (3%), 6 craft and related trades workers (2%), 4 plant and machine operators (2%), 66 students and researchers (27%), while 11 belong to other occupations (4%) with additional demographic details as contained in Table 5.1. The data were analysed with SPSS 24 version and SmartPLS 2.0 (Ringle, Wende, & Becker, 2014) for reliability analysis and variance-based structural equation modeling. The option of SmartPLS statistics software for this study is due to its easy user interface and its exploratory characteristics and its ability to handle complex models. Previous studies have established the usefulness of SmartPLS for data analysis (Almahamid, Tweiqat, & Almanaseer, 2016; Hair, Ringle, & Sarstedt, 2011; Henseler, Ringle, & Sinkovics, 2009). The study also added the interaction terms to the model to have an expanded understanding of the variables relationship.

Measurement model assessment

The study combines the theory of trust, technology acceptance, and gratification to form a model of m-banking app continuous use in an emerging market. The study tested the new model for reliability, convergent validity, and discriminant validity (see Table 5.3 for details). The factors loaded within the range of 0.54–0.93. The Composite Reliability (CR) of the variables is greater than the rule of thumb of 0.7 (0.88–0.94) (Hair et al., 2011). The Variance Extracted (AVE) values were above the threshold of 0.5 (0.63–0.81) (Hair et al., 2011; Bagozzi & Yi, 1988). Table 5.3 depicts the discriminant validity (Hair et al., 2011; Fornell & Larcker, 1981). In the data collection phase, common method bias from the self-reported data was minimized by keeping the respondents' identities confidential and by randomizing the items in the questionnaire.

Table 5.2 Items loadings and descriptive statistics

	Loading	Mean (SD)
Facilitating condition		
I have the resources necessary to use the mobile banking app	0.822	5.51 (1.41)
I have the knowledge necessary to use the mobile banking app	0.851	5.60 (1.35)
The mobile banking app is not compatible with other apps I use	0.737	5.07 (1.70)
A specific person (or group) is available for assistance with mobile banking app difficulties	0.790	5.27 (1.43)
Social influence		
People who influence my behavior think that I should use the mobile banking app	0.840	5.35 (1.50)
People who are important to me think that I should use the mobile banking app	0.886	5.38 (1.40)
The senior management of the Bank has been helpful in the use of the mobile app	0.884	5.34 (1.44)
In general, the organization has supported the use of mobile banking app	0.842	5.49 (1.40)
Privacy[a]		
I think this banking mobile app shows concern for the privacy of its users	0.863	2.51 (1.21)
I feel safe when I send personal information to this banking mobile app	0.882	2.57 (1.28)
I think that this banking mobile app will not provide my personal information to other companies without my consent	0.884	2.50 (1.25)
I think this banking mobile app abides by personal data protection laws	0.855	2.42 (1.28)
Affective[a]		
Mobile Banking app help me to derive fun and pleasure	0.906	2.84 (1.53)
Mobile Banking app stimulate my mind	0.912	2.86 (1.54)
Mobile Banking app makes me feel excited	0.884	2.71 (1.45)
I think Mobile Banking app is cool	0.801	2.45 (1.33)
Tension-free		
Mobile Banking app help me to have some enjoyable time	0.914	5.22 (1.50)
Mobile Banking app help me to have some relaxing time	0.898	5.18 (1.61)
Mobile Banking app help me to have some entertainment	0.934	5.18 (1.55)

Table 5.2 (Continued)

	Loading	Mean (SD)
Mobile Banking app multimedia features is very interesting	0.845	5.16 (1.57)
Continuous use		
I want to continue using the mobile banking app rather than discontinue	0.832	5.63 (1.30)
I plan to continue using the mobile banking app	0.901	5.63 (1.36)
I don't intend to continue using the mobile banking app in future	0.539	4.90 (1.99)
Chances are high that I will continue using the mobile banking app in future	0.857	5.78 (1.36)

Notes: SD: Standard Deviation; [a] reverse-coded.

Source: The items were adapted as follows: facilitating conditions and social influence were adapted from Venkatesh et al. (2003); affective and tension free adapted from Ha et al. (2015); privacy from Flavián and Guinalíu (2006); and continuous use adapted from Venkatesh and Goyal (2010).

Structural model assessmsent with moderation effects

Table 5.4 shows the path coefficients. The results show that facilitating conditions have the strongest effect on continuous usage (β = .43, $p < 0.01$), followed by the effects of social influence (β = .29, $p < 0.01$) and privacy concerns (β = −.26, $p < 0.01$). Affective motivation (β = 0.17, $p < 0.05$) and tension-free (β = .15, $p < 0.05$) feature of m-banking app also positively influence continuous usage, albeit their effects are weak. These findings provide support for the hypotheses H1, H3, H5, H6, and H7.

The R^2 is recommended as a viable means of assessing the model's predictive accuracy with thresholds of 0.75, 0.50, and 0.25 as being substantial,

Table 5.3 Square root of AVE (bold) on diagonal and construct correlations

Construct	CR	AVE	1	2	3	4	5	6
FC (1)	0.88	0.65	**0.8**					
SI (2)	0.92	0.75	0.7949	**0.86**				
PR (3)	0.93	0.76	−0.6357	−0.5613	**0.87**			
AM (4)	0.93	0.77	−0.6332	−0.6247	0.6356	**0.88**		
TF (5)	0.94	0.81	0.6036	0.6058	−0.5514	−0.8044	**0.9**	
CU (6)	0.87	0.63	0.8062	0.7596	−0.6673	−0.5709	0.5918	**0.79**

Notes: AVE: Average Variance Extracted; CR: Composite Reliability FC: Facilitating Condition; SI: Social Influence; PR: Privacy; AM: Affective Motivation; TF: Tension-Free; CU: Continuous Usage of M-banking App.

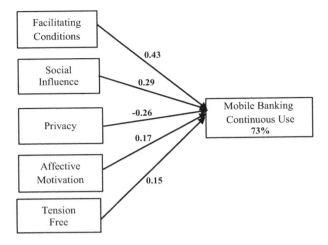

Figure 5.2 Conceptual framework and tested hypotheses

moderate, and weak sequentially (Leppäniemi, Jayawardhena, Karjaluoto, & Harness, 2017; Hair et al., 2011; Henseler et al., 2009). The overall variance of the model explains $R^2 = 73\%$, which is near substantial.

The moderation results show that the higher the education, the stronger are the links between facilitating conditions and continuous usage (moderating effect: $\beta = .13$, $p < 0.01$) and between tension-free and continuous usage ($\beta = .16$, $p < 0.01$). Thus, the results provide support for hypotheses

Table 5.4 Standardized path coefficients and corresponding hypothesis results for the study

Hypotheses	Path coefficient	Beta	TDEV	T-test	Result
H1	FC → MBCU	0.43***	0.0619	6.877	Accepted
H2	FC*Edu → MBCU	0.13**	0.0434	2.895	Accepted
H3	SI → MBCU	0.29***	0.0644	4.381	Accepted
H4	SI*Age → MBCU	0.11*	0.0566	1.953	Partially Accepted
H5	PR → MBCU	−0.26***	0.0559	4.542	Accepted
H6	AM → MBCU	0.17*	0.0773	2.082	Accepted
H7	TF → MBCU	0.15*	0.0734	2.000	Accepted
H8	TF*Edu → MBCU	0.16*	0.0792	1.993	Accepted
MBCU			R^2		
			0.729		

***$p < 0.001$;
**$p < 0.01$;
*$p < 0.05$; *the significance levels are two-tailed.*

H2 and H8. Finally, we find that the moderating effect of age on the relationship between social influence and m-banking continuous use is close to significant ($\beta = .11$, $p < 0.10$), providing partial support for hypothesis H4.

Discussion

In our study, we built a model that comprised the UTAUT2, uses and gratification, and privacy theories, and sought to determine if embedding hedonic features in m-banking apps will influence continuous use. We tested eight hypotheses comprising three moderation tests. All the hypotheses received support from the data. The model explained 73% of continuous usage of m-banking app. The findings are mostly in line with other studies.

Theoretical contributions

This research contributes to the literature on m-banking in several ways. First, the effect of facilitating conditions on m-banking continuous use was confirmed (Zhou, 2011; Venkatesh et al., 2011). This result shows that users' ability to acquire knowledge and availability of structural assurances such as the required technology will decrease their risk perception and enhance continuous use. Interestingly, the International Telecommunication Union (ITU, 2017) reports that Nigeria is the leading country in Africa with mobile cellular subscription currently above 154 million in addition to being the country with the highest Internet subscription rate, therefore, a fertile ground has already been laid for mobile Internet-enabled business transactions. Moreover, the result of the moderation test (H2) indicates that education positively moderates the relationship between facilitating conditions and continuous use. This implies that educated people will have more knowledge and innovative inclinations to operate m-banking applications than those without a similar level of education. Service providers can provide a level playing ground by increasing promotional activities geared towards training users and bank customers on how to use these applications.

Second, the effect of social influence on continuous use also shows a strong and significant relationship, indicating that the variable is a critical determinant of m-banking app continuous use, thus, H3, is accepted. This result is contrary to Venkatesh et al. (2011) and Lu (2014) who did not find support for a direct positive relationship between social influence and continuous use, but however added that the effect of social influence on continuance intention decreases as the user gains experience and knowledge in the use of the technology. Our moderation result (H4) also shows that age positively moderated the relationship between social influence and continuous use, thus, consistent with Zhou (2011), implying that the older the users are the stronger becomes the link between social influence and continuous use. This result also shades some light about the social acceptance of the aged in a collectivistic culture, implying that the older a family member becomes, the greater becomes his need of the members of the social system (Xiao, Shen, & Paterson, 2013).

Third, H5 was accepted, which shows a negative effect of privacy concern on continuous use. This implies that the higher the privacy concerns of the m-banking customers, the lower the continuous use. Cyber fraud is one of the technological dilemmas plaguing ICT-driven business transactions in Nigerians. Users' private information is important and negates the principle of fair dealing and is perceived as a betrayal of trust when a third party is given access to such information without the express approval of the user. Accordingly, as argued by Salo and Karjaluoto (2007), suppliers should make it apparently clear in such a way that users will be able to indicate which type of information they are willing to share while registering for the service. Fifth, the positive effects of the two uses and gratification variables (affective motivation, H6, and tension-free, H7) on continuous usage were both confirmed. These findings are consistent with extant studies (Zhou, 2012, 2013), underpinning the role of affective features in m-banking. Hedonic features increase interactivity and users' affective interests are likely to increase when providers embed features that promote fun, enjoyment, and pleasure, thus provide positive and relaxed feelings. Additionally, our results (H8) also show that education positively moderated the relationship between tension-free and continuous use. This implies that the higher the level of education the higher the likelihood of the user to derive pleasure as a result of personal innovativeness with the platform. From a theoretical standpoint, first, the integration and the successful confirmation of the UTAUT2, uses and gratification and privacy theories proves novel and extends the m-banking literature in this regard. Previous studies, as argued earlier, have dominantly considered the extrinsic factors as major drivers of m-banking continuous use, with few exceptions which have looked at individual-specific factors.

Ordinarily, financial-related issues are fundamentally driven by utilitarian motives, however, Kang et al. (2012) contend that enjoyment is a critical factor for m-banking continuance intention. Apparently, in an environment laced with stressors and tension-inducing socio-economic forces, avoidance-oriented mechanism is primarily escapism (Beasley, Thompson, & Davidson, 2003), which underscores desire for gratification and their effect on continuous use. To the best of our knowledge, this is one of the earliest studies that considers the effect of embedding hedonic features in m-banking app and how it influences continuous use especially in an emerging market in Africa. Second, our study's underscoring of the overarching importance of facilitating conditions as having the strongest influence on continuous use is explicit. In an emerging market context, these facilitating conditions can be summed into governmental, supplier, and individual factors (Glavee-Geo, Shaikh, & Karjaluoto, 2017). Governments must provide the right regulatory policy for the sustained use of technological innovations. This implies that a weak regulatory framework that hampers competitiveness among service providers will undermine continuous use. As an aspect of facilitating conditions, the creation of awareness and educative programs on the benefits of m-banking in addition to efficient customer-centered services are germane for sustained use of m-banking. Additionally, individual's intrinsic factors also play a role. This is underscored by the result that showed that education positively moderates the relationship between facilitating conditions and continuous use. Education imbues a user with the right skills, experience, and exposure. Thus, educated people are likely to show higher levels of personal innovativeness with m-banking app than others (Lu, 2014).

Third, our study challenges previous findings that did not support direct positive effect of social influence on continuance intention (Venkatesh et al., 2011; Lu, 2014), with not only a positive but with a significant relationship. In a collectivist culture such as Africa, reference groups such as family members, friends, colleagues, and professional group members wield enormous influence on one another through word-of-mouth. Consequently, a user can continue or discontinue technology use through peer influence. This is further enunciated by age positively moderating the relationship between social influence and continuous use.

Managerial implications

Our study also generates insights directly applicable for managers in the financial service sector responsible for m-banking services development. First, creating an enabling environment is very critical for the sustained use of m-banking. From a developing country context, erratic power supply, lack of policy framework to drive mobile telecommunication and Internet penetration are inimical to sustained use of m-banking. Governments should come up with policies to promote power supply. Power is a critical requirement for the sustainable use of electronics such as mobile phones. Smartphones come with many applications that easily drain battery and so require charging at intervals; therefore, policies that promote stable power supply are a necessity. M-banking thrives on Internet platforms; accordingly, governments should come up with policies aimed at affordable and reliable Internet access. Furthermore, service providers should constantly update the users with updates on the m-banking application. In some cases, personalized education could reduce user's complexity with the platform, for example in cases where "a bank customer, for example, perceives m-banking to be difficult to use he/she needs careful one-to-one customer education from the bank personnel. Therefore, personal communication is needed" (Laukkanen & Kiviniemi, 2010, p. 384).

Moreover, Africa, nay, Nigeria is a socially cohesive society, implying that interpersonal relationship is a rubric that mediates all societal exchanges and intercommunication. Consequently, word-of-mouth especially from the elderly and those in reputation fundamentally influences behavioral intensions. First, educative programs should be floated that espouse the benefits of m-banking, targeted at policy makers, politicians, community chiefs and title holders, church pastors, and Moslem imams; such would easily be accepted by their followers. Second, service providers should harness the power of social media by floating virtual community forums to engender discussions around m-banking applications and its benefits and the sustenance of the cashless policy of the federal government. Such forums have been found to be a great platform for the advancement of company programs, policies, and brand (Gao & Bai, 2014). Finally, service providers should build additional features into the m-banking apps to engender interactivity. Currently, a particular Nigerian bank is blazing the trail by having additional features such as booking for a cinema ticket, payment of school fees, visa fees, mobile and Internet top-up, flight and utility bills, etc. Users are likely to be fond of a mobile banking app that serves as a one-stop platform for most of their payment needs. In doing that, pleasing tones such as welcome messages and information that uniquely identifies with the user's lifestyles such as birthday greetings, Christmas, and special festivities will engender affective interest and interactivity. Not also forgetting that in all these, advanced security features that protect the user's private information should be the topmost priority.

Limitations, recommendations for future research, and conclusion

Our study has three major limitations: the sample, the data, and the variables. In terms of the sample, the generalizability of our findings is called to question as our respondents constituted of m-banking users who voluntarily accepted to respond to our questionnaires, thus, are not representative of the population especially as they were picked from a single region in Nigeria. However, some studies have argued that since specific and selective samples were used, findings from such studies could still offer insights for managers (Parra-Lopez, Bulchand-Gidumal, Gutierrez-Tano, & Diaz-Armas, 2011). Second, although the survey was carefully designed and administered, special attention was paid to reduce the potential common method bias, our data is cross-sectional, collected at one point in time. Thus, there are validity concerns of the causal inferences that can only be ruled out with a longitudinal study. Accordingly, the highly unpredictable dynamics of the Nigerian banking environment requires that a longitudinal study would be appropriate for future research. Finally, this study is particularly centered within the Nigerian m-banking context. A comparative study that incorporates other emerging markets with m-banking use such as South Africa will likely offer some important insights. Consequently, future studies should seek to incorporate also other constructs in the model such as user satisfaction as a critical determinant of continuous intention in addition to conducting a cross-cultural study within the African emerging markets.

In conclusion, in spite of the preceding limitations, this study has identified the antecedents of mobile banking services continuous usage in a developing market context. The study has found that facilitating conditions, social influence, and users' privacy concerns are critical antecedents underlying mobile banking continuous usage. This implies that with the right infrastructure and awareness, positive word of mouth and increased security features, mobile banking usage will be increased and sustained. Similarly, embedding hedonic features on mobile banking platforms influences continuous usage to a large extent. Finally, educational attainment and age are critical demographic factors service providers must take into account in their quest to ensure mobile banking continuous use in a developing market context.

Note

* *Corresponding/primary contact author*

References

Abadi, H. R. D., Kabiry, N., & Forghani, M. H. (2013, May). Factors affecting Isfahanian mobile banking adoption based on the technology acceptance model. *International Journal of Academic Research in Business and Social Sciences*, 3(5). ISSN: 2222–6990 611. Retrieved from www.hrmars.com/journals

Akinci, S., Aksoy, Ş., & Atilgan, E. (2004). Adoption of Internet banking among sophisticated consumer segments in an advanced developing country. *International Journal of Bank Marketing*, 22(3), 212–232.

Almahamid, S. M., Tweiqat, A. F., & Almanaseer, M. S. (2016). University website quality characteristics and success: Lecturers' perspective. *International Journal of Business Information Systems*, 22(1), 41–61.

Amin, H., Supinah, R., Aris, M. M., & Baba, R. (2012). Receptiveness of mobile banking by Malaysian local customers in Sabah: An empirical investigation. *Journal of Internet Banking and Commerce*, 17(1), 1.

Arnold, M. J., & Reynolds, K. E. (2003). Hedonic shopping motivations. *Journal of Retailing*, 79, 77–95.

Bagozzi, R. P., & Yi, Y. (1988). On the evaluation of structural equation models. *Journal of the Academy of Marketing Science*, 16(1), 74–94.

Bankole, F. O., Bankole, O. O., & Brown, I. (2011). Mobile banking adoption in Nigeria. *The Electronic Journal of Information Systems in Developing Countries*, 47.

Bansal, H. S., Irving, p. G., & Taylor, S. F. (2004). A three-component model of customer to service providers. *Journal of the Academy of Marketing Science*, 32(3), 234–250.

Baptista, G., & Oliveira, T. (2015). Understanding mobile banking: The unified theory of acceptance and use of technology combined with cultural moderators. *Computers in Human Behaviour*, 50, 418–430.

Beasley, M., Thompson, T., & Davidson, J. (2003). Resilience in response to life stress: The effects of coping style and cognitive hardiness. *Personality and Individual Differences*, 34(1), 77–95.

Bhattacherjee, A. (2001). Understanding information systems continuance: An expectation-confirmation model. *MIS Quarterly*, *25*(3), 351–370.

Bhattacherjee, A., Perols, J., & Sanford, C. (2008). Information technology continuance: A theoretic extension and empirical test. *Journal of Computer Information Systems*, *49*(1), 17–26.

Brown, S. A., & Venkatesh, V. (2005). Model of adoption of technology in households: A baseline model test and extension incorporating household lifecycle. *MIS Quarterly*, *29*(3), 399–426.

Chang, C. (2013). Library mobile applications in University libraries. *Library Hi Tech*, *31*(3), 478–492.

Chen, S. C. (2012). To use or not to use: Understanding the factors affecting continuance intention of mobile banking. *International Journal of Mobile Communications*, *10*(5), 490–507.

Cheng, Y., Yu, T., Huang, C., Yu, C., & Yu, C. (2011). The comparison of three major occupations for user acceptance of information technology: Applying the UTAUT model. *iBusiness*, *3*, 147–158. doi:10.4236/ib.2011.32021 2011

Childers, T. L., Carr, C. L., Peck, J., & Carson, S. (2001). Hedonic and utilitarian motivations for online retail shopping behavior. *Journal of Retailing*, *77*(4), 511–535.

Crabbe, M., Standing, C., Standing, S., & Karjaluoto, H. (2009). An adoption model for mobile banking in Ghana. *International Journal of Mobile Communications*, *7*(5), 515–543.

Cranor, L. F., Reagle, J., & Ackerman, M. S. (2014). Understanding net users attitudes about online privacy. *At & T Lab-Research Technical Report TR99.4.3*. Retrieved August 18, 2017, from http://Research.att.com

Cudjoe, A. G., Anim, p. A., & Nyanyofio, J. G. N. T. (2015). Determinants of mobile banking adoption in the Ghanaian banking industry: A case of access bank Ghana limited. *Journal of Computer and Communications*, *3*(2), 1.

De Mooij, M., & Hofstede, G. (2011). Cross-cultural consumer behavior: A review of research findings. *Journal of International Consumer Marketing*, *23*(3–4), 181–192.

Deng, S., Liu, Y., & Qi, Y. (2011). An empirical study on determinants of web based question answer services adoption. *Online Information Review*, *35*(5), 789–798. doi:10.1108/14684521111176507

Farzianpour, F., Pishdar, M., Shakib, M. D., Hashemi, S., & Toloun, M. R. (2014). Consumers' perceived risk and its effect on adoption of online banking services. *American Journal of Applied Sciences*, *11*, 47–56. http://dx.doi.org/10.3844/ajassp.2014.47.56

Flavián, C., & Guinalíu, M. (2006). Consumer trust, perceived security and privacy policy: Three basic elements of loyalty to a web site. *Industrial Management & Data Systems*, *106*(5), 601–620.

Fornell, C., & Larcker, D. F. (1981). Evaluating structural equation models with unobservable variables and measurement error. *Journal of Marketing Research*, 39–50.

Gao, L., & Bai, X. (2014). An empirical study on continuance intention of mobile social networking services: Integrating the IS success model, network externalities and flow theory. *Asia Pacific Journal of Marketing and Logistics*, *26*(2), 168–189.

Gao, L., Waechter, K. A., & Bai, X. (2015). Understanding consumers' continuance intention towards mobile purchase: A theoretical framework and empirical study: A case of China. *Computers in Human Behavior*, *53*, 249–262.

Glavee-Geo, R., Shaikh, A. A., & Karjaluoto, H. (2017). Mobile banking services adoption in Pakistan: Are there gender differences? *International Journal of Bank Marketing*, 35(7), 1090–1114.

Gu, J. C., Lee, S. C., & Suh, Y. H. (2009). Determinants of behavioral intention to mobile banking. *Expert Systems with Applications*, 36(9), 11605–11616.

Ha, Y. W., Kim, J., Libaque-Saenz, C. F., Chang, Y., & Park, M. C. (2015). Use and gratifications of mobile SNSs: Facebook and KakaoTalk in Korea. *Telematics and Informatics*, 32(3), 425–438.

Haghirian, P., & Madlberger, M. (2005). Consumer attitude toward advertising via mobile devices: An empirical investigation among Austrian users. *ECIS 2005 Proceedings*, 44.

Hair, J. F., Jr., Ringle, C. M., & Sarstedt, M. (2011). PLS-SEM: Indeed a silver bullet. *Journal of Marketing Theory and Practice*, 19(2), 139–151.

Henseler, J., Ringle, C. M., & Sinkovics, R. R. (2009). The use of partial least squares path modeling in international marketing. *Advances in International Marketing*, 20(1), 277–319.

ITU. (2017). *International Telecommunications Union*. Retrieved September 11, 2017, from www.itu.int/en/ITU-D/Statistics/Pages/stat/default.aspx

Joo, J., & Sang, Y. (2013). Exploring Koreans' smartphone usage: An integrated model of the technology acceptance model and uses and gratifications theory. *Computers in Human Behavior*, 29(6), 2512–2518.

Kaitawarn, C. (2015). Factor influencing the acceptance and use of m-payment in Thailand: A case study of AIS mPAY rabbit. *Review of Integrative Business and Economics Research*, 4(3), 222–230.

Kang, H., Lee, M. J., & Lee, J. K. (2012). Are you still with us? A study of the post-adoption determinants of sustained use of mobile-banking services. *Journal of Organizational Computing and Electronic Commerce*, 22(2), 132–159.

Kang, J. Y. M., Mun, J. M., & Johnson, K. K. (2015). In-store mobile usage: Downloading and usage intention toward mobile location-based retail apps. *Computers in Human Behavior*, 46, 210–217.

Kauffman, R. J., & Techatassanasoontorn, A. A. (2005). International diffusion of digital mobile technology: A coupled-hazard state-based approach. *Information Technology and Management*, 6(2–3), 253–292.

Koenig-Lewis, N., Palmer, A., & Moll, A. (2010). Predicting young consumers' take up of mobile banking services. *International Journal of Bank Marketing*, 28(5), 410–432.

Kumar, R. G., Rejikumar, G., & Ravindran, D. S. (2012). An empirical study of service quality perceptions and continuance intention in mobile banking context in India. *Journal of Internet Banking and Commerce*, 17(1), 1.

Laukkanen, T. (2017). Mobile banking. *International Journal of Bank Marketing*, 35(7), 1042–1043.

Laukkanen, T., & Kiviniemi, V. (2010). The role of information in mobile banking resistance. *International Journal of Bank Marketing*, 28(5), 372–388.

Lee, K. C., & Chung, N. (2009). Understanding factors affecting trust in and satisfaction with mobile banking in Korea: A modified DeLone and McLean's model perspective. *Interacting with Computers*, 21(5–6), 385–392.

Leppäniemi, M., Jayawardhena, C., Karjaluoto, H., & Harness, D. (2017). Unlocking behaviors of long-term service consumers: The role of action inertia. *Journal of Service Theory and Practice*, 27(1), 270–291.

Li, Y. M., & Yeh, Y. S. (2010). Increasing trust in mobile commerce through design aesthetics. *Computers in Human Behavior*, 26, 673–684.

Lin, H. F. (2011). An empirical investigation of mobile banking adoption: The effect of innovation attributes and knowledge-based trust. *International Journal of Information Management, 31*(3), 252–260.

Lu, H. P., & Yu-Jen Su, p. (2009). Factors affecting purchase intention on mobile shopping web sites. *Internet Research, 19*(4), 442–458.

Lu, J. (2014). Are personal innovativeness and social influence critical to continue with mobile commerce? *Internet Research, 24*(2), 134–159.

Luarn, P., & Lin, H. H. (2005). Toward an understanding of the behavioural intention to use mobile banking. *Computers in Human Behaviour, 21*, 873–891. http://dx.doi.org/10.1016/j.chb.2004.03.003

MäNtymäKi, M., & Salo, J. (2011). Teenagers in social virtual worlds: Continuous use and purchasing behavior in Habbo Hotel. *Computers in Human Behavior, 27*(6), 2088–2097.

Martins, C., Oliveira, T., & Popovič, A. (2014). Understanding the Internet banking adoption: A unified theory of acceptance and use of technology and perceived risk application. *International Journal of Information Management, 34*, 1–13.

Min, Q., Ji, S., & Qu, G. (2008). Mobile commerce user acceptance study in China: A revised UTAUT model. *Tsinghua Science and Technology, 13*(3), 257–264.

Mittal, B., & Lassar, W. M. (1998). Why do customers switch? The dynamics of satisfaction versus loyalty. *Journal of Services Marketing, 12*(3), 177–194.

Nazir, T., & Shah, S. F. H. (2014). Mediating effect of knowledge sharing between participative decision making, transformational leadership and organization performance. *Journal of Management Info, 1*(1).

Parra-Lopez, E., Bulchand-Gidumal, J., Gutierrez-Tano, D., & Diaz-Armas, R. (2011). Intentions to use social media in organising and taking vacation trips. *Computers in Human Behaviour, 27*, 640–654.

Pegueros, V. (2012). Security of mobile banking and payments. *SANS Institute InfoSec Reading Room.* Retrieved from www.sans.org/reading-room/whitepapers/ecommerce/security-mobile-banking-payments-34062

PewResearchCentre. (2017). Retrieved March 13, 2017, from www.pewglobal.org/2015/04/15/cell-phones-in-africa-communication-lifeline/

Powers, T., Advincula, D., Austin, M. S., Graiko, S., & Snyder, J. (2012). Digital and social media in the purchase decision process. *Journal of Advertising Research, 52*(4), 479–489.

Reychav, I., & Wu, D. (2014). Exploring mobile tablet training for road safety: A uses and gratifications perspective. *Computers & Education, 71*, 43–55.

Ringle, C. M., Wende, S., & Becker, J. M. (2014). Smartpls 3. *SmartPLS, Hamburg.* Retrieved from www.smartpls.com

Rosen, L. D., Whaling, K., Rab, S., Carrier, L. M., & Cheever, N. A. (2013). Is Facebook creating "iDisorders"? The link between clinical symptoms of psychiatric disorders and technology use, attitudes and anxiety. *Computers in Human Behavior, 29*(3), 1243–1254.

Salo, J., & Karjaluoto, H. (2007). A conceptual model of trust in the online environment. *Online Information Review, 31*(5), 604–621.

Shaikh, A. A., & Karjaluoto, H. (2015). Mobile banking adoption: A literature review. *Telematics and Informatics, 32*(1), 129–142.

Shaikh, A. A., & Karjaluoto, H. (2016, January). *Mobile banking services continuous usage: Case study of Finland.* System Sciences (HICSS), 2016 49th Hawaii International Conference on (pp. 1497–1506). IEEE.

Shaikh, A. A., Karjaluoto, H., & Chinje, N. B. (2015). Consumers' perceptions of mobile banking continuous usage in Finland and South Africa. *International Journal of Electronic Finance*, 8(2/3/4), 149–168.

Sjöblom, M., Törhönen, M., Hamari, J., & Macey, J. (2017). Content structure is king: An empirical study on gratifications, game genres and content type on Twitch. *Computers in Human Behavior*, *73*, 161–171.

Smith, M. G., & Urpelainen, J. (2014). Early adopters of solar panels in developing countries: Evidence from Tanzania. *Review of Policy Research*, *31*(1), 17–37.

Tam, C., & Oliveira, T. (2017). Literature review of mobile banking and individual performance. *International Journal of Bank Marketing*, *35*(7), 1044–1067.

Taylor, S., & Todd, p. A. (1995). Understanding information technology usage: A test of competing models. *Information systems research*, *6*(2), 144–176.

UNCTAD. (2007). Science and technology for development: A New paradigm for ICT. In Wayne, B. D. (2005), *Empirical investigation of the acceptance and intended use of mobile commerce: Location, personal privacy and trust*. Mississippi: Mississippi State University.

Venkatesh, V., & Davis, F. D. (2000). A theoretical extension of the technology acceptance model: Four longitudinal field studies. *Management Science*, *46*(2), 186–204.

Venkatesh, V., & Goyal, S. (2010). Expectation disconfirmation and technology adoption: Polynomial modeling and response surface analysis. *MIS Quarterly*, 281–303.

Venkatesh, V., Morris, M. G., Davis, G. B., & Davis, F. D. (2003). User acceptance of information technology: Toward a unified view. *MIS Quarterly*, 425–478.

Venkatesh, V., Thong, J. Y., Chan, F. K., Hu, p. J. H., & Brown, S. A. (2011). Extending the two-stage information systems continuance model: Incorporating UTAUT predictors and the role of context. *Information Systems Journal*, *21*(6), 527–555.

Venkatesh, V., Thong, J. Y., & Xu, X. (2012). Consumer acceptance and use of information technology: Extending the unified theory of acceptance and use of technology. *MIS Quarterly*, 157–178.

Whiting, A., & Williams, D. (2013). Why people use social media: A uses and gratifications approach. *Qualitative Market Research: An International Journal*, *16*(4), 362–369.

Xiao, L. D., Shen, J., & Paterson, J. (2013). Cross-cultural comparison of attitudes and preferences for care of the elderly among Australian and Chinese nursing students. *Journal of Transcultural Nursing*, *24*(4), 408–416.

Yang, K. (2010). Determinants of US consumer mobile shopping services adoption: Implications for designing mobile shopping services. *Journal of Consumer Marketing*, *27*(3), 262–270. doi:10.1108/07363761011038338

Yu, C. S. (2012). Factors affecting individuals to adopt mobile banking: Empirical evidence from the UTAUT model. *Journal of Electronic Commerce Research*, *13*(2), 104.

Zhou, T. (2011). Understanding mobile Internet continuance usage from the perspectives of UTAUT and flow. *Information Development*, *27*(3), 207–218.

Zhou, T. (2012). Examining mobile banking user adoption from the perspectives of trust and flow experience. *Information Technology and Management*, *13*(1), 27–37.

Zhou, T. (2013). An empirical examination of continuance intention of mobile payment services. *Decision Support Systems*, *54*(2), 1085–1091.

6 Mobile payments
Where does it come from and what does it lead to?

Mia Olsen *

Introduction

Trade that is facilitated through mobile phones and smartphones is one of the epicenters of the ongoing digitalization of our everyday lives (Pousttchi, Tilson, Lyytinen, & Hufenbach, 2015). In recent years we have in particular experienced the growth of the phenomenon of mobile payments. Mobile payments are a function of the digitalized world in which we live, and the idea of a cashless society. The work on creating electronic payment systems for implementation in situations in which cash has typically been used has been going on for the past 20 to 30 years through which many countries, local societies, and cities have developed their own such systems, although it has been with varied outcomes. In the beginning these new payment systems were based on prepaid payment cards that you could load money onto, but over the years the lead role in these new systems has been taken over by first the mobile phone and later the smartphone. The main part of the mobile payment systems that exist today, is therefore no longer based on SMS, but developed for smartphones and functioning through applications on smartphones. The use of mobile phones and smartphones for facilitating cashless payments has been predicted by both the industry and academia for years due to their diffusion throughout the world and to the fact that we carry them with us all the time.

Today, with the digitalization of payment instruments, money is to a further extent represented as information in digital form rather than in physical form. This entails that money become more abstract than previously (Giannakoudi, 1999). However, money in digital form is represented in different ways (e.g., through payment cards and mobile payments), and so far it has mainly been *payment cards*' influence on people's perception and use of money that has been studied (e.g., Feinberg, 1986; Raghubir & Srivastava, 2008; Thomas, Desai, & Seenivasan, 2010; Allgood & Walstad, 2013). These studies have demonstrated that users have a tendency towards spending more money in the case of payment card transactions, compared to when paying with cash. Meanwhile, I have only been able to find one study on *mobile payments*' influence on people's perception of money (Garrett, Rodermund, Anderson, Berkowitz, & Robb, 2014). Instead, literature on mobile payments has focused particularly on three areas (Dahlberg, Guo, & Ondrus, 2015), including strategies and ecosystems (e.g., Au & Kauffman, 2008; Pousttchi, Schiessler, & Wiedemann, 2009; Gaur & Ondrus, 2012; de Reuver, Verschuur, Nikayin, Cerpa, & Bouwman, 2015; Ondrus, Gannamaneni, & Lyytinen, 2015), technology (e.g., Konidala et al., 2012; Ma, Saxena, Xiang, & Zhu, 2013; Yang & Wu, 2013), and adoption (e.g., Alshare & Mousa, 2014; Olsen, Hedman, & Vatrapu, 2012; Zhou, 2014; Liébana-Cabanillas, Sánchez-Fernández, & Muñoz-Leiva, 2014). Corresponding with this, Sanakulov and Karjaluoto (2015) has pointed out that studies that go beyond adoption and explain the behavioral effects of mobile technology adoption are missing.

Consequently, there is a need for research on the behavioral outcome of these new mobile payment technologies. Set within this context, this chapter explores the behavioral consequences of mobile payments and it presents some of the findings from a broader study on mobile payments in Denmark.

Theoretical frame

The study presented in this chapter is theoretically based on Everett Rogers' (2003) theory of how innovations diffuse over time among the members of a social system, and which, on a tiny note includes the consequences of the innovation as well. Rogers' diffusion theory is actually not just one theory but consists of several theoretical perspectives relating to the overall concept of diffusion, which is why Rogers' theory is a meta-theory (Surry & Farquhar, 1997). Rogers (2003) presents a model, which he calls the innovation-development-process, and which explains the development an innovation goes through from the first need or problem is observed, through the research and development leading to the innovation, over commercialization, diffusion and adoption of the innovation, and the consequences it entails. The broader study on mobile payments mentioned earlier is structured around this model, whereas this chapter mainly explains the last part of the model, namely the consequences of the adoption and use of mobile payments.

Consequences are those changes experienced by an individual or a social system as a result of the adoption of the innovation. Rogers (2003) divides consequences into three classes: (1) wanted/unwanted consequences, (2) direct/indirect consequences, and (3) expected/unexpected consequences. When innovations are introduced in a social system, it is often based on an expectation that the innovation will lead to wanted, direct, and expected consequences. However, it is often the case that some unexpected, and maybe unwanted and indirect consequences arise. This may be due to the fact that the person or company behind the innovation understands and predicts the form and function that the innovation will have in a social system, but will never be able to understand and predict the *meaning* an innovation will have to the members of the system (Rogers, 2003).

Rogers' theory has been critiqued for being too simplistic (Wolfe, 1994; Robertson, Swan, & Newell, 1996; Van de Ven, Polley, Garud, & Venkataraman, 1999; Kautz & Åby Larsen, 2000; Lyytinen & Damsgaard, 2001), and even though Rogers (2003) acknowledges potential users' active role in the diffusion of the innovation, his theory fails to explain the connection between the characteristics of the innovation and the potential users' attitude towards the innovation, which ultimately leads to a decision on adoption or rejection of the innovation (Karahanna, Straub, & Chervany, 1999; Tarhini, Arachchilage, & Abbasi, 2015). Therefore, for the purpose of this study, Rogers' theory has been augmented with a theory on user behavior; more precisely, the theory of planned behavior (Ajzen, 1991), as it remedies the previously mentioned shortcoming in Roger's diffusion theory. The theory of planned behavior outlines human actions as active choices based on three factors (attitude towards the behavior, subjective norm, and perceived behavioral control) and contributes to understanding the connection between mobile payments' characteristics and the potential users' attitude towards mobile payments.

Method

With the wish to contribute with empirically based knowledge on what behavioral consequences mobile payment has to its users, the study was carried out as a qualitative, explorative, multiple case study focusing on one social system that takes advantage of mobile payments in a specific context. Point of departure was taken in a context in which mobile payments are being used; the flea market. Flea markets are considered natural laboratories in which "researchers can observe and theorize market and consumer processes 'in the wild' as forms of direct marketing and consumption" (Hansson & Brembeck, 2015). That is, at flea markets consumers are drawing on many of those conceptions and habits that they make use of when shopping in conventional retail stores (Gregson & Crewe, 1998). Studying the use of mobile payments in flea markets, leads to the possibility of generating theory that to some extent can be generalized to other use contexts. However, during the collection of the empirical material, the informants kept referring to situations of buying and selling where the contact between buyer and seller was facilitated through various apps for second-hand shopping, which is why also second-hand shopping through these apps have been explored when collecting the empirical material.

The choice of user group to focus on during the study arose from the choice of the flea market context, since women more often than men buy something from a flea market (and in second-hand shopping in general) (DBA, 2016; Chahal, 2013). What women trade most in is used clothes for children (Gregson & Crewe, 1998), which first and foremost reflects what a relatively big phenomenon trade in used clothes, toys, and equipment for children has become (DBA, 2016), and second confirms that it is mothers who most often take care of shopping for the children (Waight, 2015). Mothers' trade in used clothes and equipment has previously been studied (Clarke, 2000; Waight, 2013; Waight, 2015), but mothers as consumers is actually a quite recent phenomenon in research (see, e.g., Thomsen & Sørensen, 2006; Cairns, Johnston, & MacKendrick, 2013). Previous research has focused on women as consumers, while it has been missed that mothers as consumers stand out from these (Cook, 2013). Consequently, there is a need for research in this area of consumer culture, which is why it was decided that this study should focus on mothers who buy and sell used clothes, toys, and equipment for their children. These mothers make up what Rogers (2003) refer to as a social system (Clarke, 2000).

Research presented in this chapter is therefore based on (1) semi-structured interviews with 13 of these mothers who make use of mobile payments when buying and selling used children's stuff, and (2) self-ethnography (Alvesson, 2003) as I myself am an actor in the field of second-hand shopping for children. Self-ethnography means that the researcher is an observing participant to a higher degree than a participating observer, and I have taken advantage of this opportunity to write down notes on experiences selectively and retrospectively. The purpose of the interviews and the self-ethnographic notes was to uncover experiences with mobile payments and the sensemaking taking place when mobile payments are incorporated in everyday interactions. The interviews were carried out from April 2015 to July 2017, and each mother was interviewed once. The interviews had an average duration of around 50 minutes, and they were afterwards transcribed with focus on meaning. The interviews followed an interview-guide that was structured around the last part of Rogers' (2003) innovation-development-process, which relates to adoption, use, and consequences of the innovation, and the questions were formulated in a way that invited and encouraged the interviewee to tell about experiences she had had with mobile payments when doing second-hand shopping. Parallel to interviewing the mothers, I wrote down self-ethnographic notes on experiences and considerations I had as a second-hand shopping mother. The notes were used for remembering remarkable situations, and in the analysis, they were treated in the same way as the transcribed interviews with the mothers.

The analysis was inspired by Brinkmann and Kvale (2015) who suggest an interview analysis with focus on meaning, which involves coding, meaning condensation, and meaning interpretation. Thus, the statements from the interviews, as well as my self-ethnographic notes, were fused to some overall themes of mothers' experiences with mobile payments in second-hand shopping. The themes were *trust, opportunities with mobile payments*, and *risks with mobile payments*. During the interpretation of meaning some connections between parts of the themes had been identified, and these connections illustrate the direct and indirect consequences of mobile payments in second-hand shopping, and are presented in Figure 6.1 later in this chapter.

However, before I present to you the empirical results of these interviews and self-ethnographic notes, I would like to take a step back and explain to you the origins of mobile payments, the mobile payment situation in Denmark, and also touch upon the global perspectives on mobile payment systems.

The origins of mobile payments

In diffusion studies the dependence on previous innovations has often been overlooked, which has led to innovations being studied as if they emerge independently of what precedes and surrounds them. An innovation will most likely be part of a technology cluster, meaning that the innovation is just one among several other innovations leading in the same developmental direction (Rogers, 2003). I consider mobile payments a part of a technology cluster consisting of electronic payment solutions. This cluster appeared in the 1960s when IBM attached, the at that time most common storage medium, magnetic tape to the already existing credit cards made of plastic, thus making the ordinary plastic card much more secure. Another type of payment card, the debit card, was introduced in 1975 (Stearns, 2011) and is different from the credit card in that the money to be paid when using the card is transferred from the owner's bank account right away, instead of waiting a month to charge the money from the owner's bank account. Denmark is one of the countries in the world where the debit card, in the form of the national payment card, the *Dankort*, has gained the greatest foothold and where credit cards are only used to a lesser extent. However, as not all merchants accepted credit and debit cards, the need for withdrawing money independent of time led to the development of the ATM that became widely distributed in the western world at the end of the 1980s (Batiz-Lazo, 2009).

The next big thing in this technology cluster came with the introduction of the World Wide Web browser and server in 1990, which made it possible to spend money without having any cash and without going to a physical store. Within a few years the Internet had opened up to commercial use and online banking (Shanthi & Desti, 2015).

In the meantime, the invention of the chip payment card had begun and the idea was that instead of gaining access to an externally registered account or database, as was the case with the plastic card with the magnetic tape, the card contained a chip where data could be stored directly. The chip card was particularly popular in European countries in the mid-1990s where they were used as prepaid electronic wallets that you could load money onto and afterwards use in electronic payment systems functioning in geographically limited areas. These systems based on prepaid chip cards did not have the expected success, but the chip payment card has not been invented in vain. Together the international payment companies Europay, MasterCard, and Visa (EMV) have developed a standard for chip-nbased debit and credit cards. This standard has later on been joined by American Express, Discover, and JCB, which means that EMV compatible cards and equipment are now to be found all over the world (Sullivan, 2010). The latest development in chip cards is that they are increasingly becoming contactless and are now communicating with the card reader via RFID or NFC technology. In the middle of 2015 the Dankort with this contactless function was introduced in Denmark, and it seems to appeal to the Danes as there less than a year later had been issued 2.25 million contactless Dankort (dr.dk, 2016) (in a population of 5.7 million Danes).

Around 2010 several companies started working on implementing the chip card technology in mobile phones and smartphones in order to enable payment just by holding the phone in front of a chip reader. The idea of paying with the mobile phone is however not new; the first mobile payment transaction was carried out in 1997 when Coca Cola introduced a vending machine receiving payments by SMS. And in 1998 in Finland it became possible to buy digital services such as ringtones and games through the mobile phone, and afterwards pay for the purchase through the bill from the mobile network operator (Golden & Regi, 2013) – however, this system fitted everyday purchases poorly since the bill was only sent out on a monthly basis, and furthermore it would mix up phone bill and grocery bill making it difficult to keep track of one's finances (Heikkinen, 2008). Since then a number of mobile payment systems have been introduced throughout the world, and in the next section I elaborate on some of these.

Mobile payments in Denmark and globally: incomparable situations

The road to mobile payments has not been without obstacles and as already mentioned a number of electronic payment systems based on chip cards have been tested since the 1990s. Amongst these was the Danish *Danmønt* that was in operation from 1991 to 2005. Danmønt could be used at some kiosks, laundries, canteens, vending machines, and the like, but its mainstays were that it could be used at phone booths and vending machines for train tickets. With the introduction of the mobile phone in the late 1990s the need for payphones decreased, and as the price for train tickets increased people started using their debit card (i.e., the Dankort) when paying for tickets (Berlingske Business, 2004), thus making Danmønt redundant. That destiny does not apply to the Dankort, which is one of the most successful national payment cards in the world. Actually Denmark is one of the countries in the world with the lowest number of cash payments and the highest number of card payments per citizen; in 2015 only 20% of all payments in Denmark were made in cash (Betalingsraadet, 2016), which is far from the global average of 75% (The Guardian, 2016). Together with Danmønt and an unsuccessful attempt to introduce a mobile payment system called Mobilpenge in 2011–2014, the Dankort has prepared the Danes for new electronic payment methods.

Therefore, when the largest Danish bank *Danske Bank* launched its mobile payment app *MobilePay* in 2013, the app very quickly became popular, and today it has 3.6 million Danish users and is the second most used app in Denmark only surpassed by the Facebook app (MobilePay's Website, 2017). The app makes use of phone numbers for transferring money from one bank account to another in real-time. Almost simultaneously with the launch of MobilePay another mobile payment app named *Swipp* was introduced jointly by most of the other banks in Denmark. But this app never reached the same popularity as its competitor and in late 2016 several of the banks behind Swipp left the cooperation and partnered with MobilePay instead, and in February 2017 Swipp was closed down. MobilePay was initially marketed as an app for person-to-person (P2P) transactions and has in particular been utilized in situations that have previously been characterized by cash, such as splitting a bill, at flea markets, and collecting for charity. Due to its success and demand from the outside world the app has subsequently been extended to include among other things a solution for traders and a point of sale (POS) solution, but has never really gained a strong foothold in the latter, which might be because of the fact that the Dankort has such a strong position in the Danes' payment habits.

In April 2017 Nets, who is the issuer of the Dankort, launched a mobile version of the Dankort, which means that an electronic copy of the Dankort can now be placed in an app on the smartphone. So instead of pulling out the well-known plastic card from the wallet the payer can now pay with the electronic copy of the Dankort by holding the phone in front of a reader at POS. Consequently, the mobile payment market in Denmark is, roughly speaking, divided between MobilePay's P2P transactions and the mobile version of the Dankort at POS. The coming years will show if the mobile version of the Dankort is the solution that will make the Danes use their smartphones when paying at POS. Nets itself expects that around 50% of all transactions in Denmark in 2020 will be conducted via smartphones (Finanswatch, 2016).

Outside Denmark several relatively successful mobile payment systems have appeared over the last 15 years. Amongst these are American PayPal, which is available worldwide and can be accessed both through a browser and an app on the smartphone; M-Pesa, which started in Kenya as an SMS-based payment service, but today is available in several countries in Africa, Asia, and Eastern Europe and now can be accessed via an app on the smartphone as well; Osaifu-Keitai in Japan, which functions via an app on the smartphone; Chinese AliPay, which since 2013 has been the world's largest mobile payment system (measured in transaction volume), and which in September 2017 started using facial recognition to authorize payments (TechCrunch, 2017); and the Swedish Swish that is similar to the Danish MobilePay in how it works and has taken over transactions in situations where cash used to be king.

Besides these, we have over the last couple of years been presented with new mobile payment systems from the large international actors Apple, Samsung, and Google who are doing what they can to diffuse their systems throughout the world. Their systems Apple Pay, Samsung Pay, and Android Pay are all some sorts of digital wallet placed in the user's smartphone. Here the user can store an electronic copy of a payment card and afterwards make use of the digital wallet when paying in physical stores or shopping at the Internet. The three large companies do not really make any profit from these mobile wallets, and the wallets are not their primary business areas, but by offering these wallets the companies enhance their possibility of increased sale of their primary products (e.g., a wide diffusion of Apple Pay in a given market can lead to an increase in the number of sold iPhones in that market).

Apple Pay was launched in Denmark in October 2017, however only for customers in some banks. Apple Pay might have a fairly good chance of achieving some success in Denmark due to the Danes being heavy users of electronic types of payments. On the other hand, it might also be so that the Danes are too fond of and attached to their Dankort and MobilePay to start using Apple Pay. After all, the last 15 years with the birth and rise of mobile payments have showed us that the adoption of mobile payment systems depends on the actual need for new payment methods; in most developed countries a number of payment methods are already available, and therefore the users will only adopt a new payment method if it entails a relative advantage compared to the existing methods; whereas several developing countries are characterized by a lacking banking infrastructure and low trust in government and banks, and would benefit from a mobile payment solution that could get around these impediments. This difference in circumstances from country to country makes it difficult to offer the same mobile payment system on a global scale.

Results: consequences of mobile payment adoption in second-hand shopping

Having the background and current situation of mobile payments explained, we can move on to the results of the study of mobile payments' behavioral consequences. As presented in earlier in this chapter, I have carried out an empirical study of 13 mothers making use of mobile payments when buying and selling used children's clothes, toys, and equipment. Initially, I focused on the flea market context, as flea markets constitute one of the situations in which mobile payments have been adopted. Mobile payments' success in flea markets is probably due to their capability to substitute cash, which used to be the primary way of paying for goods at these markets; however, over the last 10 years the number of ATMs in Denmark have decreased (Betalingsraadet, 2016) and the amount of cash in the average Danish wallet has fallen, which has left a gap to be filled out by mobile payments. Moreover, flea markets are considered natural laboratories where "researchers can observe and theorize market and consumer processes 'in the wild' as forms of direct marketing and consumption" (Hansson & Brembeck, 2015, p. 92). Studying mobile payments at flea markets will therefore generate results that to some extent can be generalized to other use contexts.

Thus the interviews with the mothers specifically revolved around the flea market context and I got confirmed that mobile payments in no time have become very popular at flea markets. Several mothers further narrated how many sellers at flea markets have small homemade signs attached to their booths informing that they accept mobile payments. The mothers' choice of shopping second-hand for their children is based on various arguments extending from saving money, through minimizing the chemistry that one's own children are exposed to, and to reducing production in order to spare the environment. Some of the mothers had not been frequent flea market visitors until after they had children, and some of them bring their children to market when going there, while others prefer going alone to better concentrate on making good finds. Throughout the interviews I widened the use context from flea markets to the somewhat broader *second-hand shopping* as the mothers kept referring to other ways of shopping second-hand for their children. Especially one specific app, named Reshopper, for shopping used children's stuff in one's neighborhood was mentioned by almost all the mothers, who also explained how that app and MobilePay for the most part are used in conjunction with each other; actually if you buy or sell via Reshopper, you are expected to be a MobilePay user. Hence, in the social system of mothers buying and selling used children's stuff, MobilePay and Reshopper form a technology cluster contributing to the ease with which mothers can shop second-hand for their children.

However, as I interviewed the mothers it became clear to me that what was really interesting was the mothers' experiences with mobile payments and how the mobile payments cause changes in the mothers' second-hand shopping. Inspired by Gioia, Corley, and Hamilton (2013) and Brinkmann and Kvale (2015) I abductively analyzed the empirical material, which led to the identification of a number of general themes that illustrate the mothers' experiences with mobile payments in second-hand shopping. Three themes pointed towards changes in the mothers' second-hand shopping behavior, including opportunities with mobile payments, risks with mobile payments, and trust. To make a long story short, the mothers attitude towards mobile payments are highly positive, since mobile payments entail a number of opportunities, one of which is leading to improved trust. However, the mothers referred to incidents as well where these opportunities cause them risk.

According to Rogers (2003) an innovation will always entail consequences that cause change in the social system in which it is diffused. This is what Rogers refers to as social change. Consequences are those changes that an individual or a social system experience as a result of the adoption or rejection of the innovation. Rogers divide consequences into three classes: (1) desired/undesired consequences, (2) direct/indirect consequences, and (3) expected/unexpected consequences. When an innovation is introduced into a social system, it is done with the belief that it will cause desired, direct, and expected consequences. The reality is, however, that some undesired, indirect, and unexpected consequences often occur, probably due to the fact that the provider of the innovation is able to understand and predict the form and function that an innovation will take in a social system, but unable to understand and predict the adopter's subjective perception of the innovation (Rogers, 2003).

The diagram in Figure 6.1 illustrates how the interviewed mothers have experienced some direct consequences in second-hand shopping and how

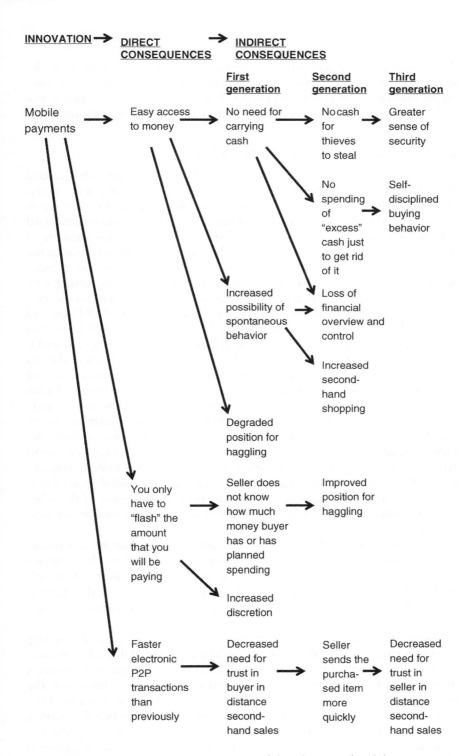

Figure 6.1 Direct and indirect consequences of the adoption of mobile payments in second-hand shopping

these direct consequences lead to generations of indirect (and maybe undesired and unexpected) consequences as well. As mobile payment is a quite recent innovation, it is not unthinkable that further indirect consequences will emerge in the future, but this is a picture of the current situation.

Direct consequence: easy access to money

If we start at the beginning, the innovation of mobile payments has caused three direct consequences, the first being the obvious easy access to money. No matter where you are or what time it is mobile payments give you access to money, and in the context of second-hand shopping it minimizes the need for carrying cash. The interviewed mothers are all fond of this attribute as most of them never carry cash and consider it time consuming to stop at the ATM on their way to the flea market or to a private home to buy second-hand for their children. One mother named Cathrin explains further why she is not fond of cash: "Before mobile payments I did not visit flea markets very often, probably because I did not want to withdraw 500 DKK and then not buy anything, meaning that I had to carry around 500 DKK that I virtually could not put in the bank again." Cathrin never uses cash and it exasperates her that it has become hard to find a bank branch where she can put her money. Here she is most likely referring to the increasing number of cashless bank branches in Denmark. Actually Cathrin is so annoyed with cash that she, if she went to visit flea markets before we had mobile payments, used to spend all her "excess" withdrawn cash on clutter just to get rid of the cash. Hence, Cathrin experiences that mobile payment helps her buying exactly what she needs, neither more nor less, which I have chosen to refer to as self-disciplined buying behavior. It should be mentioned, however, that only Cathrin and one other mother expressed this high degree of self-discipline. Later in this chapter I will come back to how most of the other mothers indicated a loss of financial control caused by the mobile payment option.

The minimized need for carrying cash leads to yet another indirect consequence, which was pointed out to me when a mother told me that "thieves go to flea markets because people carry cash when going there" (Majken). In this case mobile payments lead to the indirect consequences that there is no cash for thieves to steal, which makes the flea market visitors feel more secure.

Taking a step back, besides minimizing the need for carrying cash, the easy access to money additionally entails an increased possibility of spontaneous behavior. The majority of the interviewed mothers explained how trips to flea markets are often spontaneous and it is therefore seldom that the mothers bring cash on these trips: "If I have planned to visit a flea market I withdraw cash in advance, but if I by coincidence encounters a flea market then I have no cash" (Louise). On spontaneous trips to flea markets the mothers have, until now, had a limited possibility of buying anything due to the fact that they seldom carry cash. But with mobile payments this limit is removed, since mobile payments offer easy access to money and in that way facilitates spontaneous behavior. It is, however, not only on spontaneous flea market trips that mobile payments offer spontaneous behavior. Some of the interviewed mothers reported about situations in which they had not brought enough money to the flea market to buy an object that they came across, or situations where they had already spent their withdrawn cash and then afterwards came across an object that they wanted. Without mobile payments the only other option would be to go and find an ATM, but "if you have to go from A to B to withdraw money, then it kills that impulsive action. You know, when something that you see suddenly tempts you . . . What I mean is that it takes more than that to make you go all the way [to the ATM] and still being tempted when you get back" (Nanna). What Nanna explains here is that flea market purchases often are made spontaneously and without being thought through. If you suddenly have to spend time withdrawing money in order to be able to pay for such a flea market purchase, then that time lets you reconsider the purchase and maybe you come to the conclusion that you do not need the object. Mobile payment enables you to complete the purchase instantly, thus maintaining the spontaneous action.

It might not come as a surprise when I tell you that the mothers narrated how the easy access to money and the increased possibility of spontaneous behavior facilitated by mobile payments have caused their second-hand shopping to grow. One of the mothers Gitte describes a situation that demonstrates this: "I was at a flea market and I considered a cross. I said that I could not buy it since I had not brought any money. Then the seller said: 'Well, but I receive mobile payments.' So I actually ended up buying it anyway." Mobile payments are however not only increasing the mothers' second-hand shopping in the flea market context. Here another mother Iben explains how mobile payments increases her number of purchases made via the app Reshopper:

> If I have found something on Reshopper that I want to buy, the smart thing about mobile payment is that I have the possibility of paying right away, and through that action I have in a way secured the object. Moreover, you are to a greater extent forced to going out and pick it up (. . .) Previously you went out to inspect the object and then you might not want it. Mobile payment makes me buy more.

What Iben's statement illustrates is that there often is more than one interested buyer. By making a deal with the seller and paying right away via mobile payment Iben reserves the object. Other interested buyers represent some sort of competitors making Iben feel intimidated to quickly make a bid and a deal with seller if she wants to secure the object. On top of this, having made a deal and paid for the object, she has to go and pick it up at the seller's, whereas she previously would not have bought the object until after having seen it with her own eyes.

Even though the interviewed mothers are quite fond of the possibility of paying with their smartphones, the easy access to money entailed in mobile payment leads to some undesired consequences as well. The first undesired consequence is loss of financial overview and control. Because, even though it is nice to have easy access to money "being that easy it is a little dangerous as well" (Marie). As already illuminated some of the mothers make more spontaneous purchases. Several of the mothers used to withdraw a specific amount in cash, which they brought to the flea market, and then they only had this cash to shop for. The amount of their cash was the maximum of what they wanted to shop for. But with mobile payments the mothers are now able to spend more money than they have in cash, and they are therefore spending more money than they have planned. One of the mothers explains that "mobile payment is just like using my Dankort. I almost forget to check the amount before I accept. It is as if you are not spending any money when making use of the mobile payment option. If I had the cash in my hand it would be something completely different, I think. Then it would be my own money that I was spending" (Gitte). What Gitte refers to here is that the feeling of spending digital money on the smartphone are quite different from the feeling of spending cash, and that she therefore loses track of how much she is spending when using her smartphone for paying.

Finally, the direct consequence of easy access to money leads to an indirect consequence that some mothers experience, namely that their position for haggling is degraded. In the past a highly used argument for not wanting to pay anymore for an object than a certain amount, was that you did not have more than that amount in cash. However, mobile payments give you access to more money and the seller knows. The following quote is an example of this: "I was standing there with my coins saying: 'I only have 35 DKK' and she [the seller] wanted 50 DKK. It usually works, but not on this woman. Actually, I would say that that is the disadvantage of using mobile payments, because you cannot haggle in the same way that you used to, since you now have the money in your smartphone" (Iben).

Direct consequence: you only have to "flash" the amount that you will be paying

The second direct consequence of mobile payments identified through the interviews with the mothers is that you only have to flash the amount that you will be paying. This leads to two indirect consequences, which the mothers consider desired, as they are advantages to them. One of these indirect consequences is explained by one of the mothers who expresses how mobile payments make a higher degree of discretion possible compared to paying through a bank transfer while standing next to the seller: "If you are going to make a bank transfer in order to buy something, then you will be opening your bank app and make visible what you have, and I think that it is cumbersome and a bit private. It is easier with mobile payments where you can just show the transfer receipt to the seller" (Karoline).

The other indirect consequence of not having to flash the amount that you will be paying, is that the seller does not know how much money the buyer has or has planned to spend, which by some of the mothers is considered an advantage as they find themselves in an improved position for haggling. I know that this is the complete opposite of what other mothers explained and what I have written previously in this chapter, but Karoline explains it well in this quotation: "I do not think that it is nice to pick up 500 DKK from my wallet to buy something at a flea market, especially not if I have tried to haggle. It is more discrete [on the phone] only flashing the money that you will be paying." It seems that the difference between mobile payments improving your position for haggling and degrading your position for haggling, is caused by the amount that you have in cash.

Direct consequence: faster electronic P2P transactions than previously

The last direct consequence of mobile payments in second-hand shopping is that we now have faster electronic person-to-person transactions than previously. Here I am talking specifically about second-hand purchases where buyer and seller never meet, but where seller sends the purchased object to buyer via mail. In the past such purchases were made by means of bank transfers, but today most of the interviewed mothers make use of mobile payments for this purpose. They explained to me that one of the reasons for this shift in payment mode is that it might take a bank transfer a couple of days to go through, whereas a mobile payment transaction is in the receiver's bank account instantly. In addition to this, some of the mothers point out that it is cumbersome and associated with risk of miskeying entering the long account number that you have to enter when making a bank transfer. Moreover, the slow bank transfer meant that, unless the seller had a high degree of trust in the buyer, she would most often wait to send the object until the money had gone through to her bank account. Some of the mothers explained that if they wanted the seller to send the package with the object immediately, they had to prove to the seller that the bank transfer was initiated, which was coped with by sending a screen shot of the receipt for the transfer.

Making use of the fast electronic transactions that mobile payments constitute leads to the indirect consequence that the need for the seller to have trust in the buyer in distance second-hand purchases decreases. This is due to the instant transfer of money. With the quick transfer of money, seller sends the purchased object more quickly as well, hence making the entire second-hand purchase much faster than it used to be. And besides decreasing the need for trust in the buyer, mobile payments decrease the need for the buyer to have trust in the seller as well, as the buyer receives her purchased object more quickly than previously, thus reducing the period in which she has to have confidence that the seller is sincere.

Discussion and conclusion

According to Zelizer (1997) more money is used when money becomes digital and thus more available. This is illustrated by the rise in the number of transactions done with payment cards over the last 30 years, and it is what Zelizer would characterize a monetization. It is also what is happening right now with mobile payments in Denmark, where the possibility of mobile payment has caused its own demand; an example is that today many people settle their debts to friends and family more frequently, since they, through their smartphones, always have the right amount of money at hand.

However, with more money being used we also end up with people spending too much money as elucidated in the sections on consequences of mobile payments. However, as some of the mothers felt a loss of financial overview and control, a few of the other mothers had the experience that mobile payments could help them carrying out a self-disciplined buying behavior, not buying too much rubbish and still being able to buy whatever might catch their interest at the flea market. One interesting thing here is that those who felt the loss of financial overview and control, were very well aware of it, and yet they did not take any precautions to lower the spending, and they did not express any wish to do so.

Another central finding from this study is that mobile payments increase the feeling of trust between buyer and seller in second-hand shopping. Or rather, mobile payments decrease the need for trust, since the payments are transacted instantly and so much faster than the "old-fashioned" bank transfers. In connection to this, it is interesting that the mothers interviewed for this study experience that their second-hand shopping has increased with the emergence of mobile payments in second-hand shopping. Because even though we know that there is a recycling and reuse trend in Denmark (DBA, 2016) (and in many other places in the world), it cannot be ruled out that the easy access to money and the increased feeling of trust that mobile payments lead to, has some degree of influence on the increasing second-hand shopping, and that mobile payments therefore strengthens the economy in second-hand shopping.

Implications and future research directions

This study contributes to the area of mobile payment research and to diffusion research with knowledge of what consequences mobile payments/ an innovation can lead to. Moreover, according to McKinsey (2014) there are more than 12,000 start-ups in the payment arena, and to them, the results of the study presented in this chapter should inspire their work when developing, designing, and launching new digital payment solutions. Specifically it would be interesting if the feeling of spending money when paying in cash, could be transferred to one of the mobile payment solutions or another new electronic payment solution, e.g., through the design of the user interface. This would help people who overspend when using electronic payment instruments.

Furthermore, this study points to other directions within mobile payment research that could be interesting to follow, but which were outside the scope of the study.

As the study presented in this chapter has focused on one specific group of users, the study's results cannot be generalized to the entire population. However, the study does emphasize some possible behavioral consequences of mobile payments, and in the future it would be interesting to carry out similar studies of other user groups and other social systems, or in other countries as suggested by Dahlberg et al. (2015), in order to be able to compare the results to see if some patterns are valid for more than one user group.

As explained in the analysis, two conflicting experiences of what mobile payments can lead to were present in the studied user group; most of the mothers experienced that mobile payment can lead to loss of financial overview and control, while two mothers experienced that mobile payments can help them carry out a self-disciplined buying behavior. The two mothers experiencing this contradict previous studies of how money is spent when it is represented in an electronic form. These previous studies point towards money being spent faster when it is electronic, due to losing the feeling of letting go of the money that is present when letting go of cash (Raghubir & Srivastava, 2008). As the mothers in the present study in terms of age could be part of the generation called digital natives, new studies of the spending of various forms of money should be carried out, in order to investigate whether younger generations have the same perception of cash and money in electronic form, as found in previous studies.

Note

* *Corresponding/primary contact author*

References

Ajzen, I. (1991). The theory of planned behavior. *Organizational Behavior and Human Decision Processes*, 50(2), 179–211.

Allgood, S., & Walstad, W. (2013). Financial literacy and credit card behaviors: A cross-sectional analysis by age. *Numeracy*, 6(2), 3.

Alshare, K., & Mousa, A. (2014). *The moderating effect of espoused cultural dimensions on consumer's intention to use mobile payment devices*. Thirty Fifth International Conference on Information Systems, Auckland, (pp. 1–15).

Alvesson, M. (2003). Methodology for close up studies: Struggling with closeness and closure. *Higher Education*, 46(2), 167–193.

Au, Y. A., & Kauffman, R. J. (2008). The economics of mobile payments: Understanding stakeholder issues for an emerging financial technology application. *Electronic Commerce Research and Applications, 7*(2), 141–164.

Batiz-Lazo, B. (2009). Emergence and evolution of ATM networks in the UK, 1967–2000. *Business History, 51*(1), 1–27.

Berlingske Business. (2004). *Banker Lukker Fiaskoen Danmønt*. Retrieved from www.business.dk/diverse/banker-lukker-fiaskoen-danmoent

Betalingsraadet. (2016). *Rapport om Kontanters Rolle i Samfundet*. Retrieved from www.nationalbanken.dk/da/bankogbetalinger/betalingsraad/Documents/Betalingsraadet_Kontantrapport_juni_2016.pdf

Brinkmann, S., & Kvale, S. (2015). *Interviews: Learning the craft of qualitative interviewing*. Thousand Oaks, CA: Sage Publications.

Cairns, K., Johnston, J., & MacKendrick, N. (2013). Feeding the "organic child": Mothering through ethical consumption. *Journal of Consumer Culture, 13*(2), 97–118.

Chahal, M. (2013, October). How to snare the bargain hunters. *Marketing Week* (01419285), 1–3.

Clarke, A. (2000). Mother swapping: The trafficking of nearly new children's wear. In p. Jackson, M. Lowe, D. Miller, & F. Mort (Eds.), *Commercial cultures: Economies, practices, spaces* (pp. 85–100). Oxford: Berg.

Cook, D. T. (2013). Introduction: Specifying mothers/motherhoods. *Journal of Consumer Culture, 13*(2), 75–78.

Dahlberg, T., Guo, J., & Ondrus, J. (2015). A critical review of mobile payment research. *Electronic Commerce Research and Applications, 14*(5), 265–284.

DBA. (2016). *Genbrugsindekset 2016*. Retrieved from https://guide.dba.dk/media/378494/dba_genbrugsindekset_2016.pdf

de Reuver, M., Verschuur, E., Nikayin, F., Cerpa, N., & Bouwman, H. (2015). Collective action for mobile payment platforms: A case study on collaboration issues between banks and telecom operators. *Electronic Commerce Research and Applications, 14*(5), 331–344.

dr.dk. (2016). *Det Kontaktløse Dankort Vinder Frem Blandt Danskerne*. Retrieved from www.dr.dk/nyheder/penge/det-kontaktloese-dankort-vinder-frem-blandt-danskerne

Feinberg, R. A. (1986). Credit cards as spending facilitating stimuli: A conditioning interpretation. *Journal of Consumer Research, 13*(3), 348–356.

Finanswatch. (2016). *Nets-direktør: Mobilt dankort bliver betalingernes motorvej*. Retrieved from http://finanswatch.dk/Finansnyt/Pengeinstitutter/article8970139.ece

Garrett, J. L., Rodermund, R., Anderson, N., Berkowitz, S., & Robb, C. A. (2014). Adoption of mobile payment technology by consumers. *Family and Consumer Sciences Research Journal, 42*(4), 358–368.

Gaur, A., & Ondrus, J. (2012, August). *The role of banks in the mobile payment ecosystem: A strategic asset perspective*. Proceedings of the 14th Annual International Conference on Electronic Commerce (pp. 171–177). ACM.

Giannakoudi, S. (1999). Internet banking: The digital voyage of banking and money in cyberspace. *Information and Communications Technology Law, 8*(3), 205–243.

Gioia, D. A., Corley, K. G., & Hamilton, A. L. (2013). Seeking qualitative rigor in inductive research: Notes on the Gioia methodology. *Organizational Research Methods, 16*(1), 15–31.

Golden, S. A. R., & Regi, S. B. (2013). Mobile commerce in modern business era. *International Journal of Current Research and Academic Review*, 1(4), 96–102.

Gregson, N., & Crewe, L. (1998). Dusting down second hand rose: Gendered identities and the world of second-hand goods in the space of the car boot sale. *Gender, Place and Culture: A Journal of Feminist Geography*, 5(1), 77–100.

The Guardian. (2016). Sweden leads the race to become cashless society. Retrieved from www.theguardian.com/business/2016/jun/04/sweden-cashless-society-cards-phone-apps-leading-europe

Hansson, N., & Brembeck, H. (2015). Market hydraulics and subjectivities in the "wild": Circulations of the flea market. *Culture Unbound: Journal of Current Cultural Research*, 7(1), 91–121.

Heikkinen, p. (2008). Mobile payments breakthrough is just around the corner. *Bank of Finland*, Bulletin 1. Retrieved from https://helda.helsinki.fi/bof/bitstream/handle/123456789/10988/172237.pdf?sequence=1&isAllowed=y

Karahanna, E., Straub, D. W., & Chervany, N. L. (1999). Information technology adoption across time: A cross-sectional comparison of pre-adoption and post-adoption beliefs. *MIS Quarterly*, 183–213.

Kautz, K., & Åby Larsen, E. (2000). Diffusion theory and practice: Disseminating quality management and software process improvement innovations. *Information Technology & People*, 13(1), 11–26.

Konidala, D. M., Dwijaksara, M. H., Kim, K., Lee, D., Lee, B., Kim, D., & Kim, S. (2012). Resuscitating privacy-preserving mobile payment with customer in complete control. *Personal and Ubiquitous Computing*, 16(6), 643–654.

Liébana-Cabanillas, F. J., Sánchez-Fernández, J., & Muñoz-Leiva, F. (2014). Role of gender on acceptance of mobile payment. *Industrial Management & Data Systems*, 114(2), 220–240.

Lyytinen, K., & Damsgaard, J. (2001). What's wrong with the diffusion of innovation theory? In *Diffusing software product and process innovations* (pp. 173–190). Boston, MA: Springer.

Ma, D., Saxena, N., Xiang, T., & Zhu, Y. (2013). Location-aware and safer cards: Enhancing RFID security and privacy via location sensing. *IEEE Transactions on Dependable and Secure Computing*, 10(2), 57–69.

McKinsey. (2014). *The road back: McKinsey global banking annual review 2014*. Boston, MA: McKinsey & Company.

MobilePay's Website. (2017). Retrieved from https://mobilepay.dk/da-dk/Pages/Om-MobilePay.aspx

Olsen, M., Hedman, J., & Vatrapu, R. (2012, August). *Designing digital payment artifacts*. Proceedings of the 14th Annual International Conference on Electronic Commerce (pp. 161–168). ACM.

Ondrus, J., Gannamaneni, A., & Lyytinen, K. (2015). The impact of openness on the market potential of multi-sided platforms: A case study of mobile payment platforms. *Journal of Information Technology*, 30(3), 260–275.

Pousttchi, K., Schiessler, M., & Wiedemann, D. G. (2009). Proposing a comprehensive framework for analysis and engineering of mobile payment business models. *Information Systems and E-Business Management*, 7(3), 363–393.

Pousttchi, K., Tilson, D., Lyytinen, K., & Hufenbach, Y. (2015). Introduction to the special issue on mobile commerce: Mobile commerce research yesterday, today, tomorrow: What remains to be done? *International Journal of Electronic Commerce*, 19(4), 1–20.

Raghubir, P., & Srivastava, J. (2008). Monopoly money: The effect of payment coupling and form on spending behavior. *Journal of Experimental Psychology: Applied, 14*(3), 213.

Robertson, M., Swan, J., & Newell, S. (1996). The role of networks in the diffusion of technological innovation. *Journal of Management Studies, 33*(3), 333–359.

Rogers, E. M. (2003 [1962]). Diffusion of innovations. *Free Press.* New York.

Sanakulov, N., & Karjaluoto, H. (2015). Consumer adoption of mobile technologies: A literature review. *International Journal of Mobile Communications, 13*(3), 244–275.

Shanthi, R., & Desti, K. (2015). Consumers' perception on online shopping. *Journal of Marketing and Consumer Research, 13,* 14–21.

Stearns, D. L. (2011). *Electronic value exchange: Origins of the VISA electronic payment system.* London: Springer Science & Business Media.

Sullivan, R. J. (2010). The changing nature of US card payment fraud: Industry and public policy options. *Economic Review-Federal Reserve Bank of Kansas City, 95*(2), 101.

Surry, D. W., & Farquhar, J. D. (1997). Diffusion theory and instructional technology. *Journal of Instructional Science and Technology, 2*(1), 24–36.

Tarhini, A., Arachchilage, N. A. G., & Abbasi, M. S. (2015). A critical review of theories and models of technology adoption and acceptance in information system research. *International Journal of Technology Diffusion (IJTD), 6*(4), 58–77.

TechCrunch. (2017). *Alibaba debuts "smile to pay" facial recognition payments at KFC in China.* Retrieved from https://techcrunch.com/2017/09/03/alibaba-debuts-smile-to-pay/

Thomas, M., Desai, K. K., & Seenivasan, S. (2010). How credit card payments increase unhealthy food purchases: Visceral regulation of vices. *Journal of Consumer Research, 38*(1), 126–139.

Thomsen, T. U., & Sørensen, E. B. (2006). The first four-wheeled status symbol: Pram consumption as a vehicle for the construction of motherhood identity. *Journal of Marketing Management, 22*(9–10), 907–927.

Van de Ven, A. H., Polley, D. E., Garud, R., & Venkataraman, S. (1999). *The innovation journey.* New York: Oxford University Press.

Waight, E. (2013). Eco babies: Reducing a parent's ecological footprint with second-hand consumer goods. *International Journal of Green Economics, 7*(2), 197–211.

Waight, E. (2015). *The social, cultural and economic role of NCT nearly new sales-second-hand consumption and middle-class mothering.* Doctoral dissertation, University of Southampton.

Wolfe, R. A. (1994). Organizational innovation: Review, critique and suggested research directions. *Journal of Management Studies, 31*(3), 405–431.

Yang, C. N., & Wu, C. C. (2013). MSRC: (M)icropayment (s)cheme with ability to (r)eturn (c)hanges. *Mathematical and Computer Modelling, 58*(1), 96–107.

Zelizer, V. A. R. (1997). *The social meaning of money.* Princeton, NJ: Princeton University Press.

Zhou, T. (2014). An empirical examination of initial trust in mobile payment. *Wireless Personal Communications, 77*(2), 1519–1531.

7 Drivers of continuous usage

A consumer perspective on mobile payment service ecosystems

Robert Ciuchita, Dominik Mahr, Gaby Odekerken-Schröder and Martin Wetzels

Introduction

Mobile payment services allow consumers to use their smartphones instead of cash or bank cards to pay for products and services at registers in stores. Recent reports from consultancies (Accenture, 2016) and the business press (Groenfeld, 2017) suggest that mobile payments have the potential to revolutionize brick-and-mortar retail. With their enhanced security, faster checkouts, and a means to link with loyalty programs, mobile payments may reach volumes of $503 billion, and the number of in-store mobile payment users is expected to exceed 150 million by 2020 (BI Intelligence, 2016). Mobile payment relies on a service ecosystem of different, interconnected actors (Guo & Bouwman, 2016; Johnson, Kiser, Washington, & Torres, 2018), and the center of this ecosystem involves *users*, the consumers with smartphones who want to engage in mobile payments in stores. The ecosystem also is *enabled* by actors that provide necessary hardware or software, including financial institutions, telecommunications operators that offer mobile payment applications (apps), and technology firms that provide the mobile devices (e.g., smartphones). Finally, the ecosystem is *supported* by actors that encourage mobile payment usage, mainly the brick-and-mortar retailers (e.g., supermarkets, fashion outlets, coffee shops) that install point-of-sales (POS) payment terminals that enable mobile payments.

Early mobile payment initiatives have not been very successful in reaching critical masses of consumers though (e.g., Capgemini and BNP Paribas, 2017; Dahlberg, Guo, & Ondrus, 2015; Euromonitor, 2015; Johnson et al., 2018). It seems that consumers initially appear interested and try the mobile financial service, but they do not continue using it consistently or on a wide scale (Shaikh & Karjaluoto, 2015a). Getting people to continue using mobile payment repeatedly thus is a key determinant of the success or failure of this service ecosystem (Kujala, Mugge, & Miron-Shatz, 2017). These usage decisions appear to depend in turn on how users perceive other actors in the service ecosystem. Specifically, users' evaluations of what the other actors offer enhance or deter their continuous usage intentions (Guo & Bouwman, 2016). In this chapter, we thus ask: how do users' evaluations of the actors in the mobile payment service ecosystem affect those users' continuance intentions?

To answer this research question, we take the perspective of consumers who have used near-field communication (NFC) mobile payments – the most established and fastest-growing type (ERPB, 2015). Building on the recently proposed people–objects–physical world (POP) framework (Verhoef et al., 2017), which seeks to describe how consumers engage in service ecosystems facilitated by mobile devices, we consider three influences: (1) how users perceive themselves (i.e., people), (2) how they perceive the technology that enables their mobile payments (i.e., objects), and (3) how users perceive the service providers that support mobile payments (i.e., physical world). In particular, we study how these POP influencers affect users' intentions to continue using mobile payments (Kujala et al., 2017) and to spread positive word of mouth (WOM) about them (Oliveira, Thomas, Baptista, & Campos, 2016).

This research in turn makes two key contributions to literature on mobile services acceptance and continuance (Ovčjak, Heričko, & Polančič, 2015; Shaikh & Karjaluoto, 2015b) and mobile payments (Dahlberg et al., 2015; Gerpott & Meinert, 2017). First, we identify contextual drivers that have not been empirically explored, such as the control that users perceive they have over mobile payments in apps and the fit they sense between supporting stores and their needs, along with well-established drivers of continuance (e.g., perceived ability to use mobile payments, availability of payment apps). The conceptual model we propose, based on POP influencers (Verhoef et al., 2017), reflects how users regard the core mobile payment service ecosystem (Guo & Bouwman, 2016). Second, we focus on actual users of mobile payments, unlike most studies that rely on small convenience samples (e.g., students) or potential users (Gerpott & Meinert, 2017). Specifically, we gather perceptual and usage data from actual users, collected during a real-life, six-week mobile payment rollout. The results provide much needed insights into what leads consumers to continue using mobile payments, after their first experience with it.

The remainder of this chapter is structured as follows: first, we outline the conceptual background and present our conceptual model of how POP factors influence mobile payment continuance. Second, we describe the context and methodology employed to collect our data. Third, we present and discuss our findings. Fourth, we conclude with implications for theory and practice. In particular, we provide recommendations for different actors in the mobile payment service ecosystem, ranging from financial institutions to brick-and-mortar stores.

Conceptual background

Acceptance and continuance of mobile services

Mobile services, along with investigations of their acceptance and continuance, are undergoing tremendous development (for reviews, see Ovčjak et al., 2015; Shaikh & Karjaluoto, 2015b). Researchers from various disciplines, including information systems (e.g., Venkatesh, Thong, & Xu, 2012), human–computer interaction (e.g., Hur, Lee, & Choo, 2017), and marketing (e.g., Kim, Wang, & Malthouse, 2015), study users' motivations to adopt and continue using mobile services. In this growing field, mobile payment services represent the *transaction services* classification, which is widely researched (Ovčjak et al., 2015). As Dahlberg et al. (2015) note, most empirical studies of the acceptance and continuance of mobile payment services draw on variations of the technology acceptance model (Liébana-Cabanillas, Sánchez-Fernández, & Muñoz-Leiva, 2014), unified theory of acceptance and use of technology (UTAUT; Qasim & Abu-Shanab, 2016), or innovation diffusion theory (Oliveira et al., 2016). In operationalizing the POP influencers in our conceptual model, we include factors established by these theories.

NFC mobile payment

An NFC mobile payment is a transactional, voluntary service that allows consumers to make payments using their smartphones while they are physically present in brick-and-mortar stores (Ovčjak et al., 2015). That is, NFC mobile payment represents (1) a point-of-sale (POS) service, as opposed to a mobile app that allows users to make online purchases from their smartphones, and (2) a mobile shopping service, as opposed to a mobile bank app that allows users to access banking services from their smartphones (Khalilzadeh, Ozturk, & Bilgihan, 2017). The technology facilitates contactless communication between devices (e.g., smartphone and store register) that are within 10 cm of each other (Gerpott & Meinert, 2017). In this sense, NFC mobile payment also is a *proximity service*, as opposed to a remote service that might allow consumers to send money through their mobile devices (Gerpott & Meinert, 2017). We focus on NFC mobile payment as the most widely adopted and fastest developing type of proximity mobile payment (ERPB, 2015).

Research on NFC mobile payments from a user perspective has been sparse though, largely due to the novelty of the technology and its failure to spread as widely as expected, despite industry enthusiasm for it (Gerpott & Meinert, 2017). Khalilzadeh et al. (2017) find that attitude, security, and risk have substantial impacts on potential NFC mobile payment usage intentions, and Kujala et al. (2017) show that users' evaluations of their experience affect how their expectations influence their intentions. Gerpott and Meinert (2017) also identify differences between users and non-users in terms of socio-demographics, smartphone type and usage, and the availability of stores with NFC mobile payment capabilities. In operationalizing the POP influencers in our conceptual model, we also include the factors established by these studies.

Factors influencing mobile payment continuance

To extend research on the acceptance and continuance of mobile services, and mobile payment in particular, we examine three sets of influencers, from the perspective of actual users: the individual *users* themselves, the *technology* that enables their mobile payment, and the *service providers* that support mobile payments, in line with the POP framework (Verhoef et al., 2017). This approach also reflects a service ecosystems perspective (Guo & Bouwman, 2016) in which consumers and organizations interact and collectively create the environment. This perspective is applicable, because mobile payment requires the participation of a multitude of interconnected actors (Dahlberg et al., 2015).

The most important actors in the mobile payment ecosystem are the consumers whose smartphones are equipped for mobile payment and who make purchases in retail locations that accept mobile payments. We investigate how these people perceive themselves as users of mobile payment services. Mobile payment also is enabled by objects, including the technology involved in NFC-compatible smartphones, NFC-compatible POS registers, and mobile apps. Therefore, we assess how users perceive the technology that enables their mobile payments. Finally, mobile payments are supported by the physical world created by service providers, such as financial institutions that develop mobile payment software, telecommunications firms that develop mobile payment hardware, and brick-and-mortar retailers that install NFC-compatible POS registers in stores. We determine how users perceive service providers that support mobile payment. Our focus on the user perspective reflects our recognition that users ultimately determine the success or failure of a newly introduced service such as mobile payments (Bettencourt, Brown, & Sirianni, 2013).

Conceptual model

The proposed conceptual model is depicted in Figure 7.1.

People: how users perceive themselves

Our conceptual model accounts for users' sense of their own ability to use mobile payments, their understanding of how mobile payments work, and their experience with smartphones. Self-efficacy (i.e., ability) and experience are well established as factors that influence the acceptance and continued usage of mobile services (Dahlberg et al., 2015; Ovčjak et al., 2015). Although not usually examined in such studies, role clarity can influence users' trial of self-service technologies (Meuter, Bitner, Ostrom, & Brown, 2005), so it constitutes an appropriate individual factor to consider, alongside self-efficacy.

Objects: how users perceive the enabling technology

In our conceptual model, we account for the availability of a payment app, the privacy it provides, and the control that this payment app grants users. Perceived system quality (i.e., system availability), perceived privacy, and

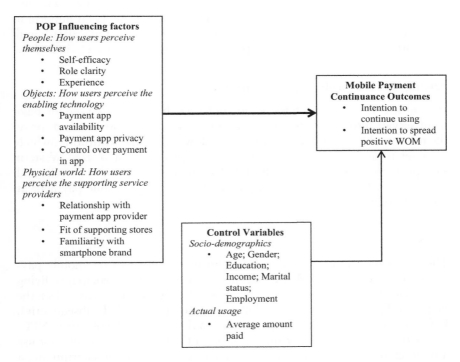

Figure 7.1 Conceptual model of the influence of POP factors on mobile payment continuance

perceived behavioral control all have been established in previous studies as factors that influence the acceptance and continued use of mobile services (Johnson et al., 2018; Ovčjak et al., 2015).

Physical world: how users perceive supporting service providers

Furthermore, our conceptual model accounts for the quality of the relationship between users and the service provider that offers the mobile payment, the fit between mobile payments and supporting stores, and users' familiarity with the brand of device they use for the mobile payment. The quality of the relationship (i.e., trust), availability, and familiarity with the brand have been identified as determinants of mobile service acceptance and continuance (Dahlberg et al., 2015; Ovčjak et al., 2015).

Continuance outcomes

Finally, the conceptual model includes intentions to continue using the mobile payment service. It is the most researched outcome in acceptance and continuance studies (Shaikh & Karjaluoto, 2015a). We also note intentions to spread positive word of mouth (WOM), which represents an important outcome variable for the diffusion of new services (Libai et al., 2010), and it recently has appeared in mobile payment research (Oliveira et al., 2016).

Setting: NFC mobile payment rollout

We capture users' perspectives before and after the rollout of a mobile payment service into a new market (i.e., no such service was available prior to the rollout). This introduction was realized by a financial institution, which we refer to as the rollout organizer; it took place in a mid-sized Western European city in the second half of 2013. The rollout lasted six weeks and involved a select group of participants who could use mobile payment at selected brick-and-mortar stores.

Users

The organizer recruited participants who were willing to try mobile payment. Specifically, a marketing agency identified 511 participants living in the city where the mobile payment was being rolled out to reflect the demographics of the country's adult population (as detailed subsequently). Before the rollout, each participant received the same model of a new, NFC-compatible smartphone. For the duration of the rollout, they could not use any other smartphone than the one they received. On each smartphone, a payment app developed by the organizer had been installed and could be linked to each participant's bank account. Thus, participants could use their new smartphones to make payments in brick-and-mortar stores, similar to using a regular bank card. That is, they could pay with the mobile device to the extent permitted by their bank account. This feature was unique at the time, because most previous mobile payment services had required a prepaid account or an intermediary service provider (e.g., telecommunications provider that would bill for mobile charges on the user's monthly invoice; Gerpott & Meinert, 2017). Contactless bank cards also had not been widely introduced at that time (Johnson et al., 2018). When they were given the smartphone, participants received an information package containing instructions about how mobile payments work and a map of stores where they could use it.

Supporting stores

The organizer recruited more than 100 stores to accept mobile payments. They represented popular shopping destinations, such as grocery stores, supermarkets, department stores, apparel stores, discounters, home and hardware stores, restaurants, bars, and cafés. All supporting stores were concentrated in the main shopping area in the city center, which minimized logistics challenges for the participants (i.e., they were the stores where participants usually shopped). The supporting stores received NFC-compatible POS terminals from the organizer, and each terminal was accompanied by a banner, advertising that mobile payment was available there. In this unique rollout, only the recruited participants could use mobile payments and only in the supporting stores.

Procedure

For participants to make a mobile payment in a supporting store, they had to tap their newly received smartphones on the newly installed POS terminals; if applicable, they also entered a mobile personal identification number (mPIN). That is, participants could choose between two settings, such that the system (1) always requested the mPIN, irrespective of the payment value (as for a regular bank card), or (2) allowed payments under €25 without entering the mPIN. For payments over €25, the mPIN was always requested. To avoid the risk of fraud, if participants made three consecutive payments of less than €25, they also were required to enter their mPIN the next time they made a payment, irrespective of its value. Participants learned about these options in the information package they received. Finally, they could use mobile payment at their own discretion but were required to use it at least once during the rollout.

Methodology

Data collection

As the research team supporting the rollout, we administered two online questionnaires to the participants: before the start of the rollout and then after it ended (six weeks later). The 511 participants had to respond to both questionnaires as a requirement for taking part in the rollout. In the first questionnaire, we sought to determine participants' socio-demographics (age, gender, education, monthly income, marital status, and employment), previous experience with smartphones, and relationship with the service provider offering the mobile payment (i.e., rollout organizer). The first questionnaire also gathered participants' perceptions of the advantages and disadvantages of the mobile payment service, before using it (i.e., expectations; Kujala et al., 2017). The list of advantages and disadvantages was developed in collaboration with the rollout organizer, based on 12 interviews and four focus group discussions conducted with 70 test users who tried the payment app one month before the start of the rollout, as well as supplemented by prior literature (Dahlberg et al., 2015).

With the second online questionnaire, we determined how participants perceived themselves, the enabling technology, and the supporting service provider after having used the NFC mobile payment service for six weeks.

We also measured their intentions to continue using it and spread positive WOM about it. The second questionnaire thus gathered the measures of the independent and dependent variables for our conceptual model. Finally, for each participant, we could observe the average amount paid across all supporting stores. During the observed six weeks, the participants paid €11.81 on average (SD = 10.29) using their NFC-compatible smartphones.

Findings

Participants' profiles

From the first questionnaire, we learned that 53% of participants were women and had an average age of 35 years. In addition, 52% were married, 55% had a monthly net household income of €2,000 or higher, and 37% were unemployed. Finally, 76% of the participants held at least a high school degree.

In terms of their experience with smartphones, before the start of the rollout, 40% of the participants had been using smartphones for at least three years; for just 12.5%, it was their first time using a smartphone. Moreover, 40% of the participants were familiar with the brand of smartphone provided by the organizer. In addition, 76% of the participants had used Internet banking through their bank's website, and 69% had previously used a mobile banking app. However, 91% of the respondents had no previous experience with NFC payments, and of those who had some experience, none had used a smartphone to make NFC payments (instead, they used contactless payment bracelets at festivals, for example).

In terms of their relationship quality with the service provider offering the mobile payment, we relied on three items from relationship management literature to assess participants' satisfaction with, trust in, and commitment to the provider (De Wulf, Odekerken-Schröder, & Iacobucci, 2001). Principal axis factoring with Promax rotation shows the three items load on one factor with item loadings greater than .7. A reliability analysis also reveals a Cronbach's alpha value of .85. Thus, the relationship quality construct is reliable and valid (DeVellis, 1991).

Perceived advantages and disadvantages of mobile payment

Based on prior literature (Dahlberg et al., 2015), 12 interviews, and four focus group discussions with 70 test users, the organizer established a set of potential advantages and disadvantages of mobile payment, before the start of the rollout. The identified advantages were convenience, ease of use, control over expenses, speed of payment, innovativeness, safety, and personalized experience. The identified potential disadvantages were risks of privacy breaches, risk of losing smartphone, faster battery discharge, higher dependence on smartphone, greater chance of impulsive shopping, and security and fraud concerns. Using a five-point Likert scale (1 = strongly disagree and 5 = strongly agree) in the first questionnaire, we asked participants about the extent to which they considered each identified aspect to be an advantage or a disadvantage of mobile payment. Figure 7.2 provides an overview of the average scores for the perceived advantages and Figure 7.3 for the perceived disadvantages from the perspective of the rollout participants.

In terms of the advantages identified, convenience (M = 4.43; SD = .62), speed of payment (M = 4.41; SD = .74), ease of use (M = 4.33; SD = .68), and innovativeness (M = 4.07; SD = .92) earned the highest average scores. Control over expenses (M = 2.70; SD = .97) and safety (M = 2.88; SD = .92) arose as potential advantages among the test users, but on average, the rollout participants did not assess them as very advantageous. They were somewhat positive about mobile payment offering a personalized experience (M = 3.51; SD = .96).

In terms of the disadvantages identified, the risk of losing the smartphone (M = 3.74; SD = 1.03) and concerns about security and fraud (M = 3.61; SD = .87) ranked highest. Participants also considered faster battery discharge (M = 3.11; SD = 1.03) and increased dependence on the smartphone (M = 3.04; SD = 1.08) as somewhat disadvantageous. Whereas the test

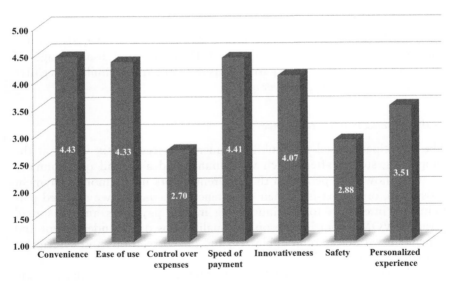

Figure 7.2 Perceived advantages of mobile payments

Notes: Sample size = 511. Each item was measured on a five-point Likert scale (1 = strongly disagree and 5 = strongly agree). Participants were asked to what extent they considered each aspect an advantage of mobile payment. Numbers on the bars indicate average scores.

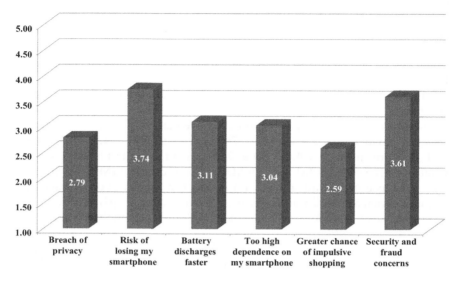

Figure 7.3 Perceived disadvantages of mobile payments

Notes: Sample size = 511. Each item was measured on a five-point Likert scale (1 = strongly disagree and 5 = strongly agree). Participants were asked to what extent they considered each aspect a disadvantage of mobile payment. Numbers on the bars indicate average scores.

users cited greater chances of impulsive shopping (M = 2.59; SD = 1.13) and breach of privacy (M = 2.79; SD = 1.02) as potential disadvantages of mobile payment services, the participants did not express similarly negative views of these elements, on average.

POP influencers of continuance

The participants used the mobile payment services for six weeks at the supporting stores, after which we administered a second questionnaire to assess how they perceived the different actors in the mobile payment ecosystem, on the basis of their experience. Specifically, we assessed participants' intentions to continue using mobile payments and to spread positive WOM about it. The operationalizations of the independent and dependent variables are in Table 7.1, and the correlations and descriptive statistics are in Table 7.2.

For brevity, most of the variable measures used single items. An exception was mobile payment app availability, which we measured with three items from the electronic service quality scale (Parasuraman, Zeithaml, & Malhotra, 2005). The principal axis factoring with Promax rotation reveals that the three items load on one factor at better than .7. The reliability analysis

Table 7.1 Overview of variables and measures

Variable	Item/Operationalization	Measurement
Influencing factors		
How users perceive themselves		
Self-efficacy	I believe I have the ability to use mobile payment.	1 = Strongly disagree, 5 = Strongly agree
Role clarity	It is clear to me how to make a payment with my smartphone.	1 = Strongly disagree, 5 = Strongly agree
Experience	Participant has been using a smartphone for three years or longer.	0 = No, 1 = Yes
How users perceive enabling technology		
Payment app availability	The mobile payment app . . .	
	. . . is always available for payment.	1 = Strongly disagree, 5 = Strongly agree
	. . . responds immediately.	1 = Strongly disagree, 5 = Strongly agree
	. . . does not crash.	1 = Strongly disagree, 5 = Strongly agree
Payment app privacy	I believe my personal information is treated confidentially in the mobile payment app.	1 = Strongly disagree, 5 = Strongly agree
Control over payment in app	I keep the setting "Always enter mobile Pin" on at all times in the mobile payment app.	0 = No, 1 = Yes
How users perceive supporting service providers		
Relationship with payment app provider	In relation to the service provider offering mobile payment . . .	
	I am satisfied with service provider.	0 = Not at all, 10 = Very much
	I trust service provider.	0 = Not at all, 10 = Very much
	I would not change service provider.	0 = Not at all, 10 = Very much
Fit of supporting stores	The participating stores meet my purchasing needs.	1 = Strongly disagree, 5 = Strongly agree
Familiarity with smartphone brand	Participant previously owned the same brand of smartphone used in the rollout.	0 = No, 1 = Yes

(*Continued*)

Table 7.1 (Continued)

Variable	Item/Operationalization	Measurement
Outcomes		
Intention to continue using	I am likely to continue using mobile payment after the rollout.	0 = Not at all, 10 = Very much
Intention to spread positive WOM	I am likely to say positive things about mobile payment to other people.	0 = Not at all, 10 = Very much
Control variables		
Socio-demographics		
Age	Participant's age.	Number of years
Gender	Participant's gender.	0 = Female; 1 = Male
Education	Participant has higher education (at least high school degree).	0 = No; 1 = Yes
Income	Participant has monthly income of €2,000 or higher.	0 = No; 1 = Yes
Marital status	Participant is married.	0 = No; 1 = Yes
Employment	Participant is employed.	0 = No; 1 = Yes
Actual usage		
Amount paid	Average amount paid via mobile during six weeks of rollout.	Amount in €

establishes a Cronbach's alpha value of .81. Therefore, the payment app availability construct is reliable and valid (DeVellis, 1991).

To test our conceptual model, we estimated two regressions, one with intention to recommend and the other with intention to spread positive WOM as the dependent variable. The independent and control variables remained the same. The unstandardized coefficients, their standard errors, and the regression summaries are in Table 7.3.

People

Self-efficacy has a significant, positive coefficient for intention to continue using (.64; $p < .01$) and intention to spread positive WOM about (.55; $p < .01$) the mobile payment service. Role clarity also reveals a significant positive coefficient on continuance intentions (.31; $p < .05$), but only a marginally significant positive coefficient for spreading positive WOM (.21; $p < .10$). Experience with smartphones has a positive significant coefficient on intentions to spread positive WOM (.29; $p < .05$).

Table 7.2 Correlations and descriptive statistics

Correlations	1	2	3	4	5	6	7	8	9	10	11	12	13	14	15	16	17	18
1. Intention to continue using	1																	
2. Intention to spread positive WOM	.70	1																
3. Self-efficacy	.35	.41	1															
4. Role clarity	.27	.29	.42	1														
5. Experience	.11	.20	.17	.04	1													
6. Payment app availability	.36	.44	.36	.31	.13	1												
7. Payment app privacy	.26	.30	.18	.19	.10	.29	1											
8. Control over payment in app	-.19	-.24	-.23	-.08	-.09	-.21	-.04	1										
9. Relationship with payment app provider	.15	.20	.18	.18	.06	.13	.28	-.03	1									
10. Fit of supporting stores	.15	.24	.16	.16	.09	.15	.14	-.05	.17	1								
11. Familiarity with smartphone brand	.08	.01	.01	.01	-.05	.02	.04	.06	.06	.06	1							
12. Age	.04	-.09	-.20	-.16	-.20	-.06	-.01	-.03	-.18	-.17	-.05	1						
13. Gender	.09	.13	.17	.02	.29	.17	.00	-.15	-.05	-.04	-.03	.05	1					
14. Education	-.17	-.16	.01	-.03	-.03	-.03	-.18	-.02	-.15	-.12	-.08	-.02	.06	1				
15. Income	.08	.00	-.07	-.07	-.05	.04	.02	-.08	-.09	-.16	-.01	.53	.06	.08	1			
16. Marital status	.10	.04	-.01	-.03	-.06	.10	.01	-.03	-.07	-.05	.02	.38	.04	.03	.60	1		
17. Employment	.05	-.02	-.08	-.02	.03	.01	.03	-.03	-.06	-.08	.01	.31	-.04	.01	.50	.34	1	
18. Amount paid	.02	-.05	-.07	.01	-.04	.01	.08	.11	.06	.04	.07	.11	-.07	-.05	.15	.11	.17	1

(Continued)

Table 7.2 (Continued)

Correlations	1	2	3	4	5	6	7	8	9	10	11	12	13	14	15	16	17	18
Descriptive statistics																		
Minimum	0	0	2	1	0	1	1	0	0	1	0	18	0	0	0	0	0	1.14
Maximum	10	10	5	5	1	5	5	1	10	5	1	72	1	1	1	1	1	145.94
Mean	8.23	7.95	4.60	4.64	.40	4.04	4.02	.34	7.82	3.13	.39	35.17	.47	.77	.55	.52	.63	11.81
Standard deviation	1.85	1.63	.59	.60	.49	.86	.75	.48	1.56	1.14	.49	14.17	.50	.42	.50	.50	.48	10.29

Notes: Sample size = 511. Correlations of .09 and higher are significant at the .05 level (two-tailed).

Table 7.3 Seemingly unrelated regressions results

Parameter	Continuance intentions		WOM intentions	
	Coefficient	Standard error	Coefficient	Standard error
Intercept	.43	.86	1.03	.71
How users perceive themselves				
Self-efficacy	.64**	.14	.55**	.12
Role clarity	.31*	.13	.21†	.11
Experience	.18	.16	.29*	.13
How users perceive enabling technology				
Payment app availability	.42**	.09	.47**	.08
Payment app privacy	.23*	.10	.26**	.09
Control over payment in app	−.31*	.16	−.36**	.13
How users perceive supporting service provider				
Relationship with payment app provider	.03	.05	.04	.04
Fit of supporting stores	.08	.07	.17**	.05
Familiarity with smartphone brand	.24†	.15	−.03	.12
Control variables				
Age	.01*	.01	.00	.01
Gender	.00	.15	.06	.13
Education	−.57**	.17	−.46**	.14
Income	.11	.21	.11	.17
Marital status	.10	.18	.08	.15
Employment	.06	.17	−.06	.14
Amount paid	.00	.01	−.01	.01
Regression summary				
R^2	.26		.35	
χ^2	181.64		278.78	
p-Value	.00		.00	

Notes: Sample size = 511.
†$p < .1$
*$p < .05$
**$p < .01$

Objects

The availability of the mobile payment app has significant, positive effects on intention to continue using (.42; $p < .01$) and intention to spread positive WOM about (.47; $p < .01$) the mobile payment service. Payment app privacy exhibits significant positive coefficients for both dependent variables: .23 ($p < .05$) for continuance intentions and .26 ($p < .01$) for positive WOM intentions. However, negative significant coefficients arise for the control participants exercised through the app for both dependent variables: −.31 ($p < .05$) for continuance intentions and −.36 ($p < .01$) for positive WOM intentions.

Physical world

The relationship users have with the payment app provider produces no significant coefficients for either dependent variable. The extent to which participants perceive that the supporting stores fit their shopping needs has a significant positive effect only for intentions to spread positive WOM (.17; $p < .01$). Finally, familiarity with the smartphone has only a marginally significant positive coefficient for intentions to continue using mobile payment services (.24; $p < .1$).

Control variables

Age has a significant, positive effect on continuance intentions (.01; $p < .05$), but education exhibits significant negative coefficients for both intentions to continue (−.57; $p < .01$) and intentions to spread positive WOM (−.46; $p < .01$). Gender, income, marital status, and employment do not produce significant coefficients. Interestingly, neither does the actual average amount paid appear to affect either dependent variable.[1]

Additional analysis

Self-efficacy implies perceived behavioral control (Shaikh & Karjaluoto, 2015b), so we tested for a potential interaction effect between self-efficacy (how users perceive themselves) and control over payment through the mPIN (how users perceive the enabling technology). With the same control variables from Table 7.3, we find significant interaction effects in both regressions, with continuance and positive WOM intentions as the dependent variables. That is, a positive, significant, interaction coefficient emerges when the mPIN setting is always on for intentions to continue using the mobile payment service (.61; $p < .05$) and intentions to recommend it (.59; $p < .01$). These interactions are depicted in Figure 7.4.

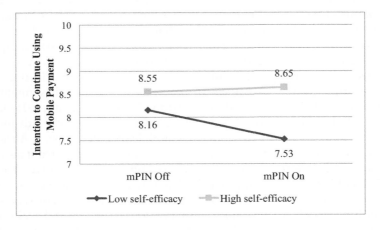

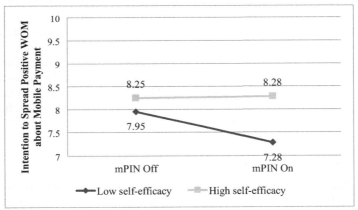

Notes: Sample size = 511. The interaction effects were tested with 5,000 bootstrap samples. The scale of the dependent variables has been truncated to facilitate interpretation.

Figure 7.4 Interaction effects of self-efficacy and perceived control

Discussion

Adoption of mobile payment

The main focus of this study is on factors that affect the use of mobile payments, but we also can make some observations about the factors that influence adoption, using the data we gathered in the first questionnaire about the advantages and disadvantages participants predicted before the rollout. These participants were recruited to reflect the demographics of the country's adult population, but they also were willing to try the mobile payment system. Thus, our users likely are early adopters, according to innovation diffusion theory (Rogers, 1995). Moreover, unlike most technology acceptance studies that expose employees in organizations or students at universities to new technology that they might not want to use (Shaikh & Karjaluoto, 2015a; Venkatesh et al., 2012), our study includes willing consumers. These users evaluated the advantages and disadvantages before using the new mobile financial service. Although these findings are only descriptive, the advantages and disadvantages that the users perceived reflect typical influences on acceptance (Ovčjak et al., 2015; Shaikh & Karjaluoto, 2015b). They regard convenience, speed of payment, and ease of use as the principal advantages; these functional and utilitarian advantages align with previously established technology acceptance determinants, such as performance and effort expectancy from the UTAUT (Venkatesh et al., 2012). The users in our study also cited the innovativeness and personalized experience of mobile payment, reflecting more hedonic and intrinsic influencers of acceptance, similar to the hedonic motivation in UTAUT (Venkatesh et al., 2012). Among the disadvantages, users in our study were mostly concerned with the potential loss of the smartphone, security, and fraud. These disadvantages resonate with perceive risks as likely influences on the acceptance of mobile financial services (Dahlberg et al., 2015).

Mobile payment continuance

After using mobile payment services for six weeks, the participants evaluated the different actors in the mobile payment ecosystem. Our results show that elements relating to the users themselves, the enabling technology, and the supporting service providers all affect users' intentions to continue using mobile payment and spread positive WOM about it.

In terms of how users perceive themselves, both ability (i.e., they believe they can use mobile payments) and clarity (i.e., they know how to use mobile payments) positively influence users' intentions to continue using the service. The more users perceive they have the ability to use mobile payments, after trying it out, and the more experienced they are with smartphones prior to the rollout, the more likely they are to say positive things about the service, which is a necessary condition for the spread of new services such as mobile payments (Libai et al., 2010). Self-efficacy is often included as a determinant of continuance (Dahlberg et al., 2015), and clarity can complement ability. But on average, our participants showed high self-efficacy and role clarity after this relatively brief usage period, which hints at their early adopter status (Rogers, 1995).

In terms of how users perceive the enabling technology, the more they believe the mobile payment app is always available, responds immediately, and does not crash, the more likely they are to continue using mobile payments and spread positive WOM. Furthermore, whether users believe their personal information is kept confidential represents a positive influence of both intentions. Prior to usage though, these participants did not regard a breach of privacy as a primary disadvantage of mobile payments. Whether users opt to require an mPIN for every mobile payment has a negative influence on their intentions to continue using and spreading positive WOM. This finding is interesting; not having to enter a mPIN for low value purchases (e.g., under €25), at the time, represented one of the main differentiators of mobile payments relative to traditional bank cards. In focus group discussions after the rollout, we learned that participants believed the disadvantages of losing their smartphone, having it stolen, or having their smartphone hacked outweighed the advantages of speedy payments and convenience. We also explored the importance of perceived control further (i.e., whether users choose to require an mPIN at all times), by combining it with their perceptions of their ability to use mobile payments. This interaction is significant only if users turn on the mPIN setting at all times. As Figure 7.4 illustrates, when users choose to be prompted for an mPIN for every purchase, they are more likely to continue using mobile payments and say positive things about it, as long as they have high perceived self-efficacy.

In relation to how users perceive supporting service providers, we find that the more they believe that the stores supporting mobile payment fit their shopping needs, the more likely they are to continue using this service. Relationship quality, a composite measure of trust in the service provider (Dahlberg et al., 2015), was not a significant influence in our analysis. On average, participants indicated that they had relatively good relationships with the payment app provider, though they were not selected on that basis. Finally, familiarity with the smartphone brand had only a marginal influence on intentions to continue using mobile payments.

Our study also presents some interesting findings related to users' socio-demographics. Specifically, users with more education were less likely to continue using the service or spread positive WOM about it. This finding is surprising, because users with less education generally are more likely to discontinue using innovations (Rogers, 1995). Age and gender influence continuance intentions in previous studies (e.g., Gerpott & Meinert, 2017) but were less important in our study. The average amount paid through mobile payment services does not drive either of the dependent variables either. Previous studies of the adoption and usage of mobile apps (e.g., Kim & Malhotra, 2005) indicate that previous usage positively influences continuance, but this finding is not supported in our research.

Conclusions

With this chapter, we consider how users' evaluations of different actors in the mobile payment service ecosystem influence the different facets of users' continuance intentions. To examine this research question, we propose a conceptual model based on a novel framework, then collect and analyze perceptual and usage data from actual users during a real-life, six-week mobile payment rollout. We thus can derive some theoretical and managerial implications from our study results.

Theoretical implications

This study offers two main contributions to literature on mobile services acceptance and continuance (Shaikh & Karjaluoto, 2015b) and mobile payments (Gerpott & Meinert, 2017). First, the user perspective on the service ecosystem captures both established and contextual influences on user continuance. Our results confirm that some well-established factors (e.g., self-efficacy, technology availability) have important roles, but others (e.g., relationship with provider, previous usage) are not as important in determining the different facets of NFC mobile payment continuance intentions. Both complementary (e.g., role clarity) and contextual (e.g., control over payment in app, fit of mobile payment supporting stores) factors should be taken into account when examining continuance influencers. By introducing and empirically testing a conceptual model based on the POP framework (Verhoef et al., 2017), we emphasize the need to take a service ecosystem perspective when investigating the continued usage of complex mobile services, such as NFC mobile payments (Guo & Bouwman, 2016).

Second, this research gathers insights from actual users who had the opportunity to experience NFC mobile payments in a real-life setting. Such a perspective is critical to expand on prior mobile payment research that employs small convenience samples (e.g., students) or potential users (Gerpott & Meinert, 2017). This approach offers unique benefits, because the factors that influence initial acceptance and subsequent usage of a technology are not necessarily the same (Kim & Malhotra, 2005), due to the effects of how users experience the technology over time (Kujala et al., 2017). For example, the risk of a privacy breach was not considered a disadvantage prior to the rollout, but the extent to which users perceived that the mobile payment app protected their privacy after having used it for six weeks emerged as an important influence on their actual continuance intentions.

Managerial implications

The results also provide implications for each of the actors in the mobile payment service ecosystem. The ways that users perceive themselves and the enabling technology represent the most important influences on their intentions to continue using mobile payment services and spread positive WOM about them. Service providers that support mobile payments should ensure that users feel as if they can use mobile payments, as well as provide clear instructions for doing so. Financial institutions can provide users with transparent information and tutorials about how to use mobile payments (e.g., branch or online advertising, video tutorials, walkthroughs when people download the app). Brick-and-mortar retailers also should make sure their NFC-equipped POS terminals are visible and that their frontline service employees receive training, so they can assist customers who might face difficulties when trying to pay with their mobile devices.

With regard to the enabling technology, the availability of a mobile payment app is a clear prerequisite; launching and maintaining a responsive, fully functioning app represents a hygiene factor for users. In light of recent data hacks (e.g., 400,000 UniCredit bank accounts breached in Italy in July 2017), financial institutions must find ways to alleviate users' fears about how their personal information will be treated and kept safe. For example, they could establish in-app notifications to remind users that their personal information will be treated confidentially and provide information about how they can help maintain security themselves. In this regard though, the extent to which service providers should encourage users to use the mPIN setting can be a double-edged sword. Not requiring the mPIN for transactions of low value might emphasize some benefits of mobile payment (e.g., speed, convenience), but it also might cause users to fear the risk of loss or theft. Financial institutions might set the mPIN option to off by default (e.g., when the app is downloaded) and inform users about its benefits, with a clear means to turn it on if they so choose.

Finally, financial institutions should make users aware of the availability of mobile payments in brick-and-mortar locations that reflect their purchasing habits, because such accessibility makes users more likely to spread positive WOM. Geolocation services within the app could send users push notifications when they enter a store that accepts mobile payments. In collaborations, financial institutions and brick-and-mortar retailers could provide in-store signage about the mobile payment option. Just as some stores host card-only registers, mobile-only registers could be added to stores, especially those that already allow self-check-out lanes.

Limitations and research directions

Several limitations of this study should be considered. First, though representative of the general adult population, the participants agreed to participate in a field study to be the first to use mobile payments. Further research should include users who are not necessarily early adopters but might adopt later. Second, all participants had to use the same model of smartphone, but some of them likely would have preferred other smartphone brands or models, as well as other smart devices (e.g., smart watches) for their mobile payments. Third, we focused on one NFC mobile payment application, provided by a financial institution. Continued research might compare this service provider with other mobile payment enablers, such as telecom or high-tech firms. Fourth, we obtained only the average amount that each participant paid through NFC. Additional studies might consider the average amount paid with other payment methods too (e.g., bank cards), to capture users' loyalty to such methods.

Notes

1 We tested the same regression models with frequency of mobile payments and total amount spent, instead of average amount spent; the results are consistent.

References

Accenture. (2016). *Consumers are pushing digital payments to the edge of a new frontier.* Retrieved March 2017, from www.accenture.com/us-en/insight-digital-payments-survey-2016

Bettencourt, L. A., Brown, S. W., & Sirianni, N. J. (2013). The secret to true service innovation. *Business Horizons, 56*(1), 13–22.

BI Intelligence. (2016). The mobile payments report: Market forecasts, consumer trends, and the barriers and benefits that will influence adoption. *Business Insider.* Retrieved June 2017, from www.businessinsider.com/the-mobile-payments-report-market-forecasts-consumer-trends-and-the-barriers-and-benefits-that-will-influence-adoption-2016-5?international=true&r=US&IR=T

Capgemini and BNP Paribas. (2017). *World payments report 2017.* Retrieved January 2018, from www.worldpaymentsreport.com/download

Dahlberg, T., Guo, J., & Ondrus, J. (2015). A critical review of mobile payment research. *Electronic Commerce Research and Apps, 14*(5), 265–284.

DeVellis, R. F. (1991). *Scale development: Theory and apps.* Newbury Park, CA: Sage Publications.

De Wulf, K., Odekerken-Schröder, G., & Iacobucci, D. (2001). Investments in consumer relationships: A cross-country and cross-industry exploration. *Journal of Marketing, 65*(4), 33–50.

ERPB. (2015). ERPB final report mobile and card-based contactless proximity payments. *Euro Retail Payments Board.* Retrieved July 2017, from www.ecb.europa.eu/paym/retpaym/shared/pdf/4th-ERPB-meeting/2015-11-26_4th-ERPB_item_6_ERPB_CTLP_working_group_final_report.pdf?726f67769d37722de341702fe5f2387a

Euromonitor. (2015). *Consumer payments 2015: Trends, developments and prospects.* Retrieved March 2017, from www.euromonitor.com/consumer-payments-2015-trends-developments-and-prospects/report

Gerpott, T. J., & Meinert, p. (2017). Who signs up for NFC mobile payment services? Mobile network operator subscribers in Germany. *Electronic Commerce Research and Apps, 23*, 1–13.

Groenfeldt, T. (2017). Mobile payments can boost growth and profitability. *Forbes*. Retrieved March 2017, from www.forbes.com/sites/tomgroenfeldt/2017/03/08/mobile-payments-can-boost-growth-and-profitability/#2e3208501396

Guo, J., & Bouwman, H. (2016). An analytical framework for an m-payment ecosystem: A merchant's perspective. *Telecommunications Policy, 40*(2), 147–167.

Hur, H. J., Lee, H. K., & Choo, H. J. (2017). Understanding usage intention in innovative mobile app service: Comparison between millennial and mature consumers. *Computers in Human Behavior, 73*, 353–361.

Johnson, V. L., Kiser, A., Washington, R., & Torres, R. (2018). Limitations to the rapid adoption of M-payment services: Understanding the impact of privacy risk on M-Payment services. *Computers in Human Behavior, 79*, 111–122.

Khalilzadeh, J., Ozturk, A. B., & Bilgihan, A. (2017). Security-related factors in extended UTAUT model for NFC based mobile payment in the restaurant industry. *Computers in Human Behavior, 70*, 460–474.

Kim, S. J., Wang, R. J. H., & Malthouse, E. C. (2015). The effects of adopting and using a brand's mobile app on customers' subsequent purchase behavior. *Journal of Interactive Marketing, 31*, 28–41.

Kim, S. S., & Malhotra, N. K. (2005). A longitudinal model of continued IS use: An integrative view of four mechanisms underlying post adoption phenomena. *Management Science, 51*(5), 741–755.

Kujala, S., Mugge, R., & Miron-Shatz, T. (2017). The role of expectations in service evaluation: A longitudinal study of a proximity mobile payment service. *International Journal of Human-Computer Studies, 98*, 51–61.

Libai, B., Bolton, R., Bügel, M. S., De Ruyter, K., Götz, O., Risselada, H., & Stephen, A. T. (2010). Customer-to-customer interactions: Broadening the scope of word of mouth research. *Journal of Service Research, 13*(3), 267–282.

Liébana-Cabanillas, F., Sánchez-Fernández, J., & Muñoz-Leiva, F. (2014). Antecedents of the adoption of the new mobile payment systems: The moderating effect of age. *Computers in Human Behavior, 35*, 464–478.

Meuter, M. L., Bitner, M. J., Ostrom, A. L., & Brown, S. W. (2005). Choosing among alternative service delivery modes: An investigation of customer trial of self-service technologies. *Journal of Marketing, 69*(2), 61–83.

Oliveira, T., Thomas, M., Baptista, G., & Campos, F. (2016). Mobile payment: Understanding the determinants of customer adoption and intention to recommend the technology. *Computers in Human Behavior, 61*, 404–414.

Ovčjak, B., Heričko, M., & Polančič, G. (2015). Factors impacting the acceptance of mobile data services: A systematic literature review. *Computers in Human Behavior, 53*, 24–47.

Parasuraman, A., Zeithaml, V. A., & Malhotra, A. (2005). ES-QUAL: A multiple-item scale for assessing electronic service quality. *Journal of Service Research, 7*(3), 213–233.

Qasim, H., & Abu-Shanab, E. (2016). Influencers of mobile payment acceptance: The impact of network externalities. *Information Systems Frontiers, 18*(5), 1021–1034.

Rogers, E. M. (1995). *Diffusion of innovations*. New York: Simon & Schuster.

Shaikh, A. A., & Karjaluoto, H. (2015a). Making the most of information technology & systems usage: A literature review, framework and future research agenda. *Computers in Human Behavior, 49*, 541–566.

Shaikh, A. A., & Karjaluoto, H. (2015b). Mobile banking adoption: A literature review. *Telematics and Informatics*, 32(1), 129–142.

Venkatesh, V., Thong, J. Y., & Xu, X. (2012). Consumer acceptance and use of information technology: Extending the unified theory of acceptance and use of technology. *MIS Quarterly*, 36(1), 157–178.

Verhoef, p. C., Stephen, A. T., Kannan, p. K., Luo, X., Abhishek, V., Andrews, M., . . . Hu, M. (2017). Consumer connectivity in a complex, technology-enabled, and mobile-oriented world with smart products. *Journal of Interactive Marketing*, 40, 1–8.

8 Stand-alone retail owners' preference on using mobile payment at the point of sales (POS)

Evidence from a developing country

Felix Adamu Nandonde

Introduction

Africa has witnessed the growth of mobile payment innovation to stimulate financial inclusions. Despite these efforts the penetration of mobile technology to the consumer market seems to be lagging behind. For example, Vodacom South Africa targeted to have 10 million subscribers of mobile payment users by 2014 when it was launched in 2010. However, up to 2014 Vodacom has had only 76,000 users; this led to the closure of the service in South Africa (Mbele, 2016). In Tanzania, mobile payment was expected to be growing faster, however it is still lagging behind up to now. For example, the country with only 10% of her population is having access to financial services, has only 17 million users of mobile payment out of a population of 53 million users. This shows that it is very important to understand the penetration of mobile payment in Tanzania with a focus on stand-alone retailers. We argue that retailers are the most important actors in the value chain of mobile service provision due to their positions and nature of the country's economy.

A literature review by Shaikh and Karjaluoto (2016) found that there are fewer studies on mobile payment. Further, the authors revealed that more of the previous studies were on m-gaming, m-ticketing, and m-government. Shaikh and Karjaluoto (2016) observe that there is no study from Africa on electronic commerce published on a creditable journal. In general, African countries such as Tanzania and Kenya are considered as pioneers of mobile payment. However, less is known on the preference of mobile payment in creditable journals. This study intends to fill that knowledge gap with a focus on stand-alone retailers in Tanzania. This goal is consistent with Szopinski's (2016) observation, which calls for more studies on mobile payment so as to understand how business people make decisions on the usage of mobile payment. With the rising use of mobile devices to facilitate payment, there is a need to understand the acceptance of mobile payment technology by retailers.

In general, previous studies on the usage of non-cash system at the point of sales (POS) focused on the debit cards, loyalty cards, and checks. Few of these studies focused on the use of mobile payment at the point of sales. For example, Trütsch (2016) investigated the choice of the facility which is used at the point of sales among consumers in Europe. Furthermore, these studies paid less attention on the influence of shop owners' on the acceptance of mobile payment at POS. One study that was conducted in Nigeria paid attention to the acceptance of business owners on the use of POS machine but not mobile payment as the tool that can facilitate a transaction. The current study intends to fill that gap with one the use of mobile devices at POS with focusing on stand-alone retailers.

In Tanzania, there is an idea of plastic cash studies which focused on mobile payment. For example, Anthony and Mutalemwa (2014) conducted a study on the acceptance of mobile payment on the case of Z-Money and found that such factors as cost, mobility, trust, and usefulness were very important. In another study, Lwoga and Lwoga (2017) found that perceived trust and social influence were the factors that motivated consumers onto using mobile payment in the country. Tossy (2012) studied the use of mobile payment for paying school fees and found that factors such as trust, social, and performance acceptance were very important. Mwanjelwa and Nandonde (2014) focused on university students' preference on buying ringtones in Tanzania and found that gospel songs are highly preferred. We acknowledge the efforts of previous studies in Tanzania; these studies paid little attention on the use of mobile device at POS. While PwC (2016) observes that mobile devices will be preferred as POS devices in developing economies, less attention has been paid by researchers on understanding how other actors in the mobile payment value chain see the technology. Nandonde and Kuada (2016,2014) call for more studies on the use of retail and ICT in developing economies following the increase of the usage of mobile payment. This study intends to fill that knowledge gap with a focus on stand-alone retailer preference on the acceptance of mobile payment in Tanzania.

To facilitate the emergence of this idea, commercial banks provide POS terminals to traders. However, the nature of Tanzania's business, which is dominated by SMEs, there is likelihood that many business owners would not manage to have POS devices. As PwC (2016) argues, the business environment is such that the adoption of mobile devices for POS transaction or mobile POS is likely to explode worldwide. The adoption of the mobile device to facilitate transaction is slow in developing countries despite the increasing number of people with mobile phones (Mbele, 2016).

Furthermore, previous studies in the country have conflicting findings on the use of mobile phones by traders. For example, a study by Chale and Mbamba (2015) shows that SMEs use mobile payment to facilitate sale transactions. While in another study, Mramba, Sutinen, Haule, and Msami (2014) found that street vendors do not use mobile devices to facilitate transaction but only for social issues. In that regard, it is very important to understand users' preference on the adaptation of innovation that facilitates the use of mobile device for POS transaction. Therefore, the objective of this study is to examine factors that influence the usage of mobile payment at the point of sales by stand-alone retailers in Tanzania. Specifically, the study intends to answer the research question, what factors influence stand-alone retailers on using mobile devices at the point of sales?

Mobile payment status in Tanzania

Mobile payment is on the rise in Tanzania. Table 8.1 shows that users of mobile payment increased by 16% between 2015 and 2016. Recently, a study by Mramba et al. (2014) showed that the use of mobile phones in Tanzania among street vendors was more for social issues and less for facilitating business transactions. Reuters (2017) indicated that in the country and found that mobile phone usage can improve the profit of business people. Up to 2016 Tanzania was estimated to have 40.17million mobile phone users (Reuters, 2017).

Up to April 2017, the number of mobile phone financial services users in Tanzania reached 17.3 million with an estimation of Tshs 50 trillion transacted during the period (TanzaniaInvest, 2017). Globally, it is estimated that 100 million people are using mobile phones to support transactions (TheCitizen, 2015). This estimation shows that Tanzania has 17% of the global users of mobile payment. In general, mobile payment is growing in the country. In that regard, understanding the factors that influence the acceptance of the system is very important.

Table 8.1 Users of mobile payment in Tanzania

SN	Year	Number of active users of mobile payment (in millions)	Number of mobile phone users (in millions)	Change in %	Value of transaction annually (Trillion in Tanzania shillings)
1	2016	17	40.17	0.9	50
2	2015	–	–	–	–
3	2014	–	31.86	16	–
4	2013	11	26.86	–	28.9
5	2012	–	19	–	17.4
6	2011	–	22.08	–	5.56
7	2010	–	19.42	–	3.4
8	2009	–	14.9	–	0.1
9	2008	0.28	7.23	–	0.6

Source: www.gsma.com/mobilefordevelopment/wp-content/uploads/2014/03/Tanzania-Mobile-Money-infographic-GSMA-MMU.pdf, Mugwe (2013), Di Castri and Lara (2014), URT (2011).

Despite this growth of mobile payment, there are some factors that limit the growth of the system in the country. For example, cybercrime has emerged and is reported as one of the limiting factors. For example, previous studies (e.g.,Taluka & Masele, 2016) cited trust as exerting some influence on the usage of mobile payment by the rural consumers in Tanzania. In that regard, it is very important to understand how these issues limit the usage of mobile payment in the country.

The Tanzania market for mobile business is quite competitive, with seven communication services providers. The major service providers are Vodafone, Tigo, Airtel, TTCL, and Halotel. M-Pesa, which is provided by Vodafone, is the market leader with a market share of 42%, followed by Tigo-Pesa with a market share of 31%. Thus Tigo-Pesa is the second leading market in Tanzania. Airtel money, which is provided by Bharti Company, is third with a market share of 24%, and Eazy Pesa by Zantel has a market share of 3%.

In general, the number of people who are using mobile payment in Tanzania is very low compared with the estimated number at the beginning. For example, in 2008 when Vodafone introduced the M-Pesa in Tanzania was expected to report successful result like Kenya. However, after one year the services had 280,000 users while during the same period Kenya had 2.7 million users (IFC, 2015). This shows that it is very important to understand the acceptance of certain technology in different markets or contexts in Africa.

Literature review

Different theories have been used to explain the acceptance of the usage of a new technology and in particular the use of mobile payment at the point of sales. A study conducted in Germany on the adoption of new technology, the diffusion of innovation theory was used (Stroborn, Heitmann, Leibold, & Frank, 2004). Other studies, which were conducted in Tanzania, extensively used utility theory, the theory of reasoned action, and the TAM model (Chogo & Sedoyeka, 2015; Chale & Mbamba, 2015).

This study is guided by the TAM model, which was proposed by Davis (1986) as the extension of the reasoned action. The model intends to measure the impact of the external environment on the preference of a new technology (Davis, Bagozzi, & Warshaw, 1989). Thus, the model is appropriate in understanding the preference of stand-alone retailers on the usage of mobile payment at the point of sales. In general, literature review in mobile payment shows that external environment has a great impact on the acceptance of a technology. For example, usability and cost or prices are some of the reasons that have been limiting the acceptance of the usage of new technology in general (see Economilades & Jeziorski, 2016)

According to Davis et al. (1989), the TAM model posits that two dimensions, which are perceived usefulness and perceived ease of use, are primary for the acceptance of a technology. The perceived usefulness of the use is based on the belief that using a certain technology will increase its performance. In general, the usage of mobile payment is likely to improve the performance of the retailers. Another element of the TAM model is the perceived easiness of use, which is the perception of the user that the system will effortlessly be used. In general, factors such as knowledge and information among the users make the technology easy to access and simple to understand. The use of mobile payment to support payment seems to be easy because it depends on the use of normal mobile devices. However, the information on the application of the technology and access to such information is subjected to a process. The assumption is that if the set of processes is easy to users then transaction would be facilitated.

The TAM model has been extensively used on the acceptance of new technology. For example, the model has been used in the context of food technology acceptance (Cox & Evans, 2008; Kim & Woo, 2016), and in the context of acceptance of computer application (Davis et al., 1989; Sanchez-Prieto, Olmos-Miguelanaz, & Garcia-Pelnavo, 2016).

Previous studies on mobile technology focused on different aspects. For example, Yueh, Lu, and Lin (2016) focused on the employees' acceptance of mobile technology at the working place.Fujimoto, Ferdous, Sekigunchi, and Sugianto (2016) focused on the effects of mobile technology and working place engagement. Despite these efforts little is known about the usage of mobile payment technology to the convenience of retail owners in developing economies. Furthermore, previous studies were more on application of mobile technology and less on the mobile payment as a tool of facilitating exchange at the point of sales. The current study covers that gap of knowledge on understanding the acceptance on the usage of mobile payment with a focus on the convenience of stores owners in Tanzania.

In general, a study by Lee, Park, Chung, and Blakeney (2012) on the usage of mobile finance technology shows that convenience and usefulness are very important for acceptance. In another study, Yen and Wu (2016) identified different factors that influence the adoption of mobile finance and these include mobility of payment, personal habit, and perceived usefulness and perceived ease of usage. However, these studies focused on the use of technology by customers with less focus on the service providers. We argued that service providers are very important to the acceptance of any technology.

Acceptance of point of sales technology

Payment at the point of sales (POS) can be performed by cash, check, debit card, credit card, loyalty cards, and mobile phones. Recently, Africa has witnessed the emergence of electronic means in facilitating payment at the point of sales; one of such means is mobile payment. Previous studies show that the usage of electronic point sales technology is influenced by factors such as price, convenience, and ease of use.

With the rise of mobile technology in Africa, mobile payment has also been turned as a means for payment at the point of sales.

Other studies on point of sales payment focused on the choice between different technologies. For example, Trütsch (2016) studied the impact of mobile payment on payment choice and found that mobile payment does not substitute physical payment methods such as cash and checks at the adoption stage.

In general, with the rising of mobile payment at the POS, the assumption is that the usage mobile payment will eventually be accepted. However, literature shows that in Africa, mobile payment at the point of purchase is very low. For example, Vodafone introduced mobile payment in South Africa but it failed. On the other hand, the level of robbery in many African countries is high. In that regard, it is likely that people would prefer to use mobile payment instead of physical cash.

Some of the studies, on the use of electronic payment at point of sales (ePOS) in Africa, focused on a number of different aspects. For example, studies that were conducted in Nigeria focused on the factors that influence consumers on using ePOS found that factors such as nativity, security, ease of use, availability, convenience, and intentions to use and complexity of technology play a great role (Adeoti &Oshotimehin, 2011).

Other studies focused on the factors that limit the usage of ePOS in Nigeria. For example, Adeoti (2013) found that power outrage, network failure, and limited number of ePOS machine limit the usage of POS tools. To minimize some of the challenges, such as a minimum number of ePOS, it is expected that the use of mobile payment at the point of sales would eventually be accepted by the business community. However, as we argued in the foregoing sections the acceptance is very low in many countries. Despite the fact that the studies do not show that cost is one of the strong factors, we believe that the cost is likely to be one of the strong factors. Another study conducted in Nigeria by Omotayo and Dahunsi (2015) found that the perceived ease of use has a significant impact on the use of machines by business organizations in the country. However, these studies paid less attention on the use of mobile technology as the tool that is used in POS. Furthermore, these studies paid less attention on the role of retailers as gatekeepers against the acceptance of technology. The current study focused on the preference of the retailer on ePOS the case of Tanzania.

Methodology

The study used a cross sectional research approach to investigate the acceptance of mobile payment at the point of sale (POS) by the retail store owners. Primary data were collected data and analyzed using quantitative analytical technique.

Development of a data collection tool

A questionnaire was developed to enable the collection of data. The used questionnaire was developed from empirical literature and theory that govern this study. Chou, Lee, and Chung (2004) argued that the development of a questionnaire on studies that focus on the usage of technology paid less attention on the influence of social and economic factors. Some of the studies conducted in Africa paid less attention on the price charges and on the usage of Internet payment (see Adeoti &Oshotimehin, 2011). The current study is in line with a study by Chou et al. (2004) that focused on understanding the preference of the usage of mobile payment technology in developing economies such as Tanzania.

In the development of questionnaire we were inspired by Chou et al. (2004), Krishen, Raschke, Close, and Kachroo (2017), Lee et al. (2012), and Davis et al. (1989). Issues that were picked were the intention to use (Davis et al., 1989;Lee et al., 2012), perceive ease of use and usefulness (Lee et al., 2012; Davis et al., 1989;Yen & Wu, 2016). Table 8.2 shows factors and authors who contributed to the development of the data collection tool.

The developed questionnaire had two parts: A and B. Part A was characterized by general information of the respondents and business information. Some of the issues which were asked in that part included the age of the respondents, life span of the firm, the form of business ownership, business that the firm deals with, how many people have been employed, knowledge on the mobile payment at the POS, usage of the mobile payment at POS and whether or not the company used or was using mobile payment. Part B of the questionnaire comprises the statement, the six-point Likert scale.

The questionnaire contained a six-point Likert scale with statements that measured fairness, perceived usefulness, perceived ease of use, and intention to use. The 26 itemized scales contain issues of fairness, attitudes towards marketing communication, cost, usefulness, and intention to use. Respondents were required to pick itemized scales from one to six; whereby one stands for *totally disagree* and six for *totally agree*.

Table 8.2 Some of the factors discussed in the previous studies

Author	Factor that influenced adoption of mobile payment
Chou et al.	Economic
Economilades and Jeziorski	Convenience
Davis et al., Sanchez-Prieto et al.	Perceived easy to use
Lee at al., Davis et al., Sanchez-Prieto et al.	Perceived usefulness
Krishne et al.	Fairness in charges

Sampling procedure and data collection techniques

Convenience sampling technique was used for data collection, because the technique is easy to administer and it was appropriate for the study that faced budget constraints (Nandonde, 2012; Malhotra et al., 2012;Zikmund, 2009). MBA-Agribusiness second year students were used as enumerators in data collection. Data were collected in Morogoro municipality. Morogoro was selected because it is the third region in the country with a good number of registered business operations (NBS, 2016). Furthermore, the region is ranked third after Dar es Salaam and Mbeya with 9,919 of the established firms in the country (NBS, 2016). According to NBS (2012), Morogoro municipality ranked second in the country as a town with a good number of private firms. The second reason for the selection of the study area is because the author is a resident in the area and this helped in minimizing traveling costs that might have been incurred during data collection.

Pilot survey was conducted and from the survey results, some amendments were made. Some of the changes made included the omission of an item on willingness of the user to pay more for the services. That question was deleted because it was difficult to be understood. The questionnaire was translated from English into Kiswahili. Three enumerators participated in the study and they were also involved in the direct translation of the questionnaire with the author before the data collection process.

Dependent variable

According to Hair, Black, Babin, and Anderson (2010), for an appropriate use of multiple regressions the selection of an dependent variable is very important. In the current study a dependent variable was used in multiple regression analysis in order to determine the usage of mobile payment among retail shop owners in Tanzania. We operationalized the usage of mobile payment in terms of the knowledge on the application of mobile payment as the means of transaction. As Hair et al. (2010) argues, the dependent variable should be nominal for multiple regressions to be an appropriate technique. Regarding the measure of *knowledge on the usage of mobile payment*, this variable was measured as nominal with category of one for *'YES I have used it'* or *'I have not used it.'*

Independent variables

Six factor scores were used as independent variables for multiple regression analysis to understand the determinant factors for the retailers' use of mobile payment instead of cash in Tanzania. The regression fitted was:

$$\text{MoPayUs} = a + b_1 FS_1 + b_2 FS_2 + b_3 FS_3 + b_4 FS_4 + b_5 FS_5 + b_6 FS_6 + e$$

Where, a is a regression constant, $b_1, b_2, b_3, b_4, b_5,$ and b_6 are the regression coefficient of the factor scores. FS is the factor scores and e is the error term.

Factors scores for each of the six variables as seen in Table 8.3 were calculated from the PCA results and used as independent variables in the multiple regression analysis.

Data analysis

The collected data were coded and analyzed using SPSS version 24. The factor analysis and multiple regression analysis were used for data analysis. Factor analysis was used as a reduction technique for variable approach.

Reliability and validity

To assess the psychometric of the measures, we first performed exploratory factor analysis. The Kaiser-Meyer-Olkin (KMO) measure of sampling adequacy was 0.876 and the Bartlett's test was significant at 0.000 level, indicating that the data matrix was sufficiently correlated to the factor analysis.

There is a debate on the acceptance threshold for the selection of the factors to be used in the analysis. Hair et al. (2010) suggest that for the selection of the loading factors that form factor scores, a researcher needs to consider a sample size too. The authors proposed a sample size range of 250 with a cutting point of .35 for factor loading. The current study has a sample size of 282; therefore we used conservative threshold of .50. This means that all factors loading with less than .50 were dropped for factor analysis stage. Table 8.3 shows six factors loaded significant with Eigen value greater than one were extracted and they explain 71.4% of the total variance. In addition, all factors were loaded significant. The six factors were named as informative education (factor one), intention to use (factor two), convenience (factor three), usability (factor four), cost (factor five), and privacy (factor six). All six factors were used for further analysis in the multiple regression analysis.

Checking for collinearity

The regression model was further tested for multicollinearity by examining collinearity statistics, the variance inflation factors (VIF), and tolerance. As a rule of thumb, if the VIF of variable exceed 10, that variable is said to be highly collinear and will pose a problem to regression analysis (Marquardt, 1970). The variables show VIF ranges from 1.460 to 7.714, which are below the threshold level.

Multiple regression analysis

Multiple regression analysis is a statistical technique that enables comparison between a continuous dependent variable and two or more continuous or discrete independent variables. The technique was used in prior mobile payment related studies with factor analysis (Shatskikh, 2013; Kishore &

Table 8.3 Factors that influence stand-alone retailers to use mobile payment at the point of sales

Variables	Components						h^2
	1	2	3	4	5	6	
Retailfair					.702		.581
Tax distribution was fair					.816		.712
Faircharges					.845		.776
Paying more					.753		.750
Helpserviceprovider					.623		.658
Taughtonhowtouse	.719						.709
Leafletswithenoughdetails	.838						.829
Educatetheircustomers	.856						.813
Motivatedbyleaflets	.859						.815
Advertisement	.869						.843
Leafletsmoreinformative	.806						.803
Botherme					−.556		.655
Locationinformation						.958	.898
Greatvalue					.601		.566
Usefulinmybus		.504					.656
Save a lot oftime			.640				.711
Easytolearn			.816				.798
Easytouse			.835				.832
Easytounderstand			.846				.863
Moresafethancash			.568				.685
Makesensetouse		.663					.680
Iwilluse		.891					.863
Recommendto		.870					.868
Encouragecustomertouse		.832					.797
Variance	39.11	10.23	9.05	5.10	4.07	3.78	
Eigen value	10.95	2.88	2.54	1.43	1.14	1.05	
Cum variance	39.11	49.43	58.46	63.55	67.62	71.37	

Sequeira, 2016; Wong, Tan, Ooi, & Lin, 2014). The technique is appropriate for use when there are multiple independent variables to predict single variable, (Hair et al., 2010).

The current study used multiple regression analysis to understand the factors that influence the usage of mobile payment among stand-alone retail owners in Tanzania. The six independent variables which were used for the study and shown in Table 8.3 were derived from factor analysis scores; and these were informative education (factor one), intention to use (factor two), convenience (factor three), usability (factor four), cost (factor five) and privacy (factor six).

Findings

Profile of the respondents

There were a total of 282 respondents surveyed in this study; among them 50.7% were males and the remaining were females (see Table 8.4). Although our finding shows a slightly lower figure of females than was the case in the previous country survey that shows that 54% of women in Tanzania are in the micro and small medium enterprises (NBS, 2012). The study findings show further that 56.4% of the respondents were aged between 26 and 45, followed by those in the age group of from 36 to 45 and these constituted 33.7%. About 52.8% of the respondents had primary education, 37% had

Table 8.4 Respondents' profile

Variable	Category	Percentage
Age	18–25	5.7
	26–35	56.4
	36–45	33.7
	46–55	4.3
	Above 55	0
Gender	Male	48.2
	Female	52.8
Education	No formal education	1.8
	Primary education	52.8
	Secondary education	37.9
	Certificate	1.1
	Diploma	3.2
	Bachelor	3.2
Number of employees	No employee	29.4
	1–4	68.4
	5–49	2.1
Years of Business Operations	1–5	79.4
	6–10	18.4
	11–15	1.8
	Above 16	.4
Forms of Business	Cooperative	2.8
	Sole proprietorship	91.8
	Company	2.8
	Partnership	1.8

secondary education, 3.2% had diploma, and another 3.2% had bachelor's degree. When respondents were asked as to whether or not they were aware of the system that allowed them to use mobile payment at the point of sales instead of cash, 95.7% indicated to have been aware of the system. When the respondents were asked whether or not they used mobile payment at the point of sales, 52.8% indicated to have been using the technology.

As for the companies' profiles, about 64.8% of the firms that participated in the study were those that employed one to four workers, 6% were those that employed 5 to 49 employees, and 29.4% were those that employed none. The firms that participated in the study dealt with different business activities from food selling to hair dressing. About 23.4% of the firms dealt with retail food stores, followed by 9.6% that dealt with motor cycle spare parts, 7.4%, dealt with clothes, 6.4% dealt with electrical items, and 5% dealt with kitchen appliances. In general, other respondents comprised less that 5%. According to NBS (2012) many of the firms in Tanzania are at micro level as presented in the study.

The current study involved firms with different forms of proprietorship. Sole proprietorship comprised 91.8% and cooperative and limited companies comprised 2.8% of the total firms studied. In general, 79.4% of the respondents stayed in the business for less than five years, 18.4% stayed in the business between six and ten years, and the remained percentage were those who stayed in business for more than11 years.

Findings of regression analysis

Table 8.5 represents the model for multiple regressions that shows the R^2 is .456 and R is .675.

Table 8.7 shows that cost (factor five) and privacy (factor six) are not significant at 0.05 with the mobile payment usage. Furthermore, 45% of the mobile payment is accounted for by these factors. Factors scores on

Table 8.5 Model summary

Model	R	R^2	Adjusted R Square	SE of the Estimate
1	.675	.456	.444	.37295

Table 8.6 ANOVA

Model	SE	Df	Mean square	F	Sig.
Regression	32.023	6	5.337	38.373	.000
Residual	38.250	275	.139		
Total	70.273	281			

Table 8.7 Regression values

Model	Unstandardised coefficients		Standardized coefficients	t	Sig.
	B	SE	B		
(Constant)	1.472	.022		66.264	.000
Education	–.282	.022	–.565	–12.694	.000
Intentiontouse	–.075	.022	–.150	–3.379	.001
Convenience	.152	.022	.304	6.842	.000
Usability	–.069	.022	–.139	–3.120	.002
Cost	–.010	.022	–.021	–.471	.638
Privacy	.021	.022	.042	.951	.342

education (factor one), intention to use (factor two), usability (factor four), and cost (factor five) have a negative sign that means that the use of mobile payment as a tool that facilitates exchange at the point of sales would decrease as the value of the scores increase.

In general, the study indicates that for convenience shop owners to accept mobile payment at the point of sales, more informative education is needed. The information can be on how to use and access the services at the registered stores. Another factor that scores negative is the cost which indicates that in general users are cost conscious and therefore the services providers should consider some of the transaction costs associated with the operations. The general assumption is that if someone can receive cash at no cost or has other alternatives means of payment, then the chances of using those services are very low.

Factor five, which is cost, is not a significant factor in influencing shop owners to use mobile payment at point of sales. In general currently in Tanzania, service providers do not charge the users for the transaction services. Another factor, which is not significant, is the privacy. In general, store owners do not find mobile payment at point of sales as violating their privacy.

Discussion and conclusion

The current study measures the acceptance of mobile payment at the point of sale; although previous studies have applied TAM model on the acceptance of mobile payment and technology in general (e.g., Davis et al., 1989; Venkatash & Davis, 1996), there is limited research that dealt with the acceptance of mobile payment at the point of sale in Africa with a focus on stand-alone retailers. The study applied TAM model to understand acceptance of stand-alone retailers on perceived ease to use and perceived usefulness in the context of stand-alone retail stores in Tanzania.

The findings of the study demonstrated that the extended TAM model has satisfactory fit with the data and that the dimensions that underlie the theory have significant impact on the retailers' perception on the usefulness. The study shows that the effect of cost on the acceptance of mobile payment is insignificant. This finding is contrast with the findings in the previous studies which show that costs have an impact on the acceptance of a new technology (see Economilades & Jeziorski, 2016). This is perhaps due to the current market practices where no charges are made on the transaction conducted at the authorized merchant. However, Tanzania is regarded as one with highest tax of 36% in Sub-Saharan Africa (Financial Times, 2017). Furthermore, studies show that cost has a negative correlation with the usage of mobile payment. That means that if the cost increases there is also a likelihood of a decrease in usage.

This study finding showed a significant relationship between usage and some of the factor scores such as informative education, intention to use, convenience, and usability. The study shows that there is a significance relationship between the intention to use factor scores and the usage of mobile payment at the point of sale. This finding is consistent with the finding in previous studies on the perceived intention to use (e.g., Davis et al., 1989; Liebana-Cabanillas, de Luna, & Montoro-Rios, 2017). This relationship shows that there is a likely chance for success of using mobile device to facilitate payment at the point of sales.

Furthermore, convenience emerged to be one of the significant factors that influence the usage of mobile payment by retailers in Tanzania. Our findings correlates with the findings of studies by Economilades and Jeziorski (2016) and Chogo and Sedoyeaka (2015) who found that convenience is one of the factors that influence the usage of mobile phones in Tanzania. This was stimulated with the desire of minimizing the risk of walking with a huge amount of money.

Limitation and managerial implications

Our work focused on the factors that influence the usage of mobile device at the point of sales in Tanzania with the case of stand-alone retailers and its importance to other developing economies. However, our study has some of the limitations; for example, we did not look at the role of employees on the acceptance of mobile payment. Furthermore, we did not focus on other forms of transaction such as the use of debit cards which has emerged in Tanzania. In spite of these limitations, our findings have some important implications for managerial considerations. One is the need for more informative education to users. The use of a mobile phone as a tool at the point of sales seems to be increasing in developing economies, however, more education should be provided by mobile service providers. The current study has shown that informative education has a significant relationship and the factor scores comprise elements such as the use of leaflets and other means for communication. So it is more important for companies to engage in informative marketing strategies to influence the use of the technology among retailers.

Another area that has an impact on the managerial consideration of the mobile payment in Tanzania is the fact that the cost is not significant. But the finding shows that the factor has a negative relationship with the usage of mobile payment which means that an increase of the cost will lead to a decrease on the usage.

Areas for further studies

Africa's economy is dominated by convenience stores that are family owned and most of these stores are a source of employment. Therefore, it is very important to understand the effects of the impact of family business on the usage of mobile payment in the continent. Furthermore, further studies can also focus on understanding the demographic background of the employees and the acceptance of the mobile payment as a means that facilitates exchange in developing economies. In general, the studies on the acceptance of mobile payment which were conducted in Tanzania and developing economies seem to have been dominated by TAM model (see Anthony & Mutalemwa, 2014) and UTAUT model (see Taluka & Masele, 2016). Furthermore, these studies relied extensively on the use of quantitative method. We propose future studies should use other theories such as the choice and diffusion of innovation theories to understand consumer preference on the emergence of these new technologies. Also, future studies can use qualitative method to study consumers' behavior on the use of mobile payment technique in the country.

Contribution to body of knowledge

The contribution of the current study to the body of knowledge on this area revolves around identification of factors that have an impact on the preferences of the retailers on the usage of mobile device at the point of sales (POS). This is because studies on the impact of mobile payment on the usage of mobile payment are lacking in Tanzania

By using the TAM model, the current study has shown information has some influence on the model, something that is not featuring in many previous studies. In this study, we managed to add the informative factors such as the use of leaflets and marketing promotion tools to show how these factors influence the usage of the new technology.

Acknowledgment

I would like to thank MBA-Agribusiness students for their assistance in data collection, namely, they are Ruth Mbilinyi, Joyce Lyimo, and Monica Kiverege.

References

Adeoti, O. O. (2013). Challenges to the efficient use of point of sale (POS) terminal in Nigeria. *African Journal of Business Management, 7*(28), 2801–2806.

Adeoti, O. O., & Oshotimehin, K. O. (2011). Factors influencing consumers adoption of point of sale terminal in Nigeria. *Journal of Emerging Trends in Economics and Management Sciences, 2*(5), 2141–7024.

Anthony, D., & Mutalemwa, D. K. (2014). Factors influencing the use of mobile payments in Tanzania: Insights from Zantel, Z-Pesa services. *The Journal of Language, Technology and Entrepreneurship in Africa, 5*(2), 69–90.

Chale, p. R., & Mbamba, U. (2015). The role of mobile money services on growth of small scale and medium enterprises in Tanzania: Evidence from Kinondoni district in Dar es Salaam. *Business Management Review*, 88–91.

Chogo, p. J., & Sedoyeka, E. (2015). Exploring the factors affecting mobile money adoption in Tanzania. *International Journal of Computing and ICT Research, 8*(2), 53–64.

Chou, Y., Lee, C., & Chung, J. (2004). Understanding m-commerce system through the analytic hierarchy process. *Journal of Business Research, 57*, 1423–1430.

Cox, D. N. & Evans, G. (2008). Construction and validation of psychometric scale of measure consumers' fears on novel food technologies: The food technology neophobia scale. *Food Quality ad Preference, 19*(8), 704–710.

The Citizen. (2015). *Number of world mobile money users hits 100m.* Retrieved August 20, 2017, from www.thecitizen.co.tz/News/Business/Number-of-world-mobile-money-users-hits-100m/1840414-2680216-ca0lqmz/index.html

Davis, F. D., Bagozzi, R. P., & Warshaw, p. R. (1989). User acceptance of computer technology: A comparison of two theoretical models. *Management Science, 35*(8), 982–1003.

Davis, F. (1986). *Perceived usefullness, perceived ease of use and user acceptance of information systems: Theory and results.* Unpublished doctoral dissertation, Massachussetts Institute of Technology.

Di Castri, S., & Gidvani, L. (2014). *Enabling mobile money policies in Tanzania.* London: GSMA. Retrieved July 20, 2017, from www.gsma.com/mobilefor development/wp-content/uploads/2014/03/Tanzania-Enabling-Mobile-Money-Policies.pdf

Economilades, N., & Jeziorski, p. (2016). *Mobile money and Tanzania.* Retrieved August 20, 2019, from www.stern.nyu.edu/networks/Mobile_Money.pdf

FSDT. (2012). *Micro and small medium enterprises in Tanzania in Tanzania.* Retrieved August 20, 2017, from www.fsdt.or.tz/wp-content/uploads/2016/05/MSME-National-Baseline-Survey-Report.pdf

Fujimoto, Y., Ferdous, A. S., Sekigunchi, T., & Sugianto, L. (2016). The effect of mobile technology usage on work engagement and emotional exhaustion in Japan. *Journal of Business Research, 69*, 3315–3323.

Hair, J. F., Black, W. C., Babin, B. J., & Anderson, R. E. (2010). *Multivariate data analysis: A global perspective* (7th ed.). London: Pearson Prentice Hall.

IFC. (2015). *M-money channel distribution case of Tanzania: Vodacom Tanzania M-PESA.* Retrieved August 20, 2017, from www.ifc.org/wps/wcm/connect/3aa858 8049586050a27ab719583b6d16/Tool+6.8.+Case+Study+-+M-PESA,+Tanzania. pdf?MOD=AJPERES

Kim, Y. G., & Woo, E. (2016). Consumer acceptance of quick response (QR) code for the food traceability system: Application of an extended technology acceptance model (TAM). *Food Research International, 85,* 266–272.

Kishore, S. V. K., & Sequeira, A. H. (2016, January–March). An empirical investigation on mobile banking service adoption in rural Karnataka. *Sage Open,* 1–21.

Krishen, A. S., Raschke, R. L., Close, A. G., & Kachroo, p. (2017). A power-responsibility equilibrium framework for fairness: Understanding consumers' implicit privacy concerns for location-based services. *Journal of Business Research, 73,* 20–29.

Lee, Y., Park, J., Chung, N., & Blakeney, A. (2012). A unified perspective on the factors influencing usage intention toward mobile financial services. *Journal of Business Research, 65,* 1590–1599.

Liebana-Cabanillas, F., de Luna, I. R., & Montoro-Rios, F. (2017). Intention to use mobile payment systems: A comparative analysis of SMS and NFS payments. *Economic Research: EkonomskaInstrazivanja, 30*(1), 891–910.

Lwoga, E. T., & Lwoga, N. B. (2017). User acceptance of mobile payment: The effects of user-centric, security, system characteristics and gender. *The Electronic Journal of Information Systems in Developing Countries, 81*(3), 1–24.

Malhotra, N. K., Birks, D. F., & Wills, p. A. (2012). *Marketing Research: An Applied Approach* (4th ed.). Harlow: Prentice Hall.

Marquardt, D. W. (1970). Generalized inverses, ridge regression and linear estimation. *Technometrics, 12,* 591–612.

Mason, C. H., & Perreault, W. D. (1991). Collinearity, power, and interpretation of multiple regression analysis. *Journal of Marketing, 28*(3), 268–280.

Mbele, L. (2016). *Why M-pesa failed in South Africa.* Retrieved August 20, 2017, from www.bbc.com/news/world-africa-36260348

Mramba, N., Sutinen, E., Haule, M., & Msami, p. (2014). Survey of mobile phone usage patterns among street vendors in Dar es Salaam city in Tanzania. *International Journal of Information Technology and Business Management, 28*(1), 1–10.

Mugwe, D. (2013, December). Tanzania's mobile pay transaction hit $ 11.1bn. *The East-African,* 11. Retrieved January 20, 2017, from www.theeastafrican.co.ke/business/Tanzania-s-mobile-pay-transactions-hit-11-1bn/2560-2108370-smt0taz/index.html

Mwanjelwa, S., & Nandonde, F. (2014). Exploring factors that influence students to buy ringtones in Tanzania. *The International Journal of Business and Public Management, 3*(1), 1–9.

Nandonde, F. A. (2012). Consumer's reactions towards involvement of large retailers in selling fair trade coffee: The case of the United Kingdom. *The Ethiopian Journal of Business Economics, 2*(2), 66–93.

Nandonde, F. A., & Kuada, J. (2014, June). *Empirical studies of food retailing in developing economies.* International Food Symposium Research (pp. 19–20), at Aarhus Business School, Denmark.

Nandonde, F. A., & Kuada, J. (2016). International firms in Africa's food retail distribution and research agenda. *International Journal of Retail & Distribution Management, 44*(4), 448–464.

NBS. (2016). *Statistical business register report, 2014–2015: Tanzania mainland.* Retrieved August 20, 2017, from www.nbs.go.tz/nbs/takwimu/Br/2014_15_SBR.pdf

NBS. (2012). *National baseline survey report: Micro small & medium enterprises in Tanzania.* Retrieved August 20, 2017, from http://www.fsdt.or.tz/wp-content/uploads/2016/05/MSME-National-Baseline-Survey-Report.pdf

Omotayo, F., & Dahunsi, O. (2015). Factors affecting adoption of point of sales terminal by business organization in Nigeria. *International Journal of Academic Research in Business Social Science, 5*(10), 115–136.

PwC. (2016). *Emerging markets driving the payments transformation.* Retrieved July 20, 2017, from www.pwc.com/vn/en/publications/2016/pwc-emerging-markets-report.pdf

Reuters. (2017, February 14). *Tanzania's mobile phone subscribers up 0.9 pct in 2016,.* Retrieved August 20, 2018, from https://af.reuters.com/article/idAFL8N1FZ0YO

Sanchez-Prieto, J. C., Olmos-Miguelanaz, S., & Garcia-Pelnavo, F. J. (2016). Informal tools in formal contacts: Development of a model to assess the acceptance of mobile technologies among teachers. *Computer Human Sciences, 55*, 519–528.

Shaikh, A. A., & Karjaluoto, H. (2016). *Mobile banking services continuous usage: Case of Finland.* Hawaii International Conference of System Sciences, pp. 1497–1506.

Shatskikh, A. (2013). *Consumer acceptance of mobile payments in restaurants.* Unpublished Master of Science in Hospitality, University of South Florida.

Stroborn, K., Heitmann, A., Leibold, K., & Frank, G. (2004). Internet payment in Germany: A classificatory framework and empirical evidence. *Journal of Business Research, 57*, 1431–1437.

Szopinski, T. S. (2016). Factors affecting the adoption of online banking in Poland. *Journal of Business Research, 69*, 4763–4768.

Taluka, E., & Masele, J. J. (2016). Influence of perceived trust in rural consumer mobile payment service adoption: And understanding of moderation effects of gender and age. *Business Management Review, 19*(2), 66–81.

TanzaniaInvest. (2017). *Mobile money transactions in Tanzania reach TZS 50 trillion in 2016–2017.* Retrieved August 20, 2017, from www.tanzaniainvest.com/telecoms/mobile-money-transactions-2016-2017

Tossy, T. (2012). Modelling the adoption of mobile payment system for primary and secondary school student examination fees in developing countries: Tanzanian experience. *International Journal of Information Technology and Business Management, 27*(1), 1–12.

Trütsch, T. (2016). The impact of mobile payment on payment choice. *Financial Markets and Portfolio Management, 30*(3), 299–336.

URT. (2011). *Tanzania communication regulatory authority: Annual report.* Retrieved August 20, 2017, from www.tcra.go.tz/images/documents/reports/TCRA%202011%20Annual%20Report%202010-2011.pdf

Venkatash, V., & Davis, F. D. (1996). A model of antecedents of perceived ease of use: Development and test. *Decision Science, 27*(3), 451–481.

Wong, C., Tan, G. W., Ooi, K., & Lin, B. (2014). Mobile shopping: The next frontier of the shopping industry? AN emerging market perspective. *International Journal of Mobile Communication, 13*(1).

Kim, Y. G., & Woo, E. (2016). Consumer acceptance of a quick response (QR) code for the food traceability system: Application of an extended technology acceptance model (TAM). *Food Research International, 85*(1), 32–48.

Yen, Y., & Wu, F. (2016). Predicting the adoption of mobile financial services: The impact of perceived mobility and personal habit. *Computers in Human Behaviour*, 65, 31–42.

Yueh, H., Lu, M., & Lin, W. (2016). Employees acceptance of mobile technology in a workplace: An empirical study using SEM and fsQCA. *Journal of Business Research*, 69, 2318–2324.

Zikmund, W. G. (2009). *Business research methods*. New Delhi: Cengage Learning.

9 The emergence of Indian mobile payments market

An institutional perspective

Sudhanshu Shekhar,* Shounak Basak and Bhupesh Manoharan

Introduction

Marketing scholars are increasingly interested in the dynamics of market creation and change (Dolbec & Fischer, 2015; Humphreys, 2010a). There are two prominent streams of research in this domain – one that views market creation as a firm-driven process (e.g., Humphreys, 2010b; Ingram & Inman, 1996; Patvardhan, Gioia, & Hamilton, 2015) and another that views market creation as a consumer-driven process (e.g., Martin & Schouten, 2014; Dolbec & Fischer, 2015). However, in emphasizing the role of either firms or consumers, extant research fails to recognize the interactive nature of market creation. We are of the view that both firms and consumers are important actors in market creation. In order to gain a comprehensive understanding of market emergence, we need to conceptualize market emergence as a dynamic process in which both firms and consumers perform important work. Further, as a result of the myopic focus on either firms or consumers, extant research has not paid due attention to other relevant factors such as regulators who also play a critical role in market creation. Regulators play an important role by setting the rules for inter-firm competition and firm-consumer interactions. In this chapter we analyze the emergence of the India mobile payments market which took place as a result of dynamic interaction between firms, regulators, and consumers.

Institutional theory is increasingly being used by marketing scholars to shed light on a variety of marketing phenomenon (Hult, Ketchen, & Hult, 2011). In this chapter, we conceptualize the Indian mobile payments market as an institutional field and analyze its emergence by drawing upon the theoretical tools from institutional theory. Mobile payments are specialized mobile financial services that allow consumers to transfer money from one account to another with the aid of mobile phones. The last decade has witnessed the growth of mobile payments in India. We investigate the role of various actors such as banking firms, nonbanking firms, regulators, and consumers in the emergence and growth of this field. Of special interest to us is the role of contradictory institutional logics (Friedland & Alford, 1991) in the emergence of this field. We show as to how the contradiction and collaboration between banking and telecom companies, both of which were driven by the respective logics of secure and inclusive payments, played a major role in the emergence of mobile payments in India. We further elaborate the institutional work (Lawrence & Suddaby, 2006) performed by macro (firms, regulators) and micro (retailers, end consumers) actors in the emergence of the field.

We draw upon a qualitative study to analyze the development of Indian mobile payment field. The Reserve Bank of India (RBI) published its first monograph on payment systems in India in 1998. This paved the way for the emergence of mobile payments field in India. The traditional commercial banks were the first movers in this segment of mobile-based financial services. Several public and private sector banks such as State Bank of India (SBI), HDFC and ICICI launched their mobile payment services with different telecom operators as their business correspondents. More recently, the demonetization of 500 and 1,000 rupee currency notes (1,000 rupees is equivalent to 15.63 USD approximately) in November 2016 gave a fillip to mobile payments. The year 2016 also saw the opening of first payments bank in India. With the opening of payment banks, nonbanking companies such as telecom operators and postal service providers have come to occupy the center stage in the field. The individual consumer has been another important actor shaping the emergence of this field. The ability of the consumers to adjust to changing systems and learn the new technology for payments, which can be termed as mobile literacy, has played a crucial role in the emergence of this field.

The chapter is divided into six sections. The first section gives the theoretical background and introduces the concept of institutional field, institutional logic, and institutional work. The second section provides a detailed descriptive narrative on the evolution of mobile payments in India. The next section discusses as to how the conflicting institutional logic of banking (security) and telecom (inclusiveness) has shaped the emergence of Indian mobile payments field. The fourth section explores the institutional work done by important macro (e.g., banking companies, telecom operators) and micro actors (e.g., retailers, consumers). The fifth section discusses the theoretical implications of the findings, and the last section concludes the chapter. The policy implications of the study and suggestions for future research are described in the conclusion section.

Theoretical background

The neo-institutional theory provides a powerful framework to study the emergence of new markets (Dolbec & Fischer, 2015). It provides important theoretical tools to analyze the role of different actors involved in the emergence of new markets. In this section we explain the three important theoretical tools from institutional theory – institutional field, institutional logic, and institutional work – that we have deployed in this chapter to analyze the emergence of mobile payments in India.

Institutional field

Institutional fields include "organizations that in an aggregate constitute a recognized area of institutional life: key suppliers, resource and product consumers, regulatory agencies, and other organizations that produce similar services or products" (DiMaggio & Powell, 1983, p. 148). The field demarcates a recognized area of social life. It consists of actors who share meanings, rules, and norms that regulate their actions (Scott, 2014). The actors in the field interact more frequently and purposefully with each other than with those outside the field. The interaction of the actors in the field leads to the development of shared norms among the actors in the field. The institutional theory scholars further point to the important role played by the State in delimiting and defining the field. The legitimacy provided by the State through legislations and regulations are important criteria that confer legitimacy to the organizational field.

The field approach allows us to study the role of different actors, both macro actors such as regulators and micro actors such as consumers, in the emergence of new fields or markets. The early studies on the emergence of new fields emphasized the role of single institutional entrepreneurs. Institutional entrepreneurs were conceptualized as hyper-masculine who could overcome the coercive, mimetic, and normative pressures in the field and act in ways that differ from other actors of the field (Battilana, Leca, & Boxenbaum, 2009). However, recent studies have taken a more pragmatic view of the field change. These studies argue that the process of institutional change is a more complex process and involves a host of actors who populate the field. The institutional change may not be always brought about individual powerful actors but can also take place as a result of the collaborative and competitive interaction of a multiplicity of actors. The action performed by these individual actors to bring about institutional change is what is referred to as institutional work.

Institutional work

Institutional work is the "purposive action of individuals and organizations aimed at creating, maintaining and disrupting institutions" (Lawrence & Suddaby, 2006, p. 215). The concept grew out of the efforts to bring back agency in institutional theory (DiMaggio, 1988) and highlighted the role of purposive human action in bringing about institutional change. The actors in an institutional field, though embedded in the normative and cognitive environment of the field are endowed with agency. The work performed by these actors plays a major role in perpetuation as well as changes in the existing field. For example, Dolbec and Fischer (2015) highlighted the important institutional work performed by consumers in maintaining the existing norms in the field of fashion. On the other hand, Zietsma and Lawrence (2010) studied the role of institutional work in the transformation of the field of forestry in British Columbia. Similarly, Gawer and Phillips (2013) highlighted the role of institutional work in enabling institutional logic changes. Following the last study on logic change, we analyze the institutional work aimed at balancing the conflicting field level logics and its implication for market creation.

Institutional logic

Institutional logics are a socially and historically constructed organizing principle of institutions (Friedland & Alford, 1991). They consist of a set of symbolic constructions and material practices that enables institutional actors to give meaning to the social reality. Institutional logic includes the "assumptions, values, beliefs, rules by which individuals produce and reproduce their material subsistence and organize time and space" (Thornton & Ocasio, 1999, p. 804). These act as both constraining and enabling factor in guiding the action of institutional actors. Institutional logics are also an important factor in bringing about institutional change. Especially, the existence of multiple contradictory institutional logics at the field level can give impetus to institutional and field change (Seo & Creed, 2002). In different studies, scholars have analyzed how the contradiction in institutional logic leads to institutional change. For example, Lounsbury (2007) analyzed how the competing logic of trusteeship and performance led to new practice creation in the mutual fund industry. Similarly, Reay and Hinings (2005) analyzed the changes in the health care industry that resulted due to the contradictions between the institutional logic of professionalism and business in the field of health care. We draw upon these studies to explore and analyze how the contradictory institutional logics has played a major role in the emergence of mobile payments field in India.

Method

Data collection

Our first source of data was newspaper reports. In order to trace the development of mobile payments market we consulted the newspaper reports related to mobile payment from 1998 to 2016. We used the Factiva newspaper database for this purpose. We searched the database for the keyword "mobile payment" and got a list of 94,401 articles. We manually went through these articles and selected 688 relevant articles for further analysis. The articles were selected based on research objective of tracing the logic changes in the mobile payment industry. The second sources of data were reports relating to mobile payments by government agencies such as Reserve Bank of India (RBI) and Telecom Regulatory Authority of India (TRAI). The other sources of data were reports by private consultancy agencies such as Deloitte and Boston Consulting Group. In addition to the various documentary sources that we utilized for tracing the historical development of the mobile payment industry, we also interviewed 18 users of mobile payment applications. These included both end consumers (12) and retailers (six). The interviews were semi-structured and each of the interviews lasted between 30 and 60 minutes.

Data analysis

The data was analyzed based on the guidelines of process theorization (Langley, 1999). The first step was to construct a database of important textual extracts from interviews and documents that showed the evolution of mobile payments market. From the database, we constructed a chronology of important events. The chronology enabled us to write a descriptive narrative of the evolution of mobile payments in India from 1998 to 2016. This narrative forms the first part of findings and has been detailed in the next section on "Evolution of mobile payments in India." The next phase of analysis consisted of coding the narrative in terms of theoretically relevant themes (Gioia, Corley, & Hamilton, 2012). Drawing upon the institutional perspective, we coded the texts in the database in theoretical terms. During this phase, there was constant comparison and iteration between the theoretical literature and the data (Corbin & Strauss, 2008). The final themes emerged after multiple iterations of comparisons between theory and data.

Evolution of mobile payments in India

The journey of mobile payments evolution in India can be divided into four phases.

1   Emergence of mobile banking and payments: 1998–2003
2   Formation of specialized mobile payment companies: 2004–2010
3   Growth of mobile payment companies: 2011–2014
4   Formation of payment banks: 2015-present

These phases are based on the chronology of events that brought about the revolution of mobile payment services in India. Each of these phases has its own characteristics and has made definitive contributions in the evolution of mobile payments in India. A brief overview of these phases is presented next.

Emergence of mobile banking and payments: 1998–2003

The beginning of mobile payments in India was made in the year 1998 when Reserve Bank of India, the monetary regulator, published its first monograph on the payments systems in India. The monograph highlighted the status of electronic payments in the country till date. Till then retail electronic fund transfer (EFT) which enabled a consumer to transfer funds to another person having an account with the commercial bank were active only in four metropolitan cities of India, namely Delhi, Kolkata, Chennai, and Mumbai. It was also in the year 1998 that Housing Development Finance Corporation (HDFC) bank started its initiative to accept utility bills such as telephone and electricity bills through its Automated Teller Machines (ATMs). This marked the beginning of electronic payments revolution in India. HDFC bank collaborated with telecom operator Hutchison Max to provide mobile banking in the form of balance inquiry, requesting mini statements, and check books. The customers could avail the facilities by sending a short message (SMS) to the bank through their Hutchison Max mobile phones (Business Line, 1999). Other banks like ICICI Bank and Federal Bank followed suit. The bank even floated a stand-alone company ICICI Infotech Services Ltd. to design the software and technological support for these services. Similarly, Federal Bank collaborated with software company Infosys and launched the net-banking and telephone bill payment services in collaboration with telecom companies Escotel and BPL Mobile (Sanandakumar, 2000). It can be noted that this period witnessed the beginning of online bill payments and rudimentary online banking services (The Times of India, 2002).

Formation of specialized mobile payment companies: 2004–2010

This period witnessed a shift from a mere collaboration between banks and telecom operators to the establishment of specialized mobile payment companies. The growth of mobile subscriber base in India during this period gave a boost to the creation of such companies. The mobile subscriber base during the period rose from 33.69 million in 2004 to 584.32 million in 2010 (Telecom Regulatory Authority of India, 2011). Passage of Payment and Settlement Systems Act in the year 2007 provided the regulatory framework for electronic payments (Reserve Bank of India, 2016a). Another significant change was the introduction of core banking which led to the electronic interconnection of bank branches. This period also marked the introduction of mobile wallets (explained in next subsection) in India (Business Line, 2004a, 2004c). One of the significant entrants in this domain was ICICI bank which launched the mCheck services in collaboration with Visa and Airtel (Business Line, 2005). The service could be used to purchase goods in retail stores. The service was greatly expanded over the years with Airtel entering into a partnership with other banks and online/off-line retail outlets. The chairman of mCheck commented on the popularity of this service among the consumers in initial days:

> The initial response has been very encouraging. Users have been proactively using mCheck for transactions such as postpaid bill payments/prepaid top-up. We have tied up with Airtel and will be announcing tie-ups with other mobile service providers shortly. We also work closely with banks including ICICI, HDFC, State Bank of India, Citibank and Corporation Bank and will be adding more banks in the coming days.
>
> (Murali, 2008)

Table 9.1 Active mobile payment companies

C-sam in partnership with Tata Consultancy Services
Seges (an Indian consultancy firm) used the Slovenian mobile payment technology M-Pay
Mcheck launched by ICICI Bank in collaboration with Visa
Paymate (Indian company founded in 2006)
Tarang (Indian company launched in 2009)
Tyfone partnered with Satyam (Indian software company)
Oxigen (Norwegian mobile payments company)
Obopay (US based company) partnered with Yes Bank (Indian Bank) to launch mobile wallet

Table 9.1 provides a list of mobile payment companies active in this period (Business Line, 2004b). New mobile-based services such as recharging of the prepaid accounts was also introduced in this period. Airtel, in collaboration with banks such as Citibank, HDFC, UTI, IDBI, and SBI, was the first one to launch such a service in 2004 (M2 Presswire, 2004). Telecom operators collaborated with individual firms to provide mobile payment gateways to their customers. For instance, Reliance Infocom (a telecom operator in India) joined hands with Indian Airlines (government owned airlines of India) to introduce the first mobile-based booking of airline tickets.

Another important development during this period was related to the security of mobile payments. The security issue was prominently raised in various seminars and conferences organized on mobile payments. Due to the security concerns, RBI only permitted the operation of semi-closed wallets (explained in the next subsection).

Growth of mobile payment companies: 2011–2014

This period was marked by competition between the banks and mobile operators in the mobile payment field. The telecom operators became increasingly active and launched a variety of mobile-based financial services, in addition to mobile payments, to woo the large unbanked population in India. This led to increased regulatory concerns about the role of telecom operators as financial service providers. However, the rapid rise of mobile-based financial services had the advantage of coverage and scalability. The banks were constrained by their limited rural presence whereas the telecom operators were able to cater to even the most far flung areas of the country. Already, telecom operators had been hugely successful in turning India into the fastest-growing telecom market with 900 million users (one-third of them in rural areas). Based on this, Reserve Bank of India approved 50 banks to provide mobile-based banking services to enable rural outreach of financial services. However, Reserve Bank of India did not allow the telecom

Table 9.2 Active firms providing mobile financial services

Bharti Airtel, mCheck India Payment Systems
PayMate India, State Bank of India
Vodafone India, ICICI Bank
HDFC, Canvas M Technologies, Netxcell
Yes Bank
Bharat Sanchar Nigam
Union Bank of India
Obopay Mobile Technology India
Axis Bank

---

operators to launch their mobile wallets without partnering with Banks (Kar, 2012). This move, on the part of regulator, was driven by security concerns of the consumers. The proponents of mobile-based financial services criticized this move. The consumers, however, were increasingly becoming comfortable with the mobile-based financial services. As per a contemporary survey, 64% Indian respondents used mobile phones for making payments, as compared to 66% Chinese respondents, 30% US respondents, and 23% UK respondents in 2012 (Trak.in, 2012).

MasterCard, working in collaboration with Comviva, Sybase 365, and Utiba, announced the MasterCard Mobile Money Partnership program in 2012 to cater to more than 2.5 billion financially underserved people of India (India Retail News, 2012). MasterCard predicted great prospects for mobile payments in India based on the demographic advantage and the overall telecom infrastructure (Joshi, 2012). Table 9.2 shows the major players engaged in mobile financial services in this period.

In a turn of events, the Reserve Bank of India approved many companies to provide mobile wallet facilities in 2013 (The Financial Express, 2013). The mobile wallet is a way to use the mobile phone in lieu of the plastic cards to carry out monetary transactions. That is to say, consumers can use the smartphone or tablet to pay the retailer while making a purchase, instead of cash or credit/debit card. These firms providing mobile wallet facility aspired to provide simple money services for all users. Small businesses needed to adapt to the changing requirement of accepting money through the mobile wallets to relieve customers from the hassles of hard cash. From the urban high-rises to the rural landscape, mobile payments allowed everybody to complete a secure and assured transaction with the help of a mobile phone. Many of the cash-based transactions were increasingly replaced by electronic payments. For example, before this period, every trip in an Ola Cab (a popular app based Taxi service in India) was paid in cash, while the advent of Ola money changed the landscape. The mobile wallet also replaced debit/credit cards with the smartphone (Wood, 2014). Table 9.3 lists some of the mobile wallet companies active in India during this period.

Table 9.3 Types of mobile wallet companies in India

Four types of mobile wallets in India		
Type of wallet	*Features*	*Example*
Open wallet	• Allow customers to buy goods and services • Withdraw Cash at ATMs or Banks • Transfer Funds	M-Pesa by Vodafone and ICICI
Semi-open wallet	• Allows to transact with merchants in contract with the service provider • Money transfer from Airtel money wallet to any bank account or another Airtel money wallet • Cannot withdraw Cash	Airtel Money
Semi-closed wallet	• Can be used for transactions for goods and services including financial services at select merchant locations that have contract with the wallet provider • No cash withdrawal or redemption	Paytm, Mobikwik
Closed wallet	• For in-house transactions with the merchant only • No cash withdrawal or redemption	Amazon Pay Balance

Formation of payment banks: 2015–2017

Formation of payment banks is the defining phenomenon of this period. Payments bank is a concept mooted by the Reserve Bank of India. It has approved a set of telecom and mobile payment companies to provide basic banking services to their customers, such as savings/current account and remittance and bill payment facilities. The payments banks are, however, barred from providing a credit of any sort including loans and credit cards. The business model of payment banks relies on transaction and merchant fees. Essentially, the business model is based on high volume and low value of such transactions. The participation of telecom operators as payment banks is expected to increase the banking coverage in the country. The optimism is justified to some extent keeping in view the existing large consumer base of telecomm companies. Table 9.4 lists the payments banks approved by Reserve Bank of India.

The Reserve Bank of India has stipulated the payments bank to service the rural unbanked populace. The general idea behind the formation of payments banks was to increase the reach of the banking system to the remote corners of the country which was left out by the current commercial banking system (Robello & Roy, 2015). With the aim of keeping their operating costs low, payments bank outlets have adopted a light asset model without large physical branches.

Table 9.4 Approved payments banks in India

Reliance Industries Limited (one of largest industrial agglomerates in India)
Paytm (mobile wallet)
Sun Pharma founder Dilip Shantilal Shanghvi (who partnered with Telenor and IDFC)
Fino Paytech (a payments company)
Department of Posts (postal service of Indian government)
Cholamandalam Distribution services (a financial services company)
National Securities Depository Limited (Indian central securities depository)
Aditya Birla Nuvo (fashion and lifestyle company)
Tech Mahindra (software service company)
Airtel (telecom operator)
Vodafone (telecom operator)

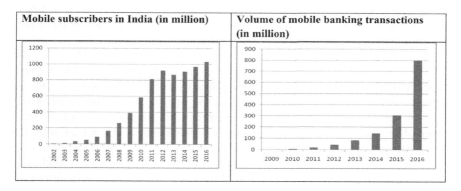

Figure 9.1 Growth of mobile banking in India

Rapid expansion in coverage of mobile phone networks has led to an exponential increase in the mobile phone user base (Figure 9.1). Telecom operators, mobile wallets companies, traditional banks and now payments banks have leveraged this user base to launch a variety of mobile-based financial services. The mobile payment services constitute an important aspect of these mobile-based financial services. We analyze the dynamics underlying the emergence of this mobile payment services in the next sections.

Conflicting institutional logics in an emerging field

The emergence of institutional field is a dynamic process in which the contradiction between different institutional logics can play an important role (e.g., Reay & Hinings, 2005; Dunn & Jones, 2010). In the case of mobile

Table 9.5 Institutional logics in mobile payments market

	Banking logic	*Telecom logic*
Main characteristics	Security of transaction is the main concern.	Inclusiveness is the main concern.
	Telecom companies could operate only as business correspondents of banks.	Telecom companies can operate stand-alone payment system.
	Banking services were reserved for traditional banks.	Telecom companies can provide banking services through payment banks.
Central actors	Banking companies	Telecom operators

payments, we notice that the emergence of the field has been characterized by the conflict between the "secure or banking logic" and "inclusiveness or telecom logic." On the one hand, there has been a concern with security due to which the regulator has been cautious in scaling up mobile payment services. This is what we refer to as banking or secure logic. On the other hand, the advent of mobile payments has the advantage of reaching out to a large consumer base. This is a huge advantage, especially in the Indian context where a large segment of the population has remained unbanked. Thus mobile payments have emerged as the provider of inclusive banking services whereby it reaches out to consumers who are not a part of the traditional mainstream banking. This logic of inclusiveness is what we refer to as the telecom logic. Our findings highlight the contradictions between the banking and telecom logic in the evolution of the mobile payment field and suggest that there has been a gradual shift towards the telecom logic in the recent years (Table 9.5).

Banking logic

The concern with the security of monetary transactions was paramount in the initial years when the regulator RBI made provisions for mobile payments. It was the banking companies such as HDFC and ICICI that launched the mobile payment and banking services in the early years. The telecom companies acted as junior partners of the mainstream banking companies in launching the mobile payment services. The telecom companies could launch mobile payment services only in collaboration with the mainstream banks and could function only as the business correspondent of the mainstream banks. For example, Obopay functioned as the business correspondent of YES bank (Indiainfoline, 2010). Further, there was greater stress on the security of the mobile payments. The RBI's vision document for payment systems in the year 2009 listed safety and security as the most important component (Reserve Bank of India, 2009). During the early years, the telecom operators could not launch the open mobile payments due to the regulatory emphasis on security of mobile payments (Dataquest, 2010).

Telecom logic

The recent years, however, has shifted the game in favor of the telecom companies. The recent vision document by the RBI lists coverage and convenience as the most important components of payment systems (Reserve Bank of India, 2016b). This is not to say the security is no longer a concern for the regulators. It is only the emphasis that has changed. In keeping with this change in emphasis, various telecom operators and specialized mobile payment companies have been granted licenses to operate payment banks (Robello & Roy, 2015). These payment banks operate savings account, accept deposits, and provide remittance services. Thus the telecom and mobile payment companies are now encroaching on the turf of banking companies. The facility of payment banks also makes it easier for the telecom operators to launch mobile payment services without the collaboration of traditional banking companies.

The conflict between the banking and telecom logic has shaped the emergence of the Indian mobile payments field till now. The field remains in a state of dynamic equilibrium as the disruption brought about the payments banks is yet to unfold completely. The realignment that these payments bank will bring in the relationship between telecom operators, traditional banking companies, and specialized payment companies remains to be seen. However, it seems certain that the future of the field, similar to the past, will now be increasingly shaped by conflict between the two institutional logics of banking and telecom.

Institutional work by macro and micro actors

Institutional emergence, maintenance, and change is a result of the institutional work performed by field level actors (e.g., Lawrence & Suddaby, 2006, p. 215; Zietsma & Lawrence, 2010). As Gawer and Phillips (2013) have argued shifts and changes in institutional work can also lead to shifts in institutional logics. Lawrence and Suddaby (2006) enlist the various types of institutional work involved in the creation of newer practices. They define vesting, defining, and advocacy as forms of political work by the institutional players to redefine the rules and challenge the boundaries of the extant practices. Institutional actors are also involved in constructing identities, changing norms, and constructing networks to facilitate institutional change (Lawrence & Suddaby, 2006). In this section, we elaborate the institutional work performed by the macro and micro actors that led to the emergence of mobile payments field in India. In this section, we also try to show that the work of institutional actors played an important role in balancing the conflict between the institutional logic and over a period of time led to a shift from banking to telecom logic.

Institutional work by macro actors

The macro level actors who have played an important part in the emergence of mobile payments field are the regulator (RBI), mainstream banking companies, telecom operators, and specialized mobile payment service providers.

Enabling

Mainstream banking companies, especially private banks, played an important role in the emergence of mobile payments field (Goyal, Pandey, & Batra, 2012). They carried out the political institutional work of initiating and advocating the need for mobile payments in India (Malhotra & Singh, 2007). They were also the first ones to launch this service and collaborated with telecom operators and specialized mobile payment service providers to launch these services. The adoption of new technological innovation required the creation of newer systems and structures to facilitate the transition from the old logic to the new logic. The banking firms played the role of innovators in the transition process. Further any logic transition is confronted with resistance from the internal institutional actors (Rojas, 2010). These firms had to overcome the internal institutional resistance to the logic change. The banking firms enabled the logic change not merely thorough external collaboration but also through internal structural and process changes (Selvan, Arasu, & Sivagnanasundram, 2012).

Regulating

The regulator, RBI, responded to the changing situation in the mobile payment sector from time to time. It served as an institution builder for the launch of electronic and mobile payment services. The RBI mandated the presence of a bank and a mobile service provider for a mobile platform based exchange (Indian Government News, 2011) and facilitated the collaboration between banking and telecom companies. The RBI also played an important role in the passing of mobile payment related legislations (Chakrabarty, 2009). These legislations played an important role in balancing the twin objectives of increasing the banking coverage in the country and ensuring the security of financial transactions. The government of India also played a proactive role in the creation and regulation of mobile payments. Through the Digital India policy and the Telecom Regulatory Authority of India (TRAI), it simplified the rules and regulations to facilitate the mobile payments systems in the country (Telecom Regulatory Authority of India, 2016).

Educating

The telecom operators and specialized mobile payment companies played an important role in educating the consumers about the availability and attractiveness of mobile payments. The unprecedented diffusion of mobile phones and the mammoth growth of the telecommunication sector in India gave a huge impetus to the mobile wallet firms to enter the e-banking domain (Singh, 2008). Positioning the use of mobile payments as a convenience option and a youthful lifestyle indicator, the mobile payment firms effectively captured the psyche of the changing Indian consumer who wanted to emulate a fashionable and modern lifestyle (Thakur & Srivastava, 2014). In some cases, the mobile wallet firms also appealed to the consumers to learn and adopt mobile wallets for national development and to improve the technological competence of India at the global level. A mobile wallet provider (Paytm) reached out to 850,000 off-line merchants (especially during the demonetization phase). In its communications, it also targeted daily wage workers such as electricians or plumbers with a do-it-yourself (DIY) print ad. The advertisement by a mobile wallet provider (Paytm) captures this theme:

'Drama band k\aro, Paytm karo' (Stop being melodramatic, use Paytm)
'Chinta nai, Paytm karo' (Do not worry, use Paytm).
'Ab ATM nahin, #Paytm karo' (Don't use ATM, Use Paytm)

(**Source:** Paytm website)

Though it forms a part of their advertising portfolio, these activities have nonetheless played an important role in generating awareness about the mobile payments. The DIY print advertisements made in the vernacular and English languages facilitated the adoption of the mobile wallets among the semi-literate consumers.

Institutional work by micro actors

The micro level actors who have played an important part in the shift in the emergence of mobile payment field are the retailers (B2B consumers) and end consumers.

Collaborating

On the retail side, the adoption of mobile payments by restaurants, cinema halls, buses, and taxis played a prominent role in the increase of mobile payments (Thakur & Srivastava, 2014). The early adopters of these facilities collaborated with the mobile payments companies to offer an innovative value proposition to their customers (Al-Bawaba News, 2006). They also helped the mobile payments providers with feedback to improve their systems. The early adopters identified the barriers to the adoption of mobile payments and conveyed their concerns to the platform providers so that they could improve their service (Thakur, 2013). A retailer noted:

> I always wanted my firm to be at the forefront to provide great service to the consumers. I was one of the first in my business to adopt Paytm in this vicinity. When the Paytm distributor came to demonstrate others were skeptical but I adopted it early. Paytm was also incentivizing us to adopt the payment system. So I thought why not adopt it. . . . There were few glitches but I established a good rapport with the providers so they were able to sort out the problems whenever they happened. They also asked for continuous feedback to improve their service. Today if you see Paytm service is much better than what it was two years back and our constant feedback played an important role to make Paytm better.

The other consumer segment that was at the forefront of adopting mobile payments was the non-government organizations (Gupta, 2013). They played an important role in designing innovative mobile payment based solutions to foster inclusive banking (Contify.com, 2009). Many of them also worked with the bottom of the pyramid (BoP) end consumers and were instrumental in bringing financial inclusion (Chavan et al., 2009).

Learning

The end consumers facilitated the emergence of mobile payment field by quickly learning and adopting mobile payments solution (Dasgupta, Paul, & Fuloria, 2011). The demography of the Indian consumers has played an important role in this regard (Joshi, 2012). The preponderance of a young population has led to the faster adoption of mobiles and consequently mobile payments. A young consumer noted:

> Mobile payments have made life a lot simpler for us. It provides great convenience. I need not bother about taking my purse or my cards. Today even my grandfather uses mobile wallets. Earlier he was skeptical and worried about the transaction fearing the loss of money. But once I taught how simple and convenient to use it, he has now adopted it readily.

Figure 9.1 shows the astonishing growth in a number of mobile users and mobile banking transactions over the years. The growth in the number of mobile users signifies a readiness on the part of consumers to adopt mobile-based value-added services and mobile payments (Sha & Mohammed, 2017). A consumer mentioned:

> Today everything is moving into the digital domain. All the apps I use like Ola, Uber etc. . . . are on my phone itself. Most of these give great

offers too when we use Paytm or other mobile wallets as they collaborate with each other. When it is convenient to get all the value added services at your fingertips, why should I stand in the banks and ATMs to get my own cash? The mobile wallets have given me greater independence and are saving me a lot of time which I unnecessarily spend in the banks.

The young age of the population has been an asset in the sense that they have been quick to learn the mobile applications and use them in their day to day transactions.

Discussion

Conflicting institutional logics and market emergence

Marketing researchers have shown increasing interest in the emergence of new markets (Dolbec & Fischer, 2015; Humphreys, 2010a). The conflict and contradiction between institutional logics are recognized as an important mechanism of field evolution (Reay & Hinings, 2009; Lounsbury, 2007; Dunn & Jones, 2010). However, marketers have not paid enough attention to the dynamics of institutional logics in market emergence. By examining the conflicts and contradictions in the emergence of Indian mobile payments market, this chapter addresses an important gap in market emergence literature. The emergence of Indian mobile payments market has been driven by the conflict between the banking and telecom logic. On the one hand there has been the concern with providing banking facilities to the large percentage of the unbanked population. The logic of increasing the coverage of banking facilities has played an important part in the evolution of this market. The concern is similar to that faced by other countries such as Kenya, where the emergence of mobile payments market has been driven solely by the logic of increased coverage and inclusive banking (Muthiora, 2015). However, in contrast to the Kenyan mobile payment market, the institutional logic of banking or secure payments has played an equally important role in the Indian context.

The regulators have played an important role in balancing these contradictory institutional logics of secure and inclusive mobile payments. Our findings, therefore, point to the important role of regulatory authorities in situations where the market is structured by conflicting and contradictory logics. Extant research on market dynamics points to the role of regulations in the emergence of new markets (Humphreys, 2010b). This stream of research conceptualizes regulation in terms of granting legitimacy to certain illegitimate practices such as casino gambling. Our findings complement this stream of research and suggest that regulation is not a passive process of granting legitimacy but an active process of balancing the contradictory logics. The regulators have to engage in active institutional work in order to balance the logics or confer legitimacy on illegitimate practices.

Institutional work plays an important role in bringing about shifts in institutional logics (Gawer & Phillips, 2013). In the case of Indian mobile payments market, institutional work by regulators has played an important role in structuring the market. A significant section of the population in India has remained unbanked till now. On the contrary, the mobile phones have spread rapidly over a very short span of time. The tele-density in India increased from 36.9% in 2009 to 83.36% in 2016 (Telecom Regulatory Authority of India, 2011, 2016). This increase in tele-density has caught the eye of banking regulators who view it as an opportunity to increase the banking density of the country. Though security of banking transactions remains a concern, the RBI of India has given greater importance to coverage and inclusiveness in the recent years. This has led to the entry of nonbanking companies such as telecom regulators and mobile payment companies in the banking field. Many of these companies have given licenses to open payment companies which in some ways are competitors of traditional banks. This shift towards mobile payments has been driven by the logic of inclusive banking.

Firm–consumer interaction and market emergence

There are two prominent approaches for understanding the emergence of new markets. One stream of literature emphasizes the role of firms in market emergence (e.g., Russo, 2001; Patvardhan et al., 2015; Ojha & Rao, 2014). The firms play a lead role in introducing new technology (Garud, Jain, & Kumaraswamy, 2002) and in taking collective action to legitimize the new market category (Russo, 2001; Patvardhan et al., 2015). The other stream of research emphasizes the role of consumers in the emergence of new markets (e.g., Ansari & Phillips, 2011). Extant research suggests that consumers can create new markets either through their deliberate actions (e.g., Sandikci & Ger, 2010; Giesler, 2008) or new markets can emerge as unintended consequences of consumer activity (e.g., Ansari & Phillips, 2011; Dolbec & Fischer, 2015). However, in both the cases, the extant research has been focused only on the role of end consumers in market emergence. The role of B2B consumers such as retailers has remained understudied. Our findings suggest that B2B consumers have an important role to play in market emergence. Our study further complements the firm and consumer based approaches by emphasizing the firm-consumer interaction in market emergence.

The foremost aspect of the interaction between consumers and firms has been the constant feedback between the mobile payment firms and the consumers. The mobile payment companies have been in constant interaction with the consumers to understand their needs and rollout relevant products. The feedback from consumers, who were apprehensive of using mobile payments due to security concerns, has led to firms paying greater attention to security features of mobile payments. The present case study further shows that the collaboration between consumers and firms can play an important role in market emergence. In the current context, this was especially true of B2B consumers such as retailers and the mobile payment service providers. Our findings suggest that collaborative institutional work by retailers played a significant role in the creation of mobile payments market. This firm–consumer collaborative view of market emergence complements the extant studies which emphasize the collaboration only among similar firms (e.g., Russo, 2001). The interaction between end consumers and B2B consumers has also been important in the emergence of this market. In the year 2016, when demonetization was announced many of the end consumers persuaded the retailers to adopt the mobile payments. In addition to the push by mobile payment firms, this too played a catalytic role in the diffusion of mobile payment technologies. These findings suggest that market creation needs to be seen not in binary terms – either as a firm or consumer driven process – but as an interactive process of co-creation.

Conclusion

This longitudinal case study of Indian mobile wallet industry has enabled us to bring together three important streams in institutional theory, namely, institutional logic, logic change, and institutional work, to understand the dynamics of market creation. Our work shows that conflict and shift in the institutional logics play an important role in the emergence of new markets. Furthermore this research also throws light on the institutional work performed by macro and micro actors as they interact with each other in the market emergence process. The role of regulators is as important as the role of other macro and micro actors. They help in balancing the conflict between the competing institutional logics which characterize a market in its emerging phase. This study further throws light on macro (firm)–micro (both B2B and end consumers) interaction in the market emergence and suggests that market creation needs to be conceptualized as an act of co-creation.

The current study sheds light on the importance of regulators and policy makers in the market creation, particularly in the situation of competing institutional logics. Our findings suggest that policy makers should be cognizant of underlying institutional logics in framing in new rules and regulations. Additionally, they should also take into account the interactions between macro and micro actors and the impact of such interactions on the process of market creation and disruption.

There are many limitations to our study. Although, we have performed a longitudinal analysis to understand the emergence of new markets and their underlying institutional logic, our results are limited to a single case study. Similar research needs to be conducted in other contexts to test the generalizability of our findings. The current study is further limited by its focus on a technology intensive market of mobile payments. Another promising research area is the study of the logic change and the dynamics associated with culturally embedded markets. Our findings further suggest that role of regulatory authorities in market emergence needs to be explored in greater detail.

Note

* The corresponding author is Sudhanshu Shekhar

References

Al-Bawaba News (2006, August 30). An average Indian spends more than 100 hours per year to buy movie tickets. *Al-Bawaba News*. Retrieved from https://global.factiva.com

Ansari, S. S., & Phillips, N. (2011). Text me! New consumer practices and change in organizational fields. *Organization Science*, 22(6), 1579–1599.

Battilana, J., Leca, B., & Boxenbaum, E. (2009). How actors change institutions : Towards a theory of institutional entrepreneurship. *The Academy of Management Annals*, 3(1), 65–107.

Business Line (1999, December 30). HDFC Bank, Hutchison Max announce mobile banking. *Business Line*. Retrieved from https://global.factiva.com

Business Line (2004a, April 8). C-Sam develops mobile wallet. *Business Line*. Retrieved from https://global.factiva.com

Business Line (2004b, February 21). enStage e-payment solution for banks. *Business Line*. Retrieved from https://global.factiva.com

Business Line (2004c, October 18). TCS, C-SAM in pact for wireless payment platform. *Business Line*. Retrieved from https://global.factiva.com

Business Line (2005, September 20). Bharti, ICICI Bank, Visa launch mobile wallet. *Business Line*. Retrieved from https://global.factiva.com

Chakrabarty, K. C. (2009). Mobile commerce, mobile banking: The emerging paradigm. In *India telecom 2009* (pp. 1–11). New Delhi: Government of India.

Chavan, A., Arora, S., Kumar, A., & Koppula, p. (2009). How mobile money can drive financial inclusion for women at the Bottom of the Pyramid (BOP) in Indian Urban Centers. In *International conference on internationalization, design and global development* (pp. 475–484). Berlin, Heidelberg: Springer.

Contify.com (2009, June 1). ZERO MASS Foundation. Contify.com. Retrieved from https://global.factiva.com

Corbin, J., & Strauss, A. (2008). *Basics of qualitative research: Techniques and procedures for developing grounded theory* (3rd ed.). Thousand Oaks, CA: Sage Publications.

Dasgupta, S., Paul, R., & Fuloria, S. (2011). Factors affecting behavioral intentions towards mobile banking usage : Empirical evidence from India. *Romanian Journal of Marketing*, 1(1), 6–28.

Dataquest (2010, November 2). Realizing Indias dream. *Dataquest*. Retrieved from https://global.factiva.comDiMaggio, p. J. (1988). Interest and agency in institutional theory. In L. G. Zucker (Ed.), *Institutional patterns and organizations: Culture and environment* (pp. 3–21). Cambridge, MA: Ballinger.

DiMaggio, p. J., & Powell, W. W. (1983). The Iron Cage revisited : Institutional isomorphism and collective rationality in organizational fields. *American Sociological Review*, 48, 147–160.

Dolbec, P.-Y., & Fischer, E. (2015). Refashioning a field ? Connected consumers and institutional dynamics in markets. *Journal of Consumer Research*, 41(6), 1447–1468.

Dunn, M. B., & Jones, C. (2010). Institutional logics and institutional pluralism: The contestation of care ad science logics in medical education, 1967–2005. *Administrative Science Quarterly*, 55, 114–149.

The Financial Express (2013, May 10). Cell me money. *The Financial Express*. Retrieved from https://global.factiva.com

Friedland, R., & Alford, R. R. (1991). Bringing society back in: Symbols, practices, and institutional contradictions. In W. W. Powell & p. J. DiMaggio (Eds.), *The new institutionalism in organizational analysis* (pp. 232–263). Chicago: The University of Chicago Press.

Garud, R., Jain, S., & Kumaraswamy, A. (2002). Institutional entreprenuership in the sponsorship of common technological standards: The case of Sun Microsystems and Java. *Academy of Management Journal*, 45(1), 196–214.

Gawer, A., & Phillips, N. (2013). Institutional work as logics shift : The case of Intel's transformation to platform leader. *Organization Studies*, 34(8), 1035–1071.

Giesler, M. (2008). Conflict and compromise: Drama in marketplace evolution. *Journal of Consumer Research*, 34(April), 739–753.

Gioia, D. A., Corley, K. G., & Hamilton, A. L. (2012). Seeking qualitative rigor in inductive research: Notes on the Gioia methodology. *Organizational Research Methods*, 16(1), 1–17.

Goyal, V., Pandey, U. S., & Batra, S. (2012). Mobile banking in India : Practices, challenges and security issues. *International Journal of Advanced Trends in Computer Science and Engineering*, 1(2278), 56–66.

Gupta, S. (2013). The mobile banking and payment revolution. *European Financial Review*, 2, 3–6.

Hult, T., Ketchen Jr., D. J., & Hult, G. T. M. (2011). Marketing and organization theory: Opportunities for synergy. *Journal of Academy of Marketing Science*, 39, 481–483.

Humphreys, A. (2010a). Megamarketing : The creation of markets as a social process. *Journal of Marketing*, 74(March), 1–19.

Humphreys, A. (2010b). Semiotic structure and the legitimation of consumption practices: The case of casino gambling. *Journal of Consumer Research*, 37(3), 490–510.

Indiainfoline (2010, December 27). 2011 . . . The year of mobile payments. *Indiainfoline*. Retrieved from https://global.factiva.com

Indian Government News (2011, August 11). RBI deputy governor Khan speaks at FICCI-IBA conference on global banking. *Indian Government News*. Retrieved from https://global.factiva.com

India Retail News (2012, February 23). MasterCard launches partnership program to enhance mobile money services for underbanked consumers in developing markets. *India Retail News*. Retrieved from https://global.factiva.com

Ingram, P., & Inman, C. (1996). Institutions, intergroup competition, and the evolution of hotel populations around Niagara Falls. *Administrative Science Quarterly*, 41(4), 629–658.

Joshi, S. (2012, May 21). Payment at fingertips. *The Hindu*. Retrieved from https:// global.factiva.comKar, S. (2012). Of Micropayments, why Boku failed in India and the road ahead. *PluGGd.in*.

Langley, A. (1999). Strategies for theorizing from process data. *Academy of Management Reivew, 24*(4), 691–710.

Lawrence, T. B., & Suddaby, R. (2006). Institutions and institutional work. In S. R. Clegga et al. (Eds.), *The Sage handbook of organization studies* (pp. 215–254). London: Sage Publications.

Lounsbury, M. (2007). A tale of two cities: Competing logics and practice variation in the professionalizing of mutual funds. *Academy of Management Journal, 50*(2), 289–307.

M2 Presswire (2004). AirTel prepaid top-up is now powered by SmartTrust DP(tm). *M2 Presswire.*

Malhotra, P., & Singh, B. (2007). Determinants of Internet banking adoption by banks in India. *Internet Research, 17*(3), 323–339.

Martin, D. M., & Schouten, J. W. (2014). Consumption-driven market emergence. *Journal of Consumer Research, 40*(February), 855–870.

Murali, D. (2008). Pay through the mobile phone. *Business Line.*

Muthiora, B. (2015). *Enabling mobile money policies in Kenya: Fostering a digital financial revolution.* London: GSM Association

Ojha, A. K., & Rao, R. A. (2014). The emergence of an organizational field: The case of open source software. *Vikalpa, 39*(2), 127–144.

Patvardhan, S. D., Gioia, D. A., & Hamilton, A. L. (2015). Weathering a meta-level identity crisis: Forging a coherent collective identity for an emerging field. *Academy of Management Journal, 58*(2), 405–435.

Reay, T., & Hinings, C. R. B. (2005). The recomposition of an organizational field : Health care in Alberta. *Organization Studies, 26*(3), 351–384.

Reay, T., & Hinings, C. R. B. (2009). Managing the rivalry of competing institutional logics. *Organization Studies, 30*(6), 629–652.

Reserve Bank of India (2009). Payment systems in India–Vision 2009–12: Introduction. *Payment Systems in India–Vision 2009–12.* Retrieved September 15, 2017, from https://rbi.org.in/scripts/bs_viewcontent.aspx?Id=2144

Reserve Bank of India (2016a). *Payment and Settlement Systems Act, 2007: Frequently asked questions.* Retrieved September 14, 2017, from https://rbi.org.in/scripts/FAQView.aspx?Id=73

Reserve Bank of India (2016b). *Payment and settlement systems in India: Vision-2018.* Retrieved September 15, 2017, from https://rbi.org.in/Scripts/PublicationVisionDocuments.aspx?Id=842

Robello, J., & Roy, A. (2015, August 19). Reliance, Airtel, nine others get RBI nod to open payments banks. *Live Mint.* Retrieved from https://www.livemint.com

Rojas, F. (2010). Power through institutional work: Acquiring academic authority in the 1968 third worl strike. *Academy of Management Journal, 53*(6).

Russo, M. V. (2001). Institutions, exchange relations, and the emergence of new fields: Regulatory policies and independent power production in America, 1978–1992. *Administrative Science Quarterly, 46*(1), 57–86.

Sanandakumar, S. (2000, May 11). Let the bank pay your bills. *The Economic Times.* Retrieved from https://global.factiva.com

Sandikci, O., & Ger, G. (2010). Veiling in style : How does a stigmatized practice become fashionable ? *Journal of Consumer Research, 37*(1), 15–36.

Scott, W. R. (2014). *Institutions and Organizations: Ideas, Interests and Identities* (4th ed.). Thousand Oaks, CA: Sage Publications.

Selvan, N. T., Arasu, B. S., & Sivagnanasundram, M. (2012). Behavioral intention towards mobile banking in India : The case of State Bank of India (SBI). In *Mobile opportunities and applications for E-service innovations* (pp. 98–100). Hershey, PA: IGI Global.

Seo, M., & Creed, W. E. D. (2002). Institutional contradictions, praxis, and institutional change: A dialectical prespective. *Academy of Management Review*, 27(2), 222–248.

Sha, N., & Mohammed, S. (2017). Virtual banking and online business. *Banks and Bank Systems*, 12(1), 75–81.

Singh, S. K. (2008). The diffusion of mobile phones in India. *Telecommunications Policy*, 32(9–10), 642–651.

Telecom Regulatory Authority of India (2011). *Annual report 2010–11*. New Delhi.

Telecom Regulatory Authority of India (2016). *Annual report 2015–16*. New Delhi.

Thakur, R. (2013). Customer adoption of mobile payment services by professionals across two cities in India: An empirical study using modified technology acceptance model. *Business Perspectives and Research*, 1(2), 17–30.

Thakur, R., & Srivastava, M. (2014). Adoption readiness, personal innovativeness, perceived risk and usage intention across customer groups for mobile payment services in India. *Internet Research*, 24(3), 369–392.

Thornton, p. H., & Ocasio, W. (1999). Institutional logics and the historical contingency of power in organizations: Executive succession in the higher education publishing industry, 1958–1990. *American Journal of Sociology*, 105(3), 801–843.

The Times of India (2002, February 5). Timesofmoney.com launches bill payment hotline. *The Times of India*. Retrieved from https://global.factiva.com

Trak.in (2012, May 15). India's mobile banking adoption highest in world. *Trak.in*. Retrieved from https://global.factiva.com

Wood, M. (2014, August 4). Easier ways to make payments with smartphones. *The Financial Express*. Retrieved from https://global.factiva.com

Zietsma, C., & Lawrence, T. B. (2010). Institutional work in the transformation of an organizational field: The interplay of boundary work and practice work. *Administrative Science Quarterly*, 55(2), 189–221.

10 Institutional logics as inhibitors or levers? The case of mobile payments in Finland

Mikko Riikkinen,* Ilkka Lähteenmäki and Satu Nätti

Introduction

Across the world, digital communication technologies are changing how people communicate. This disruptive technology-driven change has been shown to affect the business environment, where interaction increasingly involves computer-mediated networks: machine to machine, human to machine, and human to human (Oviatt & Cohen, 2015). Along with this ongoing change in communication practices, digitalization is revolutionizing how value is created in customer interactions. While much human-to-human interaction already occurs through digitalized channels, new and emerging technologies (e.g., 5G, Internet of Things, blockchain) further radically amplify the information intensity of products and processes and increase the connectivity of actors and processes in customer interactions with service providers.

Westerlund, Leminen, and Rajahonka (2014) argued that, if utilized proficiently, these new tools would facilitate new approaches to value creation and service interaction in all knowledge-intensive industries. Indeed, enhancing interaction and value creation with customers is claimed to be among the keys to success in the digital age (Haas, Snehota, & Corsaro, 2012; Vargo & Lusch, 2014). The digital revolution demands greater attention to customers' idiosyncratic needs, along with the reorganization and reinvention of operations to improve customer-perceived value in unique and customer-specific interaction situations (e.g., Matthyssens & Vandenbempt, 2008). As information is increasingly gathered by technological means, customer interaction must focus on making sense of what is of value to the beneficiaries of service users (Vargo & Lusch, 2014). In addressing these changes, companies have yet to understand how and when digital tools and channels can effectively be used for customer interaction while remaining focused on value creation.

Digital interaction is no longer just one of a business's activities; it is the central means by which companies systematically relate and combine their activities, knowledge, and resources with other actors (Håkansson, Ford, Gadde, Snehota, & Waluszewski, 2009; Ulaga & Eggert, 2006; Blocker et al., 2012; Haas, Snehota, & Corsaro, 2012). However, the institutional environment in service-intensive industries means that technology utilization poses certain challenges. *While organizations must continue to perform well in their technical domain, managers must also ensure that their organization adapts to provide services in a viable and sustainable manner, maintaining value creation and intensive interaction with customers.*

The challenge is formidable; in many traditional industries, companies must undergo radical change to incorporate increasingly connected, customer-centered, and service-based modes of operation (Gebauer & Kowalkowski, 2012). This transformation means redirecting attention from the firm's resources and production processes to support customer value creation (cf. Grönroos & Ravald, 2011; Ballantyne & Varey, 2008; Grönroos, 2008). In other words, both sales and service production activities must be adapted to support a customer-centric approach (see, e.g., Heinonen, Jaakkola, & Neganova, 2015), and service providers must learn new ways of enhancing value creation. Organizations need to be increasingly sensitive and responsive to emergent opportunities and must be able to react flexibly to emergent situations (Borg & Johnston, 2013).

The digitalization of customer interaction is a matter of strategic concern at organizational level, requiring change in the broader, taken-for-granted assumptions, values, beliefs, and culture shared by the organization's actors (Scott, 2014). In this context, it is important to comprehend how value creation is guided and constrained by institutions embodied in the customer and in organizations involved, and how organizational practices and established management models are deployed (Spohrer & Maglio, 2010; Lusch & Vargo, 2014; see also DiMaggio & Powell, 1983).

As noted earlier, many factors within and between companies and their customers can impede development toward the new business logic of digital services. In addition, industry-specific cultural, cognitive, and regulative issues can hamper comprehension or implementation of this new logic. These issues are not yet well understood, not least because of the novelty of this phenomenon in many businesses. To shed light on this strategic challenge, the present study addresses the following question:

How do institutional factors affect the innovations of new payment services?

Empirically, the study examines the kinds of institutional barrier that a newly established enterprise, for example, must overcome in developing digitalized customer interaction. In so doing, the present study deepens current understanding of new digital service innovation adoption in the financial sector, encompassing consumers, participating companies, and retail banks.

Because there is still scarce understanding of this phenomenon, a qualitative case study of mobile payment development in Finnish financial sector was conducted (e.g., Kovács & Spens, 2005). This kind of an explorative approach provides an extremely informative starting point for the study.

Payment services is a context in which institutional logics play out, but the theoretical mechanism must be understood at the higher industry level. Our approach is further informed by the fact that practices and beliefs concerning payments have been strongly institutionalized within the Finnish banking sector and among consumers. To find out these barriers to innovation in payment services, we interviewed business experts and start-up representatives. They all have the experience of payment service development, some of them from several decades. In addition, multiple sources of secondary data were used.

In terms of both theory development and empirical analysis, we focus here on institutional logic, which has been defined as the socially constructed sets of material practices, assumptions, values, and beliefs that shape cognition and behavior (Thornton, Ocasio, & Lounsbury, 2012). To understand institutional development in the present case, we address the adoption of digital communication technologies and practices in the interaction between firms and consumers in terms of three aspects: (1) *cultural-cognitive*, (2) *normative*, and (3) *regulative*. Analysis of these three aspects helps in understanding institutional logic and change.

The chapter is organized as follows. First, the core analytical framework is described, addressing institutional factors and their logic in service provider–customer interactions. The aim of this theoretical section is to identify relevant concepts for the analysis of institutional factors that create barriers to payment digitalization. After outlining the research design and methodology, the study findings are presented. The final section discusses theoretical and managerial implications, limitations of the study, and directions for future research.

Theoretical foundation; institutional logic

Institutional logic has been defined as the socially constructed set of material practices, assumptions, values, and beliefs that shape cognition and behavior (Thornton et al., 2012). At the individual level, this includes norms and values; at the organizational level, institutional logic includes culture, politics, regulation, and industry-side norms (Oliver, 1996). A shared understanding of acceptable norms of activity creates institutions (Suddaby et al., 2010) organized by a dominant logic, and institutional change is understood as a transition from one dominant logic to another (Helfat et al., 2007). Institutional logic can be observed in many domains (Friedland & Alford, 1991), including markets, industries, organizations, and networks of organizations.

Organizations are tightly embedded in their social and political environment, and their actions and constructions reflect the rules, values, beliefs, and practices determined by that environment (e.g., Powell, 2007). Actors are not isolated but interact constantly, which is why actors' institutional behavior is not explained by solely rational or market economy factors (e.g.,

Marsh & Stoker, 2002). In the broader sense, institutions can be defined not only as visible organizations and constructions but in terms of routines, manners, and established models of action (including rules, laws, and agreements). For this reason, the concept of *established* is central to understanding and defining institutions (e.g., Hodgson & Knudsen, 2006). Because institutions reflect and describe their surrounding society, they must be established and stable, and they affect the behavior of actors either by restraining or changing it (Peters, 1999).

In the present study of institutional barriers to innovation in payment services, the institutions that influence the development are not only formal, organizational, and visible but may be also informal, non-organizational, and invisible. For example, cooperation among established Finnish banks is an informal and even invisible institution that is highly influential in the development of local payment services in Finland. Customer behaviors and their established assumptions about how to pay (or about accepted payment methods) can also form an institution that affect payment procedure development.

To understand the institutional barriers that can hamper change (and also, in this case, the potential accelerators of change when tackled), the adoption of new digital service and practices between firms and consumers is examined in terms of the following aspects: (1) cultural-cognitive, (2) normative, and (3) regulative.

Cultural-cognitive aspects refer to the shared conceptions that constitute the given social reality and the frames used to construct meaning (Thornton et al., 2012). From an institutionalist perspective (Scott, 2008), institutions embody common and self-evident beliefs and meanings that are both subjective and objective (that is, external to the actor). Cultural-cognitive meanings vary among different actors, depending on the level of embeddedness in routines and patterns, which can make them difficult to understand (Scott, 2008). It is often the case that rules are obeyed because they are based on a 'taken-for-granted' mental model, and contradictory behavior is not seen as an option. In the present context, how consumers habitually pay, or believe they must pay, may be determined by cultural-cognitive factors, for example.

Normative aspects refer to rules prescribing rights and privileges, as well as responsibilities and duties, grounded in the institution's experience (Jackall, 1988; Ocasio, 1999). Norms are based on rules describing how things should be done in order to achieve goals. Normative institutions are values that internalize desirable behavior (Meyer & Rowan, 1977; Zucker, 1983). A normative system specifies both the *goals* of each action and the *ways* of reaching them (Scott, 2008). Norms depend on the actor's role in the institution; only some values and norms are common to all actors (Scott, 2008). In the context of payments, while established players may share common norms for goals and execution, new players may have different values and norms challenging status quo.

Regulative aspects refer to an institutions' ability to constrain and regularize behavior, encompassing legal systems (laws) and policies and rules within the organization or industry (e.g., Barnett & Carroll, 1993). These are often formal rules such as laws, but they may also be informal, as in the case of general norms of behavior (Meyer, Rowan, & Scott, 1983). In banking and payment services, government supervision has traditionally been strong, and for this reason, regulative aspects and related influences are of particular interest here.

Organizations tend to legitimize their operations in their extended social environment, leading typically to *institutional isomorphism* – that is, they become more homogenous in their cultural-cognitive, normative, and regulative aspects (Meyer & Rowan, 1977). While competition and open markets should lead to differentiation of organizations in the same market, strong institutionalism may serve as a counterforce. If regulation plays a strong role in a given business area, business legitimation and continuity may be even stronger drivers than economic outcomes (DiMaggio & Powell, 1983; Hall & Taylor, 1996), and consolidating the company's existence becomes more important than profits (see Meyer & Rowan, 1977). This is seen in the current offering of financial products by the Finnish banks, which is limited, especially within the areas of payments, lending, and wealth services.

Despite the many sources of friction mentioned above, institutions are, in one way or another, in continuous flux. Change is determined both by rule makers and by rule takers – that is, by those who form institutions and those for whom institutions are made. Institutions may change by chance or for no discernible reason. Change may also be a natural process of evolution, arising from competition or social development. When change is goal-oriented, it may also be driven by a few powerful actors (Goodin, 1996). Formal institutions are more easily influenced than informal ones (North, 1990), and regulative changes seem to influence institutions more rapidly than cultural customs. Certainly, legal obligation can be forceful; in the payments area, for example, the second Payment Services Directive (PSD2) seems likely to change business models and services at a more rapid pace than any other current institutional driver.[1]

While informal institutions may change without the conscious action of actors, formal institutions need to commit resources to implement change, and earlier decisions may lock development on a certain path. In other words, path dependency is caused by historical actions, and by an attitude of 'this is the way we have always done it.' Because many institutionalized habits and traditions are strongly embedded, they steer decision-making (Thoenig, 2003), and even irrational behavior or business decisions may be explained by this institutional path dependency. Conversely, institutional entrepreneurs modify old institutions and create new ones, as do new entrants, creating a competing institutional logic. Institutional entrepreneurs have the resources to change existing institutions or to exploit the status quo of institutional position (Lawrence & Phillips, 2004). Shi, Shambare, and Wang (2008) have used institutional theory to analyze the adoption of Internet banking. According to them, both normative and coercive forces have significant influence on attitude and intention to use new digital banking services.

Methodological aspects

The single case study method facilitates the collection of rich data in respect of a target phenomenon that is not yet well understood (Eisenhardt & Graebner, 2007; Yin, 2009). In adopting this approach, we employed abductive logic (e.g., Dubois & Gadde, 2002), which is appropriate given the nature of the target phenomenon and the objective of developing theory based on the case study (Locke, 2010). The single case setting of mobile payment development in Finland enabled us to develop an in-depth understanding of a complex phenomenon in question (Gummesson, 2000; Yin, 2009; Patton, 1990).

Since it was clear from early on that our study will be qualitative, interviews were an obvious choice of method. Data collection included interviews, relevant documents, and participant observations. The interviewing process started in March 2015 with the start-up company interviews and ended in January 2016 with the industry experts.

The aim for the start-up firm interviews was to collect data of its founders' entrepreneurial activity through which they strive to alter how value is created in this context. Furthermore, we wanted to understand how new entrant form competitive edge against an established bank. In particular, we focused on their introduction of a novel practice for mobile payments. This was extremely informative part of the data, for institutional barriers really become explicit during the launch process.

The chosen industry expert interviews were conducted with banking industry representatives from three different organizations that represents large established banks in the Finnish market (Table 10.1). These interviewees were selected on the basis of their firsthand experience of institutional barriers when digitalizing payments and of related institutional factors that affect the adoption of new practices for customer interaction with service providers. Interviews with industry experts indeed augmented the view of payments development in Finland over a long period of time and clarified why payment services have encountered certain institutional barriers that newly established firms have been able to overcome. The saturation point of data collection was reached in quite early stage of data collection, and it seemed that informants hold quite homogenous understanding of the phenomenon under scrutiny.

All the interviews were recorded and transcribed. Thematic analysis was conducted to categorize the data according to chosen theoretical perspectives and pre-understanding of institutional logic. The interviews were conducted using a narrative method where the interviewee was given the

Table 10.1 List of interviewees, interview times, interviewee roles, and duration of interview

Date	Interviewee	Company	Role	Duration
04.04.2015	Miki Kuusi	Wolt	CEO	55 min
04.04.2015	Oskari Petas	Wolt	Payment technology	50 min
01.05.2015	Elias Pietilä	Wolt	CTO	40 min
21.10.2015	Miki Kuusi	Wolt	CEO	45 min
17.01.2016	Erkki Poutiainen	Nordea	Head of transaction banking	60 min
18.01.2016	Hannu Kuokka	Danske Bank	Head of cards	55 min
19.01.2016	Päivi Heikkinen	Bank of Finland	Head of cash department	60 min

context of *mobile payments* and then asked to reflect from their perspective. This lead to a discussion which mostly started from the background of the interviewee and continued further to the fundamentals of payments. After the first round of interviews we analyzed the collected data and found out that there are few key themes that repeat over and over again in all the interviews and therefore the saturation of data collection was reached.

Although the interviewees have given the permission to publish their names, we have decided to use their quotes anonymously. This is due to the means of research and putting the stress on the content.

We also collected *secondary data* to support the interviews (Table 10.2). In these 30 events in Finland and in Germany, themed around FinTech and payments, we spoke with dozens of FinTech entrepreneurs, bankers, and other industry experts. Although these talks were not recorded, we assembled the key findings and presentations to gain a fuller understanding of the relevant institutional barriers. Furthermore, these discussions supported our preliminary findings of the key themes detected in the interviews.

Thus, in the following empirical section, we consider the barriers from the differing perspectives of the industry experts and the institutional entrepreneurs. Analysis of these two complementary views provides a fuller understanding of the actual institutional barriers encountered to the existing payments space. In analyzing these barriers, we also aim to illuminate the associated change of institutional logic and how cognitive, normative, and regulative logics may both constrain and support the process of change (Scott, 1995). Before that, a short description of payment service development as an empirical setting of the study and how our company example Wolt (from which start-up interviews are collected) relates to this entity.

Table 10.2 Secondary data

Date	Location	Event
27.01.2015	Berlin	FinTech Meetup
12.02.2015	Berlin	Berlin Tech meetup
27.02.2015	Berlin	Startup Weekend Future of shopping
10.03.2015	Helsinki	Kasvu Open
25.03.2015	Berlin	Startup Night – Pitches, Traction & Funding
26.03.2015	Berlin	Valley in Berlin – You Is Now
07.04.2015	Berlin	Startup Confessions by BSC Accelerators Edition
15.04.2015	Berlin	Fundraising workshop
05.05.2015	Berlin	Startup Next Berlin
11.05.2015	Berlin	Seedcamp Berlin
12.05.2015	Berlin	interact.io & myContacts launch
20.05.2015	Berlin	FinTech & Payment Stammtisch
10.06.2015	Berlin	2nd hu:braum Portfolio Days
11.06.2015	Berlin	Axel Springer Plug n play pitching
17.06.2015	Berlin	FinTech Berlin Meetup
06.08.2015	Berlin	Inbot Sales Conversion Workshop & Penthouse Party
02.09.2015	Helsinki	Exit Only event by Frontier
03.09.2015	Helsinki	AVP Talk – "Get Ideas Out of Your Head and Into the World"
08.09.2015	Helsinki	Nordea Startup Accelerator info session
06.10.2015	Berlin	Silicon Allee Breakfast Meet Up
06.10.2015	Berlin	Itembeer Happy Hour @ "Making Customers Happy MeetUp"
22.10.2015	Berlin	Explore the latest FinTech trends on Top of Berlin
11.11.2015	Helsinki	Slush 11.11–12.11
11.11.2015	Helsinki	Startup Sauna Fall '15 Demo Day
17.11.2015	Berlin	FinTech Stammtisch
19.11.2015	Frankfurt	FinTech Forum
25.11.2015	Helsinki	OP Hoksaamo – day
01.12.2015	Helsinki	Fintech Finland Community Launch
03.12.2015	Berlin	Rockstart Answers Berlin #2
08.12.2015	Berlin	FinTech Berlin December Meetup

Empirical setting; mobile payment service development in Finland

The radical changes in technology have created opportunities for Financial technology (FinTech) start-ups to enter the market with alternative payment offerings. While the estimated proportion varies according to the source, payment start-ups are generally considered to be the largest FinTech sector.

Table 10.3 Categories of payment start-ups

Category	Purpose	Examples
Online payment services	To help businesses to move their payment processing online, making it more accessible, secure, and inexpensive	Stripe, WePay
Billing automation and streamlining	To streamline invoicing and automate financial processes and billing	Zuora, Paymentus
Point-of-sale payments	To offer point-of-sale products and services, including card readers, stands, and digital storefronts	iZettle, Revel Systems
Personal payment services	To provide consumers with more convenient payment platforms	MobiKwik, Affirm
Bitcoin payments	To use digital currency to make payments faster and more secure	Coinbase, BitPay
E-commerce payments	To provide payment solutions for the e-commerce market that are geared to the challenges facing online merchants	Klarna
Connected card payments	To offer all-in-one connected credit cards as a key link in the payments value chain	Coin, Stratos
Money transfer services	To provide digital solutions for sending money quickly and cheaply across borders	Transferwise, Remitly

Source: Adapted from CB Insight 2015.

CB Insights is an online database for venture capital and based on their company data, they suggest dividing payment start-ups into eight sub-categories (Table 10.3).

Although the categories in Table 10.1 are not confirmed through academic researchers, it illustrates the complexity of payments as a whole. The largest category is online payments, which has grown rapidly since offering payment processing. Because of the high costs of sending and following up on invoices, some of the new market entrants have concentrated on using technology to automate invoicing. Point-of-sale systems (POS) were formerly provided by large hardware suppliers, but the latest developments in hardware technology has made it possible to offer cheaper integrated solutions, e.g., to attach to a smartphone or pad. Personal payment services make transactions stress-free while also reducing the time spent on banking platforms. Using Bitcoin for payments has become more common, and numerous start-ups are building supporting services for that market. Furthermore, there are several e-commerce payment providers concentrate on making payments easy for merchants. As the number of plastic cards in our wallets increases, a number of start-ups have created 'all-in-one' cards that combine these. Finally, money transfer services offer international payment transactions at a fraction of the service fee charged by traditional providers.

In order to understand the phenomenon in Finland, we reviewed payment related companies in the Finnish market. Most of the companies are working solutions that are not in direct customer contact but instead work around areas such as webshop payments and offer it as a solution. However, there was one exception: Wolt, which is a Helsinki-based high tech start-up founded in October 2014. Wolt has developed a 'simple to use' mobile application that allows consumers to order and prepay for products from nearby restaurants, cafeterias, and bars. The major value-add of this application is that it enables customers to pick up orders quickly and avoid queueing. During data collection for this study (in summer 2015), Wolt expanded their service offering to home delivery. At that time, the company was less than a year old but had expanded the number of restaurants covered by their service to more than 200, including well-known Finnish brands such as Kotipizza.

In Wolt's case, simplicity is the key for both consumer and merchant; the process needs to be logical for both parties, and payment should not be the main focus. Ownership of the purchased good is transferred while the process is ongoing, and all documentation (such as receipts) is delivered automatically in digital format. The service comprises two separate apps: one for the consumer and one for the merchant. The consumer app enables complicated orders to be placed in a matter of seconds. Being a Wolt user is free of charge, and their loyalty as well new user acquisition for Wolt is rewarded in the form of credits. On the merchant side, one major enabler of Wolt's early success was the ability to integrate into any existing point-of-sale system without additional technology. As Wolt's revenue is generated by a small transaction fee, there is no signup cost for new merchants. Wolt's business model is facilitated by direct contracts with banks and card issuers, which makes it possible to offer the service with a competitive price.

Looking at the categories of payment services in Table 10.3, it is challenging to locate Wolt within this framework. This is because, rather than being just a stand-alone payment option, Wolt has built its business model around the core consumer process of ordering food or beverages. The salient category, then, is 'personal payment services,' as customers provide their payment card information when signing up with Wolt and subsequently use their Wolt account when paying for orders. From data collection point of view, Wolt representative interviews were valuable, for institutional barriers really become explicit during the launch process of this new kind of payment service.

Institutional logic as a barrier to digitalizing payments

Cultural-cognitive aspects

Cultural-cognitive aspects refer to the shared conceptions that constitute a given social reality and the frames through which meaning is created

(Thornton et al., 2012). In a payments context, for example, how consumers usually pay, or how they believe they must pay, is closely linked to their cultural-cognitive background. In the present case, this influence could be seen among both service providers and consumers. One typical explanation for the stagnation of payment service development or consumer expectations was 'this is how we are used to paying.' Our research identified two central cultural-cognitive barriers to digitalization of payments in Finland: consumer behavior and bank dominance.

Consumer behavior

Consumers are used to concrete payments; when you pay, you use some established means or device. For centuries, cash has been the standard means. More recently, credit and debit cards preceded mobile phone payments, using the same chip as in cards. Payment integration and embedding in the primary consumer action lies beyond traditional payment institutions. In the case of Wolt, for instance, the consumer makes a contract with the service provider for future payments by giving permission to complete the payment automatically at the moment of purchase. Based on that permission, the service provider then takes care of the payment process.

> *Old local infrastructure and (consumer) habits have blocked out new players like PayPal and Klarna.*
>
> *(Payments Expert A)*

> *Consumers are so deeply into card schemes. Since the 1970s, they have been used to withdrawing money from ATMs to pay for everything they buy, and now to make person-to-person payments as well. – There was the old infrastructure, and the old habits.*
>
> *(Payments Expert C)*

Bank dominance

Traditionally in Finland banks have dominated the relationship with consumers, who seem to have accepted that position. Banks have had authority over their customers because what they brought to the market determined the standard for payment services. In general, the institutional position of banking and banks c.f. customers is the historic reason why banks have dominated the relationship. Banks have not been service firms as such, but legitimated institutions under strict regulation without real competitive threat until new entrants and FinTech firms entrance since the 1990s. In Finland, payments development and the use of digital means have been modern compared to many other markets. Customers have been pleased to digital services, e.g., for the removal of checks already in the 1980s. However, it does not diminish the influence of bank dominance, which might be due to cultural drivers.

> *Customers have been steered toward using payment methods favored by the bank.*
>
> *(Payments Expert A)*

> *Card payment services have been dominated by US schemas; Visa, MasterCard, Amex.*
>
> *(Wolt founder C)*

> *Banks have huge sales organisations; they can always sell more their own products.*
>
> *(Wolt foinder A)*

> *Banks directed customers to withdraw money from ATMs rather than at a branch.*
>
> *(Payments Expert C)*

Normative aspects

Normative aspects refer to the rules prescribing rights and privileges, as well as responsibilities and duties, based on the institution's experience (Jackall, 1988; Ocasio, 1999). In the payments area, for example, established players may share common norms for goals and their execution while new players may have different values and norms (Scott, 2008). In the present study, we identified the following normative barriers to payments development: security, lack of cooperation inside the banking industry, lack of competencies, technological lock-in, and path dependency of payment-action-related choices.

Security

All market parties, including regulators, banks, and consumers, emphasize the importance of security as a feature of payments. This implicitly suggests that new payment methods are not necessarily perceived as secure. Banks are considered to be reliable and therefore customers are confident to use payments offered by incumbent banks. In Finland, the share of digital payments is already vast, and therefor services like PayPal or Apple Pay offered outside of the traditional sector have not reached notable market share. However, to an average consumer, it is challenging to evaluate the risk level of services, regardless if they are offered by an incumbent or a new market entrant, for example a FinTech start-up.

Customers see online payments insecure. They do let their cards to be taken at the back-office in kebab-pizzeria out of their sight but are not willing to give their card information when shopping on-line.

(Wolt founder D)

It is not possible for consumers to estimate the risks of payment security. – Security is perhaps the most significant barrier to payments development.

(Payments Expert A)

If the service provider is known for reliability, that refers also to the trustworthiness of the service.

(Payments Expert C)

Cooperation inside the banking industry

Until 1994, the Finnish banking system was very closed, with no real competition outside the local market. The 1994 EEA agreement opened the market, but entry by foreign banks remained slow (Lähteenmäki, 2006). Local banks have been used to close cooperation through the banking association. Our data indicates that this has led to normative, mutually reinforcing thinking among industry experts.

You need a kind of consortium or value chain to offer [a payment service]; you can't operate alone.

(Payments Expert B)

The payment system was highly structured and defined by the cooperation between banks in the banking association. – The bank card scheme was a cooperative effort to reduce the amount of cash in the payment system.

(Payments Expert A)

Clearly, earlier payment service development was based on the needs of the banking sector rather than the needs of consumers. The choices made created a strong path dependency for development in a relatively stagnant environment. Innovations in payments were rather incremental than disruptive for the banking industry. Cost efficiency was more important driver than for example competition and service differentiation. An interesting question is how financial technology can change the current status quo of consortium or value chain need (the need of scale) rather than service differentiation (scope). Furthermore, the role of Finnish Banking Association as a vocal union is unclear since FinTech firms are questioning the traditional role of cooperative effort.

Lack of competencies

From a normative perspective, one of the issues was the lack of business development competencies in established banks. Our qualitative analysis shows that this formerly regulated and protected business area did not need the same level of competencies before as it does in the current more open and competitive environment. Because of the protected position, established banks did not need to concentrate on differentiating service offering. Partly this might have been due to the lack of suitable competences. Markets opening, changes in regulation, new market entrants, and FinTech phenomenon in general have changed the competitive environment. Therefore, new employee competencies needed, such as innovativeness, flexibility, customer centricity, and open-mindedness have caught the attention of incumbents.

> *Banks have not been very flexible because of the lack of competition. –*
> *It was not critical to consider other development options.*
>
> *(Payments Expert B)*

Technological lock-in

Banks have often been early adopters of new technology. However, early innovations have led too easily to lock-in to a certain technology, restricting further development in this regard. In particular, early investment in mobile technology at the end of 1990s in Finland was seen as a strong barrier to benefiting from next-generation technologies now.

> *Strong investment in electronic purses, mobile payments, and WAP*
> *(wireless application protocol) at the beginning of the Millennium may*
> *have locked us into that legacy of first-wave electronic payments.*
>
> *(Payments Expert B)*

> *It's as if things are concreted in – you can't touch them, and our world*
> *goes no further.*
>
> *(Payments Expert C)*

Path dependency of payment-action-related choices

In a long history, the digitalization of first payments transactions began in the 1960s, and transactions have since been automated by established banks in many ways. However, the actual payment action has been locked into cash or cards, and the consumer always uses some means or device.

> *Consumers got used to cards – first with ATMs, then to pay for their*
> *groceries shopping, and later for online purchases.*
>
> *(Payments Expert A)*

NFC [near field communication] technology for paying without a PIN code for both in cards and smartphone payments, was seen as a great innovation. However, you still need to use some kind of device to pay.
(Payments Expert C)

Regulative aspects

Payment regulation causes huge amount of costs in the form of compliance.
(Wolt founder A)

The first meaningful regulative event in this payments context was the Single European Payments Area (SEPA) initiative to improve cross-border payments efficiency for the euro. The aim was to increase competition between banks inside the Eurozone. However, our data indicate that the effect of SEPA for consumers was more negative than positive. Earlier (pre-SEPA) Finland, along with several other European countries, had their proprietary, internal payment systems offering fast and cheap money transfers inside their respected country. SEPA harmonized payments in euros under the same basic conditions, rights, and obligations, but also steered payment transfers to circle outside of the home country. Our experts did not see this being only beneficial for consumers.

SEPA did not improve the user experience. On the contrary, consumers who make payments mostly within their own home country have more to do when making a wire transfer.
(Payments Expert B)

PSD2 is expected to impact on the payments industry, as banks will be required to open APIs to third-party providers. This means that start-ups can exploit institutional barriers to offer their services to consumers using the same bank payment API.

PSD2 will open access to customer bank accounts [data] for third party players.
(Payments Expert B)

The issues outlined earlier serve to clarify the formation and difficulty of renewing institutional logic in the payments context, offering distinct reasons for the legitimation of institutions. According to Powell (2007), it is important to understand which factors are most important in strengthening or weakening the current social order. Our research confirms that Finnish banks, authorities, banking associations, banking employees, and customers have together formed an institutionalized community with common and shared values and meanings, increasing the sense of security and trust for actors inside that community as compared to those outside (cf. Wooten & Hoffman, 2008). This institutionalization may lower transaction costs by virtue of higher reliability and internal communication between actors (North, 1990). On the other hand, institutions may also increase transaction costs (Goodin, 1996); for example, payment services card schemes and technologies originally designed for ATM withdrawal became the status quo for all kinds of payment, preventing the emergence of more cost-effective methods.

New entrants versus institutionalized beliefs

The preceding analysis describes the barriers limiting or preventing new forms of payment service emerging. However, the payments experts (representing the established banking industry) also mentioned several respects how new entrants could compete against the traditional banks, using existing barriers as levers for their own capabilities and new approaches. Based on our analysis of the interviews with established bank experts, we were able to identify four perspectives that help to understand the advantages for new entrants: *consumer, payment, bank,* and *technology.*

From the consumer perspective, the experts referred repeatedly to millennials and to younger consumers' using smartphones for everyday purposes. Being a digital native has given them greater control but also higher expectations towards the service providers.

> *This generation of mobile phone users always carry their mobile phones; the user experience is already in place.*
>
> *(Payments Expert C)*

> *Consumers have noticed that they can tender payments services.*
>
> *(Payments Expert B)*

> *I believe that payments will be abstracted in long term.*
>
> *(Wolt founder C)*

From the payment perspective, the role of the payment practice itself is diminishing, which means that location and time are no longer relevant. It has also become easier for consumers to compare different services and to find the most convenient solution without thinking about the payment per se.

> *Payment is never the primary origin [of the process]; modern technology allows payment integration into the basic thing: what you want to do.*
>
> *(Payments Expert B)*

> *To some extent, these new services make location and time of day irrelevant. At the same time, consumers have realized that they can compare different services.*
>
> *(Payments Expert C)*

> *Convenience [of the payment process] is more important for consumers.*
> *It can even be a little more expensive if it is easier to use.*
>
> *(Payments Expert A)*

From a bank perspective, the barriers are obvious. Banks used to lead technological development, however lost that position because of their existing technical and cultural set-up. Banks are not familiar with rapid changes in the market. This means that their responses take time and this creates window of opportunity to the new market entrants.

> *Banks were early adopters of technology and the Internet. However,*
> *the situation has been stagnant for the last fifteen years. – Banks are not*
> *used to competition. Traditional banks are not flexible environments*
> *[for new innovation]. – Banks are tied to massive payment systems*
> *[Swift, card schemes].*
>
> *(Payments Expert B)*

> *Banking business is so shielded by regulation.*
>
> *(Wolt founder C)*

> *We have that "can't touch that one" attitude; we are cemented in, and*
> *this world goes no further.*
>
> *(Payments Expert C)*

> *Visa has announced that when regulation (referring to PSD2) forces into*
> *competition, it weakens innovation, makes things more expensive, and*
> *complicates customer service.*
>
> *(Wolt founder B)*

From a technology perspective, the experts saw increasing possibilities, and FinTech start-ups were not seen as a negative factor. Instead, moving toward more flexible platforms and structures is seen as an opportunity also for banks to innovate. PSD2 will enhance this development, and FinTech may be the long-awaited catalyst for financial industry.

> *PSD2 opens up access to customers' account information and payment*
> *processes. – In a way, you can open a bank without being a bank. – When*
> *we start to use account transfers for our purchases, and for person-to-*
> *person payments as well, it introduces new possibilities and maybe also*
> *brings banks back to better payments innovation. – There is increasing*
> *'Intel Inside' kind of thinking.*
>
> *(Payments Expert B)*

> *Electronic wallets, mobile payments, WAP . . . locked us into that legacy –*
> *FinTech is a great opportunity to break the old legacy infrastructure.*
>
> *(Payments Expert C)*

Overall, although the established banks have enabled the opportunity for new entrants and FinTech firms, several institutional factors were identified as barriers to development for all payment service providers. These include *consumer behavior, lack of competencies within established banks, technological lock-in, path dependency*, and *issues of regulation*. The findings indicate that all three institutional aspects (cultural-cognitive, normative, and regulative) contribute to the success of new payment methods offered by new entrants. In addition, our analysis identified entry factors related solely to the competencies of new entrants and FinTech firms.

New entrant's competitive edge

What can be new entrants' competitive edge against the incumbents in this new situation? Our analysis highlights especially four differentiating competencies, which are *customer centricity, simplicity, innovativeness*, and *technological edge*.

> *Banks prefer to focus all their efforts on satisfying institutional investors or shareholders, and no bank seems to specialize in user experience design.*
>
> *(Wolt founder A)*

> *User interfaces do not seem to be specialty of any bank.*
>
> *(Wolt founder C)*

This view concurs with banking industry experts that originally development of payment services was driven by internal needs of banks rather than consumer needs.

Simplicity combined with customer centricity was also brought up. This further highlights the focus to customer experience.

> *We have everything as little as possible. Customer does not use any payments mean, and the shop-keeper does not handle money or money transfer. Shop-keeper uses his/her old point-of-sales devices. Customer gets electronic receipt and no paper is needed.*
>
> *(Wolt founder C)*

> *Our focus is on user experience. There are two user experiences in our case: the customer and the sales-person in the restaurant.*
>
> *(Wolt founder A)*

Simplicity is important for merchant as well as customer's processes. Hence, payment is understood being in a supportive role not as core service per se. Furthermore, payment is not the primary process for either of the parties, and the less they have to manage it, the better is the user experience.

Finally, *innovativeness* seems to be a significant feature.

> *Banks have concentrated on payments processes for decades. However, we noticed that there is nothing wrong with existing processes, but the main challenge is payment transactions as such (the actual payment execution at the point-of-sale).*
>
> (Wolt founder D)

> *On-boarding is very complicated process of traditional banking service. We used Facebook application programming interfaces (APIs) to on-board the customer with SMS message confirmation.*
>
> (Wolt founder B)

Wolt's founders suggested that a bank with an API-based strategy could prove to be very successful, since many start-ups seek for a partner to build in-app payments. In addition, Wolt's founders envisage that the institution of payment will increasingly be integrated in the core service process, and actually many recent services have moved in this direction. As an example the Wolt's founders mentioned Uber, where the consumer does not even notice the payment, as it is integrated in the process. Wolt's founders also believe that the future of grocery stores will involve home delivery rather than going to the supermarket. They anticipate that smaller merchants will join the service first, with larger corporations following once the critical mass of users is reached. Branded apps such as Starbucks they do not consider as a threat because:

> – *In the long term, consumers would prefer to use one app for several shops and restaurants.*
>
> (Wolt founder A)

Discussion and conclusions

This study sought to identify the main institutional barriers in developing digitalized customer interaction and through one case example understand what kind of challenges a newly established enterprise has to overcome when launching a mobile payments service. In particular, our empirical data clearly show that institutional factors (cultural-cognitive, normative, and regulative) affect adoption of new digital service innovations in the highly institutionalized payments setting. Our study confirms that while status quo institutions create many barriers that can block innovation, those barriers can also serve as catalysts for the creation of new services by institutional entrepreneurs. Hence, services that are relevant for the consumers can be created by the new market entrant although the institutional barriers have been keeping the incumbents from doing them. In other words, incumbents and also consumers have been locked-in the old institutional way of thinking, while new entrants are free of the same barriers. In line with Greenwood and Hinings (1996), our research supports the view that institutional logic offers an appropriate framework for understanding the factors that influence adoption of such innovations in highly institutionalized settings.

The current study identifies *consumer behavior* and *bank dominance* as cultural-cognitive factors influencing payment service innovation, likewise *security, cooperation within the banking industry, lack of competencies, technological lock-in*, and *path dependency of payment-related choices* as being influential normative factors. Regulative aspects are characteristically EU-level rules as strong regulative factors that hinder development of the new business logic of digital services. However, while institutional logic limits the need for established actors to change within their traditional context, it also creates opportunities for new players. Our study reinforces the view of Battilana (2006) and DiMaggio (1988) that institutional entrepreneurs can create entirely new procedures without the burden of the past, enabling them to challenge the institutions.

According to DiMaggio (1988), institutional entrepreneurs modify old institutions and create new ones by accessing resources that support their own interests. To understand how start-up firms have been able to break the institutional barriers, we have to understand how those resources enable innovation. As all those resources were also within the reach of established banks, start-ups' main resource was their ability to think outside the box, which we characterize here as the start-up mental model. For example, Wolt's founders believe that the user experience of paying will change and the payment element of the process will disappear; when smoothly integrated into the process, the consumer does not even notice the payment. Figure 10.1 encapsulates our key findings regarding the differences between an incumbent and a start-up in terms of institutional barriers.

Figure 10.1 shows how *cultural-cognitive* and *normative* reasons have hindered the innovation of customer-centric new services in payments area, which explains also why established banks can be described as goods-dominant by their business logic. Furthermore, regulation has been protecting the traditional banking sector, thus strengthening the goods-dominant logic. During our research, we observed how recent changes in regulation have enhanced the move from *goods-dominant* to *service logic* by opening the competition for new entrants.

The present study demonstrates strong managerial implication that innovation can be created with relatively few resources and within a limited timeframe. Corporate executives should explore different ways of cooperating with promising start-ups and should fully assess the cost of creating new services in-house. Examples that our Wolt example has demonstrated to create better customer experience in payments area are such as easier and faster onboarding process of the service, integration and abstraction of secondary service (i.e., payment) into primary service (food ordering), real-time

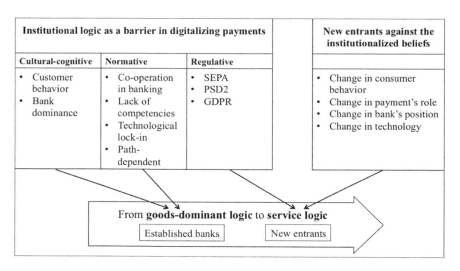

Figure 10.1 Institutional logic as barrier and enabler of new innovation

follow-up of the service process, reverse use of customer data, automatic registration of transaction (no use of concrete payment device or receipt), integration of new service into existing legacy (no need for new point-of-sale device), and the use of social media (group 'Wolt&Friends' was created before the launch operating as a platform for early adopters). Wolt's core team of just six people was able to turn their concept into a functioning and scalable business model in less than six months. This confirms that, with the right thinking and allocation of resources, big companies could in principle develop several Wolt-like ideas for serving existing customers or acquiring new ones. However, big organizations need to find some effective means of generating new ideas, as many are invented outside the organizational context. In general, Wolt's idea is not groundbreaking, and it can be assumed that some bigger corporation has already had a similar idea; what matters is that the capability to execute ideas.

Furthermore, this research paves the way for future research. While this chapter looked at one market and one informative company, it is important to acknowledge that this is only one case study within a particular market (Finland), with its own special characteristics. The study could usefully be repeated in other markets to compare results and develop a better understanding of this phenomenon. As there are several other companies building their service around a similar kind of 'hiding-the-payment' approach, a multi-case study could be done within the same industry. Additionally, a cross-industry study would provide a broader view of these issues.

Notes

* Corresponding/primary contact author
1 PSD2 is intended to create a more integrated and efficient European payments market, encouraging innovation and protecting consumers by making payments safer and more secure. It seeks to open payment markets to new entrants, leading to more competition, greater choice, and better prices for consumers. The directive was approved by the European Parliament and the European Council in late 2015 and came into force on January 13, 2016. Market participants will have to comply with most of the requirements set out in the legislation from January 13, 2018.

References

Ballantyne, D., & Varey, R. (March, 2008). The service-dominant logic and the future of marketing. *Journal of the Academy of Marketing Science*, 36(1), 11–14.

Battilana, J. (2006). Agency and institutions: The enabling role of individuals' social position. *Organization*, 13: 653–676.

Barnett, W. P., & Carroll, G. R. (1993). How institutional constraints affected the organization of early US telephony. *Journal of Law, Economics, & Organization*, 9, 98.

Blocker, C. P., Cannon, J. P., Panagopoulos, N. G., & Sager, J. K. (2012). The role of the sales force in value creation and appropriation: New directions for research. *Journal of Personal Selling & Sales Management*, 32(1), 15–27.

Borg, S., & Johnston, W. (2013). The IPS-EQ model: Interpersonal skills and emotional intelligence in a sales process. *Journal of Personal Selling & Sales Management*, 33, 39–51.

DiMaggio, p. J. (1988). Interest and agency in institutional theory. In L. G. Zucker (Ed.), *Institutional patterns and organizations: Culture and environment* (pp. 3–21). Cambridge, MA: Ballinger.

DiMaggio, p. J., & Powell, W. W. (1983). The Iron Cage revisited: Institutional isomorphism and collective rationality in organizational fields. *American Sociological Review*, 48(2), 147–160.

Dubois, A., & Gadde, L. E. (2002). Systematic combining: An abductive approach to case research. *Journal of Business Research*, 55(7), 553–560.

Eisenhardt, K. M., & Graebner, M. E. (2007). Theory building from cases: Opportunities and challenges. *Academy of Management Journal*, 50(1), 25–32.

Friedland, R., & Alford, R. R. (1991). Bringing society back in: Symbols, practices, and institutional contradictions. In W. W. Powell & p. J. DiMaggio (Eds.), *The new institutionalism in organizational analysis* (pp. 232–263). Chicago: The University of Chicago Press.

Gebauer, H., & Kowalkowski, C. (2012). Customer-focused and service-focused orientation in organizational structures. *Journal of Business & Industrial Marketing*, 27(7), 527–537.

Goodin, R. (1996). Institutions and their design. In R. Goodin (Ed.), *The theory of institutional design*. Cambridge: Cambridge University Press.

Greenwood, R., & Hinings, C. R. (1996). Understanding radical organizational change: Bringing together the old and the new institutionalism. *The Academy of Management Review*, 21(4), 1022–1054.

Grönroos, C. (2008). Service logic revisited: Who creates value? and who co-creates? *European Business Review*, 20(4), 298–314.

Grönroos, C., & Ravald, A. (2011). Service as business logic: Implications for value creation and marketing. *Journal of Service Management*, 22(1), 5–22.

Gummesson, E. (2000). *Qualitative methods in management research*. Thousand Oaks, CA: Sage Publications.

Haas, A., Snehota, I., & Corsaro, D. (2012). Creating value in business relationships: The role of sales. *Industrial Marketing Management*, 41(1), 94–105.

Håkansson, H., Ford, D., Gadde, L.-E., Snehota, I., & Waluszewski, A. (2009). *Business in Networks*. Chichester: John Wiley & Sons.

Hall, P., & Taylor, R. (1996). Political Science and the three new institutionalisms. *Political Studies*, 44(5), 936–957.

Heinonen, K., Jaakkola, E., & Neganova, I. (2015). *Foundations and manifestations of customer-to-customer value creation in Service dominant logic*. Network and Systems Theory and Service Science, pp. 58–58.

Helfat, C., Finkelstein, S., Mitchell, W., Peteraf, M. A., Singh, H., Teece, D. J., & Winter, S. G. (2007). *Dynamic capabilities: Understanding strategic change in organizations*. Cambridge, MA: Blackwell.

Hodgson, G. M., & Knudsen, T. J. (2006). Dismantling Lamarckism: Why descriptions of socio-economic evolution as Lamarckian are misleading. *Journal of Economic Issues (Association for Evolutionary Economics)*, March, 40(1), 1–25, 25p.

Jackall, R. (1988). *Moral mazes: The world of corporate managers*. New York: Oxford University Press.

Kovács, G., & Spens, M. (2005). Abductive reasoning in logistics research. *International Journal of Physical Distribution & Logistics Management*, 35(2), 132–144.

Lähteenmäki, I. (2006). *The development of the Finnish banking industry from a partnership perspective*. Oulu University. Acta Univ. Oul. G 23.

Lawrence, T., & Phillips, N. (2004). From Moby Dick to free Willy: Macro-cultural discourse and institutional entrepreneurship in emerging institutional fields. *Organization*, 11(5), 689–711.

Locke, K. (2010). Abduction. In A. Mils, G. Durepos, & E. Wiebe (Eds.), *Encyclopedia of case study research*. Thousand Oaks, CA: Sage Publications.

Lusch, R. F., & Vargo, S. L. (2014). *Service-dominant logic: Premises, perspectives and possibilities*. Cambridge, MA: Cambridge University Press.

Marsh, D., & Stoker, G. (2002). *Theory and methods in political science*. Basingstoke: Palgrave, Macmillan.

Matthyssens, P., & Vandenbempt, K. (2008). Moving from basic offerings to value-added solutions: Strategies, barriers and alignment. *Industrial Marketing Management*, 37(3), 316–328.

Meyer, J. W., & Rowan, B. (1977). Institutionalized organizations: Formal structure as myth and ceremony. *American Journal of Sociology*, 83, 340–363.

Meyer, J., Rowan, B., & Scott, W. R. (1983). *Organizational Environments: Ritual and rationality*. Beverly Hills, CA: Sage.

North, D. C. (1990). *Institutions, institutional change, and economic performance*. Cambridge, UK: Cambridge University Press.

Ocasio, W. (1999). Institutionalized action and corporate governance: The reliance on rules of CEO succession. *Administrative Science Quarterly*, 44(2), 384–416.

Oliver, C. (1996). The institutional embeddedness of economic activity. *Advances in Strategic Management*, 13, 163–186.

Oviatt, S., & Cohen, p. R. (2015). The paradigm shift to multimodality in contemporary computer interfaces. *Synthesis Lectures on Human-Centered Informatics*, *8*(3), 1–243.

Patton, M. (1990). *Qualitative evaluation and research methods*. Beverly Hills, CA: Sage Publications, pp. 169–186.

Peters, B. G. (1999). *Institutional theory in political science: The new institutionalism*. London: Pinter.

Powell, W. (2007). The new institutionalism. In *The international encyclopedia of organization studies*. Thousand Oaks, CA: Sage Publications.

Scott, W. R. (1995). *Institutions and Organizations: Ideas, Interests and Identities*. Thousand Oaks, CA: Sage Publications.

Scott, W. R. (2008). *Institutions and Organizations: Ideas and Interests* (3rd ed.). Los Angeles, CA: Sage Publications.

Scott, W. R. (2014). *Institutions and Organizations: Ideas, Interests and Identities* (4th ed.). Thousand Oaks, CA: Sage Publications.

Shi, W., Shambare, N., & Wang, J. (2008). The adoption of Internet banking: An institutional theory perspective. *Journal of Financial Services Marketing*, *12*(4), 272–286.

Spohrer, J., & Maglio, p. (2010). Toward a science of service systems: Value and symbols. In p. P. Maglio, C. A. Kieliszewski, & J. C. Spohrer (Eds.), *Handbook of service science*. Boston, MA: Springer.

Suddaby, R. (2010). Challenges for institutional theory. *Journal of Management Inquiry*, *19*(1), 14–20.

Thoenig, J. (2003). Institutional theories and public institutions: Traditions and appropriateness. In p. Guy & J. Pierre (Eds.), *Handbook of public administration* (p. 22). Thousand Oaks, CA: Sage Publications.

Thornton, p. H., Ocasio, W., & Lounsbury, M. (2012). *The institutional logics perspective: A new approach to culture, structure, and process*. New York, MA: Oxford University Press.

Ulaga, W., & Eggert, A. (2006, January). Value-based differentiation in business relationships: Gaining and sustaining key supplier status. *Journal of Marketing*, *70*(1), 119–136.

Vargo, S. L., & Lusch, R. F. (2014). Inversions of service-dominant logic. *Marketing Theory*, *14*(3), 239–248.

Westerlund, M., Leminen, S., & Rajahonka, M. (2014). Designing business models for the Internet of Things. *Technology Innovation Management Review*, *4*(7).

Wooten, M., & Hoffman, A. (2008). Organizational fields past, present and future. In R. Greenwood, C. Oliver, K. Sahlin, & R. Suddaby (Eds.), *The SAGE handbook of organizational institutionalism* (pp. 130–148). London: Sage Publications. Ross School of Business Paper No. 1311.

Yin, R. K. (2009). *Case study research: Design and methods*. Thousand Oaks, CA: Sage Publications.

Zucker, L. G. (1983). Organizations as institutions. In S. B. Bacharach (Ed.), *Research in the sociology of organizations* (pp. 1–48). Greenwich: JAI Press, 2.

Part III

Branchless banking services

11 Branchless banking and financial inclusion

Agents as facilitators of financial access

Olayinka David-West, Immanuel Ovemeso Umukoro and Nkemdilim Iheanachor*

Introduction

Sarma and Pais (2011) define financial inclusion as a process that ensures the ease of access and use of a formal financial system for all members of an economy. Financial inclusion encompasses the access to and use of affordable formal financial services to disadvantaged and low-income segments of an economy (Krishnakumar & Vijayakumar, 2013). Financial inclusion is also defined as a state in which all members of an economy (including disabled, poor, and rural populations) have access to quality financial products and services at an affordable cost in a convenient manner, and with dignity for clients (Kasprowicz & Rhyne, 2013). The importance of financial inclusion is further emphasized by Asktrakhan (2016) who posits that people without access to formal financial services are often exposed to transact in ways that are risky, costly, wasteful, and inconvenient, and which do not improve their economic security and sustainability. While access to employment, regular income, financial literacy, and awareness are enablers of financial inclusion on the one hand, inadequate bank branch distribution, absence of credit history, and low financial literacy remain substantive inhibitors.

Access to formal financial services such as credit for investments is a key link between economic opportunities and outcomes; and by empowering individuals and families to take advantage of such economic opportunities, financial inclusion becomes a powerful tool for strong and inclusive growth (Lagarde, 2014). In light of this, Tuesta (2016) reported that increased financial inclusion positively affects a population's welfare and can potentially reduce the likelihood of poverty. This can have a significant positive impact on a country's macro-economy as well as contribute towards growth in gross domestic product (GDP) through increased productivity. Financial inclusion also provides members of the economy the benefits of a variety of financial products, which are not only standardized but provided by regulated financial institutions, thus ensuring safety and security of investment (Kama & Adigun, 2013).

The IFC (2011) reports that low level of financial inclusion represents an obstacle to economic development, and as such, many governments have made efforts to enhance access to formal financial services by reducing both pecuniary and non-pecuniary costs associated with conducting transactions using formal financial services. This is because the informal mechanisms are not only risky but increase the cost of being financially excluded (David-West et al., 2017b; Demirguc-Kunt & Klapper, 2012; Ivatury, Lyman, & Staschen, 2006). The migration from informal to formal financial services can mitigate financial risks involved in keeping money with relatives, use of thrifts, money guards, piggybanks, and other unregulated informal mechanisms.

Addressing the multifaceted problems of financial exclusion has culminated in several efforts at global, regional, and national levels. Led by the World Bank, several nations have spearheaded ambitious reforms to reduce the number of financially excluded since 2011 (Demirguc-Kunt, Klapper, Singer, & Van Oudheusden, 2015). One of such is the Universal Financial Access (UFA) initiative that aims to reduce the number of underserved adults in the financial system to one billion by 2020. Notwithstanding the emergence of new technologies and innovative business models, there are still about two billion adults globally that do not have access to formal financial services. Of this number, about 60% work in the informal economy where there is substantial reliance on cash and other informal financial services, such as money guards, thrifts, rotation savings, local money lenders, and the like.

According to the IFC (2011), banks have recognized their dearth of capabilities or incentives to expand services to the base of the pyramid rapidly and as such require alternative service delivery channels. The deployment of such alternative channels such as online banking, mobile banking, payment cards, ATMs, and POS has given rise to a digital financial service (DFS) ecosystem. According to David-West, Iheanachor, and Kelikume (2018), the term 'digital financial services' (DFS) refers to a wide range of innovative technologies used primarily in developing countries to deliver essential financial services to consumers – especially women and the most vulnerable people the society, given their inability to access formal financial services. Yu and Ibtasam (2018) add that DFS refers to the use of technological and financial solutions including but not limited to mobile money, and can be enabled to engage disadvantaged segments of the population such as the underbanked unbanked. These innovative tools range from simple mobile phones to diverse information technologies in the form of structured electronic payment platforms and mobile phone-enabled solutions such as mobile money services (David-West et al., 2018; Peruta, 2015; Martinez, Hidlago, & Tuesta, 2013). Given the ubiquity of mobile communications systems and the possibility of delivering financial services via mobile phones, the use of mobile money services in serving the bottom of the pyramid has become a reality.

In many developing economies, the lack of infrastructures like transportation, electric power, security, and telecommunications presents several challenges to business and the economy. The pecuniary and non-pecuniary costs associated with route-to-market and time-to-market have significant implications for low-income earners who must bear the cost-to-serve transferred to consumers as cost-to-use. Many producers in both the manufacturing and the agricultural sectors rely on licensed business agents (LBAs) for buying raw materials as evident in fast moving consumer goods (FMCG) producing firms where these agents serve as links between remotely located local farmers and the corporate production sites. In their capacity as middlemen, the business agents also provide payments to the farmers for the goods and services. This concept of agency in financial services is the basis of agency banking.

Agency banking, also known as branchless banking is an arrangement that involves the use of agents and technology to transmit details of financial transactions (Lauer, Dias, & Tarazi, 2011). This arrangement typically involves mobile technologies such as mobile phones, tablets, laptops, and cellular networks. Using these technologies, agents, instead of physical bank branches, provides financial services. The Central Bank of Nigeria (2013) further defines agency banking as the provisioning of financial services to customers by a third-party (known as an agent) on behalf of a licensed deposit-taking financial institution or non-bank financial services provider. Wairi (2011) adds that agency banking is a branchless banking model that allows financial institutions to use third-party retail agents and leverage ICT to provide financial services outside the traditional brick and mortar bank premises. This definition acknowledges the fact that the agency banking model has undergone different maturity and transformational changes from the use of post offices and other accredited centers to encompass the adoption of ubiquitous mobile technologies.

On the other hand, the term, agent refers to a third party or individual authorized by a principal to act on its behalf and for whom such principal is liable concerning activities undertaken by the agent within the scope of its agent relationship or contract (Tarazi & Breloff, 2011; Lauer et al., 2011). In some markets like India, agents are synonymous with a customer service point, meaning an individual acting on behalf of a bank or non-bank financial service providers to serve customers that may not readily and easily access physical bank locations. The Central Bank of Nigeria (2013) also defines an agent as an entity engaged by a financial institution or non-bank financial institution to provide specific financial services on its behalf at the agent's location. Furthermore, Njunji (2013) notes that an agent could be a retailer or postal outlet contracted by a bank or non-bank financial institution to act as a financial access point on its behalf. In this regard, agents are the face of the financial institutions they represent and make branchless banking possible for customers to transact either in cash or electronically. Barasa and Mwirigi (2013) opine that the use of agents as financial access points can provide commercially viable banking services by reducing fixed costs and encouraging enterprise and additional revenues. Furthermore, Mas and Siedek (2008) propose that achieving universal access to financial services requires financial services providers adapt their systems to cater to a low value – high volume transaction environment as well as build more flexible and scalable retail networks of access points where customers can conveniently cash-in or cash-out from bank accounts or wallets.

It is important to note the difference between agency banking (branchless banking delivered via use of individuals equipped with mobile technology) and mobile branches. While the two concepts are designed to enhance ease of access to financial services, agency banking makes use of third parties (agents) who are not employees of the financial institution. On the other hand, the mobile branch is an extension of the bank's financial services using existing workforce. Examples of mobile bank branches include the use of vans, boats, or other moving vehicles that circulate among communities to provide the services of standard bank branches (CGAP, 2009).

This chapter examines the role of agents as critical actors in the financial services ecosystem and agency banking models for financial inclusion. It presents the role of agents and agency banking in changing consumer behaviors regarding the adoption (purchase), use, and/or disuse of financial services (traditional and digital).

Methodology

This chapter presents a review of literature on the role of agency banking and agents in facilitating access to financial services – both traditional and digital. The chapter employed an integrative literature review approach in identifying themes relevant to financial inclusion (access to formal financial services), agency banking, and consumer behavior. A literature search was performed in order to aggregate scholarly works on the themes related to agency banking and access to financial services. Internet keyword searches were performed on dedicated databases such as JSTOR, Google Scholar, Emerald Insights, and Ebscohost between March and November 2017. This integrative approach allowed us to objectively critique, summarize, and draw conclusions (Christmals & Gross, 2017; LoBiondo-Wood & Haber, 2010) about themes on agents, agency banking, access to financial services, and consumer behavior. Relevant and related themes were further clustered, analyzed, and synthesized for coherence based on the distribution of financial services to low-income groups, financial inclusion concepts, and measures found in national and industry-focused reports, journal articles, and blog posts using a 'Best Fit' approach (Carroll, Booth, Leaviss, & Rick, 2013) involving a two-phase analysis. Phase 1 involved clustering of similar themes and a synthesis of same for coherence to arrive at an academic viewpoint; while Phase 2 involved a synchronization of the output of Phase 1 to achieve a well-structured review.

Table 11.1 Thematic focus and related literature

Theme focus	Literature*
Financial inclusion/ access to financial services	Sarma and Pais (2008, 2011), David-West et al. (2017b), David-West et al. (2016), Demirguc-Kunt et al. (2015), Donovan (2012), Demirguc-Kunt and Klapper (2012), Kama and Adigun (2013), Park and Mercado (2015), Mbiti and Weil (2011)
Agency banking: overview	Lyman, Pickens, and Porteous (2008), Krishnakumar and Vijayakumar (2013), Tarazi and Breloff (2011), CGAP (2012, 2009), Demirguc-Kunt et al. (2015), Wairi (2011)
Agency banking: benefits	Njunji (2013), CGAP (2009), Kitaka (2001), Barasa and Mwirigi (2013)
Agency banking: challenges	CGAP (2012), Lauer et al. (2011), Davidson and McCarty (2015), David-West et al. (2016), Venkatesh, Morris, Davis, and Davis (2003)
Access to finance: inhibitors	Ivatury et al. (2006), George, Bhat, and Gupta (2016)
Access to finance: benefits	Shi (2011), David-West, Umukoro, and Muritala (2017a), CGAP (2009)
Agency banking and consumer behavior	Kardes, Cronley, and Cline (2011), Bankole, Bankole, and Brown (2011), Wessels and Drennan (2010), Torelli and Rodas (2017), Lewis (1991), Parasuraman, Zeithaml, and Berry (1994), Gu, Lee, and Suh (2009), Kardes et al. (2011)

* Complete details available in reference section.

Source: Authors' compilation.

Table 11.1 shows the key themes and related literature.

Following this methodology, we present an overview of agency banking as a tool for financial inclusion, agent dynamics, and consumer behavior.

Agency banking: a tool for financial inclusion

Agency banking is a driver of financial inclusion that has been adopted by different financial markets to address market-specific peculiarities. The agency banking model delivers financial services traditionally confined within brick and mortar bank branches using non-bank retail agents equipped with supported technologies such as mobile phones, point of sale (POS) terminals, card readers, etc. Through this delivery approach, customers can access formal financial services with the same customer experience without necessarily visiting a traditional bank branch.

The intermediation of mobile technology in delivering financial services through agents has redefined agency banking as a more technology-oriented concept. Given this, the term agent is commonly used in agency banking literature and synonymous with mobile money agent. Lyman et al. (2008)

submit that the convergence of technology and non-bank retail channels such as agents can reduce the cost of delivering financial services to clients beyond the reach of traditional banking. With the involvement of non-bank financial institutions (mostly mobile money operators and more recently, FinTechs) in the delivery of financial services via mobile telephones, the term mobile money agent further establishes itself firmly in financial inclusion and branchless banking discourse.

An assessment of agency banking across developing economies, such as Nigeria, Brazil, Kenya, Bangladesh, India, Tanzania, Pakistan, and Uganda, helps provide an insight on the operational framework and landscape of agency banking deployment for financial inclusion.

Agents as drivers of agency banking

Agency banking requires a viable agent network driven by well-trained, competent, and trustworthy agents. With agents manning financial access points, the ease of conducting financial transactions becomes possible especially for payments and remittances flowing between locations geographically disconnected from formal financial institutions. George et al. (2016) report that one of the primary pain points in enabling financial access through agents has been the need to build efficient distribution systems. When combined with adequate equipment, this system enables agents to serve as the intermediary between financial services providers and customers that lack access to formal financial services.

As attention is given to agency banking, developing the capabilities of agents will also ensure the realization of the objectives of this approach. In consonance, Stuart (2013) asserts that beyond customer recruitment and uptake, financial inclusion efforts must also focus on tactics that increase the financial capabilities of customers. By implication, mobile money agents can be developed and deployed as resource persons for building customers' financial, digital, and literacy capabilities for their efficient use of financial products and services.

Agency banking in the DFS ecosystem

Agents, representing the agency banking model, operate in the broader DFS ecosystem. The ecosystem mapping shown in Figure 11.1 shows three distinct layers of ecosystem participants: the core business, extended enterprise, and broader DFS business ecosystem (David-West et al., 2016). The core business layer consists of mobile money operators (bank and non-bank), super-agents, and agents. The mobile money operators act as the e-money issuer and payment service provider, while the super-agents play the role of agent network manager. The extended enterprise layer comprises service providers to the innermost core. Noteworthy in this layer is the deposit money banks that hold all wallet and account deposits as well as the mobile

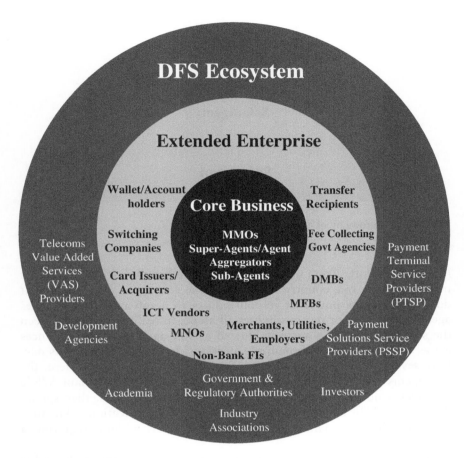

Figure 11.1 DFS ecosystem map

Source: David-West et al. (2016).

network operators that provide the telecommunications channel to consummate transactions. The outer layer of the ecosystem map comprises other supporting or compliance enforcing stakeholders, such as development agencies, regulators, and academia (David-West et al., 2016).

Taxonomy of agents

Figure 11.2 presents the taxonomy of agents in a hierarchical arrangement that depicts potential volumes and scale. Sub-agents, at the base of the pyramid, are typically individuals manning a single location/storefront. While sub-agents are either directly recruited and managed by the financial institution or super-agents, qualification criteria are often country-specific

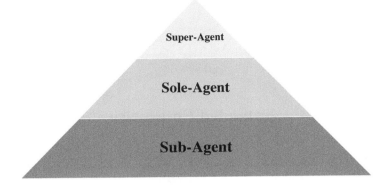

Figure 11.2 Taxonomy of agents

(Tarazi & Breloff, 2011). Also, the roles and responsibilities of sub-agents may vary from one country to another. The sole-agent is an agent that does not delegate power or responsibilities to a sub-agent but assumes agent relationship or responsibilities all alone. In reality, the line between the sole-agent and sub-agent is blurred as sole-agents in most instances act as sub-agents but with multiple locations. In essence, sole-agents may have several outlets which they oversee and monitor directly. Here, the sole-agents own, fund and manage all outlets within their domain. While sole-agents do not acquire nor aggregate other sub-agents, they spread their network of agent outlets at strategic business locations akin to a store franchise or small-scale super-agent (SMSA) without requiring a super-agent.

The super-agent sits at the apex of the pyramid. Super-agents are defined as aggregators or acquirers of sub-agents and referred to as business correspondents in India (CGAP, 2012). While financial service providers may also act as super-agents, super-agents are licensed and independent entities that own and manage the agent networks and may after that sub-contract to other sub-agents. The super-agent retains the overall responsibility for maintaining relationships with the client financial institution and other sub-agents. Other super-agent responsibilities include training, technical assistance in term of liquidity management, branding, rebalancing, and other services deemed necessary.

Agents operations

Agents, on behalf of their principals, provide access to formal financial services. The complement of services offered is limited, with country-level variations as may be defined by the financial services regulators. In the case of mobile money, the core services provided by agents are categorized using the ACTA four-part framework (BMGF, 2013).

Accounts: Agents conduct account-related activities covering the relationship between the account holder and financial service providers such as account opening and maintenance. In this capacity, agents enforce the requirements for each account type that is permissible under the operational guidelines of the provider. This service includes know-your-customer (KYC) and other customer-due diligence (CDD) compliance. Agents may also provide information services such as account balance; albeit without custody of the customer security credentials.

Cash-In, Cash-Out (CICO): These are account deposits and withdrawals made at the agent location. In the case of cash-in services, an agent receives cash deposits on behalf of account holders. The agent debits the e-money equivalent from his/her wallet account and credits the account holder's wallet. On the other hand, cash-out is akin to a cash withdrawal where the agent receives e-money into his wallet account from the customer or sender and pays out the cash equivalent. Clearing and settlement of the CICO transactions follow transaction processing guidelines. Depending on the e-wallet balance, cash-on-hand, and volume of operations, the agent may need to visit a bank to rebalance (deposit cash-in-hand for e-money) his/her account.

Transactions: Transactions are direct transfers of funds between accounts (BMGF, 2013) through different payment instruments. Utility payments and remittances typify such transactions.

- Utility Payments: These are payments for utilities such as electricity, satellite TV subscription, water, waste management, and other fees payments – school, hospital, and the like. Although customers may perform these transactions directly (self-service tool), low technology sophistication warrants the use of over-the-counter (OTC) assistance.
- Remittances: Agents are customer service points for inbound and outbound payment flows to third-parties, domestic and international. Different regulations guide foreign remittances.

Adjacencies: These could be financial or non-financial. Financial adjacencies are non-payment services that could be provided by agents for additional revenue. Micro-credit disbursement and repayments at agent locations are examples of such adjacencies.

Mobile money agents depend on high-volume low-value transactions to attain the necessary critical mass that guarantetees profitability and sustainability. The process of driving scale at the agent location requires the agent to facilitate a diverse portfolio of financial services typically available at the bank branch. Examples include the disbursement of social credits, access to micro-credit, loan repayments, and the disbursement of facilities to small-holder farmers and MSMEs. Many governments are channeling payments of this kind through mobile money agents to eliminate the cost-to-use incurred by beneficiaries. CGAP (2009) reports that many agents are now allowed to accept loan applications and subsequent disbursement as well as a collection of repayment from customers. It is important to note that the approval of small loan facilities is the exclusive right of the financial services providers that the agents represent. At best, agents only serve as points of processing, disbursement, and repayment.

On the other hand, non-financial adjacencies are strategies for customer acquisition and retention, cross-selling services, improving collections, or powering other businesses with consumer insights (BMGF, 2013). An agent's involvement in non-financial adjacencies is usually very high and forms a vital component of the revenue streams.

Benefits of agency banking

The agency banking model remains an essential component in driving financial inclusion. Demirguc-Kunt et al. (2015) report that a significant number, about 46%, of financially excluded adults live in rural areas and developing regions of the world. David-West et al. (2017a) characterize these excluded as low-income earners with basic literacy and education as well as low financial literacy. Hence, addressing the financial services' needs of this population profiles requires delivery mechanisms that individuals can trust, feel, and relate to. Agents, in the value chain, facilitate the delivery of financial services to the millions of potential customers with low literacy levels and those that may lack the requisite technology nor have the needed capabilities to use formal financial services.

With over 60% of the world's financially excluded population living in rural areas and below the poverty threshold, low literacy levels (Demirguc-Kunt et al., 2015) and an averseness to the use of sophisticated technologies (Shi, 2011; David-West et al., 2017a), self-service financial transactions are limited. Thus, agents become the bridge to financial services by eliminating additional access costs, facilitate the adoption of financial services, and enhance customer-provider experience. David-West et al. (2017a) and CGAP (2009) suggest that the use of agents equipped with mobile technology in the delivery of digital financial services can bridge the access gap to formal financial services. Specifically, agency banking is designed to meet the following:

> *Access to formal financial services*: Access to formal financial services may be delimited by various factors, including but not limited to, urban-rural migration (temporary or permanent), and displacement resulting from natural disasters and remote bank branch closure. Agents can

thus serve individuals who lack access to formal financial services, make financial services more affordable and hence reduce the associated cost-to-use.

Last mile: The geographic distribution and spread of agents make them a cost effective and readily available channel and last mile access point for serving the excluded population. Agents, most often live among and share similar socio-cultural norms and values with the consumer segments they serve. Thus, they serve as 'banks in the neighbourhood.'

Brand enhancement: Through agency banking interactions, agents enhance the provider-customer experience and build trust in the providers' brand.

Liquidity management: Agents supporting cash-based transactions (cash-in, cash-out) provide an additional channel for cash dispense and lodgments, especially outside regular banking hours.

Financial services awareness: Using below-the-line (BTL) marketing tools, agents can promote awareness of financial services offered. Agents may also engage in cross-selling and up-selling financial services. While this increases awareness of financial services, agents also win more customers thereby increasing sign-on and ultimately scale up transaction volumes and values.

Lower cost of delivery and cost of utility: The lower cost structures of agents supports the closure of more expensive bank branches, especially in rural locations with low commercial activities. This reduced structure could also translate to lower transaction fees. Beyond the reduction in the delivery costs incurred by providers, agents at the edge of the customer reduce costs associated with travel and time (Njunji, 2013; CGAP, 2009; Kitaka, 2001). Njunji (2013) further asserts that through agency banking, financial service consumers can benefit from lower transaction costs, and access financial services very close to their homes.

Branch decongestion: Njunji (2013) posits that agency banking can help financial institutions to divert existing customers from congested branches thereby providing a complementary and more convenient channel for accessing financial services. This option provides an efficient route-to-market structure for financial institutions in developing countries that serve large adult population segments that are either rural or semi-urban with no or little presence of modern infrastructures.

Service quality: Banks can also reduce queues, improve and personalise customer relationship, cater to customers with low literacy level, and increase customer base and geographical coverage with a low-cost solution for low volume transaction areas. This benefit can also help win customer loyalty and serves as of competitive advantage.

Agency banking: opportunities and challenges

The opportunities associated with the efficient deployment of the agency banking model include but are not limited to:

Financial services awareness: The ability of agents to drive transaction volumes and educate financial services consumers on the use of financial services can significantly impact the success of agency banking and financial inclusion at large (David-West et al., 2016; Demirguc-Kunt et al., 2015; Faye & Triki, 2013; CGAP, 2009). Governments and financial service providers can also leverage the agency banking arrangement towards educating consumers and altering negative perception on use of formal financial services. The diffusion of financial services among the under-banked and unbanked segments requires influencing and changing user or would-be user's attitude towards adoption. Agents, being first adopters, and then marketers of these financial services are strategic change agents needed to sensitize individuals on the benefits of formal financial services and product served at agent locations.

Resource optimization: In economies where the spread of formal financial institutions is mostly inadequate, the use of agents to serve as financial access points between sellers and buyers is commonplace. The recruitment of these agents or business correspondents into the mobile money domain by leveraging the agency banking model is feasible. With this financial service providers can optimize their resources by deploying low-cost business models in serving customer segments that would have been unprofitable using traditional banking approaches.

Job creation: Agency banking does not only reduce both pecuniary and non-pecuniary cost for the low-income unbanked and underbanked segments of the population but can boost their economy through the provision of jobs for the unemployed.

The challenges associated with the efficient deployment of the agency banking model include:

Agent activity supervision: Agent due diligence and the proportionality principle set by the regulator – usually the apex bank are the most rigorous regulatory frameworks available. The former ensures that satisfactory background checks are carried out on prospective agents to mitigate fraud and other related risks. On the other hand, the proportionality principle ensures that transactions carried out by agents are not above set thresholds or guidelines on agent operations (CGAP, 2012). However, there are reported frauds carried out by agents on customers ranging from collection of unapproved commissions, non-crediting of cashed-in transactions to customers' accounts, absconding, and other related sharp practices. Although the apex bank (as is in most countries) establishes the guidelines for agent banking, supervision of agent activities remains fragmented without a holistic framework. Lauer et al. (2011) report that although some countries have issued regulations defining terms and conditions for the use of agents, there is lack of global guidance on supervision mechanism that directly addresses how best to supervise agents. While this may be lacking, country-specific guidelines and regulations on the conduct of agents have been the prerogative of regulators whose best efforts end in issuing licenses to operators without monitoring agents activities while leaving the supervision efforts to operators. As such, operators can exploit agents to their advantage and may not take drastic measures except an agent's conducts affect their brand(s).

Consumer protection: Trust is a necessary precondition for the adoption of digital financial services which service providers must guarantee (Davidson & McCarty, 2015). For most account holders, this is necessary because their first interaction with an agent may be to hand over cash. Where consumer complaints occur, agents are incapable of providing redress without the intervention of their principals. Hence, the efficient reporting and feedback management of customers' grievances requires a robust complaints management platform that keeps the agent and customer in the loop before customers get disgruntled and lose confidence in the provider's brand. In some instances, agents often bear the brunt of customer dissatisfaction. Evidence from Nigeria (David-West et al., 2016) has shown that where transactions fail, some operators do not reverse the interchange fees that are part of the commission charged to the customers. Agents must then refund the customer's full amount while incurring the lost. The need for regulators to disincentivize service providers for failed transactions can be one of many remedies to this while interactive and functional platforms that monitor and facilitate these processes are essential.

Platform interoperability: Interoperability allows payments and remittances to be carried out across multiple platforms (different service providers, channels, instruments, store of value, etc.) in a seamless and cost-efficient manner by leveraging existing infrastructure. With this, products offered by financial services providers can be accessed on a single platform while agents can also serve multiple service providers. CGAP (2012) reports that interoperability can enhance higher product and service efficiency, convenience for customers, and transaction efficiency. However, interoperable platforms come with challenges of high cost, compliance risk, risks associated with systemic failure and threat to competition – all of which may deter financial services providers from riding on interoperable platforms. These affect agent efficiencies in the delivery of financial services as they regularly interface with customers of different financial service providers whom agents must serve if they are to operate at scale and remain profitable.

Agent exclusivity: The need for shared agents as an attempt to promote interoperability remains a threat to the competitive advantage of service providers that consider it unfair to share agents they have committed resources to develop. Hence, cost-sharing the agent development expenses are mandatory. While such policies are often not fully enforced, the use of super-agents that assume the responsibility of agent network development and management can be a long-term solution. However, the choice to contract the services of super-agents is a commercial decision of financial services providers.

Agent value proposition: Although agents serve as an intermediary between financial services providers and customers, the value offered by service providers must also benefit agents who are the enablers of the services. Providers may embellish their services with the right customer value proposition (CVP) such as affordability, accessibility, ease of use, product fit, customer-centricity, service reliability and security to win and retain customers. On the other hand, the value proposition for agents may be somewhat different. Agent profitability is dependent on the volume and value of transactions conducted. To drive volume, agents need service providers to build brand awareness and integrity to attract and retain customers. As such, services must be reliable, secure and interoperable, to ensure brand integrity. Furthermore, agents need an interactive and cost-free customer relationship system for handling customer complaints and adequately handle consumer protection. Oftentimes, these value propositions are not practically available to support agents' operations.

Agent network size: Across emerging markets where digital financial services like mobile money are evolving, qualified agents are not always available. In most cases, agents lack higher education qualifications, and where more-educated graduates have taken up the agency businesses, the lack of scale and low-profit margins may discourage active and continued participation.

Agent development: Insufficient investments in agent development could also compel agents to become short-term focused on agency business (David-West et al., 2016), and may inhibit consumer's adoption and continued use. Investment in agent network development must also focus on agent capacity building in managing liquidity, handling complaints (mainly relating to failed transactions), developing the agent-customer relationship, as well as building trust. Developing viable agent networks also requires financial service providers to collaborate with telcos (in markets where the telcos are limited to service carriers only) to strengthen network connectivity especially. These development efforts are critical in rural locations where infrastructural challenges may further inhibit access to formal financial services.

Illiquidity: The liquidity level of an agent may restrict the number of transactions that can be carried out. Although financial services regulators in developing countries are pushing for a cashless economy, cash is still king in most developing economies, and accounts for over 100% of transactions undertaken within the informal sector. As such, agents complement ATMs and their access to cash, especially during the weekends and holidays is imperative. In Nigeria, some financial service providers have commenced issuing interest-free e-float to their agents who are unable to carry out rebalancing or make cash withdrawals before banking hours elapse while others are getting innovative on how agents can rebalance without necessary visiting the bank. On the other hand, while their principals may have topped agents e-float, cash-out services may be disrupted where the agent runs out of physical cash.

Insecurity: Security concerns range from unauthorized access to personal accounts, customer fraud, failed transaction authorization and authentication, as well as physical cash theft at the agent locations. In the absence of a customer compliants platform, agents may not be able to provide real-time and up to date transaction information and may be compelled to refund monies of spurious customer claims of undelivered remmittances. In some cases, agents engage private security to protect cash in store or transit, therefore increasing operational costs. These experiences translate to modeling social and peer influences that deter prospective individuals from subscribing as mobile money agents. David-West et al. (2017a) note that intending adopters ascertain trust and security as they often inquire from peers, friends and family members. The impact of social influence is well documented under the unified theory of acceptance and use of technology by Venkatesh et al. (2003).

Despite the benefits and opportunities, these challenges describe factors that inhibit the adoption of both digital and non-digital financial services, and further impede the viability of the agency banking model. Various combinations and permutations of these constraining factors may force agents out of business if not adequately resolved by financial service providers. In all, regulators on their part must strengthen efforts on policy and regulatory compliance to create an enabling environment for agents involved in driving access to financial services.

Agents and consumer behavior

Consumer behavior is the study of individuals, groups, or organizations and all the activities associated with the purchase, use, and disposal of goods and services, including the consumer's emotional, mental, and behavioral responses that precede or follow these activities.[1] Kardes et al. (2011) define consumer behavior as encompassing all activities relating to the purchase, use, and disposal of goods and services – activities such as consumer's emotional, mental, and behavioral responses that influence the purchase, use, and disposal of services. At the purchase or acquisition phase, the series of activities such as decision-making, information search about product availability, cost, fit, and accessibility, and other activities that enhance or reduce consumers' appetite for acquiring the product (in this case, financial products and services) define consumer behavior.

From the use perspective, consumer behavior refers to all activities and thought processes that a consumer carries out concerning where and when to get the needed products and services. This description includes who is offering what (brand, durability, cost, and after sales experience); how accessible, easy to use and the anticipated benefits derived from consuming products or services. On the other hand, a consumer's behavior towards the disposal of product or services has to do with his disposition towards discontinuation of the use of products and services given certain conditions which may include dissatisfaction, availability of better and cheaper alternatives, change in customer needs, and the like.

Bankole et al. (2011) reported that culture could influence adoption of financial services served at agent locations. Similar studies also show that customers behavioral intention to adopt financial services are influenced by relative advantage, compatibility, communication, and trialability (Brown, Cajee, Davies, & Stroebel, 2003; Suoranta, 2003; Cruz, Barretto Filgueiras Neto, Munoz-Gallego, & Laukkanen, 2010; Püschel, Afonso Mazzon, & Hernandez, 2010; Koenig-Lewis, Palmer, & Moll, 2010), as postulated by Rogers (1995) diffusion of innovation theory. Other factors that influence consumers behavior towards the adoption of traditional and digital financial services at agent locations include perceived usefulness, perceived risk, cost, and compatibility (Wessels & Drennan, 2010); self-efficacy, perceived ease-of use, and perceived usefulness (Gu et al., 2009; David-West et al., 2017a).

Agents, given their proximity to consumers and shared cultural beliefs (especially for those living in rural and remote settlements) can influence consumer behavior quicker than external change drivers (Torelli & Rodas, 2017). Given that agents may have an existing relationship with customers, they can likely influence the underbanked and unbanked individuals by serving as the initiator of the adoption process and influence their decision to adopt and use financial services served at the agent location. In some instances, consumers with low education and awareness profiles entrust the agent with their financial decisions given the level trust and reputation the agent has built with the customer over time.

As individual needs for financial services grow, they seek mechanisms that address their needs reliably, affordably, and efficiently. While formal financial services served at bank branches may not be readily available or affordable, alternative channels, which are mainly informal become the options for meeting financial services' needs. Thus, the role of an agent as a facilitator of access to financial services becomes undoubtedly essential in meeting consumers' financial service needs. In countries such as India, Nigeria, Bangladesh, Pakistan, Kenya, Tanzania, and Peru that have deployed agency banking models, regulators require that prospective agents or business correspondents (in the case of India) must own an existing business before being recruited as agents. By operating other businesses, agents can influence consumers' behavior towards adoption and use of financial services offered by financial service providers at the agent location.

Impact of agent banking on consumer behavior

In a CGAP report,[2] agents are considered to play a critical role not only in handling transactions but in identifying, acquiring, and educating new customers, as well as delivering customer experiences that enhance customer retention. Such customer experiences are needed by services providers and agents to win consumer trust and loyalty towards building a brand as well as remaining competitive. When properly deployed, agents have the potential of changing consumer behavior regarding how consumers purchase, use, or dispose off financial services.

Purchase: While many financial services providers may not be able to locate branches in every location, agents as financial service points deliver services to targeted customers. As earlier noted, agents serve as change agents within the cultural settings, thereby facilitating the true spirit of inclusion. Also, agents are well placed to cross-sell and upsell other financial products, thereby deepening financial services adoption. Through positive word of mouth and leveraging on existing customer networks, they can influence customers' behavioral intention to adopt digital financial services. Given their presence at the edge of the customer, agents can impact customer adoption decisions, first-level customer support and assistance as well as customer training.

Use: Although adoption and use are sometimes synonymous, adoption or purchase of a product does not always amount to use. For instance, customers may open an account at a bank branch or agent location and may not use it given certain conditions such as low self-efficacy, lack of income, lack of trust, system or product complexity, and so on. Agents can enhance the utilisation of financial services by offering customers the needed assistance. This assistance could be the provision of education and demonstrations on the use of the financial services. Hence, agents serve to onboard and develop customers that can later migrate to self-service provision. Product or service design limitations that may constrain the use and are beyond the control of the agent would still impact utility despite the agent's accessibility and willingness. Notwithstanding, use may also be enhanced as customer trust is won by an agent. This is because people would readily transact with those they have existing relationships with, than those not very well known to them.

Disposal: Several factors account for customers' disuse of financial services. Customer satisfaction which represents the actual service quality rendered compared to the quality of service expected (Lewis, 1991; Parasuraman et al., 1994) is a determinant of customer loyalty and retention. While the factors of customer satisfaction vary, inadequate customer satisfaction levels can deter customers from using already adopted financial services. This phenomenon also applies to the agent and financial service provider relationship. Agents may change representing financial services providers as a result of poor service quality which impacts their reputation, profitability, and other such factors. However, agents can be the missing link between financial service providers and consumers by providing seamless customer facing experience that may be missing at the bank branch due to overcrowding or as a result of alternative self-service channels. Well-trained agents can attend to customer grievances and escalate those that are too complex, yet following up with the redress process on behalf of the customers, thus reducing the level of financial services disposal.

Although agents are vital to the adoption and use of both traditional and digital financial services, they also have the propensity to encourage customer disuse of financial services served at the agent location. While there are guidelines for the recruitment and management of agents such as due diligence and agents periodic performance evaluations, literature suggests that there are pockets of agent-related fraud activities that may deter customers from using agents for accessing financial services. Similarly, peer influence from existing customers on prospective customers (Venkatesh et al., 2003) can also lead to the disposal of financial services as well as inhibits potential adoption of financial services due to agents' fraudulent practices.

Through agency banking arrangements, agents can play a significant role in the distribution of financial services. Their proximity to customers further highlights the role of agents in the adoption and use of digital financial services, enhance financial inclusion and ultimately change customer behaviors.

A high-level summary of reviewed literature showing key focused areas, study objectives, key findings and identified gaps is presented in Table 11.2.

Table 11.2 Summary of key literature

Literature*	Focus area	Summary	Key findings	Gaps
Sarma (2008); Sarma and Pais (2008)	Financial inclusion and development	Accessed indices for measuring financial inclusion	i. Identified access, availability, and usage of financial products as indices for measuring financial inclusion	i. Access is proxied by number of bank accounts per 1,000 population without considering other forms of account such as e-wallets. ii. Availability of financial access points was limited to bank branches and ATMs; and do not consider mobile money agents.
Sarma and Pais (2011)	Financial inclusion and development	Understudied the relationship between human development and financial inclusion	i. Found that human development and financial inclusion are positively related; and that income, inequality, literacy, urbanization, and physical infrastructure for connectivity and information determine a nation's financial inclusion and human development.	i. The study was largely based on data on financial activities of the banked population, and only proxied for the underbanked and excluded segments.
David-West et al. (2016)	Digital financial services in Nigeria	i. Focused on sustainable business models for delivering DFS to low-income citizens. Also assessed the use of traditional and digital financial services in Nigeria. ii. Determined the cost-to-serve using activity based approach for DFS.	i. Formal financial service (savings, insurance, investment, credit, pension) penetration still very low. On the contrary, informal financial service adoption remains prevalent especially among the underbanked/unbanked. ii. DFS operators' assets, resources, and capabilities were still in their nascent stages of development but more advanced among bank-led MMOs.	i. Data on mobile money agents covered only four of the 36 states and the Federal Capital Territory (FCT). ii. Supply side only focused on assets, resources, and capabilities of eight of the 23 mobile money providers.

(Continued)

Table 11.2 (Continued)

Literature*	Focus area	Summary	Key findings	Gaps
		iii. Assessed the assets, resources, and capabilities needed by operators to deliver DFS to low-income segments.	iii. Cost-to-serve was relatively high in Nigeria and was inhibitive to DFS adoption and agents' viability.	
David-West et al. (2017a)	Digital financial services in Nigeria	i. Focused on DFS market enabling policies and regulatory frameworks. ii. Also focused on gender-based assessment the use of traditional and digital financial services uptake in Nigeria.	i. Absence of DFS laws, regulations, and policies. Where present, policies are ineffective and not DFS-specific. ii. DFS uptake requires broader ecosystem partnership among operators, regulators, and other ecosystem partners.	i. Narrative on consumer insights was high level. ii. Beyond market enabling policies, agent banking as last mile financial access point was not explored.
David-West et al. (2017b)	Mobile money adoption	i. Assessed factors inhibiting adoption of mobile money services in Nigeria.	i. Technology adoption drivers such as social influence, facilitating conditions, effort expectancy, and performance expectancy were all found to be determinants of mobile money uptake in Nigeria.	i. Did not provide the impact level of each factor, which is needed to guide operators, regulators, policy makers, and industry players in determining how best to deploy limited resources towards driving adoption.
Demirguc-Kunt et al. (2015)	Measuring global financial inclusion indicators	Financial services penetration assessment providing in-depth data on how people save, borrow, make payments, and manage risks.	i. About 62% of adults globally have accounts at a bank, or formal financial institution or mobile money provider as at 2014. ii. Between 2011 and 2014, 700 million adults worldwide became account holders. iii. Number of adults without an account dropped by 20% to two billion.	i. Sample size per country was 1,000 respondents, which is unrepresentative for a country such as Nigeria with about 170 million (as at 2014). ii. There was hardly any mention of agency banking as a financial service delivery channel.

Torelli and Rodas (2017)	Consumer and branding	Implications of tightness-looseness and how the collective consensus about brand meanings might differ in tight and loose cultures, as well as on how these differences impact acceptance of brand extensions and consumers' reactions to negative publicity.	i. To reach a strong social consensus, members of a given culture need to pay more attention to cues regarding norms in their surroundings. ii. Situational influence on individual's attitudes and behaviors is stronger in tight cultures than in loose ones.	i. Factors that enable or inhibit brand dilution (adoption) were limited to socio-cultural factors without accounting for individual factors.
Barasa and Mwirigi (2013)	Agency banking and financial inclusion in Kenya	Study explored role of agency banking in driving financial inclusion in emerging markets.	i. Agency banking is a viable model for scaling financial inclusion. ii. The viability of the model is however challenged by privacy issues, insecurity, poor customer service, and fraud at agent locations.	i. There is a methodological concern as the authors reported a qualitative approach yet mentioned a sample size of 400 respondents for which result was not presented.
Bankole et al. (2011)	Adoption of mobile banking	Factors affecting mobile adoption in Nigeria using a mixed methodology.	i. Culture is the most important factor influencing users' behavior towards mobile banking adoption in Nigeria.	i. Focused on mobile banking, which takes into consideration the banked population only, and does not explore inhibitors to adoption among the excluded.

(Continued)

Table 11.2 (Continued)

Literature*	Focus area	Summary	Key findings	Gaps
David-son and McCarty (2015)	Customer adoption and usage of mobile money services among the unbanked		i. Customers are aware of the mobile money service, but lack understanding on how it could be beneficial to them. ii. Rigorous onboarding process, lack of trust in operators' brand, and product use complexity were inhibitive to adoption. iii. There is need for operators to develop a viable agent network and incentivize agents for efficiency and sustainability.	i. The role of the regulator in building an enabling environment for DFS uptake and scalability was not explored. This is important as the success of operators and agents' activities are largely dependent on an enabling environment.
Wessels and Drennan (2010)	Consumer behavior and mobile banking acceptance	Examined motivators and inhibitors of consumers' attitude towards acceptance, and intention to use mobile phone banking.	i. Consumer attitude affects intention to adopt m-banking. ii. Perceived usefulness, risk, costs, and technology compatibility also influence m-banking adoption.	i. Sample only included participants with web-enabled phones and do not include the broad definition of mobile phone enabled banking, which includes basic and feature phones. ii. Survey was via email and excluded non-digital literate adults. iii. Study did not include 'actual use.' Although the authors argue that this is not a limitation, acceptance of a technology does not necessarily mean usage and such factors that account for use may be different (unless otherwise established empirically).

* Complete details available in reference section.

Source: Authors' compilation.

Conclusion – making agency banking work for all

The potential of agency banking and the role of agents is significant and remains key to driving financial inclusion. Demirguc-Kunt et al. (2015) report that across Sub-Saharan Africa (SSA), the use of agents in delivering financial services drove account ownership by one third – up to 34%. Through agents, 12% of adults across SSA now have access to a mobile money account, which is four times the developing world average. Making agency banking work requires collaborative efforts of all stakeholders in the financial service industry. The following are some recommendations for various ecosystem participant.

- Regulators: The viability and sustainability of the agency banking model require a clear regulatory framework that addresses issues around liquidity management, liability to customers, agent operations, agents' security, and consumer protection. Regulators must also ensure that appropriate frameworks are put in place to implement policies and regulatory guidelines that improve agent value proposition and realize the imperatives of agency banking. Other areas that need regulatory attention include pricing transparency and disclosure (CGAP, 2009), trust and fidelity, customer grievance redress, interoperability and network connectivity (David-West et al., 2017b) that may deter existing and potential customers from adopting financial services, especially digital financial services delivered at agent locations. Furthermore, enforcement of regulatory guidelines on agency banking is paramount to curb poor services, compliance failure, and other agents' sharp practices.
- Financial Services Providers: As the adoption of digital financial services grows with changing customer behavior, the capabilities required by agents in meeting consumers' financial service needs have to be developed and enhanced by the service providers they represent. Financial service providers on their part must provide strict security requirements needed to safeguard customers and agents. While providers must promote their brand, periodic agents' due diligence (ADD) required to reduce agent-related fraud activities as well as build trust in providers' brands (Shi, 2011; Davidson & McCarty, 2015; David-West et al., 2017a) is paramount. For agents, the possibility of representing a provider (by existing and prospective mobile money agents) could be low if issues around trust, service reliability, security, interoperability, and profitability are not resolved by service providers as this could inhibit the efficacy of agents and financial inclusion at large. Financial institutions must also seek mechanisms to enhance service delivery, especially in the management of issues affecting customer transactions. Offering toll-free services to agents and customers is good, yet resolving complaints within 48 hours from when reported is preferable for all. This way, agents are motivated to serve providers and customers without having to contend with trust related issues.

- Operators: Given that agency banking is a tool for achieving the global vision of financial inclusion, the active participation of all stakeholders remains critical (David-West et al., 2016). Agents rely on services of multiple operators such as payment switches, mobile network operators, payment systems and services providers, card issuers, and so on to serve consumers. To achieve platform interoperability, the need to have multiple handshakes among ecosystem operators cannot be overemphasised.

- Super-agents: Although service providers and other operators are responsible for product and platform design, implementation, and branding, the super-agent holds the responsibility of agent network development (recruitment, training, supervising, liquidity management and many more) needed to drive the agency banking model. While regulators define the appropriate policies and guidelines, the super-agent is in a better position to enforce agent-based compliance. The mobile money license in some markets enables operators to be agent network developers and managers, thus making the involvement of a super-agent a business decision for operators.

- Agents: Agents serve as the face of the financial service and financial service provider, and also provide the face-to-face, over the counter (OTC) interactions with financial service consumers (David-West et al., 2016). Consequently, agents' ability to engage customers in a friendly manner influences consumers' adoption behavior of financial service (traditional and mobile). Agents' interpersonal relationship with customers is also dependent on trust, integrity, empathy, literacy level, service efficiency, and such other factors that customers may look for before patronizing financial services delivered through agents. Agents must, therefore, be able to display the preceding qualities to be able to win and retain customers in order to operate at scale and profitable.

Theoretical and managerial implication

This chapter provides insights into agency banking as a tool for financial inclusion (access to and use of formal financial services) and changing consumer behaviors towards driving financial inclusion. From a theoretical perspective, the chapter draws attention to the role of agents in promoting access to financial services while influencing customer purchase, use and disuse behavior. The need to situate studies of this nature in consumer behavior and financial services adoption theories is apt. There is, however, an absence of theories and models that underpin studies in financial inclusion. The insights shared will provide a deeper understanding of how peer influence and local change agents can alter consumer behavior in the adoption and use of financial services primarily to economically and educationally disadvantaged population segments. For managers and policy-makers, the chapter further highlights the need for financial services providers to identify, understand, and leverage the collaborative efforts of ecosystem participants towards the efficient deployment of agency banking in promoting access to financial services. This requirement is essential because while service providers remain at the core of the ecosystem, the efficient delivery of financial services to target population segments depends on the different roles played by different ecosystem participants.

Direction for future research

Agency banking has proven to be a viable model for driving financial inclusion across several financial markets. While evidence exists on the role of agents in driving access to financial services, there is little evidence on the application of consumer behavioral theories in explaining how agents influence the different elements of consumer behavior (purchase, use and disposal) towards adoption and use of digital financial services. Further studies should as such be carried out in establishing the relationships between agency banking and consumer behavior towards adoption and use of digital financial services. The need to develop theories, metrics, and models that support and explain enablers and inhibitors of financial services, and rooted in consumer behavior also creates an area for future research.

Notes

1 Consumer Behavior. Available at https://en.wikipedia.org/wiki/Consumer_behaviour
2 Agent Networks. Available at www.cgap.org/topics/agent-networks

References

Asktrakhan, I. (2016). *Universal financial access by 2020? Look to Africa for inspiration.* [Online] Retrieved June 3, 2016, from http://blogs.worldbank.org/africacan/universal-financial-access-by-2020-look-to-africa-for-inspiration

Bankole, F. O., Bankole, O. O., & Brown, I. (2011). Mobile banking adoption in Nigeria. *The Electronic Journal of Information Systems in Developing Countries*, 47(1), 1–23.

Barasa, D. A., & Mwirigi, F. M. (2013). The role of agency banking in enhancing financial sector deepening in emerging markets: Lessons from Kenyan experience. *European Journal of Business and Management*, 5(21), 27–34.

BMGF (2013). *Fighting poverty, profitably: Transforming the economics of payments to build sustainable, inclusive financial systems.* Retrieved July 14, 2016, from https://docs.gatesfoundation.org/Documents/Fighting%20Poverty%20Profitably%20Full%20Report.pdf

Brown, I., Cajee, Z., Davies, D., & Stroebel, S. (2003). Cell phone banking: Predictors of adoption in South Africa: An exploratory study. *International Journal of Information Management*, 23(5), 381–394.

Carroll, C., Booth, A., Leaviss, J., & Rick, J. (2013). "Best fit" framework synthesis: Refining the method. *BMC Medical Research Methodology*, 13(1), 37, 1–16.

The Central Bank of Nigeria. (2013). *Guidelines for the regulation of agent banking and agent banking relationships in Nigeria.* [Online] Retrieved April 16, 2017, from www.cbn.gov.ng/out/2013/ccd/guidelines%20for%20the%20regulation%20 of%20agent%20banking%20and%20agent%20banking%20relationships%20 in%20nigeria.pdf

CGAP. (2009). *Financial access 2009: Measuring access to financial services around the world.* Washington, DC: The World Bank Group.

CGAP. (2012). *Advancing financial access for the world's poor: Annual report 2012.* Washington DC. [Online] Retrieved August 20, 2016, from http://documents. worldbank.org/curated/en/616911468320667224/pdf/75163020120CGA0Box0 374307B00PUBLIC0.pdf

Christmals, C. D., & Gross, J. J. (2017). An integrative literature review framework for postgraduate nursing research reviews. *European Journal of Research in Medical Sciences*, 5(1), 7–15.

Cruz, P., Barretto Filgueiras Neto, L., Munoz-Gallego, P., & Laukkanen, T. (2010). Mobile banking rollout in emerging markets: Evidence from Brazil. *International Journal of Bank Marketing*, 28(5), 342–371.

Davidson, N., & McCarty, M. Y. (2015). *Driving customer usage of mobile money for the unbanked.* [Online] Retrieved July 14, 2016, from www.gsma.com/ mobilefordevelopment/wp-content/uploads/2012/03/drivingcustomerusagefinal-lowres.pdf

David-West, O., Ajai, O., Umukoro, I. O., Salami, D., Isheyemi, O., & Ihenachor, N., et al. (2016). *Digital financial services in Nigeria: State of the market report 2016.* 1–112. [Online] Retrieved January 27, 2017, from http://doi.org/10.13140/ RG.2.2.24491.23849

David-West, O., Ajai, O., Umukoro, I. O., Salami, D., Kelikume, I., & Ihenachor, N., et al. (2017b). *Digital financial services in Nigeria: State of the market report 2017.* 1–112. [Online] Retrieved January 6, 2018, from www.researchgate.net/ publication/322315266_Digital_Financial_Services_in_Nigeria_State_of_the_ Market_Report_2017

David-West, O., Iheanachor, N., & Kelikume, I. (2018). A resource-based view of digital financial services (DFS): An exploratory study of Nigerian providers. *Journal of Business Research*, 88, 513–526.

David-West, O., Umukoro, I. O., & Muritala, O. (2017a). Adoption and use of mobile money services in Nigeria. In M. Khosrow-Pour (Ed.), *Encyclopaedia of information science and technology* (4th ed., pp. 2724–2738). [Online] Hershey, PA: IGI Global. Retrieved April 25, 2017, from doi:10.4018/978-1-5225-2255-3. ch237

Demirguc-Kunt, A., & Klapper, L. (2012). *Measuring financial inclusion: The global findex database.* World Bank Policy Research Working Paper 6025.

Demirguc-Kunt, A., Klapper, L., Singer, D., & Van Oudheusden, p. (2015). *The global findex database 2014: Measuring financial inclusion around the world.* Policy Research Working Paper 7255, World Bank, Washington, DC. [Online] Retrieved April 12, 2016, from http://documents.worldbank.org/curated/ en/187761468179367706/pdf/WPS7255.pdf#page=3

Donovan, K. (2012). Mobile money for financial inclusion. *Information and Communications for Development.* Conference Edition.

Faye, I., & Triki, T. (2013). Financial inclusion in Africa: The role of technology. In T. Triki & I. Faye (Eds.), *Financial inclusion in Africa* (p. 148). Tunis: African Development Bank (AfDB).

George, D., Bhat, S., & Gupta, A. K. (2016). *Re-imagining the last mile: Agent networks in India.* Retrieved from www.microsave.net/files/pdf/PB_15_Re_Imagining_the_Last_Mile_for_Agents.pdf

Gu, J. C., Lee, S. C., & Suh, Y. H. (2009). Determinants of behavioral intention to mobile banking. *Expert Systems with Applications, 36*(9), 11605–11616.

IFC. (2011). *IFC Mobile Money Study 2011: Nigeria.* [Online] Retrieved April 25, 2016, from www.ifc.org/wps/wcm/connect/da61a9004a052da18b11ffdd29332b51/Mobile+Money+Study+2011+-+Nigeria?MOD=AJPERES

Ivatury, G., Lyman, T., & Staschen, S. (2006). Use of agents in branchless banking for the poor: Reward, risks and regulations. *Consultative Group tom Assist the Poor.* [Online] Retrieved July 31, 2017, from www.cgap.org/sites/default/files/CGAP-Focus-Notes-Use-of-Agents-in-Branchless-Banking-for-the-Poor-Rewards-Risks-and-Regulation-Oct-2006.pdf

Kama, U., & Adigun, M. (2013). *Financial inclusion in Nigeria: Issues and challenges.* Occasional Paper No. 45. [Online] Retrieved May 3, 2016, from www.cenbank.org/out/2014/rsd/occasional%20paper%20no.%2045%20issues%20and%20challenges.pdf

Kardes, F., Cronley, M., & Cline, T. (2011). *Consumer behavior.* Mason, OH: South-Western Cengage, p. 7.

Kasprowicz, P., & Rhyne, E. (2013). Looking through the demographic window: Implications for financial inclusion. *Centre for Financial Inclusion,* Publication 18.

Kitaka, p. (2001). *A Survey of the use of financial performance indicators by microfinance institutions in Kenya.* MBA Research Project, University of Nairobi.

Koenig-Lewis, N., Palmer, A., & Moll, A. (2010). Predicting young consumers' take up of mobile banking services. *International Journal of Bank Marketing, 28*(5), 410–432.

Krishnakumar, R. & Vijayakumar, L. (2013). Financial inclusion: A demographic perspective. *International Journal of Current Research, 5*(12), 3835–3837.

Lagarde, C. (2014). Empowerment through financial inclusion. *Address to the International Forum for Financial Inclusion: The International Monetary Fund.* [Online] Retrieved August 22, 2016, from www.imf.org/external/np/speeches/2014/062614a.htm

Lauer, K., Dias, D., & Tarazi, M. (2011). Bank agents: Risk management, mitigation, and supervision. *CGAP Focus Note.* [Online] Retrieved January 25, 2017, from www.cgap.org/sites/default/files/Focus-Note-Bank-Agents-Risk-Management-Mitigation-and-Supervision-Dec-2011.pdf

Lewis, B. R. (1991). Service quality: An international comparison of bank customers' expectations and perceptions. *Journal of Marketing Management, 7*(1), 47–62.

LoBiondo-Wood, G., & Haber, J. (2010). Understanding research findings. In G. LoBiondo-Wood & J. Haber (Eds.), *Nursing research: Methods and critical appraisal for evidence-based practice* (7th ed.). St Louis: Mosby Elsevier.

Lyman, T., Pickens, M., & Porteous, D. (2008). Regulating transformational branchless banking: Mobile phones and other technology to increase access to finance. *Consultative Group to Assist the Poor.* [Online] Retrieved June 21, 2017, from www.cgap.org/sites/default/files/CGAP-Focus-Note-Regulating-Transformational-Branchless-Banking-Mobile-Phones-and-Other-Technology-to-Increase-Access-to-Finance-Jan-2008.pdf

Martínez, C. H., Hidalgo, X. P., & Tuesta, D. (2013). *Demand factors that influence financial inclusion in Mexico: Analysis of the barriers based on the ENIF survey.* BBVA Research, 13/37 Working Paper.

Mas, I., & Siedek, H. (2008). Banking through networks of retail agents. *Consultative Group tom Assist the Poor.* Retrieved July 31, 2017, from www.cgap. org/sites/default/files/CGAP-Focus-Note-Banking-Through-Networks-of-Retail-Agents-May-2008.pdf

Mbiti, I., & Weil, D. (2011). *Mobile banking: The impact of M-Pesa in Kenya.* NBER Working Paper 17129.

Njunji, A. (2013). *A survey of adoption of agency banking by commercial banks in Nakuru CBD.* Master's Thesis in Business Administration in Finance, University of Nairobi, Nairobi, Kenya.

Parasuraman, A., Zeithaml, V. A., & Berry, L. L. (1994). Reassessment of expectations as a comparison standard in measuring service quality: Implications for further research. *The Journal of Marketing,* 111–124.

Park, C., & Mercado, R. V. (2015). Financial inclusion, poverty, and income inequality in developing Asia. *ADB Economics Working Paper Series No. 426.* [Online] Retrieved July 14, 2016, from www.adb.org/sites/default/files/publication/153143/ewp-426.pdf

Peruta, M. D. (2015). *Mobile money adoption and financial inclusion objectives: A microeconomic approach through a cluster analysis.* GREDEG Working paper, No. 2015-49. [Online] Retrieved May 3, 2016, from www.gredeg.cnrs.fr/working-papers/GREDEG-WP-2015-49.pdf

Püschel, J., Afonso Mazzon, J., & Hernandez, M. C. J. (2010). Mobile banking: Proposition of an integrated adoption intention framework. *International Journal of Bank Marketing, 28*(5), 389–409.

Rogers, E. M. (1995). Diffusion of innovations: Modifications of a model for telecommunications. In *Die Diffusion von Innovationen in der Telekommunikation* (pp. 25–38). Berlin, Heidelberg: Springer.

Sarma, M. (2008). Index of financial inclusion. *Indian Council for Research on International Economic Relations,* Working Paper No 215. Retrieved June 22, 2016, from http://icrier.org/pdf/Working_Paper_215.pdf

Sarma, M., & Pais, J. (2008, September). *Financial inclusion and development: A cross country analysis.* Annual Conference of the Human Development and Capability Association, New Delhi (pp. 10–13).

Sarma, M., & Pais, J. (2011). Financial inclusion and development. *Journal of International Development, 23,* 613–628.

Shi, X. (2011). *Exploring factors that hinder the adoption of mobile services in China: A qualitative user analysis with special focus on mobile financial services.* Master's thesis, School of Economics, Aalto University. [Online] Retrieved June 29, 2016, from https://aaltodoc.aalto.fi/bitstream/handle/123456789/782/hse_ethesis_12650.pdf?sequence=1&isAllowed=y

Stuart, G. (2013). *From financial literacy to financial capabilities: Implications for practitioners.* Center for Financial Inclusion, ACCION. [Online] Retrieved March 14, 2017, from https://cfi-blog.org/2013/04/17/from-financial-literacy-to-financial-capabilities-implications-for-practitioners/

Suoranta, M. (2003). *Adoption of mobile banking in Finland.* Jyväskylän yliopisto, 84–89.

Tarazi, M., & Breloff, p. (2011). *Regulating banking agents.* Consultative Group to Assist the Poor. [Online] Retrieved August 15, 2017, from www.cgap.org/sites/default/files/CGAP-Focus-Note-Regulating-Banking-Agents-Mar-2011.pdf

Torelli, C. J., & Rodas, M. (2017). Globalization, branding and multi-culturalism in consumer behavior. In C. V. Jansson-Boyd & M. J. Zawisza (Eds.), *Routledge International Handbook of Consumer Psychology* (pp. 43–52). Abingdon, UK: Routledge.

Tuesta, D. (2016). *The importance of financial inclusion.* [Online] Retrieved August 22, 2016, from www.bbva.com/en/news/economy/macroeconomics/the-importance-of-financial-inclusion/

Venkatesh, V., Morris, M. G., Davis, G. B., & Davis, F. D. (2003). User acceptance of information technology: Towards a unified view. *MIS Quarterly, 27*(3), 425–478. [Online] Retrieved May 27, 2017, from http://dx.doi.org/10.2307/3250981

Wairi, D. K. (2011). *Factors influencing the adoption of agent banking innovation among commercial banks in Kenya.* MBA Dissertation at the School of Business, University of Nairobi. Retrieved January 4, 2018, from http://erepository.uonbi.ac.ke/bitstream/handle/11295/12479/Wairi_Factors%20influencing%20the%20adoption%20of%20agent%20banking%20innovation%20among%20commercial%20banks%20in%20kenya-1.pdf?sequence=3

Wessels, L., & Drennan, J. (2010). An investigation of consumer acceptance of M-banking. *International Journal of Bank Marketing, 28*(7), 547–568.

Yu, S., & Ibtasam, S. (2018). *A qualitative exploration of mobile money in Ghana.* Proceedings of ACM SIGCAS Conference on Computing and Sustainable Societies (COMPASS), Compass '18, June 20–22, Menlo Park and San Jose, CA, USA.

12 How is the use of mobile money services transforming lives in Ghana?

Aijaz A. Shaikh,* Richard Glavee-Geo,
Heikki Karjaluoto and Robert Ebo Hinson

Introduction

John is working on a construction site which is located 300 miles away from his home in Sawla, a small town located in northern Ghana. The citizens of Sawla town are largely 'unbanked,' and the town has very limited access to formal banking services such as Internet and ATM services. Most of the town's population relies on mobile money (MM) services in sending and receiving funds. John does not maintain a bank account but considers a cell phone as a 'blessing' to communicate with his family members and to send them money through a nearby MM agent found in a kiosk on a street corner. John visits the MM agent, deposits money into his MM account and then transfers the money to his wife in Sawla at his convenience after performing a few simple steps on his basic handset. John pays a very nominal transaction fee, and to his satisfaction, he also receives immediate funds delivery confirmation on his cell phone. Nowadays, John has adopted the MM services to pay the tuition fee for his daughter. MM plays a very important role in the life of John in effectively managing his finances and payment needs.

The preceding synopsis shows a glimpse of how MM services are transforming the lives of the poor in Ghana and in most developing countries where this new form of business model has been introduced.

Mobile money (MM) is considered a revolutionary phenomenon in the developing world and relies on basic mobile handsets capable of voice and SMS or text, not Internet-enabled smartphones (Lepoutre & Oguntoye, 2017; Maurer, Nelms, & Rea, 2013). As we learned from the story of John, in most of the African countries, including Ghana, a considerable population cannot access formal banking services but own a cell phone. Against this increasing financial exclusion situation, many African countries are considered important research sites, particularly in MM systems and services. This necessity for academic research is due to a large scale usage of MM services by underbanked consumer segment living mostly in rural or remote areas where the provision of formal banking services has always been financially unviable and a mammoth challenge for the banking industry, government agencies, and the regulatory authorities. Nonetheless, in the opinion of CGAP (2006), the provision of formal banking services such as MM is considered safer and cheaper than informal alternatives.

Historically, the development and deployment of SMS-based MM provider called M-PESA first started its operations in Kenya in 2007. Following this lead, many developing markets introduced branchless banking or 'mobile money' products on cell phones to largely underbanked, and unbanked population segment. This innovative arrangement allows the mobile network operators (MNOs) and banks to develop an agent network and other value chain elements, and collaborate with each other to allow the remotely located population to access banking systems as well as information using their cell phones. This innovation also allows the conduction of various transactions such as salary receipt and payments, remittances transfers, airtime purchase, utility bill and school fee payments, and savings (Murendo, Wollni, De Brauw, & Mugabi, 2018). We argue that banking institutions should understand the changing consumer behavior and the factors including their decision as to when to prolong the usage of a specific banking channel such as MM. Unlike formal banking services, the MM technology relies on agent network.

Nonetheless, since 2003 MM sector has expanded to over 32 countries in the developing world (Tobbin, 2011). Here, prior literature has extensively examined various antecedents of acceptance and post-acceptance in the mobile banking context. However, the field of research in MM (also known as branchless banking) is disparate (Muthinja & Chipeta, 2017) and the MM research is still in an incipient stage of development worldwide (Dermish, Kneiding, Leishman, & Mas, 2011). Nonetheless, most of the studies conducted in the field of MM were available in the shape of ground-level surveys and white papers written for a specific purpose by practitioners. Consequently, the academic research and conceptual understanding of portable devices such as mobile phones in the development of innovative mobile financial services for the underprivileged class is lagging behind the rapid pace of change on the ground (Duncombe & Boateng, 2009). Similarly, the MM as a phenomenon of interest is contemporary and scarcely researched (Tobbin, 2011).

To fill this gap in the literature, the purpose of this chapter is threefold. Frist, we assess the potential of mobile phones as a delivery mechanism for financial services (Duncombe & Boateng, 2009) in a developing country, Ghana. Second, we highlight the significance of the role played by the MM agent in providing branchless banking services to the poor. Third, we investigate various consequences that influence the consumer decision-making process and their continued usage of mainstream MM or micro-financial services. Here, we developed a theoretical model consisting of two independent variables (MM agent credibility, MM agent service quality) and examined their influence on the endogenous variables (consumer engagement, continuous usage of MM services, WoM). The overarching research question is: how do MM agent credibility and service quality drive consumer engagement and continuous usage of MM services?

To answer our research question, the theoretical model (Figure 12.2) depicts that MM agent credibility and service quality have a positive direct effect on consumer engagement as well as both direct and indirect effects (via engagement) on continuous usage of MM services in Ghana. We also hypothesized that continuous usage has a positive direct effect on WOM. Finally, in the proposed model, we control for the effects of perceived risk, age, gender, education, duration, frequency of usage, income, and cell phone usage duration.

Next, we provide the review of past literature and discuss the role played by MM agent as well as the state of MM services in Ghana. We then explain the research model and present the hypotheses. This will be followed by a discussion of the research methodology and results. Finally, we conclude with a brief discussion of the results, limitations, implications, and future research directions.

Literature review

The literature review section has been divided into two subsections. The first subsection provides a brief overview of different MM models in place and how they differ from each other. The second subsection explains the MM usage in Ghana and the context of study.

MM services and MM agent

MM is an evolving sector, and it has an economic impact, especially in the emerging and developing world (Tobbin, 2011). Resultantly, Africa's branchless banking or MM market has expanded and diversified in recent years (Chironga, De Grandis, & Zouaoui, 2017). This diversification in MM sector is based on a very simple notion: Who manages the MM value chain elements? i.e., either bank or mobile network operator (MNO).

In MNO-based MM model, the majority of the value chain elements – deposit holding, MM issuer, payment platform, the recruitment of local MM agents who act as resellers, telecommunication channels – are owned and managed by the MNO. The bank here acts only as a deposit holder. The scope of the MM services under the MNO-led model largely concentrates on payments. Nonetheless, if there is no particular legislation for non-bank-actors such as MNO engaging in payment systems, the implementation of the purely MNO-led model in those countries require the collaboration of MNOs and the banking entity for such deployment. Another type of MM model is called MNO-bank partnership. Here MNOs in partnership with a banking company deploy the MM services. This collaboration with a financial institution expands the scope of the MM services from simple payments to loans and deposits.

Bank-led MM models are different from the MNO-led models. According to Chironga et al. (2017), the bank-led MM models require banks to develop banking apps and other value chain elements. These MM services typically require the sender to be a customer of the bank providing the service, while the beneficiary or recipient does not need to be a bank customer.

Because the banking companies are considered mature organizations with well-established business practices and a reassuringly cautious attitude to change (Lepoutre & Oguntoye, 2017), bank-led and MNO-bank-partnership MM models provide several benefits to the consumers as well as develop a strong consumer trust in the MM services.

In MM, also known as branchless banking (Reaves et al., 2017), the agent network plays an important role, and it has been explicitly considered, for example by Cobert, Helms, and Parker (2012), as the most critical success factor in MM. Here, designated agents provide financial services to low-privileged consumer segments on behalf of banking institutions, and these agents are considered the face of service to the consumers. Research (e.g., Maurer et al., 2013; Davidson & Leishman, 2011) has referred these agents as 'human ATMs' or 'bridges to cash,' 'front-line, human face.' According to the explanation provided by Baptista and Heitmann (2010), agent is regard as an individual or business that is designated by the bank or mobile network operator (MNO) to facilitate the transactions for MM users, provide front-line customer services, register new prospects, and so forth.

Elaborating the significance of paying close attention to managing the agent network, prior research (Cobert et al., 2012; Chironga et al., 2017) has reported that since customers interact with MM agents for conduct cash-in and cash-out functions, the customers consider the MM agent as the face of the company such as bank. In this situation it is safe to conclude that a MM agent can either build or destroy trust and credibility of MM services. Also, Vodafone pioneered the MM business in Africa with its highly successful and popular MM service called M-Pesa. The firm recognized that the critical actors in the MM ecosystem are actually the agents that constitute the M-Pesa network (Lepoutre & Oguntoye, 2017).

The branchless banking systems and their usage in Ghana

Africa, earlier known as the unbanked continent, is widely considered the global leader in MM technology and services, which has become an important component of Africa's financial services landscape (Chironga et al., 2017). People in Africa use more mobile phones than in any other part of the world (Dogbevi, 2010). According to Africa Mobile Trends (2016), by the year 2020, the mobile subscriptions across African continent will increase to 50%. In terms of mobile phone subscriptions, Sub-Saharan Africa will became the third biggest region, now accounting for 10% of the global subscriber base (Africa Mobile Trends, 2016). Sub-Sahara Africa recorded 420 million mobile subscribers at the end of 2016. (GSMA, 2017). Africa is credited with the invention of MM (Botsman, 2014). The platform first emerged in 2007 when Vodafone developed M-PESA for Vodacom and

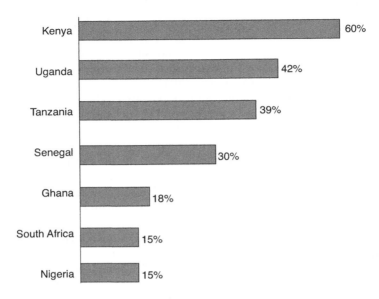

Figure 12.1 Mobile payment usage of top seven African countries
Source: African Business Central, 2015.

Safaricom in Kenya (; Mbele, 2016) for money transfers. Currently, the continent leads the rest of the world in respect of MM usage. According to Botsman (2014), a survey conducted by the Gates Foundation, the World Bank, and Gallup World Poll revealed that out of the top 20 countries that employ MM, 15 are African. Additionally, Kenya has 80% of the world's MM transactions (Botsman, 2014). Figure 12.1 depicts the mobile payment usage of the top seven African countries.

The liberalization of Ghana's mobile telephone sector has resulted in dramatic transformation. The sector currently comprises five firms (MTN, Vodafone, Airtel Tigo, Glo, and Expresso) (NCA, 2016). MTN, the market leader as at July 2017, accounted for 47.54% and 56.29% of mobile voice and mobile data subscription, respectively (see Table 12.1 for details).

The introduction of MM to the Ghanaian economy has played a key role in the push for financial inclusion (Ghana Banking Survey, 2016). According to the World Bank, the majority of Ghanaians (a whopping 76%) is unbanked (Segbefia, 2016) and MM has aided in extending some form of financial assistance to rural Ghana where traditional banks have not been able to operate. MM is currently being employed in transferring money, making payments, and other transactions traditionally deemed to be the reserve of banks (Ghana Banking Survey, 2016). MTN, Ghana's largest telecom company, started the MM concept in August 2009 and by 2014, the patronage

Table 12.1 Market shares of mobile phone operators by voice calls and data

Firm	Voice (%)	Data (%)
MTN	47.54	56.29
Vodafone	24.02	16.48
Millicom (Tigo)	14.84	13.70
Airtel	11.36	12.37
Glo	2.18	1.11
Expresso	0.06	0.02

NB: Expresso's mobile voice and data subscriptions beyond April 2017 is unavailable.

Source: NCA, 2017.

of MM had gained momentum, and the volumes were rising astronomically across income groups (Opare, 2018; citifmonline, 2016). In August 2016, there were 16.4 million registered MM accounts in Ghana (GBN, 2016). In respect of the value and volume of transactions, the Bank of Ghana reported that MM transactions amounted to GH¢11.6 billion in 2014 and GH¢9.2 billion in 2013 from an amount of GH¢2.4 billion. Additionally, the total number of registered agents reached 108,531 in June 2016 as against 36,000 agents in the same period the previous year (citifmonline, 2016;). The number of transactions has almost quadrupled since 2012; from 30 million to about 106.4 million in 2014 (citifmonline, 2016). The exponential rate at which MM patronage is rising is arguably due to the benefits that the service offers subscribers. MM provides a cheap and relatively safe means of transferring money, shorter transaction times and reduces the transaction cost of financial services to the poor and unbanked (Ahiabenu, 2010; Ghana Banking Survey, 2016). Additionally, the proliferation of mobile phones in the country could be a factor (Anderson, 2013).

Research model and hypotheses

The research model is depicted in Figure 12.2. It includes five main constructs and six hypotheses in total. We investigate the effects of MM agent credibility as well as MM agent service quality on the unbanked consumer engagement. We also investigate the effect of consumer engagement on consumer continuance usage of MM services and WOM.

The effects of MM agent credibility on consumer engagement with MM services

The term 'credibility' is defined as the extent to which a person believes that the use of any financial service will have no security or privacy threats

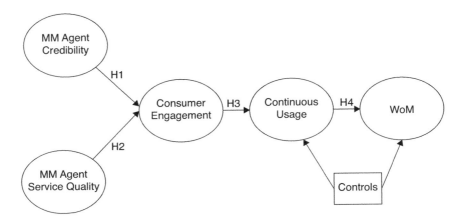

Figure 12.2 Theoretical model

(Luarn & Lin, 2005). According to Kim, Shin, and Lee (2009) and Kim and Prabhakar (2004), structural assurances promise the reliability of monetary or financial transactions, the protection of individual privacy, and transactional confidentiality. Since MM is a financial service, the credibility and the usage of this newly developed service for the unbanked or underbanked can be enhanced if MM agents are deemed trustworthy by consumers (Maurer et al., 2013; Davidson & Leishman, 2011). Conversely, if an agent commits a fraud, misguides the consumer, or makes mistakes, it will tarnish the image of the banking system and the credibility of the service. Resultantly, this will reduce (and may eliminate) the continuous engagement with the MM services.

In relation to consumer engagement, mobile-based developments created two major challenges for research and service organizations, especially banks. First, the use of technology demands a structured rather than an unstructured approach. Second, technology usage in the everyday lives of consumers changes consumer behavior, making consumers more fickle and more skeptical than ever before (Shaikh & Karjaluoto, 2016). Based on that premise, there is a need to move beyond customer satisfaction and loyalty with an underlying purpose to evolve to a higher level, a level of desired differentiation and sustainable competitive advantage (Pansari & Kumar, 2017). This led to the rise of the term engagement among marketing academics and practitioners (Pansari & Kumar, 2017).

Customer engagement has been considered an emerging and interesting topic in the marketing research (Marketing Science Institute, 2014; Hepola, Karjaluoto, & Shaikh, 2016). The term 'customer engagement' has also been referred to as customer brand engagement, brand engagement, and consumer engagement (Puriwat & Tripopsakul, 2014). According to Vivek,

Beatty, Dalela, and Morgan (2014) and Hepola et al. (2016), consumer engagement goes beyond purchase of a service or product, and refers to the level of the customer's (or potential customer's) interactions and connections with the brand or firm's offerings or activities, often involving others in the social network created around the brand, offering, or activity. In the mobile services context, Hollebeek, Glynn, and Brodie (2014) have defined customer engagement as a consumer's positively valenced mobile services (including mobile application) related to cognitive, emotional, and behavioral activity or related to focal consumer and mobile services interactions.

Prior research (e.g., Imlawi, Gregg, & Karimi, 2015; Yang, Kang, & Johnson, 2010) has confirmed the relevance of credibility as an antecedent to customer engagement in the context of online blogs. This direct correlation between the credibility and customer engagement implies that the higher the credibility, the higher the consumer engagement. Nonetheless, this relationship between credibility and consumer engagement is not investigated in the context of mobile-based services such as MM, but considering the adjacent association between the online blogging and mobile-based services, this correlation is expected to be present also in the context of MM services. It is, therefore, hypothesized:

H1: *Agent credibility positively influences consumer engagement with MM services.*

The effects of MM agent service quality on consumer engagement with MM services

In the backdrop of increasing competition among service companies such as banks, the nature and the quality of service provided to customers have received immense attention from companies with or without web presences. The basic argument emanating from an extended literature on service quality (e.g., Goyal & Chanda, 2017; Salanova, Agut, & Peiró, 2005; Sureshchandar, Rajendran, & Anantharaman, 2002; McLachlin, 2000) explains that superior service quality creates a great customer experience. It is considered as an important antecedent of customer loyalty and retention; a positive perception of firm's service quality which promotes the positive word of mouth for the service provider such as agent and bank. A strong correlation is found between service quality and customer satisfaction (Farooq, Salam, Fayolle, Jaafar, & Ayupp, 2018). The most important dimension of service quality is reliability, and the only appropriate judge of service quality is the customer.

Literature has segregated the definition of web-based service quality or e-SQ and off-line service quality that involves physical or face-to-face interaction. Parasuraman, Zeithaml, and Berry (1988) defined service quality as global judgment, or attitude, relating to the superiority of the service. On the other hand, e-SQ is defined as the extent to which a website facilitates efficient and effective shopping, purchasing, and delivery of products and services (Zeithaml, Parasuraman, & Malhotra, 2000).

The scope of this study considers face-to-face service quality provided by agents in MM services to largely unbanked consumer segment and its effect on the customer engagement. Investigating the service quality, customer engagement, commitment, and customer loyalty of service providers of the mobile network, Thailand, Dhasan and Kowathanakul (2017) found that service quality, promotional offers, commitment, and customer engagement have positive associations with customer loyalty. Their study also found a direct relationship between service quality and online customer engagement. A similar study by Puriwat and Tripopsakul (2014) found that service quality significantly influences customer engagement's three dimensions: cognitive, emotional, and behavioral engagement. Considering this direct effect between service quality and customer engagement, we hypothesized that:

H2:   *Agent service quality positively influences consumer engagement with MM services.*

The effects of consumer engagement on continuous usage of MM services

Considering the effects of MM agent credibility and service quality on customer engagement, we now determine how customer engagement affects continuous usage behavior; an increasing customer engagement will prolong the usage of MM services.

A review of contemporary literature revealed a positive and significant relationship between consumer engagement and continuous usage. For example, Hepola et al. (2016) examine the effects of consumer engagement (cognitive, affection, and activation) and perceived risk on continuous usage intention of consumers using m-banking and m-payment applications. We extend this relationship between the consumer engagement and the continuous usage intention in the context of branchless banking or MM services considered closely associated with the mobile payment services. We, therefore, posit that

H3:   *Consumer engagement positively influences continuous usage behavior.*

The effects of continuous usage of MM services on word of mouth

The relationship between continuous usage of service and positive e-WOM is quite obvious, since a satisfied customer will provide a positive recommendation. In this study, however, we have considered WOM more pressing after considering the nature of the MM services that serve a different consumer segment, i.e. unbanked and underbanked. Unlike social media and e-service, MM services demand traditional face-to-face interaction with the MM agent and, therefore, it is considered different from the e-WOM, which is shared online with a larger consumer segment using online or social media channels. Thus, e-WOM is considered more influential than traditional WOM (Ring et al., 2016).

WOM is predominantly verbal and informal communication between private parties concerning evaluations of goods and services (Anderson, 2013; Ring et al., 2016). In services marketing, prior research (Brown, Barry, Dacin, & Gunst, 2005, p. 123) has described WOM as "a dominant force in the marketplace." Similarly, WOM has been considered a vital element in influencing purchase decisions of potential consumers (Ring et al., 2016; Shaikh & Karjaluoto, 2016). After all, when customers believe they are satisfied and get more out of a product or service, they say positive things about this particular product or service.

Given its assigned importance, it is surprising to find relatively few studies (Brown et al., 2005) directed at understanding relationship between the increasing usage of service and WOM. Nonetheless, in the marketing (consumer behavior) literature (e.g., Shaikh & Karjaluoto, 2016), some evidences confirm the relationships between continuous usage intention and WOM. Thus, we hypothesize:

H4: *Continuous usage produces positive word of mouth.*

Research methodology

Sample and data collection procedure

Consistent with a previous study examining customer usage of MM service (Chauhan, 2015; Upadhyay & Jahanyan, 2016; Cobla & Osei-Assibey, 2018), we conducted a survey of customers to test our conceptual model. The data for this research was collected from college student cohorts who were existing subscribers of MM services. University of Ghana executive masters' students were conveniently selected for the empirical investigation. Three teaching assistants randomly approached the students on the university campuses to ask if they would be willing to fill out a questionnaire. In all, 869 students were approached, out of which 595 responses were received from September 12, 2016, to October 11, 2016. Two hundred and sixteen declined to participate because they had not subscribed to MM services. Appendix A presents the sample characteristics.

Measurement

We adapted our measures from established scales. When necessary, items were modified to suit the MM context. WOM was captured with three items borrowed from Zeithaml, Berry, and Parasuraman (1996). Consumer engagement was modeled as first order components of the three dimensions of it: activation, affection, and cognition. Two items were used to measure activation, four items measured affection and three items measured cognitive. These nine items were adapted from Hollebeek et al. (2014). Continuous usage of MM services was measured with three items adapted from Zhou (2013). All the remaining constructs were measured with four items. Items of MM agent service quality were adapted from Kim et al. (2009). Items of MM agent credibility were taken from Tang, Lin, Wang, & Wang (2004). The scales for perceived risk (of using MM services) were taken from Karjaluoto, Töllinen, Pirttiniemi, & Jayawardhena (2014). All items were measured on a seven-point Likert scale, ranging from strongly disagree (1) to strongly agree (7). The measurement items are shown in Appendix B.

Findings

The data were analyzed using SmartPLS 3.2.7 (Ringle, Wende, & Becker, 2015). We first assessed the measurement model regarding the reliability of the scales, and checked for convergent and discriminant validity. All factor loadings were significant at $p < 0.001$ (two-tailed) and ranged from 0.497 to 0.947 (see Appendix B). Values of 0.5 are considered acceptable (Barclay, Higgins, & Thompson, 1995) although loadings above 0.7 were preferred and considered as the rule of thumb. The composite reliability indices (Fornell & Larcker, 1981) were all above the acceptable value of 0.7 (Hair, Sarstedt, Ringle, & Gudergan, 2018). Convergent validity was assessed by average variance extracted (AVE), where a value of 0.5 and above indicates an acceptable level (Fornell & Larcker, 1981). The AVE values ranged from 0.61 to 0.89 (Table 12.2) and were all above the cut-off value of 0.5. Discriminant validity was performed using Fornell and Larcker's (1981) criterion, which requires that the square root of each latent variable's AVE is greater than the latent variable's correlation with any other construct in the model (Glavee-Geo, Shaikh, & Karjaluoto, 2017). A comparison of the square root of the AVE (diagonal values) and the correlations among the constructs are presented in Table 12.2, showing support for discriminant validity. Further, discriminant validity was also assessed by using the *heterotrait-monotrait ratio of correlations (HTMT)* (Henseler, Ringle, & Sarstedt, 2015). The HTMT values were below .85, demonstrating that discriminant validity was established between any two of constructs (Hair et al., 2018; Henseler et al., 2015).

Assessment of the path coefficients was done by bootstrapping to assess the significance of the path coefficients. Table 12.3 shows the results of the path analysis of the initial model. In the proposed model as depicted in Figure 12.2, we hypothesized the structural relations between MM agent credibility, service quality, consumer engagement, continuous usage, and WOM. We hypothesized a positive association between MM agent credibility (H1), MM agent service quality (H2), and consumer engagement.

Table 12.2 Discriminant validity coefficients (*n* = 595)

	CR	AVE	1	2	3	4	5	6	7	8
Continuous usage (1)	.81	.61	.78							
Agent credibility (2)	.88	.66	.44	.81						
Perceived risk (3)	.89	.68	−.19	−.26	.83					
Agent service quality (4)	.89	.67	.34	.44	−.07	.82				
Word of mouth (WOM) (5)	.93	.81	.50	.29	−.17	.25	.89			
Activation (6)	.94	.89	.46	.34	−.11	.21	.39	.95		
Affection (7)	.95	.81	.54	.45	−,18	.38	.59	.45	.90	
Cognitive (8)	.88	.71	.30	.28	.07	.27	.41	.26	.61	.84

Note: *Bold values on the diagonal are square root of the AVEs. CR Composite reliability; AVE Average variance extracted.*

We proposed the outcome of consumer engagement to be continuous usage (H3), while WOM is posited to be the outcome of continuous usage (H4). The results of the structural model are shown in Figure 12.3.

MM agent creditability significantly influence activation (β = 0.31, p < 0.001), affection (β = 0.36, p < 0.001), and the cognitive (β = 0.21, p < 0.001) components of engagement. However, although MM agent service quality significantly influence affection (β = 0.22, p < 0.001) and the cognitive (β = 0.18, p < 0.001) components of engagement, the influence of MM agent service quality on activation was not supported (β = 0.07, p > 0.05). We found

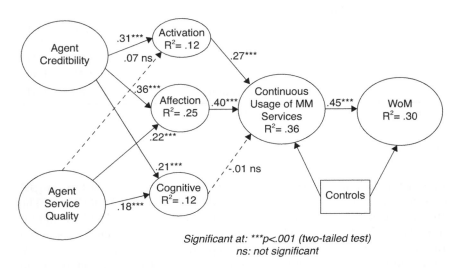

Significant at: ***p<.001 (two-tailed test)
ns: not significant

Figure 12.3 Results of respecified structural model (*n* = 595)

Table 12.3 Path coefficient and VIF (*n* = 595)

Criterion	Predictor	Path coefficient	t-values	VIF
Activation	Agent credibility	.31***	6.72	1.23
	Agent service quality	.07 ns	1.52	1.23
Affection	Agent credibility	.36***	7.71	1.23
	Agent service quality	.22***	4.39	1.23
Cognitive	Agent credibility	.21***	4.28	1.23
	Agent service quality	.18***	3.88	1.23
Continuous usage	Activation	.27***	5.08	1.41
	Affection	.40***	7.09	2.05
	Cognitive	−.01 ns	.24	1.70
	Perceived risk	−.10**	2.66	1.12
	Age	−.03 ns	.55	1.63
	Gender	−.04 ns	1.30	1.04
	Education	.02 ns	.44	1.12
	Mobile money usage experience (duration)	.05 ns	1.45	1.22
	Frequency of usage	−.04 ns	.93	1.31
	Income	.03 ns	.58	1.44
	Cell phone usage duration	.02 ns	.58	1.41
Word of mouth (WOM)	Continuous usage	.45***	10.62	1.10
	Perceived risk	−.06 ns	1.41	1.07
	Age	.04 ns	.66	1.61
	Gender	−.01 ns	.23	1.04
	Education	−.04 ns	1.29	1.11
	Mobile money usage experience (duration)	.09**	2.36	1.21
	Frequency of usage	.08**	2.05	1.21
	Income	.10**	2.21	1.43
	Cell phone usage duration	.04 ns	.88	1.41

Note: # *based on 1,000 bootstrapping samples*

****p < 0.001*
***p < 0.05 (two-tailed), ns – not significant*

support for the effect of activation (β = 0.27, p < 0.001) and affection (β = 0.40, p < 0.05) on continuous usage of MM services (see Table 12.3). The effect of the cognitive component of engagement was found to be insignificant (β = −0.01, p > 0.05). H4, which states a positive association between continuous usage and WoM, is also supported (β = 0.45, p < 0.001). We controlled for the effects of perceived risk, age, gender, education, duration of MM usage, frequency of usage, income, and cell phone usage duration on both endogenous variables (continuous usage and WOM). We found that perceived risk and duration of MM usage significantly influence continuous usage while income significantly influences WOM. Table 12.3 shows the results of the path analysis. In this chapter, the terms 'cognitive' and 'cognition' are used interchangeably. In addition, the control variables MM usage experience, usage experience of cell phones, and income were significantly related to WOM while perceived risk was found to be negatively related to continuous usage of MM services.

Discussion and conclusion

It is considered important to reach the underbanked and unbanked consumer segment when the consumption of formal banking products and services is considered as an important prerequisite to improving economic activities, helping the less privileged to increase their household income, building their asset base, and improving their resilience to shocks (Abramovay, 2004; Morawczynski, 2009). Consequent to these benefits, the MM service initiatives receive a considerable amount of attention from marketing executives, regulators, and government agencies, as well as from FinTech start-ups and MNOs.

The purpose of this chapter was to provide an overview of the consumer MM financial sector in Africa with an empirical focus on the role of service agents in Ghana. We sought to achieve this purpose with an overarching research question stated as: how do MM agent credibility and service quality drive consumer engagement and continuous usage of MM services? Specifically, we sought to find answers two research questions: (1) what are the factors that affect MM usage behavior of consumers in a developing country? and (2) how does the credibility of MM agent play a decisive role in the success of branchless banking? In total, we hypothesized six structural relations and developed a model that we tested to answer our research questions.

Theoretical implications

Previous research has established the relevance of trust and credibility in customer engagement (e.g., Imlawi, Gregg, & Karimi, 2015) and behavioral intention to adopt and use m-banking (Cudjoe, Anim, & Nyanyofio, 2015). Thus, in the context of m-banking, credibility has been found to be of topmost concern (see also Tang et al., 2004). Our support for the effect of MM agent credibility on all the three components of customer engagement provides strong support for the important role of credibility in mobile financial services delivery and adoption intention. Credibility strongly stimulate all the three dimensions of consumer engagement in terms of activation, affection, and cognition. Consequently, activation and affection predict continuous usage. However, our analysis shows that MM agent service quality only had significant influence on the affection and the cognitive process of consumer engagement and not on activation.

Service quality is the extent to which the service delivered matches customer expectations (Chen, 2012). The level of service has been found to have a significant impact on trust in the usage of MM services (Zhou, 2013) while Chen (2012) found support for its indirect effect on continuous intention. The level of service is key in engaging consumers of MM services as supported by our study. Our study shows the importance of the quality of service delivered by agents in enhancing customer engagement and the continuous use of service. This is very important due to the variability of services delivered on behalf of financial institutions. Thus, engagement has an impact on the continuous use of MM service. Customer engagement is an important link to continuous usage. Our study on MM services confirms the linkages between customer engagement on WOM (cf. Hepola et al., 2016). Thus, the manner in which MM service agents engage customers and potential customers have implication on how these customers foretell their experiences to other potential customers.

Prior research has shown that an increased use of mobile and other e-services will result in positive e-WOM or recommendation intention (Noori, Hashim, & Yusof, 2016; Shaikh & Karjaluoto, 2016). The effect of continuous usage on WOM has also been supported by the present study of MM services. The importance of risk in the m-banking adoption process has been the focus of recent studies (e.g., Shaikh, Glavee-Geo, & Karjaluoto, 2018). Thus, the significant negative effect of perceived risk on continuous usage found from our study highlights the risk-continuous usage link. In using the service, gender, age, level of education and income levels were found not to have any impact. This presupposes that the continuous usage of MM is irrespective of age, gender, level of education and income. However, regarding age, one can argue that a certain minimum age is required to transact financial services. All the respondents to this study were above 18 years.

Managerial implications

It is widely accepted and reported that over two billion people in the world do not have access to formal banking and financial services such as branch, ATMs, and Internet. This motivates the banking industry to expand its outreach by developing and deploying banking services which can be conveniently accessed using cell phones by a largely unserved and unexplored consumer segment which is often referred to as the underbanked or unbanked.

For managers, it is a valuable piece of information to understand that the transformational services such as MM are aimed at bringing the financial and payment services to the unbanked and, according to Tobbin (2011), this phenomenon is spreading throughout emerging economies at a rate that is unprecedented. MM services are unique and follow a different business model that allows the designated agents to provide financial services to less-privileged segments of a population. MM agents are intermediaries working on behalf of banking institutions. They are considered the 'frontline' contact persons for the co-creation of services to be 'consumed' by consumers. The credibility and trustworthiness of these intermediaries, therefore, have a significant impact on the service delivery designed and deployed by banking companies or the MNOs.

Moreover, the quality of service delivered by intermediaries/agents on behalf of financial institutions and MNOs is another critical issue worth consideration if the 'branchless banking' business model is to become successful as an alternative delivery channel. Of the three dimensions of engagement, affection's influence on continuous usage has the greatest impact compared to activation and cognitive. This means that more should be done to stimulate the engagement process. Marketing communications and promotional campaigns of MM services targeted at consumers should emphasize the 'feeling positive,' 'happy,' 'good,' and 'proud' about MM services. The actual service delivery by service agents should also aim at stimulating these 'emotions' in the consumers of MM services.

In addition, the significant effect of MM agent service quality on the affection and the cognitive process of consumer engagement and the insignificant effect on activation means that MM service agents, FinTechs and the banks need to do more in terms of customer service. This will require training and retraining of service agents who are the main intermediaries between the financial institutions (herein the banks), the FinTechs and the MM customers. Thus, improving MM agent service quality should be able to 'activate' users of the service in terms of using MM services regularly and very often. The effect of the cognitive dimension on continuous usage is insignificant in the study and this also means that targeted marketing communication strategies should be rolled out to help in educating the users and potential consumers. These communication and promotional strategies should aim at creating awareness of the service since this is a new service design and should help stimulate the cognitive processes of consumers to 'think,' and to develop 'interest' in using the service. Subsequently, these strategies will culminate in increasing usage of MM services to the underbank and unbank segments of the population.

Limitations and future research directions

Our study is not without any limitations. First and the foremost limitation is that the generalization of our study results is difficult to establish because of two major reasons: First, the cross sectional nature of our study does not provide the definitive information about the cause-and-effect relationships but a snapshot of a geographic location where the study was conducted. Second, the measurement of the constructs in order to study the consumer behavior in using MM services was survey-based administrated at a single point in time, and descriptive. These limitations in our study can be overcome if the future research considers conducting studies with larger samples sizes and experimental research design. The generalizability of the findings can also be achieved by involving different demographics and age groups of the participants in multiple countries where MM services are currently in use in Africa.

Another limitation is the demographic profile of the study participants. The majority of the study participants were college students from rural Ghana. Therefore, examining the consumption intention, behavior, and beliefs of the people living in urban Ghana is out of the scope of this study. Future research may conduct a detailed comparative study in examining the behavior of consumers living in rural and urban areas that use MM services. This will give an interesting insight to determine consumers in urban Ghana, despite having access to other banking channels, consider MM services and how their attitude, as well as MM service consumption pattern, differs from consumers living in rural Ghana.

Asian countries have recently been developing and deploying several MM models and applications in both MNO-led and bank-led. Another future research advice could be to replicate our research model in other developing markets in Asia.

Note

* *Corresponding/primary contact author*

References

Abramovay, R. (2004). As finanças na luta contra a pobreza. *Desafios do Desenvolvimento, 1*(3), 66–67.

Africa Mobile Trends (2016). *Smartphone adoption is gaining momentum.* Retrieved from www.agyp.co/. . ./31717ccb1e3d-Jumia_White_Paper_Africa_Moblie

Ahiabenu, K (2010). *Beyond the Bank: The Rise of Mobile Money in Ghana.* Retrieved December 14, 2017, from https://www.modernghana.com/news/301842/beyond-the-bank-the-rise-of-mobile-money-in-ghana.html

Anderson, E. W. (2013). Customer satisfaction and word of mouth. *Journal of Service Research, 1*(1), 5–17.

Baptista, P., & Heitmann, S. (2010). *Unleashing the power of convergence to advance mobile money ecosystems.* Washington, DC: IFC and the Harvard Kennedy School.

Barclay, D., Higgins, C., & Thompson, R. (1995). The partial least squares approach to causal modeling: Personal computer adoption and use as an illustration. *Technology Studies*, Special Issue on Research Methodology 2(2), 285–324.

Botsman, R. (2014, February 14). *Mobile Money: The African Lesson We Can Learn.* Retrieved December 14, 2017, from www.rachelbotsman.com

Brown, T. J., Barry, T. E., Dacin, p. A., & Gunst, R. F. (2005). Spreading the word: Investigating antecedents of consumers' positive word-of-mouth intentions and behaviors in a retailing context. *Journal of the Academy of Marketing Science, 33*(2), 123–138.

CGAP (2006). *Use of agents in branchless banking for the poor.* Retrieved from www.cgap.org/publications/use-agents-branchless-banking-poor

Chauhan, S. (2015). Acceptance of mobile money by poor citizens of India: Integrating trust into the technology acceptance model. *Info, 17*(3), 58–68.

Chen, S. C. (2012). To use or not to use: Understanding the factors affecting continuance intention of mobile banking. *International Journal of Mobile Communications, 10*(5), 490–507.

Chironga, M., De Grandis, H., & Zouaoui, Y. (2017). *Mobile financial services in Africa: Winning the battle for the customer.* Retrieved from www.mckinsey.com/industries/financial-services/our-insights/mobile-financial-services-in-africa-winning-the-battle-for-the-customer

Citifmonline (2016). *Mobile Money records over 100 % increase in 2016 first quarter.* Retrieved April 13, 2018, from http://citifmonline.com/2016/06/09/mobile-money-records-over-100-increase-in-2016-first-quarter/

Cobert, B., Helms, B., & Parker, D. (2012). *Mobile money: Getting to scale in emerging markets.* Retrieved from www.mckinsey.com/industries/social-sector/our-insights/mobile-money-getting-to-scale-in-emerging-markets

Cobla, G. M., & Osei-Assibey, E. (2018). Mobile money adoption and spending behaviour: The case of students in Ghana. *International Journal of Social Economics, 45*(1), 29–42.

Cudjoe, A. G., Anim, p. A., & Nyanyofio, J. G. N. T. (2015). Determinants of mobile banking adoption in the Ghanaian banking industry: A case of access bank Ghana limited. *Journal of Computer and Communications, 3*, 1–19.

Davidson, N., & Leishman, p. (2011). *Building, incentivising and managing a network of mobile money agents.* Retrieved from www.gsma.com/mobilefordevelopment/wp-content/uploads/ 2011/02/Agent-Networks-full.pdf

Dermish, A., Kneiding, C., Leishman, P., & Mas, I. (2011). Branchless and mobile banking solutions for the poor: A survey of the literature. *Innovations: Technology, Governance, Globalization, 6*(4), 81–98.

Dhasan, D., & Kowathanakul, S. (2017). *Building customer loyalty through service quality, customer engagement and commitment: The case of mobile network providers in Thailand.* XVI International Business & Economy Conference (IBEC), Chile.

Dogbevi, E. K. (2010). *More in Africa use mobile phones than on any other continent.* Retrieved from www.ghanabusinessnews.com/2010/01/04/more-in-africa-usemobile-phones-than-on-any-other-continent

Duncombe, R., & Boateng, R. (2009). Mobile phones and financial services in developing countries: A review of concepts, methods, issues, evidence and future research directions. *Third World Quarterly, 30*(7), 1237–1258.

Farooq, M. S., Salam, M., Fayolle, A., Jaafar, N., & Ayupp, K. (2018). Impact of service quality on customer satisfaction in Malaysia airlines: A PLS-SEM approach. *Journal of Air Transport Management, 67*, 169–180.

Fornell, C., & Larcker, D. F. (1981). Evaluating structural equation models with unobservable variables and measurement error. *Journal of Marketing Research, 18*(1), 39–50.

GBN (2016). *Ghana registers 16.4 million mobile money accounts.* Retrieved April 13, 2018, from https://www.ghanabusinessnews.com/2016/08/11/ghana-registers-16-4-million-mobile-money-accounts/

Glavee-Geo, R., Shaikh, A. A., & Karjaluoto, H. (2017). Mobile banking services adoption in Pakistan: Are there gender differences? *International Journal of Bank Marketing, 35*(7), 1090–1114.

Goyal, P., & Chanda, U. (2017). A Bayesian Network Model on the association between CSR, perceived service quality and customer loyalty in Indian Banking Industry. *Sustainable Production and Consumption, 10,* 50–65.

GSMA (2017). *The mobile economy Sub-Saharan Africa 2017*. Retrieved from www.gsma.com/mobileeconomy/sub-saharan-africa-2017

Hair Jr., J. F., Sarstedt, M., Ringle, C. M., & Gudergan, S. p. (2018). *Advanced issues in partial least squares structural equation modeling.* Thousand Oaks, CA: Sage Publications.

Henseler, J., Ringle, C. M., & Sarstedt, M. (2015). A new criterion for assessing discriminant validity in variance-based structural equation modeling. *Journal of the Academy of Marketing Science, 43*(1), 115–135.

Hepola, J., Karjaluoto, H., & Shaikh, A. A. (2016). *Consumer engagement and behavioral intention toward continuous use of innovative mobile banking applications: A case study of Finland.* Thirty Seventh International Conference on Information Systems, Dublin. AISel.

Hollebeek, L. D., Glynn, M. S., & Brodie, R. J. (2014). Consumer brand engagement in social media: Conceptualization, scale development and validation. *Journal of Interactive Marketing, 28*(2), 149–165.

Imlawi, J., Gregg, D., & Karimi, J. (2015). Student engagement in course-based social networks: The impact of instructor credibility and use of communication. *Computers & Education, 88,* 84–96.

Karjaluoto, H., Töllinen, A., Pirttiniemi, J., & Jayawardhena, C. (2014). Intention to use mobile customer relationship management systems. *Industrial Management & Data Systems, 114*(6), 966–978.

Kim, G., Shin, B., & Lee, H. G. (2009). Understanding dynamics between initial trust and usage intentions of mobile banking. *Information Systems Journal, 19*(3), 283–311.

Kim, K. K., & Prabhakar, B. (2004). Initial trust and the adoption of B2C e-commerce: The case of Internet banking. *ACM SIGMIS Database, 35,* 50–64.

Lepoutre, J., & Oguntoye, A. (2017). The (non-) emergence of mobile money systems in Sub-Saharan Africa: A comparative multilevel perspective of Kenya and Nigeria. *Technological Forecasting and Social Change, 131,* 262–275.

Luarn, P., & Lin, H. H. (2005). Toward an understanding of the behavioral intention to use mobile banking. *Computers in Human Behavior, 21*(6), 873–891.

Marketing Science Institute (2014). *2014–2016 research priorities*. Retrieved from www.msi.org/research/2014-2016-research-priorities

Maurer, B., Nelms, T. C., & Rea, S. C. (2013). "Bridges to cash": Channelling agency in mobile money. *Journal of the Royal Anthropological Institute, 19*(1), 52–74.

Mbele, L. (2016, May 11). Why M-Pesa failed in South Africa. *BBC Africa Business Report*, Johannesburg.

McLachlin, R. (2000). Service quality in consulting: What is engagement success? *Managing Service Quality: An International Journal, 10*(3), 141–150.

Morawczynski, O. (2009). Exploring the usage and impact of "transformational" mobile financial services: The case of M-PESA in Kenya. *Journal of Eastern African Studies, 3*(3), 509–525.

Murendo, C., Wollni, M., De Brauw, A., & Mugabi, N. (2018). Social network effects on mobile money adoption in Uganda. *The Journal of Development Studies*, *54*(2), 327–342.

Muthinja, M. M., & Chipeta, C. (2017). What drives financial innovations in Kenya's commercial banks? An empirical study on firm and macro-level drivers of branchless banking. *Journal of African Business*, 1–24.

NCA. (2016). *Telecom voice subscription for December 2016*. Retrieved April 13, 2018, from http://www.nca.org.gh/assets/Uploads/Voice-Statistics-December-2016.pdf

NCA. (2017). *Telecom voice subscription for December 2016*. Retrieved April 13, 2018, from http://www.nca.org.gh/assets/Uploads/Voice-Statistics-December-2017.pdf

Noori, A. S., Hashim, K. F., & Yusof, S. A. M. (2016). The conceptual relation of electronic word-of-mouth, commitment and trust in influencing continuous usage of social commerce. *International Review of Management and Marketing*, *6*(7S).

Opare, E. A. (2018). The Advantages and Disadvantages of Mobile Money on the Profitability of the Ghanaian Banking Industry. *Texila International Journal of Management*, *4*(2), 1-8.

Pansari, A., & Kumar, V. (2017). Customer engagement: The construct, antecedents, and consequences. *Journal of the Academy of Marketing Science*, *45*(3), 294–311.

Parasuraman, A., Zeithaml, V. A., & Berry, L. L. (1988). SERQUAL: A multipleitem scale for measuring consumer perceptions of service quality. *Journal of Retailing*, *64*(1), 12–40.

Puriwat, W., & Tripopsakul, S. (2014). *The investigation of the influence of service quality toward customer engagement in service dominant industries in Thailand*. International Proceedings of Economics Development and Research, 82, 42.

Reaves, B., Bowers, J., Scaife, N., Bates, A., Bhartiya, A., Traynor, P., & Butler, K. R. (2017). Mo(bile) money, mo(bile) problems: Analysis of branchless banking applications. *ACM Transactions on Privacy and Security (TOPS)*, *20*(3), 11.

Ring, A., Tkaczynski, A., & Dolnicar, S. (2016). Word-of-mouth segments: Online, offline, visual or verbal? *Journal of Travel Research*, *55*(4), 481–492.

Ringle, C. M., Wende, S., & Becker, J.-M. (2015). *SmartPLS 3. Boenningstedt: SmartPLS GmbH*. Retrieved April 18, 2018, from www.smartpls.com

Salanova, M., Agut, S., & Peiró, J. M. (2005). Linking organizational resources and work engagement to employee performance and customer loyalty: The mediation of service climate. *Journal of Applied Psychology*, *90*(6), 1217.

Segbefia, L. (2015). *70% Of Ghana's Population Is Unbanked*. Retrieved December 14, 2017, from https://www.newsghana.com.gh/70-of-ghanas-population-is-unbanked/

Shaikh, A. A., Glavee-Geo, R., & Karjaluoto, H. (2018). How relevant are risk perceptions, effort, and performance expectancy in mobile banking adoption? *International Journal of E-Business Research (IJEBR)*, *14*(2), 39–60.

Shaikh, A. A., & Karjaluoto, H. (2016, January). *Mobile banking services continuous usage-case study of Finland*. System Sciences (HICSS), 2016 49th Hawaii International Conference on (pp. 1497–1506), Koloa, HI. IEEE.

Shaikh, A. A., & Karjaluoto, H. (2016). On some misconceptions concerning digital banking and alternative delivery channels. *International Journal of E-Business Research*, *12*(3), 1–16.

Sureshchandar, G. S., Rajendran, C., & Anantharaman, R. N. (2002). The relationship between service quality and customer satisfaction: A factor specific approach. *Journal of Services Marketing, 16*(4), 363–379.

Tang, T. I., Lin, H. H., Wang, Y. S., & Wang, Y. M. (2004). *Toward an understanding of the behavioral intention to use mobile banking services*. PACIS 2004 Proceedings, 131.

Tobbin, p. (2011). *Understanding mobile money ecosystem: Roles, structure and strategies*. Mobile Business (ICMB), 2011 Tenth International Conference, Como, Italy, 185–194. DOI: 10.1109/ICMB.2011.19.

Upadhyay, P., & Jahanyan, S. (2016). Analyzing user perspective on the factors affecting use intention of mobile based transfer payment. *Internet Research, 26*(1), 38–56.

Vivek, S. D., Beatty, S. E., Dalela, V., & Morgan, R. M. (2014). A generalized multidimensional scale for measuring customer engagement. *Journal of Marketing Theory and Practice, 22*(4), 401–420.

Yang, S. U., Kang, M., & Johnson, p. (2010). Effects of narratives, openness to dialogic communication, and credibility on engagement in crisis communication through organizational blogs. *Communication Research, 37*(4), 473–497.

Zeithaml, V. A., Berry, L. L., & Parasuraman, A. (1996). The behavioral consequences of service quality. *Journal of Marketing, 60*(2), 31–46.

Zeithaml, V. A., Parasuraman, A., & Malhotra, A. (2000). *A conceptual framework for understanding e-service quality: Implications for future research and managerial practice*. Working Paper No. 00–115. Marketing Science Institute, Cambridge, MA.

Zhou, T. (2013). An empirical examination of continuance intention of mobile payment services. *Decision Support Systems, 54*(2), 1085–1091.

Appendix A

Sample demographic characteristics

Demographic characteristics	Frequency	Percent
Gender		
Males	316	53.1
Females	279	46.9
Age (years)		
18–25	356	59.8
26–35	173	29.1
36–45	48	8.1
46–55	15	2.5
56–65	3	0.5
Highest level of education		
Junior high school	9	1.6
Senior high school	137	23
O level/A level	11	1.8
Polytechnic	17	2.9
Teacher training	4	.7
Bachelor/Master	414	69.5
PhD	3	.5
Current employment status		
Student	346	58.2
Employee/professional	229	38.5
Unemployed	7	1.2
Entrepreneur	13	2.2
Usage frequency of cell phones		
< 1 year	117	19.7
1–3 years	159	26.7
4–6 years	150	25.2
7–9 years	74	12.4
10–12 years	32	5.4

(*Continued*)

Demographic characteristics	Frequency	Percent
13–15 years	17	2.9
> 15 years	46	7.7
MM Usage experience		
< 1 month	85	14.3
1–4 months	92	15.5
5–8 months	82	13.8
9–12 months	118	19.8
13–16 months	69	11.6
17–20 months	37	6.2
> 20 months	112	18.8

Appendix B

Item means, standard deviations, and factor loadings

Items	Indicators	M	SD	Loadings[a]
Activation				
I usually use MM services regularly.	ACT2	4.23	1.76	.947***
I use MM services very often.	ACT3	4.19	1.84	.945***
Affection				
I feel very positive when I am using MM service.	AFF1	4.93	1.40	.883***
Using MM service makes me happy.	AFF2	4.83	1.42	.923***
I feel good when I am using MM service.	AFF3	4.88	1.41	.920***
I am proud to use MM service.	AFF4	4.87	1.49	.872***
Cognitive				
Using MM gets me to think about the service.	COG1	4.67	1.51	.812***
I think about MM a lot when I'm using this service.	COG2	4.46	1.48	.872***
Using MM stimulates my interest to learn more about this service.	COG3	4.52	1.50	.849***
Continuous usage				
I intend to continue using MM rather than discontinue its use	CON1	5.22	1.66	.910***
My intentions are to continue using MM rather than use any alternative means	CON2	4.64	1.67	.860***
I would like to continue my use of MM.	CON3	2.78	1.70	.497***
Agent credibility				
Using MM agent service would not divulge my personal information.	CRD1	4.49	1.40	.816***
I would find the MM agent service secure in conducting my MM transactions.	CRD2	4.50	1.42	.857***
The MM agent is like a friend to me because of his truthfulness.	CRD3	4.03	1.46	.805***

(*Continued*)

(Continued)

Items	Indicators	M	SD	Loadings[a]
The MM agent can always be relied on when doing cash transactions.	CRD4	4.22	1.49	.776***
Perceived risk				
The decision of whether to use MM service is risky.	RISK1	3.52	1.58	.798***
Using MM service puts my privacy at risk.	RISK2	3.72	1.61	.839***
MM service has more uncertainties.	RISK3	3.77	1.52	.828***
In general, I believe using an MM service is risky.	RISK4	3.74	1.60	.848***
Agent service quality				
MM agent provides on-time services.	SRQ1	4.54	1.50	.832***
MM agent provides prompt responses.	SRQ2	4.68	1.42	.884***
MM agent provides professional services.	SRQ3	4.35	1.44	.813***
MM agent provides personalized services.	SRQ4	4.40	1.43	.738***
Word of mouth (WOM)				
I say positive things about MM to other people.	WOM1	5.25	1.47	.883***
I recommend MM to someone who seeks my advice.	WOM2	5.28	1.43	.912***
I encourage friends and relatives to use MM.	WOM3	5.29	1.53	.903***

Note: a based on 1,000 bootstrapping samples.
Significant at *** $p < 0.001$ (two-tailed)
M: Mean SD: Standard Deviation

13 Mobile financial services

Conclusion

Aijaz A. Shaikh * *and Heikki Karjaluoto*

Mobile financial services have received the highest attention from the consumers and the service industry due to rapid diffusion of mobile devices across different regions and their extensive usage for information, communication, and payment. According to Statista (2017), the cell phone user in the world is expected to cross five billion by the end 2019, which brings over two-thirds of the world population within the mobile usage net, and this ration is increasing steadily. This immense diffusion of the mobile technology and usage, on one hand, has inspired a huge digital migration from traditional to digital channels and, on the other hand, has undeniably created a lucrative business proposition for the banking and other sub-sectors of the economy.

Historically, SMS banking started to dominate the mobile financial services in the developed world during the early 1990s. Later on, the advent of the smartphones and other smart devices in 2007 provided new business propositions and motivation to the banking and nonbanking industry to design, develop, and deploy new banking and payment solutions for the consumers. Mobile-based financial services provide useful and timely financial information to consumers on portable devices and allow the consumers to conduct a variety of transactions, ranging from payments to buying insurance to investments, using various methods such as SMS or downloadable applications with improved features and functionality.

In this development, mobile financial services (MFS) have escalated into a topic of major importance for both academics and practitioners. The underlying objective of this edited volume is to provide in-depth and relevant empirical research that investigates users' perspectives when using MFS and other technologies, including downloadable applications. Specifically, this edited volume presents historical as well as contemporary developments, innovations, laws and legislations, research, and analysis on the usage of mobile devices for banking and payment purposes as well as factors and consequences that impact the attitude, behaviors, beliefs, and abilities of consumers who adopt and continuously use MFS. Additionally, this edited volume provides an in-depth look at how the fast-emerging field of MFS contributes to the well-being of society, especially in developed and emerging market context, by exploring the significant benefits to consumers as well as financial institutions, FinTech, and other service providers.

This edited volume maintains a strong focus on all three major MFS domains (see Figure 13.1) throughout its 12 chapters. Notable themes that were considered and included in this book were divided into these three major domains and include but are not limited to mobile banking, mobile payments, mobile wallet, mobile money, mobile contactless payments, branchless banking, Omni-channels, etc.

This edited volume is beneficial for the academics who are investigating and teaching the topic as well as for professionals in the financial industry. In addition, regulators, policy makers, and marketing executives in general are the expected audience. Another potential beneficiary will clearly be service providers, FinTech firms, and start-ups that develop and deploy innovative banking and payment solutions for consumers in collaboration and/or partnership with banking and other financial institutions. The usability as well as the value of this book will further increase after the promulgation of open banking or revised payment systems directives (PSD2) prepared, issued, and implemented by the European Commission in the year 2018.

The conclusions drawn from this edited collection are discussed next:

Prior research has divided the MFS into two major domains, i.e., m-banking and mobile payments. The contributions in this edited volume have endorsed these two domains with a projection for the third domain entitled 'mobile money or branchless banking,' which according to our analysis will soon be recognized as the separate digital domain within the fertile ambit of MFS.

The analysis of the chapters included in this edited volume suggests that the global trends including mobile devices and social media have led to a revolutionary change bringing drastic decline in traditional 'brick and mortar' business models (Moorhouse, tom Dieck, & Jung, 2018). Similarly, the research on the adoption and usage of mobile financial services, products,

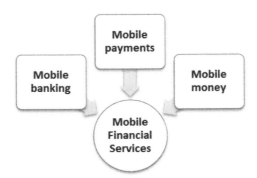

Figure 13.1 Segregation of mobile financial services in three major domains

and applications is ongoing; mobile financial and payment market is flooded with portfolio of offerings including banking, payment, and value-added services (Chawla & Joshi, 2017); and additional work as well as further research in this emerging field is essential for the financial services sector and nonbanking companies as the mobile financial technology gains adoption and usage in consumer research.

Here, this necessity of research is because of three major reasons. First, the relationship between a customer and an organization changes over time. This dynamic customer relationships demands proactive approach from the industry including financial and insurance (Bolton & Lemon, 1999). Academic research in this direction provides important leads to the industry. Second, a huge investment underpins mobile telephone and technology development and implementation. The purpose of this investment is to create a sustainable and a long-term relationship with the consumers, which could only be possible when the consumer accepts as well as continuously uses the technology, service, or product. Third, the FinTech explosion and open banking regulations, including the PSD2, have created a highly competitive and disruptive environment for the banking industry, i.e., banks could not anymore retain the customer data and maintain their sole ownership on the customer relationship. In the understanding of Deloitte (2017), the term 'open banking' is used to describe the shift from a closed banking model to one in which data is shared between different members of the banking ecosystem with a formal consent from the customer. Here, academic research on mobile financial services could provide a valuable consumer insight on their adoption and usage behavior, attitude, and beliefs.

This edited volume first paid attention to introduce, define, and conceptualize the term 'mobile financial services' and seeks to answer there critical research questions: what are MFS and how they are conceptualized in the marketing and IT literature? How prior literature has segregated MFS into different types such as mobile banking, mobile payments, and mobile money? How these different types of MFS differ from each other? Over 25 various definitions on mobile banking, 13 definitions on mobile payments, and a few definitions on mobile money were identified, discussed, and synthesized in this edited volume thereby providing a detailed overview of the field under investigation. This effort has also highlighted the major difference between the three mobile financial technologies, i.e., m-banking, m-payments, and m-money.

In addition to the MFS users, some attention is also paid to the non-active consumers segment with an objective to examine how to convince a non-active consumer to start using and engaging in continued usage of mobile financial services. Empirical data was collected through 24 semi-structured theme interviews and three focus groups during 2015 and 2016. Theory-based content analysis was used to analyze the data. The findings derived from this research present a diverse set of factors that influence consumers' attitudes and behaviors in relation to MFS. For example, the reason why some consumers are not using MFS largely based on the fact that banking institutions have somehow failed to clearly communicate the value proposition and the benefits of using the MFS to non-active consumer segment. In addition, a highly secure, simple, and easy-to-use MFS that does not contain anything 'extra' (e.g., advertisements, animations, and an overload of information) is highly favored by the non-active potential consumer. A complete list of research questions developed and discussed in this edited volume are summarized in Table 13.1.

More recently, the role played by nonbanking actors – including telecoms, financial technology (FinTech) firms, and other market participants, such as

Table 13.1 Research questions addressed in this edited volume

Research questions	Chapter no.
• What is the mobile financial services (MFS) landscape?	01
• What are MFS and how they have been conceptualized in the marketing and IT literature?	01
• How has prior literature segregated MFS? How do these types of MFS differ from each other?	01
• How to get non-active consumers to engage and continuously using mobile financial services?	02
• How emotions are considered crucial in Omnichannel banking environment and in gaining customer loyalty?	03
• How customer perspectives are considered in developing m-banking services and applications?	04
• What are the antecedents of m-banking continuous usage in a Sub-Sahara Africa?	05
• To what extent the hedonic features embedded on m-banking platforms influence the continuous usage?	05
• How do users' evaluations of the actors in the mobile payment service ecosystem affect the users' continuance intentions?	07
• What factors influence stand-alone retailers in Tanzania on using mobile devices at the point of sales?	08
• How the contradiction and collaboration between banking and telecom companies, both of which were driven by the respective logics of secure and inclusive payments, played a major role in the emergence of mobile payments in an emerging country context?	09
• How do institutional factors affect the innovations of new payment services?	10
• How the agents are considered critical actors in the financial services ecosystem and agency banking models for financial inclusion?	11
• What is the role of agents and agency or branchless banking in changing consumer behavior regarding the adoption, usage, or resistance of financial services?	11
• How do mobile money gent credibility and service quality drive consumer engagement and continuous usage of mobile money services in Africa?	12

PayPal and Amazon (Shaikh, Glavee-Geo, & Karjaluoto, 2017) – in developing and deploying innovative financial and payment services has also been recognized. Perhaps, this recognition for nonbanking actors is largely motivated after the promulgation of open banking and revised payment system directives (PSD2) issued by the European Commission in the year 2018.

This edited volume has included three chapters discussing the MFS adoption and usage in the African continent. The attitude and behavior of the consumers when adopting and using MFS in African countries such as Ghana, Nigeria, and Tanzania present a unique scenario. For example, in addition to banks and other financial institutions, the non-bank agent network plays a significant role in increasing the financial inclusion in Africa through mobile banking and mobile money technology and services. It is considered important to reach the underbanked and unbanked consumer segment when the consumption of formal banking products and services is considered as an important prerequisite to improving economic activities, helping the less privileged to increase their household income, building their asset base, and improving their resilience to shocks (Abramovay, 2004; Morawczynski, 2009).

Assessing the significance of the mobile money agents in providing branchless banking services to the poor in Ghana, research examined how do mobile money agent credibility and service quality drive consumer engagement and continuous usage of mobile money services in Ghana? Data were collected using the survey instrument. Findings placed strong emphasize on the credibility of mobile money agent and considered it a topmost concern. Here agent credibility found to be a significant driver of consumer engagement and continuous usage. In addition, agent service quality is considered another significant driver of customer engagement and the continuous use of mobile money services in Africa.

In the developed world, mobile payments have already revolutionized the payment landscape and created a cashless society. These developments radically changed the consumer behavior and resulted in the creation of a new consumer segment called 'de-banked' consumer. As we learned about the presence of unbanked and underbanked consumers in developing world, the de-banked consumer in developed world is creating serious ripples in the payment industry and challenges for the traditional banking industry thereby increasing the need for incorporating the consumer opinion when developing a new product or service. Using the qualitative research approach, 23 semi-structured in-depth interviews were conducted in a developed market with an underline objective to understand how banking institutes and developers regard and incorporate consumer perspectives in developing and deploying m-banking services so that service adoption can take place effortlessly and encouraging the use of m-banking services right from its first deployment. Interesting findings emerged from this research effort. For example, even if customer feedback demands bank branches be retained, consumers still prefer using m-banking as their primary, e-banking (such as ATMs) as secondary, and bank branches only as the last resort channel to handle their bank affairs. The flipside is that digital and m-banking services have diluted the human interaction, which challenges the rationale of improving the customer experience.

From the research design perspective, the chapters included in this review have sought to adopt and deploy various research methods such as qualitative, quantitative, and also the mix-method (see Figure 13.2) for data collection in all three domains: mobile banking, mobile payment, and branchless banking. In chapters that follow the qualitative research approach, authors used various research tools such as in-depth semi-structured interviews. Qualitative interviews were usually conducted to learn about the research participants' feelings, thoughts, and experiences. Other qualitative research tools, such as secondary analysis of qualitative data, focus groups, self-ethnography, participant observations, and so forth, were also used in the studies included in this edited volume. In quantitative research method, online and on-site survey instruments were used to collect the data.

Among the major theoretical and managerial implications derived from this edited volume, we observed that this volume is useful for the academic and the industry in several ways. For example, MFS are required to be easy to use, function flawlessly and be tailorable for diverse customer segments and their varying needs. Security issues are highly emphasized because the service is closely related to customers' money and privacy. The social aspects are important because recommendations, suggestions, evaluations, and encouragement from others may have a strong impact on the decision to start (or not to start) using and continuing the use of the service. The potential of agency banking and the role of agents are significant and remain

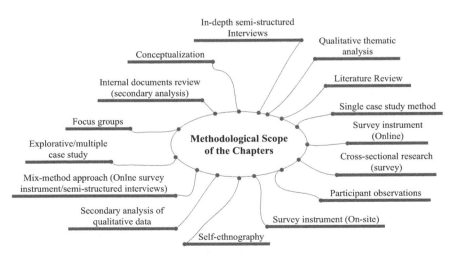

Figure 13.2 Methodological scope of the chapters

key to driving financial inclusion in developing countries mostly in Africa. Nonetheless, the viability and sustainability of the agency banking model require a clear regulatory framework that addresses issues around liquidity management, liability to customers, agent operations, agents' security, and consumer protection.

In sum, the development of the mobile financial services as well as the fast changes seen in the consumer behavior and attitude towards more convenient and always available services, the digital customer acquisition and providing low-friction customer experience have become a daunting task for the banks and other service providers globally. Either its banked or de-banked consumer or an unbanked or underbanked consumer, each consumer segment occupies a distinct position, revenue probability, and a different set of customer relationship. Understanding the core factors influencing the customer behavior and attitude is a key to the successful implementation of marketing and business strategy.

Note

* *Corresponding/primary contact author*

References

Abramovay, R. (2004). As finanças na luta contra a pobreza. *Desafios do Desenvolvimento, 1*(3), 66–67.

Bolton, R. N., & Lemon, K. N. (1999). A dynamic model of customers' usage of services: Usage as an antecedent and consequence of satisfaction. *Journal of Marketing Research*, 171–186.

Chawla, D., & Joshi, H. (2017). Consumer perspectives about mobile banking adoption in India: A cluster analysis. *International Journal of Bank Marketing, 35*(4), 616–636.

Deloitte. (2017). *How to flourish in an uncertain future-open banking and PSD2.* Retrieved from www2.deloitte.com/content/dam/Deloitte/cz/Documents/financial-services/cz-open-banking-and-psd2.pdf

Moorhouse, N., tom Dieck, M. C., & Jung, T. (2018). Technological innovations transforming the consumer retail experience: A review of literature. In *Augmented reality and virtual reality* (pp. 133–143). Cham: Springer.

Morawczynski, O. (2009). Exploring the usage and impact of "transformational" mobile financial services: The case of M-PESA in Kenya. *Journal of Eastern African Studies, 3*(3), 509–525.

Shaikh, A. A., Glavee-Geo, R., & Karjaluoto, H. (2017). Exploring the nexus between financial sector reforms and the emergence of digital banking culture: Evidences from a developing market. *Research in International Business and Finance, 42*, 1030–1039.

Statista. (2017). *Number of mobile phone users worldwide from 2013 to 2019 (in billions).* Retrieved from www.statista.com/statistics/274774/forecast-of-mobile-phone-users-worldwide/

Index

For Product Safety Concerns and Information please contact our EU
representative GPSR@taylorandfrancis.com Taylor & Francis Verlag GmbH,
Kaufingerstraße 24, 80331 München, Germany

Printed and bound by CPI Group (UK) Ltd, Croydon, CR0 4YY
01/05/2025
01858413-0002